OXFORD EARLY CHRISTIAN STUDIES

EVAGRIUS OF PONTUS

THE OXFORD EARLY CHRISTIAN STUDIES series includes scholarly volumes on the thought and history of the early Christian centuries. Covering a wide range of Greek, Latin, and Oriental sources, the books are of interest to theologians, ancient historians, and specialists in the classical and Jewish worlds.

Titles in the series include:

Evagrius of Pontus

The Greek Ascetic Corpus

Translation, Introduction, and Commentary by
ROBERT E. SINKEWICZ

OXFORD
UNIVERSITY PRESS

OXFORD
UNIVERSITY PRESS

Great Clarendon Street, Oxford, OX2 6DP

Oxford University Press is a department of the University of Oxford.
It furthers the University's objective of excellence in research, scholarship,
and education by publishing worldwide in

Oxford New York

Auckland Bangkok Buenos Aires Cape Town Chennai
Dar es Salaam Delhi Hong Kong Istanbul Karachi Kolkata
Kuala Lumpur Madrid Melbourne Mexico City Mumbai Nairobi
São Paulo Shanghai Taipei Tokyo Toronto

Oxford is a registered trade mark of Oxford University Press
in the UK and certain other countries

Published in the United States
by Oxford University Press Inc., New York

British Library Cataloguing in Publication Data

Data available

Library of Congress Cataloging in Publication Data

Data available

ISBN 0-19-925993-3

1 3 5 7 9 10 8 6 4 2

Typeset by Regent Typesetting, London
Printed in Great Britain
on acid-free paper by
T. J. International,
Padstow, Cornwall

To my wife

PREFACE

The writings of Evagrius appear to have been widely known and read in antiquity. His disciple, Palladius, reports briefly on his literary activities in the *Lausiac History* (38. 10) and in the Coptic *Life of Evagrius* (BV 161). In a letter of 414 (*Ep.* 133. 3) Jerome complains that Evagrius is read by many, not just in the East but in the West as well, thanks to the translations made by Rufinus. At the end of the fifth century, Gennadius of Marseille in his *Lives of Illustrious Men* (11) could still produce a list of Evagrius' major works, which he probably had in hand, since he claims that he translated into Latin both the *Gnostikos* and the *Antirrhetikos*. The Evagrian literary corpus survives today in several forms, reflecting the circumstances surrounding the condemnations of Origenism at the end of the fourth and beginning of the fifth century by Epiphanius of Salamis, Jerome, and Theophilos of Alexandria and then again in the sixth century at the Second Council of Constantinople (553).

As Claire Guillaumont suggested in her preliminary study of the transmission history of the Evagrian corpus (SC 170), Palestine was probably the first major dissemination point, for it was there that Evagrius maintained close links with the monasteries of Melania and Rufinus on the Mount of Olives in Jerusalem. Not long afterwards, Constantinople probably became the second major transmission point, when Palladius and the other Origenist monks sought refuge there with John Chrysostom. Finally, from the tenth century onwards it was primarily the monks of Mount Athos who preserved and transmitted the works of Evagrius. With the condemnations of Origenism, those works of Evagrius considered most 'tainted' dropped out of the Greek transmission history and were preserved primarily in the Syriac and Armenian versions. The Byzantine monasteries continued to copy and read the ascetic works of Evagrius, sometimes passing them on under his own name and sometimes under the name of Nilus of Ancyra.

The early printed editions of the Evagrian Greek ascetic corpus by Suarès (1673), Bigot (1680), Cotelier (1686), Galland (1788), and Nikodemos of the Holy Mountain and Makarios of Corinth (1782) appeared in the seventeenth and eighteenth centuries. Relying on some of these prior editions, Jacques-Paul Migne incorporated the Evagrian texts into volumes 40 (Evagrius: 1863) and 79 (Nilus: 1865) of his *Patrologia Graeca*. These editions have presented scholars with two difficulties, namely, that of determining Evagrian authorship and that of the varying reliability of the text witnesses used by these editions. Nilus of Ancyra had himself read the works of Evagrius and assimilated his teaching with the result that it has taken scholars well into the twentieth century to determine with some certainty which works ascribed to Nilus in fact belong to Evagrius. The delimitation of the Evagrian corpus is now reasonably clear. Problems of the text, however, remain. In some cases, the editions report incomplete witnesses with a portion of the text missing, namely, for *Vices* and *Exhortations*. In others (viz. *Eulogios*, *Eight Thoughts*, and *Thoughts*), the text given is that of a short recension, while a longer and probably original recension exists in the manuscripts. Finally, the texts of these early editions sometimes reproduce imperfect text witnesses, in one case, at least, rendering the text almost unreadable (viz. *Eulogios*). Through the efforts of Antoine and Claire Guillaumont along with Paul Géhin, the Sources Chrétiennes series has now published critical editions of two works of the ascetic corpus, the *Praktikos* and *Thoughts*, as well as two volumes of the biblical scholia for Ecclesiastes and Proverbs. The *Gnostikos* volume is not fully a critical edition in that it reports only the surviving Greek fragments, but not the Syriac texts.

Although most of the surviving works of Evagrius of Pontus have been known in the West for almost two centuries, there is still no complete English translation for the entire corpus. Indeed, for some works there is no English translation at all. The present translation endeavours to provide an English version of the entire Greek ascetic corpus of Evagrius exclusive of the biblical scholia. The latter have been omitted in part for practical reasons, as they would make the length of the book unwieldy, and in part because they constitute a distinct category and deserve their own volume. I would also add the further reason that the Greek ascetic corpus, as defined in this way, has its own separate transmission history, whether under the name of Evagrius himself or under the name of Nilus of Ancyra. In this sense, the present translation covers the Byzantine monastic collection of Evagrius' ascetic works. I have decided not to include the *Gnostikos* in my translation of the ascetic corpus, because there is no complete text in Greek and only four manuscripts supply the text for nineteen chapters (seventeen in one case). Where no Greek text survives either in these manuscripts or in citations by other authors, the task of translation is especially problematic as there are three Syriac versions and the Armenian version. For these reasons I have decided to leave the translation of this text for another occasion.

To ensure a reasonably reliable textual basis for the translation, all the texts without critical editions have been collated against the principal manuscripts. Thus, for *Vices* and *Exhortations* a translation is given for the completed texts and for *Eulogios, Eight Thoughts*, as well as *Thoughts*, translations are given for the long recension. In this sense, nine of the thirteen texts of the Greek ascetic corpus are given English translations for the first time. Detailed information on the textual basis of the translation is provided in an appendix. To assist the reader in the understanding and study of these texts, I have provided a general introduction to the life of Evagrius and his ascetic doctrine as well as particular introductions to each of the works. The translations have been provided with an extensive commentary, which attempts to guide the reader through the intricacies of Evagrian thought by providing explanatory comments and references to other Evagrian texts. Finally, detailed indexes have been provided for the translation to allow the reader to identify and study the numerous themes of Evagrian teaching.

I should like to thank the officers and editors of the Oxford University Press for their assistance and fine work in preparing my book for publication, with special mention to Hilary O'Shea, Lucy Qureshi, Lavinia Porter, and Enid Barker. Finally, I want to express my appreciation to the editors of the Early Christian Studies Series, Gillian Clark and Andrew Louth, for considering my book for publication.

R.E.S.

Toronto
2002

CONTENTS

ABBREVIATIONS

WORKS OF EVAGRIUS

Admonitions 1–2   *Admonition 1 (CPG 2440. 1).* Syriac: Wilhelm Frankenberg, *Euagrius Ponticus,* Abhandlungen der königlichen Gesellschaft der Wissenschaften zu Göttingen, Philologisch-historische Klasse, new series, 13. 2 (Berlin: Weidmannsche Buchhandlung, 1912), 554–6
Admonition 2 (CPG 2440. 2). Syriac: W. Frankenberg, 556–62

Antirrhetikos   *Antirrhetikos against the Eight Thoughts.* Syriac: W. Frankenberg, 472–545

Chapters 33   *Thirty-Three Ordered Chapters (CPG 2442).* PG 40. 1264D–1268B; Paul Géhin (ed.), *Évagre le Pontique, Scholies aux Proverbes,* Sources Chrétiennes, 340 (Paris: Cerf, 1987), 486–9 (for nos. 17–33)

Eight Thoughts   *On the Eight Thoughts (CPG 2451).* Long recension: Lavra Γ 93, fols. 308r–315v; short recension: PG 79.1145D–1164D

Eulogios   *To Eulogios: On the Confession of Thoughts and Counsel in their Regard (CPG 2447).* Long recension: Lavra Γ 93; short recension: PG 79. 1093D–1140A. The number references are to my new paragraph numbering, followed by the old PG paragraph numbering, and then by the PG column number. Where only one numerical reference is given, it is to my new paragraph numbering.

Exhortations 1–2   *Exhortations to Monks (CPG 2454).* Complete text: Lavra Γ 93, fols. 304r–307r; PG 79. 1235A–1240B

Foundations   *Foundations of the Monastic Life: A Presentation of the Practice of Stillness (CPG 2434).* PG 40. 1252D–1264C; *Philokalia* 1. 38–43

Gnostikos   Antoine and Claire Guillaumont, *Évagre le Pontique. Le Gnostique,* Sources Chrétiennes, 356 (Paris: Cerf, 1989)

Imitation Ct.   *In Imitation of the Canticle of Canticles (CPG 2463).* Paul Géhin, 'Evagriana d'un manuscrit basilien (*Vaticanus gr. 2028; olim Basilianus 67*)', *Le Muséon,* 109 (1996), 71–2

Imitation Eccles.   *In Imitation of Ecclesiastes (CPG 2464).* P. Géhin, *Le Muséon,* 109 (1996), 76

Instructions (Prov.)   *Instructions:* Joseph Muyldermans, *Evagriana. Extrait de la revue Le Muséon 44, augmenté de: Nouveaux fragments grecs inédits*

(Paris: Paul Geuthner, 1931), 20–1 (nos. 50–67). This is a partial edition only; for the complete text see Lavra *Γ* 93, fols. 307r–308r. Syriac: *An Explanation of the Parables and Proverbs of Solomon*, ed. J. Muyldermans, *Evagriana Syriaca. Textes inédits du British Museum et de la Vaticane*, Bibliothèque du Muséon, 31. (Louvain: Publications Universitaires, 1952), 135–8

KG   *Kephalaia Gnostika* (*CPG* 2432). A. Guillaumont, *Les Six Centuries des 'Kephalaia Gnostica' d'Évagre le Pontique,* Patrologia Orientalis, 28. 1 (Paris, 1958)

CG   C. Guillaumont, 'Fragments grecs inédits d'Évagre le Pontique', *Texte und Untersuchungen,* 133 (1987), 209–21

G2   P. Géhin, 'Evagriana d'un manuscrit basilien (*Vaticanus gr. 2028; olim Basilianus 67*)', *Le Muséon,* 109 (1996), 64–5

HNF   Irénée Hausherr, 'Nouveaux fragments grecs d'Évagre le Pontique', *Orientalia Christiana Periodica,* 5 (1939), 229–33

M1   J. Muyldermans, *Evagriana. Extrait de la revue Le Muséon 44, augmenté de: Nouveaux fragments grecs inédits* (Paris: Paul Geuthner, 1931), 52–9

M2   J. Muyldermans, *À travers la tradition manuscrite d'Évagre le Pontique. Essai sur les manuscrits grecs conservés à la Bibliothèque Nationale de Paris,* Bibliothèque du Muséon, 3 (Louvain: Bureaux du Muséon, 1932), 74, 85, 89, 93

Letters   *Letters* 1–64

F   Syriac: W. Frankenberg, 564–610

G1   P. Géhin, 'Nouveaux fragments grecs des Lettres d'Évagre', *Revue d'Histoire des Textes,* 24 (1994), 117–47

G2   P. Géhin, 'Evagriana d'un manuscrit basilien (*Vaticanus gr. 2028; olim Basilianus 67*)', *Le Muséon,* 109 (1996), 66–7

CG   C. Guillaumont, 'Fragments grecs inédits d'Evagre le Pontique', *Texte und Untersuchungen,* 133 (1987), 209–21

Letter on Faith (*CPG* 2439)   Marcella Fortin Patrucco (ed.), *Basilio di Cesarea, Le lettere,* i ('Turin: Società editrice internazionale, 1983), 84–112

Letter to Melania (*CPG* 2438)   Syriac: W. Frankenberg, 610–19; Gösta Vitestam, *La second partie du traité qui passe sous le nom de 'La Grande Lettre d'Évagre le Pontique à Mélanie l'Ancienne,* Scripta Minora Regiae Societatis Humaniorum Litterarum Lundensis, 1963–4, no. 3 (Lund: Glerrup, 1964)

Lord's Prayer   *An Exposition of the Lord's Prayer* (*CPG* 2461). Paul de Lagarde, *Catenae in Euangelia aegyptiacae,* (Göttingen 1886), 13

Maxims 1–3   *Maxims 1–3* (*CPG* 2443–5). PG 79. 1249C–1269D; A. Elter (ed.), *Gnomica,* i: *Sexti Pythagorici, Clitarchi, Evagrii Pontici sententiae,* (Leipzig, 1892), pp. lii–liv

Monks   *To Monks in Monasteries and Communities* (*CPG* 2435).

	H. Gressmann, 'Nonnenspiegel und Mönchsspiegel des Euagrios Pontikos', *Texte und Untersuchungen,* 39 (1913), 152–65
Praktikos	*The Monk: A Treatise on the Practical Life (CPG* 2430). A. and C. Guillaumont, *Évagre le Pontique, Traité Pratique ou Le Moine,* Sources Chrétiennes, 170–1 (Paris: Cerf, 1971)
Prayer	*Chapters on Prayer (CPG* 2452). PG 79. 1165–1200; *Philokalia* 1. 176–89
Reflections	*Reflections (CPG* 2433). J. Muyldermans, 'Note additionnelle à *Evagriana*', *Le Muséon,* 44 (1931), 369–83; repr. in *Evagriana. Extrait de la revue Le Muséon 44, augmenté de: Nouveaux fragments grecs inédits* (Paris: Paul Geuthner, 1931) 33–47
S-Eccles.	*Scholia on Ecclesiastes (CPG* 2458). P. Géhin, *Évagre le Pontique, Scholies à l'Ecclésiaste,* Sources Chrétiennes, 397 (Paris: Cerf, 1993)
S-Prov.	*Scholia on Proverbs (CPG* 2456). Paul Géhin, *Évagre le Pontique, Scholies aux Proverbes,* Sources Chrétiennes, 340 (Paris: Cerf, 1987)
S-Ps.	*Scholia on the Psalms (CPG* 2455). PG 12:1053A–1686A; J. B. Pitra, *Analecta sacra,* ii–iii (Paris 1867–83), ii. 444–83 and iii. 1–364. For the numbering of the scholia see M.-J. Rondeau, 'Le commentaire sur les Psaumes d'Évagre le Pontique', *Orientalia Christiana Periodica,* 26 (1960), 327–48
Thoughts	*On Thoughts (CPG* 2450). Long recension: A. and C. Guillaumont and P. Géhin, *Évagre le Pontique. Sur les Pensées,* Sources Chrétiennes, 438 (Paris: Cerf, 1998); short recension: PG 79.1200D–1233A
Vices	[*To Eulogios*] *On the Vices opposed to the Virtues (CPG* 2448). Complete text: Lavra Γ 93, fols. 295v–298r; PG 79. 1140B–1144D
Virgin	*Exhortation to a Virgin (CPG* 2436). H. Gressmann, *Texte und Untersuchungen,* 39 (1913), 146–51

OTHER ABBREVIATIONS

Am	Émile Amélineau, *De Historia Lausiaca, quaenam sit huius ad Monachorum Aegyptiorum historiam scribendam utilitas* (Paris, 1887)
Apophthegmata Patrum	
A	Alphabetical Collection: PG 65. 71–440, cited according to the number system of *Les sentences des pères du désert. Collection alphabétique,* trans. Lucien Regnault (Abbaye de Solesmes: Sablé-sur-Sarthe, 1981)
S	Systematic Collection: ed. Jean-Claude Guy, *Les Apophtegmes*

des Pères: Collection Systématique I, Sources Chrétiennes, 387
(Paris: Cerf, 1993)

N   Anonymous Collection (for editions see *CPG* 5561), cited
according to the numbering system of *Les sentences des pères
du désert. Série des anonymes,* trans. Lucien Regnault, Spiritualité
Orientale, 43 (Bégrolles-en-Mauges: Abbaye de Bellefontaine,
1985)

Bu   E. A. Walis Budge, *The Paradise, or Garden of the Holy Fathers,* ii
(London: Chatto & Windus, 1907). The roman numeral
indicates series I or II, and the arabic numeral the number of
the saying

AS   J. B. Pitra, *Analecta sacra,* vols. ii–iii (Paris 1867–83), ii. 444–83
and iii. 1–364

BV   Gabriel Bunge and Adalbert de Vogüé, *Quatre ermites égyptiens
d'après les fragments coptes de l'Histoire Lausiaque,* Spiritualité
Orientale, 60 (Bégrolles-en-Mauges: Abbaye de Bellefontaine,
1994)

CPG   *Clavis Patrum Graecorum,* ed. Maurice Geerard, 6 vols.
(Turnhout: Brepols, 1974–98

CSCO Corpus Scriptorum Christianorum Orientalium (Louvain,
1903–)

CSEL Corpus Scriptorum Ecclesiasticorum Latinorum (Vienna
1866–)

Études A. Guillaumont, *Études sur la spiritualité de l'Orient chrétien,*
Spiritualité Orientale, 66 (Bégrolles-en-Mauges: Abbaye de
Bellefontaine, 1996)

HE   *Historia Ecclesiastica,* of Socrates, PG 67. 33–841; of Sozomen,
ed. J. Bidez and G. C. Hansen, *Sozomenus Kirchengeschichte,* Die
Griechischen christlichen Schriftsteller, 50 (Berlin: Akademie
Verlag, 1960)

HL   Palladius, *Historia Lausiaca,* ed. Cuthbert Butler, *The Lausiac
History of Palladius,* Texts and Studies, 6.1–2 (Cambridge:
Cambridge University Press, 1898–1904), cited according to
the chapter and paragraph number, followed by the page and
line numbering

HM   *Historia monachorum in Aegypto,* ed. A. J. Festugière, Subsidia
Hagiographica, 53 (Brussels: Société des Bollandistes, 1961)

OCD *The Oxford Classical Dictionary,* 3rd edn., ed. Simon
Hornblower and Antony Spawforth (Oxford: Oxford
University Press, 1996)

Origines A. Guillaumont, *Aux origines du monachisme chrétien. Pour
une phénoménologie du monachisme,* Spiritualité Orientale, 30
(Bégrolles-en-Mauges: Abbaye de Bellefontaine, 1979)

PG   Patrologia Graeca, ed. J. P. Migne *et al.* (Paris, 1857–66).

Philokalia   Φιλοκαλία τῶν ἱερῶν νηπτικῶν, ed. Nikodemos the
                      Hagiorite and Makarios of Corinth, i (Athens: Aster, 1974)
PL   Patrologia Latina, ed. J. P. Migne *et al.* (Paris, 1844–80)
PO   Patrologia Orientalis, (Paris and Turnhout, 1904–)
SC   Sources Chrétiennes, (Paris: Cerf, 1942–)

Abbreviations for Biblical references follow the standard Oxford University Press conventions, with the exception of references to 1–2 Sam. and 1–2 Kgs., which are given as 1–4 Kgs., following the Septuagint. Psalm references are to the Septuagint numbering.

INTRODUCTION

THE LIFE OF EVAGRIUS

Evagrius was born in the town of Ibora in Helenopontus, probably in the year 345.[1] He was the son of a rural bishop and was himself ordained a lector by Basil, bishop of Caesarea. After the death of Basil in 379, he attached himself to Gregory of Nazianzus who ordained him a deacon. Evagrius then appears in the company of Gregory in Constantinople, where the latter became bishop of the orthodox community in November of 380. After Gregory's resignation in 381 during the Council of Constantinople, Evagrius continued to serve the new bishop, Nektarios, in the conflict with the Arians. At some point during this period Evagrius fell in love with a married woman of the aristocratic class, but even though he recognized the danger of scandal and the use the heretics might make of this, he found himself unable to break off the relationship. Then, while at prayer, Evagrius had a vision in which he was imprisoned by the soldiers of the governor, presumably at the instigation of the woman's husband. An angel appeared to him in prison and advised him to leave Constantinople as soon as possible. Evagrius agreed and swore an oath on the Gospel. Warned by this experience, Evagrius packed his bags and boarded a ship for Jerusalem. These events probably took place in 382.

In Palestine he met Melania the Elder who offered him hospitality, presumably in the neighbouring monastery of Rufinus. Evagrius' resolve seems to have faltered at this point, for he is said to have turned to his old ways that were characterized as displays of vainglory and pride. God then afflicted him with a six-month fever which wasted his flesh and thereby tamed his unruly passions. When the doctors could not cure his fever, Melania suspected the real nature of his illness and demanded to know what was troubling him. Evagrius told her the whole story. She then made him promise to take up the monastic life. Evagrius accepted her counsel and recovered within a few days, receiving the habit from Rufinus and then departing for Egypt.

---

[1] Palladius notes in *HL* 38. 1 (116. 11–12) that Evagrius was 54 when he died on the feast of Epiphany (*HL* 38. 13, (122. 14–15)) at the beginning of 399 or possibly 400. Palladius in his *Dialogue* does not mention him among the monks persecuted by Theophilus in 400.

Evagrius arrived in Egypt probably in 383, spending two years in Nitria before moving on to Kellia where he lived for fourteen years until his death. His two principal monastic teachers were Makarios of Egypt (the Great) and Makarios of Alexandria.[2] Evagrius speaks of Makarios of Egypt with great veneration as his true teacher in the spiritual life, even though he lived some distance away in the desert of Sketis. Indeed, he calls both Gregory of Nazianzus and Makarios the Great 'vessels of election', thus placing them on an equal footing for the role they played in his religious formation.[3] Although it is difficult to isolate the particular teachings that Evagrius received from his spiritual mentors, Gabriel Bunge has argued convincingly that it is possible to identify several points of common teaching that Evagrius shares with and perhaps received from his teachers. Makarios of Egypt may have offered Evagrius special guidance in spiritual prayer, for the sources identify this domain as one where Makarios was especially gifted. Palladius, for example notes that 'he was said to be in continual ecstasy. He occupied himself much more with God than with earthly things.'[4] Evagrius himself cites the authority of Makarios of Egypt on the subject of anger, the great obstacle to prayer, and this citation accords quite closely with a saying attributed to Makarios in the *Apophthegmata*.[5] The theme of humble abandonment to the will of God is found in both.[6] Bunge has also suggested a link between the early history of the practice of monologic prayer and the teaching of Makarios and Evagrius.[7] Monologic prayer consists of the use of a short phrase or sentence, usually based on scripture, which may be recited repetitively either in a time of difficulty or as a regular practice. In the *Apophthegmata* Makarios recommends the practice of a monologic prayer, based on two psalm verses, Ps. 40: 5 and 93: 18):

Some questioned Abba Makarios, saying: 'How should we pray?' The elder said, 'There is no need to speak at great lengths; it is enough to stretch out one's hands

---

[2] On his relationship with his two mentors see, G. Bunge, 'Évagre le Pontique et les deux Macaire', *Irénikon*, 56 (1983), 215–27; 323–60.

[3] For his part, Gregory remembered Evagrius with fondness in his will: 'To Evagrius the deacon, who shared with me many common labours and concerns, and on numerous occasions demonstrated his kindness, I acknowledge my thanks both before God and before others. And God will grant him great rewards, but that he may not want for the little tokens of our friendship, I wish him to be given one shirt, one tunic, two cloaks, and thirty gold nomismata' (PG 37. 393B).

[4] *HL* 17.5 (44. 25–7).

[5] A489 (Makarios 36).

[6] Evagrius, *Prayer* 31; *Apophthegmata*, A472 (Makarios 19).

[7] See *Irénikon* 56 (1983): 341–7.

and say, 'Lord, as you will and as you know, have mercy on me.' And if the warfare grows pressing, say, 'Lord, help me!' He knows very well what we need and he acts mercifully towards us.'[8]

Evagrius also recommends a short and intense prayer in times of temptations.[9] And he even suggests a possible formula at one point:

Take heed lest he (Satan) deceive you with praises, that he may not exalt you in your own eyes, lest you become proud of your attainments like the Pharisee. Rather, strike yourself like the Publican, beat your breast like him, saying: 'O God, have mercy on me a sinner. O God, forgive me my debts.[10]

The relationship between these texts is at least suggestive of a teaching that was passed on from master to disciple.

The six references to Makarios of Alexandria in Evagrius' writings are all concerned with ascetic practice: monastic abstinence (*Praktikos* 94), warfare against the thoughts or the demons (*Antirrhetikos* 4. 23, 4. 58 and 8. 26; *Thoughts* 33 and 37). Palladius himself was living at Kellia during the last three years of Makarios' life (390–3) and he represents him primarily as a great ascetic, renowned for his physical discipline. Further, the Coptic versions of the *Lives* of Evagrius and Makarios of Alexandria represent the two men as strikingly similar in their practices of corporeal asceticism. Makarios followed a strict regimen and he recommended a similar dietary discipline to Evagrius.[11] The latter eventually had to modify his diet, on the order of the elders, as he suffered from a gastro-intestinal ailment in the latter years of his life.[12] Both monks recited 100 prayers each day.[13] Sleep deprivation is also mentioned among their practices. Evagrius himself would sleep only one third of the night (4 hours) while during the day he would fend off drowsiness by walking back and fourth in his courtyard and keeping his mind occupied with appropriate considerations.[14] Makarios and Evagrius both resorted on occasion to extreme practices of physical asceticism in order to defeat some particularly recalcitrant demonic temptation. There is a story that Makarios was stung by a gnat and killed it in revenge (or according to another version, he was troubled by the passion of fornication). He therefore condemned himself to sit naked in the marsh of Sketis for six months, where he was severely bitten by mosquitoes and became barely recognizable.[15] When Evagrius was

---

[8] Ibid.   [9] *Prayer* 98.   [10] *Admonition* 1, F556. 15–17; cf. *Prayer* 102.

[11] *HL* 18. 1–2; BV 158 (Am 122).   [12] *HL* 38. 13; BV 159 (Am 122).

[13] Evagrius—*HL* 38.10 (120.11) and BV 159 (Am 112); Makarios—*HL* 20. 3 (63.13–14).

[14] Evagrius—BV 159 (Am 113), cf. *Antirrhetikos* 2. 55.

[15] *HL* 18. 3 (48–9).

tempted by fornication, he spent the entire night praying, while standing naked in a cistern of water in mid-winter, and on another occasion when he was tormented by a spirit of blasphemy he spent forty days in the open air till his body was covered with vermin.[16]

In addition to the similarities in their physical austerities, both Makarios of Alexandria and Evagrius show a particular interest in the workings of the demons. In discussing the ability of the demons to tempt monks through certain types of physical contact, Evagrius cites Makarios' authority.[17] On another occasion he cites the caution of his teacher about revealing too much regarding the demons' ingenuity in guessing the thoughts or attitudes in people's minds.[18] Both Palladius and Rufinus (in his translation of the *Historia monachorum*) have much to say about the encounters of Makarios with demons and the techniques he deploys in routing them. Here too in the matters of ascetic demonology there is some suggestion of the influence of Makarios of Alexandria on his student.

During his years in the desert Evagrius never forgot the kindness and hospitality shown him by Melania and Rufinus, for he continued to correspond with them throughout the remainder of his life. If we accept Bunge's attribution of the letters to various addressees, seventeen letters in total were addressed to Rufinus and Melania.[19] Judging from the tone and content of its prologue, Evagrius' great treatise on *Prayer* was very probably addressed to Rufinus.[20] Some twenty-nine letters in all were addressed to other monastics. Interesting also are the five letters addressed to John the bishop of Jerusalem (386/7–417), a friend of Rufinus and a pro-Origenist.[21] Evagrius' close relationship with his friends in Palestine is further confirmed by a second occasion when he sought refuge with Rufinus and Melania. At one point bishop Theophilos of Alexandria sought to make Evagrius bishop of Thmuis, but, unwilling to accept, he fled to Palestine.[22] Bunge has suggested that this event should be dated to about 391–4.[23] Within Egypt itself, Evagrius maintained close relationships with a number of monks who later became embroiled in the outbreak of the Origenist controversy shortly after his death. Among the so-called Tall Brothers (Ammonios, Euthymios, Dioskoros and Eusebios), Evagrius was associated in a particular way

---

[16] BV 163 (Am 116).   [17] *Thoughts* 33.   [18] *Thoughts* 37.
[19] G. Bunge, *Evagrios Pontikos: Briefe aus der Wüste*, Sophia, 24 (Trier: Paulinus, 1986), 176–207. Unfortunately, very few of the attributions can be made with certainty.
[20] Cf. Bunge, *Briefe*, 181.   [21] *Letters* 2, 9, 24, 50, 51.
[22] Cf. BV 162 (Am 115); Socrates, *HE* 4. 23 (PG 67. 521A).
[23] Bunge, *Briefe*, 187.

with Ammonios. Palladius mentions the two of them together in the phrase, 'those in the company of saints Ammonios and Evagrius'.[24] Evagrius also reports a visit that he and Ammonios made to visit John of Lykopolis in the Thebaid.[25] Palladius himself arrived in Kellia *c.*390/1 and was closely associated with Evagrius until the latter's death. During those years Palladius lived in a cell close to that of Evagrius and met with him at the weekend gatherings of the brothers. He acknowledges Evagrius as his teacher in 'the life in Christ, in the spiritual interpretation of scripture and in the discernment of false teaching'. Palladius is thus able to claim in the Coptic *Life* that his testimony regarding Evagrius and his virtues is an eyewitness account.

THE TEACHING OF EVAGRIUS ON THE ASCETIC LIFE

Foundations

The works of Evagrius are for the most part not systematic in their presentation of a teaching on the ascetic life, but rather are composed of short sentences grouped around individual themes or of more detailed and extended discussions of particular topics. Nevertheless, the thought of Evagrius is highly ordered in its understanding of the ascetic life as a progression of stages that the monk must pass through in order to attain the ultimate goal of the knowledge of God. Further, there is a set of teachings appropriate to each of these stages, which will aid the ascetic in his practice, but the teacher must be diligent in not offering any instruction before its time to those who are not yet prepared to receive it.[26]

Two Evagrian treatises speak most directly to the initial stages of a monk's training, namely, *Foundations* and *Eulogios*.[27] The full title of the former, as it is given in the manuscript Lavra *Γ* 93, is *The Foundations of the Monastic Life: A Presentation of the Practice of Stillness*. The Greek word *hesychia* I have translated either as 'stillness' or as 'the practice of stillness'; it refers to a state of calm or tranquillity, resulting from the avoidance of all external circumstances that might upset the internal balance and equanimity

---

[24] *HL* 24. 2 (78. 1).

[25] *Antirrhetikos* 6. 16, F524; cf. *HL* 35. 3 (101. 4–13), where some manuscripts mention also Ammonios and Albanios in addition to Evagrius and the interlocutor Palladius.

[26] This subject is treated in some detail in the *Gnostikos.*

[27] A. Guillaumont treats the subject of the initial stages of monastic practice in 'Les fondements de la vie monastique selon Évagre le Pontique', *Annuaire du Collège de France,* 78 (1977–8), 467–77.

of the mind. It is an ascetic 'practice' in the full, active sense of the term in that the monk must attentively work at establishing and maintaining it; this is further indicated by the frequent use of the verbal form (*hēsuchazein*) both in Evagrius and in the *Apophthegmata Patrum*.[28]

Hesychia is thus the principal topic of *Foundations*, and Evagrius devotes his attention to describing how this ascetic practice is to be established in the life of the new initiate and how it is to be pursued and protected. The fundamental requirement for acquiring a state of stillness in one's life is the withdrawal from all circumstances that give rise to anxieties, worries and concerns: the ascetic must seek a life free from anxieties, what Evagrius calls *amerimnia*, a close synonym for *hesychia*.[29] The first expression of this conversion of life is the renunciation of marriage and family with all its attendant distractions and the adoption of the solitary life, which constitutes the necessary precondition for the practice of stillness.[30] As we know from a variety of sources, the practice of monastic life in the desert settlements of Nitria, Kellia, and Sketis was not one of absolute solitude. The monks lived apart in separate cells during the week, gathering for a common assembly or *synaxis* on Saturday and Sunday, which included a common meal, a liturgical office, and the eucharist, as well as opportunities for consultation with elders or even a conference. Even during the week, monks would occasionally receive visitors or go off to look after a sick neighbour.[31]

The remainder of *Foundations* reviews the various practices that will serve the monk in guarding his state of stillness both externally and internally. The diet must be kept frugal and simple in order to avoid distractions (probably sexual); basic fare is sufficient for hospitality. Any accumulation of goods or wealth is to be avoided as a source of idle preoccupation; any surplus should be given to the poor. Evagrius also counsels against the practice of maintaining a serving boy (or a young disciple) as this may be both a source of scandal and a further cause for worry over having to provide for someone else. Caution must be exercised in human relationships: the monk should associate only with like-minded brothers, truly committed to the ascetic life, and he should avoid meetings with

---

[28] e.g. Evagrius, *Foundations* 3. 1253C; 5. 1257A; 6. 1257B. *Apophthegmata Patrum* A11 (Antonios 11); A34 (Antonios 34); A40 (Arsenios 2); A138 (Anoub 1); A390 (Ioseph of Panepho 7).

[29] Cf. *Foundations* 2. 1253B; *Eulogios* 12. 11. 1108B1, 26. 27. 1129B, 26. 28. 1129D; *Vices* 3. 3. 1141D.

[30] *Foundations* 1–3.

[31] Cf. A. Guillaumont, 'Histoire des moines aux Kellia', *Orientalia Lovaniensia Periodica*, 8 (1977), 187–203 (repr. *Origines* 10: 151–67).

parents and relatives. Frequent social contacts can distract the mind and disturb stillness.[32]

Ultimately, if the location of the cell is unsuitable for the practice of stillness, the monk must consider voluntary exile (*xeniteia*), leaving the local region or even his native country to find a place that will allow for sufficient solitude.[33] At the same time, Evagrius recognizes that such an option should only be taken after very careful consideration and the monk must discern whether or not he is properly motivated. He must be wary of the ever present danger of acedia that will inspire within him a kind of boredom, a feeling of the tedium of ascetic practice and ultimately dissatisfaction with his cell and his current circumstances. Acedia is countered with the regularity of manual labour and the firm commitment to 'remain seated in one's cell'. To renew his zeal and foster the interior dimension of stillness the monk can meditate on the death, judgement, reward, and punishment that may await him. His efforts can be further fortified by fasting, ascetic austerities, and prayer.

The Evagrian advocacy of the practice of stillness is mirrored in the later collections of the *Apophthegmata Patrum*. There too the primary emphasis of the practice is the establishment of the necessary external conditions to promote an interior state of tranquillity. The greatest threat to stillness is frequency of social contacts or inappropriate relationships (with secular people, with relatives, or with worldly-minded brothers). Although the emphasis is on the external conditions, the goal is to maintain one's interior life free of unnecessary agitation or distraction.[34]

Eulogios, the second longest work in the Greek ascetic corpus, is also devoted to discussion of the initial stage of the ascetic life.[35] Evagrius here draws attention to a traditional recommendation of the elders that the monastic novice undertake *anachoresis* by degrees, first proving his virtue in community and only then seeking greater solitude. Evagrius himself followed this pattern, spending two years at Nitria before withdrawing to the greater isolation of Kellia.[36] Another element of practice deemed essential for the monk throughout his ascetic vocation was submission

---

[32] *Foundations* 3–5.

[33] *Foundations* 6 and especially *Eulogios* 2. 2, where Evagrius expounds at length the benefits of voluntary exile and the temptations the aspiring ascetic may have to face.

[34] See e.g., *Apophthegmata Patrum* A10 (Antonios 10 = *Life of Antony* 85), A34 (Antonios 34), A76 (Arsenios 38), A154 (Ammonathas), A194–5 (Doulas 1–2), A423 (Isaak the Theban), A475 (Makarios of Egypt 22), A793 (Paul Kosmetes 2), A831 (Sisoes 28).

[35] For a detailed discussion of the doctrine in this work see the introduction to the translation below.

[36] *Eulogios* 29; cf. *Thoughts* 23; Palladius, *HL* 38. 10 (120. 5–8).

to a spiritual guide. Evagrius recognizes that the monk will, on occasion, experience a variety of temptations whose purpose is to alienate him from the influence and guidance of his 'father'.[37] As the aspiring ascetic begins to make some progress in his practice, he will inevitably be tempted to take some pride in his achievement and even expect to receive the recognition of others for it. Indeed such thoughts can quickly become overweening preoccupations and lead the monk into the dangers of vainglory and ultimately pride. The best weapon against such temptations is the 'lightning-bolt of humility'.[38] Even within the semi-anchoretic context of life at Nitria and Kellia, the monk must learn to live harmoniously with his brothers: this will mean accepting personal offences in a spirit of humility and without harbouring any resentment; any malicious gossip must be avoided; the service of hospitality must be offered ungrudgingly and with sincere generosity; and finally the monk must at all costs avoid irascibility and cultivate the virtue of gentleness. The importance of charitable relations among the brothers is highlighted by the extensive treatment that Evagrius devotes to the subject in *Eulogios*.[39] All these facets of the initial stages of the monastic life Evagrius shares in common with what we know of the traditions of the monastic settlements of Nitria, Kellia, and Sketis. He is thus among the very first to codify and commit to writing these oral teachings of the desert fathers.[40]

Evagrian *Ascesis*

Once *hesychia* has been established as the precondition, the ascetic embarks on the long road of the practical life that will lead eventually to the attainment of impassibility and thereby enable him to enter upon the gnostic life whose final goal is the knowledge of the Holy Trinity. For Evagrius, the practical life refers not to the active life (as it did from the time of Plato to the Cappadocian Fathers), but to that stage of the ascetic life, subsequent to the monk's withdrawal from the world, in which he will engage in the struggle against the vices in an unrelenting effort to establish the virtues within himself.[41] This stage is truly an agonistic one

---

[37] Evagrius details these temptations at some length in *Eulogios* 15 and 26.

[38] *Eulogios* 3, 14, 25, 31.   [39] *Eulogios* 4–5, 11, 16–17, 24.

[40] Further details on these subjects and on the contemporary monastic traditions can be found below in the introductions to the individual treatises of the Evagrian corpus and in the footnotes to the translations.

[41] A. Guillaumont treats the subject of the practical life in 'L'ascèse évagrienne', *Annuaire du Collège de France*, 79 (1978–9), 395–9. See also his lengthy treatment and study of the sources in SC 170, 38–112.

to which Evagrius applies the abundant imagery of the athletic contest and the military engagement.

Evagrius accepts the commonplace Platonic tripartite division of the soul and locates the passions in the 'passionate part' with its two components, the concupiscible and the irascible. The passions derive their source material ultimately from the perceptions of the sensible world, and when they are active in the soul they impede the mind in its natural activity of spiritual knowledge. Although the monk has to a large extent abstracted himself from the multiplicity of sensations in the secular world, he must still deal with the impressions left by the senses on his mind, whether stored in the memory or actualized in the mental representations (*noēmata*) of his thoughts. As Evagrius would indicate in his *Antirrhetikos*, such thoughts could take innumerable different forms: some would remind him of his former life and its comforts, or of his present life and its discomforts; other thoughts would recall the face of a brother who had been the cause of some irritation; still others might turn into obsessive fantasies about becoming an ascetic of great repute who would attract crowds of visitors, who in turn might compel him to accept the priesthood or even the episcopacy.[42] Thus for Evagrius the terms 'thoughts' (*logismoi*) and 'fantasies' (*phantasiai*) took on a strongly negative cast, with the latter term bearing much of its modern psychological connotations. Behind each thought there stood a demon at work, to the extent that Evagrius would frequently use the terms 'thought', 'demon', and 'evil spirit' interchangeably. Although at times it seems almost as if Evagrius has reduced the demonic reality to a mere psychological manifestation, at other times he makes it abundantly clear that he perceives the demons as individual, rational beings that seek with savage ferocity to pervert the human mind from its natural activity, the contemplation of God.[43] When the demons cannot turn the monk's thoughts to wickedness, they will seek to instil terror and panic through horrible nightmares or daytime hallucinations, all with the purpose of moving the solitary to abandon his monastic commitment. At times the demons may even attack the monk physically, touching his head or back or brain, even leaving visible wounds upon the body.[44]

The best-known hallmark of the Evagrian system is his categorization

---

[42] Cf. *Praktikos* 7, 10, and 11; *Eulogios* 21.

[43] It is interesting that the language of demons and evil spirits is almost entirely absent from *On the Eight Thoughts*.

[44] Evagrius provides details of these phenomena in *Antirrhetikos* 4 (On Sadness).

of all evil thoughts under eight generic thoughts: gluttony, fornication, avarice, sadness, anger (sometimes reversed: anger–sadness), acedia, vainglory, and pride. The monk must learn to discern the presence of each of these thoughts in all their various manifestations. Evagrius devoted several entire treatises to detailing the operations of the eight thoughts: *Vices, Eight Thoughts, Praktikos,* and the *Antirrhetikos.*

Gluttony. For monks who ate only one meal a day, which frequently consisted of no more than dry bread with water and, occasionally, a little olive oil, the thought of gluttony was not a temptation to bulimic excess, but rather a stirring of anxiety over the body's health and well-being or, more simply, a feeling of boredom with an unvaried diet. Under the rigours of such dietary restrictions the monk would become fretful about contracting illnesses of the stomach and digestive tract, especially when he knew of other monks who were afflicted with such sufferings. This concern was especially acute in the absence of medical assistance.[45] The boredom of the diet would drive the solitary to think of the delicacies of the table he had known in the past or to long for a few vegetables and some cooked food, at least on a feast day.[46] Anxieties about food and clothing might lead to miserliness in offering hospitality and leave the monk unwilling to give alms to those in need.[47] But there was also the temptation to become over-attached to a strict regimen of fasting which might lure an individual to ascetic extremes that would be harmful to the body or that would make him reluctant to have more than one meal when hospitality or sickness required it.[48] Above all, food abstinence was important because food fuelled the desires of the body and ineluctably enticed the monk towards indulging in carnal pleasures. Controlling the unruly impulses of the body at the basic level of food consumption was the first step in mastering the disordered movements of the soul.[49]

Fornication. According to Evagrius, it was a common experience for monks to be plagued with erotic images induced by demons either in daytime fantasies or dreams during the night.[50] The purpose of the demons was to discourage the ascetic practitioner to the point of abandoning his commitment. When such demonic attacks were particularly persistent, it was tempting to think that it was beyond nature to resist the intensity of sexual desires, especially in youth. This in turn produces sadness

---

[45] *Praktikos* 7 and 16.
[46] *Antirrhetikos* 1. 3, 1. 29–30, 1. 35–6, 1. 39, 1. 53, 1. 60.
[47] *Antirrhetikos* 1. 49, 1. 58, 1. 66.
[48] *Foundations* 10; *Antirrhetikos* 1. 37.
[49] *Eight Thoughts* 1. 2, 1. 5–6, 1. 11–12, 1. 28–9, 1. 30.
[50] See the numerous cases cited by Evagrius in *Antirrhetikos* 2.

and a feeling of hopelessness about the ascetic enterprise.[51] To counter such temptations the monk must remain committed to the exercises of physical asceticism, especially the restriction of food and water. Vigils and intense prayer are recommended. Here too anger and irascibility can be put to their natural use in being directed against the demons who provoke desire. Needless to say, the monk must avoid all occasions where he might encounter women.[52] Any laxity in such exercises may result in the monk gradually succumbing to the allurement of pleasures and forming a habit that may seem unbreakable. The demons will then tempt him to think that controlling the fire of one's nature is virtually impossible, but he can take consolation in the fact that after sin there is always the opportunity to repent. This of course places the individual in a position of ultimate risk of his salvation, for he may die before having a chance to repent.[53] For Evagrius, the perniciousness of the demon of fornication even extends to its ability, when all else fails, to touch the human body directly and inflame sexual desire.[54]

Avarice. The thought of avarice also involves basic human anxieties and worries over the body's fortune and well-being. Avarice arises out of obsessive concern with old age and sickness that might render the monk unable to provide for his needs through his manual labour or unable to look after himself in the case of illness. There is then the shame of having to rely on the charity of others for basic material needs.[55] Avarice represents all ties to the transitory things of this world and to the material values of the dominant society. The monk must therefore seek to free himself from these attachments and their attendant anxieties so that his mind might rise unencumbered to the contemplation of spiritual things. For Evagrius, the possession of material goods beyond basic necessities is contrary to charity. The avaricious monk hoards his possessions and is unwilling to help those in need lest he deprive himself either in the present or the future. Even the monastic elder must be cautious about possibly avaricious motives in imposing unreasonable burdens of manual labour on his disciple or on younger monks.[56] The demons deploy a whole array of tactics to tempt the ascetic to avarice, arguing for example that amassing a few possessions or some extra food is legitimate if one's intention is to have something to give to the poor; or in the fantasy

---

[51] *Praktikos* 8; *Antirrhetikos* 2. 2, 2. 4–5, 2. 8, 2. 18, 2. 25, 2. 31, 2. 43.

[52] *Praktikos* 17; *Eight Thoughts* 2 (*pass.*); *Eulogios* 18. 19; *Thoughts* 16.

[53] *Eulogios* 21. 22–3.

[54] *Antirrhetikos* 2. 25, 2. 27, 2. 45, 2. 55, 2. 63.

[55] *Praktikos* 9 and 18; *Eight Thoughts* 3. 3–5, 3. 7.

[56] *Praktikos* 18; *Antirrhetikos* 3. 4–10, 3. 28, 3. 30, 3. 37–8, 3. 40, 3. 44, 3. 49, 3. 52, 3. 55.

world of the monk's own mind, the demons may depict him as a generous benefactor of the poor and those in prison, who goes about collecting donations from wealthy women. This in turn may lead to the temptation of vainglory; above all, the monk will be tempted to remember all that he has given up in the world—the inheritance he left behind, the prosperity of other family members, or concerns about whether or not relatives will send money.[57] All such attachments weigh heavily on the monk, who, like a ship with a heavy cargo, easily sinks in a storm, or like a leaky boat, is continually awash with material concerns. On the other hand, one who is free of possessions can soar to the heights like an eagle.[58]

Sadness. The first three thoughts of gluttony, fornication and avarice are all involved with the transitory pleasures of the body and the material world. The thought of sadness arises from the frustration of any pleasure or appetite whether of the body or of the soul.[59] Indeed, every passion is associated with an appetite, except for sadness. For example, anger produces the appetite for revenge and the frustration of revenge leads to sadness. Vainglory arises from a desire for human esteem, which will also produce inevitable frustration.[60] Unfulfilled desires and appetites give birth to sadness, and sadness deprives the soul of all pleasures both material and spiritual. If sadness feeds on the other passions and draws strength from them, it can ultimately be eliminated only by the complete extirpation of the passions.[61] A moderate attack of sadness, if properly discerned, can actually be beneficial because it can prompt the monk to abandon all attachment to the pleasures of this world. However, if the attack is persistent, it can cause discouragement and tempt the monk to abandon his commitment.[62] Sadness also seems to have another dimension, which Evagrius reveals fully only in the *Antirrhetikos*, where he indicates that it can eventually place the monk in the danger of suffering a severe agitation of the soul resulting from direct demonic manifestations. These can provoke utter terror and profound psychological disturbance, suggesting to the monk that he has been abandoned by God and his angels and there is now no hope for him.[63] These demonic manifestations can be visual (both daytime apparitions and nightmarish phantoms), auditory, or even physical interventions. They may take such bizarre forms as snakes entwining round the body or flying and hissing through the air, scorpions

----

[57] *Foundations* 4–5; *Thoughts* 21.
[58] *Eight Thoughts* 3. 3, 3. 5.   [59] *Praktikos* 10 and 19.
[60] *Eight Thoughts* 5. 10, 5. 17–18; for the relationship between sadness and anger see *Eulogios* 7. 6–7 and *Eight Thoughts* 5. 1.
[61] *Eight Thoughts* 5. 5, 5. 11–14.   [62] *Thoughts* 12.
[63] *Antirrhetikos* 4. 1–2, 4. 4, 4. 8–10, 4. 16, 4. 27 and *pass.*

attacking the flesh, demons applying branding irons to the skin, lightning flashes on the walls of the cell, and so forth.[64] Evagrius does describe such machinations of the demons elsewhere, especially in *Thoughts*, but he associates them with other conditions, especially anger and pride.[65]

Anger. The thought of anger is the most dangerous passion of the soul and the greatest obstacle in the gnostic life and in the path to pure prayer. Anger is the unnatural movement of irascibility against another human being. The only natural and proper use of irascibility is anger directed against the demons.[66] Prolonged anger turns into resentment, moving the soul towards the wild bestial ferocity that is characteristic of the demons.[67] It darkens and 'thickens' the mind, rendering it incapable of contemplation and pure prayer.[68] A long-harboured and obsessive anger makes the mind susceptible to frightful demonic apparitions.[69] The monk must therefore make every effort to cultivate within himself an attitude of gentleness, patience, humility, and charity. These virtues must govern his relationships with his brothers, where he may be tempted to reply angrily to an unkind word or deed, to harbour suspicions about others, to quarrel over transitory goods, to indulge in malicious gossip, or even to take a brother to court over some possessions.[70]

Acedia. This temptation draws the monk to relax his efforts and ultimately to abandon his commitment to the monastic life. Overcome by

[64] *Antirrhetikos* 4. 5 (visions and touches induced by the demons), 13 (demons hissing in the air), 14 (a demon with eyes glowing like fire), 18 (demons entwining round the body like snakes), 23 and 38 (a demon brandishing a sword), 33 (demons in the form of scorpions wounding the body), 34 (demons spying on the monk from the air in the form of Indians (or, 'Ethiopians')), 36 (demons that fall upon the skin of the body and set upon it branding irons, leaving rounded impressions on the skin as from a cupping glass—a phenomenon that Evagrius saw with his own eyes), 41 (demons who scorch the nerves of the body), 45 (snakes flying through the air and coming down the walls), 47 (demons appearing in the likeness of the idols of the old gods), 48 (demons who burst into flame and dissipate in smoke), 53 (stars appearing in the cell at night and burning the eyes and face), 56 (demons who irritate the hair, neck, ears, or nostrils during the monk's prayer), 62 (lightning flashes appearing on the walls), 65 (demonic touches), 15, 24, 32 (demons who make various noises).   [65] *Thoughts* 27, 33; cf. *Eulogios* 27. 29 and 31. 34; *Praktikos* 11, 21.

[66] *Praktikos* 10, 24; *Eulogios* 11. 10; *Thoughts* 5.

[67] *Vices* 5 ('mother of wild beasts'); *Eight Thoughts* 4. 1; *Prayer* 5, 91; S9-Ps. 73: 19 (12. 1532C), '*Give not over to the wild beasts the soul that makes confession to you.* If the demons are called beasts and irascibility predominates in beasts, then irascibility predominates in the demons. And in Job it says, "The wild beasts will be at peace with you" (Job 5: 23)'; *KG* 1. 53 (HNF 230), 'The demons that fight with the mind are called birds; wild animals those that trouble the irascible part; and those that set desire in motion are named domestic animals.'

[68] *Eight Thoughts* 4. 5, 4. 6; *Prayer* 12–13, 21–2.

[69] *Praktikos* 10, 21; *Antirrhetikos* 5. 12.

[70] See especially *Eulogios* 5. 5, 11. 10, 16. 16–17, 24. 25–6; *Thoughts* 32.

dissatisfaction with his manual labour, with his cell, and with his spiritual practice, he finds himself constantly distracted whether at work or at prayer.[71] Readily will he relieve the boredom with a visit to the sick or the performance of a service for a brother.[72] The monastic life appears like such a lengthy and unnecessarily harsh undertaking, when surely one could live a good life in the world.[73] Evagrius counsels that at such times the monk must exercise perseverance and patient endurance, while committing himself to the regular, attentive exercise of his daily tasks of manual labour and prayer. Above all he must remain seated in his cell and reject all temptation to abandon it.[74]

Vainglory. As the neophyte begins to make progress in the struggle against the passions, there is the ever-present temptation to find satisfaction in such accomplishments and to seek the esteem and praise of others. Any success in the practice of the virtues is an opportunity for vainglory. It is a danger at every step of the way from the newest beginner to the experienced ascetic of many years.[75] It is a temptation to reveal one's ascetic practices to others in the hope of a word of praise, and for those more advanced it is a call to begin teaching others, whether brothers or seculars, before one has attained complete health of soul.[76] The thought of vainglory incites fantasies of receiving the charism of healing, of acquiring a notable reputation for holiness and being carried off to be made a priest by the people of a nearby town or city.[77] The ascetic must remain vigilant in discerning the presence, however subtle, of this destroyer of the virtues, until the moment arrives when the pleasant fruit of spiritual knowledge is granted him and he loses all taste for the values of the world.[78]

Pride. The prolonged entertainment of thoughts of vainglory leads ultimately to pride, which suggests to the ascetic that his achievements were attained through his own efforts and without the help of God, while at the same time having him look with arrogance on the less noteworthy achievements of the brothers.[79] This refusal to acknowledge the assistance of God and the mercy of Christ is in the end a withdrawal from God.

---

[71] *Praktikos* 12, 28; *Eulogios* 9. 8–9.
[72] *Eight Thoughts* 6. 6–7, 8.
[73] *Antirrhetikos* 6. 14, 6. 25, 6. 27, 6. 41.
[74] *Praktikos* 28; *Eight Thoughts* 6. 2–3, 6. 5, 6. 17–18.
[75] *Praktikos* 13, 31; *Eulogios* 14. 14–15, 19. 20, 21. 22; *Thoughts* 14–15.
[76] *Eight Thoughts* 7. 10–13,19; *Antirrhetikos* 7. 1, 7. 9, 7. 13, 7. 17, 7. 29
[77] *Thoughts* 21; *Antirrhetikos* 7. 3, 7. 8, 7. 10, 7. 26, 7. 35, 7. 40, 7. 42.
[78] *Praktikos* 32.
[79] *Praktikos* 14; *Eight Thoughts* 8. 5–6; *Eulogios* 14. 14–15, 31. 33–4.

Such an attitude is nothing less than blasphemy.[80] The monk overcome by pride is abandoned by God and has left himself open to demonic fantasies, terrifying visions, and nightmares, which can destroy his mental and emotional balance, driving him to madness.[81] He must remember that every good he has ever received and any attainment he has ever realized have come to him from God's gracious assistance and the mercy of Christ. It is only in deep humility that the monk will find refuge from the dangers of vainglory and pride.[82]

Once the monk had gained some experience in discerning the thoughts in their basic manifestations, he would be taught by his spiritual guide to recognize the more subtle tactics employed by the demons in their warfare against the soul. In the treatise *On Thoughts* Evagrius treats at length of the various stratagems of the demons and the ways in which the monk can unmask and counter them.[83] As the monk discovers in his own thoughts the various passions of the concupiscible and irascible parts of the soul, he must apply to them the therapeutic remedies recommended by his spiritual father: these will involve such ascetic exercises as fasting, vigils, manual labour, almsgiving, psalmody, and prayer. Above all, for the healing of the soul the monk must cultivate the virtues that stand opposite the vices, and in particular the two principal virtues, chastity for the healing of the concupiscible part and gentleness for the healing of the irascible part.

After much effort and with the assistance of God, the monk gradually achieves some degree of control over the passions and approaches the threshold of impassibility. For Evagrius, impassibility itself represents a progression of growth from the 'little (or imperfect) impassibility' to 'perfect impassibility'.[84] The first stage involves a mastery of the passions of the concupiscible part of the soul, principally gluttony and fornication. Progress through the second stage advances with the gradual control of the passions of the irascible part, but perfect impassibility remains a goal that is not fully attainable in this life.[85] The passions of the irascible part of the soul persist in the human person until death. Impassibility is not, however, a purely negative concept, for it ultimately involves a restoration of these two parts of the soul to their proper nature: the

---

[80] *Eight Thoughts* 8. 4; *Eulogios* 31. 33.

[81] *Praktikos* 14; *Eight Thoughts* 8. 10; *Eulogios* 31. 34; *Thoughts* 21.

[82] *Praktikos* 33; *Eight Thoughts* 8. 12–13, 18–21, 32.

[83] For a detailed treatment of the subject see below, the introduction to the translation of this treatise.

[84] *Praktikos* 60; *Thoughts* 35; *Gnostikos* 2.

[85] *Praktikos* 36.

concupiscible is turned towards desire for the knowledge of God and the irascible develops an aversion to all evil and an utter hostility towards the demons. Evagrius proposes a variety of tests of discernment that will enable the monk to recognize the signs of approaching impassibility.[86] The monk should carefully observe his thoughts to determine the strength of the temptations they pose and whether these can be avoided with relative ease. Dreams can also be used as a diagnostic for one's state of spiritual progress: the presence of erotic images indicates that warfare is still strong in the concupiscible part and the occurrence of nightmares and terrifying dreams suggests that there is need for further purification in the irascible part. Further, the clarity or obscurity of the dream images is helpful in determining the relative strength or weakness of the passions.[87] Finally, the state of the mind during prayer can be an important indicator of impassibility. When the mind is able to practise prayer without distraction, with its imagination untouched by the things of this world, when it is able to practise undistracted psalmody, then it is making progress in impassibility.[88] When the mind is no longer troubled by thoughts arising from the impassioned memories, it returns to is natural state and beholds itself as luminous.

The Gnostic Life

Although Evagrius has a great deal to say about prayer, especially in his treatise on the subject, we ultimately know very little about the precise nature of his practice. Did he stand or sit? Were there particular times of the day or night devoted to prayer practice? What was the relationship between psalmody and prayer, or the repetitive recitation of scripture verses and prayer?

In several places Evagrius recommends psalmody for the calming effect it has on the wildness of the passions, especially irascibility. In *Eulogios*, he also speaks of psalmody at the synaxis during the night and of how one ought to prepare properly for it from the first moment of waking so as to avoid the incursion of thoughts during psalmody and prayer. Undoubtedly Evagrius followed the common desert practice of two periods of psalmody, an office of twelve psalms after the meal at the ninth hour and another morning or vigil office just after midnight.[89] Still

---

[86] *Praktikos* 63–70; *Thoughts* 20.
[87] *Praktikos* 54–6; *Thoughts* 27–9.
[88] *Praktikos* 63–70.
[89] For the psalmody at the ninth hour see Palladius, *HL* 7. 5; the usage of twelve psalms

discussing the office, he recommends two methods of psalmody: one apparently involves the recitation of the psalms of the synaxis in a soft whispered voice and the other requires simply persevering through the course of the synaxis (or meditation on the meaning of the psalm).[90] It also seems that the psalms were recited in a standing position.[91] The same passage from *Eulogios* implies a very close relationship between psalmody practice and prayer. The appropriate preparation ('practising thoughts of light') as one rises for the office prevents the demon of acedia from rendering the soul torpid or agitated during psalmody and prayer and thus blind to contemplation. Evagrius also recommends the use of a short, intense prayer for moments when one is beset with temptation.[92] On one occasion he mentions as an example the simple prayer of the Publican in the Gospel.[93] This practice is closely allied with the exercise of 'counter-saying' the thoughts, for which Evagrius offers a full panoply of examples in his *Antirrhetikos*. This involves responding to each particular temptation (or demon) with an appropriate text of scripture.

In the sixth century, when John of Gaza describes the practice at Sketis, he indicates first that there was no strict rule, for the monks would engage in manual labour, meditation, and periods of prayer throughout the day. Prayer and meditation was practised during the course of the monk's manual work. From time to time he would stand up to make a brief prayer or say the Our Father and then sit down again. While working, the monk might repeat to himself the scripture he had memorized or ponder the *Lives of the Fathers* that he had read or he might simply examine

is mentioned by John Cassian, *Institutes* 2. 4 and by Barsanouphios and John of Gaza, *Letter* 143. 30–3 (SC 427). The latter refers specifically to the practice at Sketis.

[90] Both the interpretation and the text itself are uncertain at this point.

[91] In *Praktikos* 40 Evagrius mentions that the demons will sometimes tempt the sick to try to follow the habitual rule even when it is beyond their strength. In this context he mentions the practice of standing during psalmody.

[92] *Prayer* 98, 'In times of temptations such as these, use a short and intense prayer.'

[93] *Admonition* 1, F556. 15–17, 'Take heed lest he (Satan) deceive you with praises, that he may not exalt you in your own eyes, lest you become proud of your attainments like the Pharisee. Rather, strike yourself like the tax-collector, beat your breast like him, saying: "O God, have mercy on me a sinner. O God, forgive me my debts"'; *Prayer* 102, 'Do not pray like the Pharisee but like the tax-collector in the holy place of prayer so that you too may be justified by the Lord (Luke 18: 10–14).' Makarios the Egyptian recommended a similar practice of 'monologic' prayer. Cf. *Apophthegmata* A472 (Makarios the Egyptian 19), 'Abba Makarios was asked, "How should one pray?" The old man said, "There is no need at all to make long discourses; it is enough to stretch out one's hands and say, 'Lord, as you will, and as you know, have mercy.'" And if the conflict grows fiercer say, "Lord, help!" He knows very well what we need and he shows us his mercy."'

his thoughts. John also reports the Sketiote practice of saying twelve psalms at vespers and at the night office. At the end of each psalm there was an alleluia and a prayer.[94] Perhaps it is in these periods of prayer following each psalm that we should locate the Evagrian practice of 'pure prayer'.[95]

For Evagrius, then, the monk's life is deeply imprinted with prayer that passes repeatedly through the different modalities of petition, vow, intercession and pure prayer.[96] The nature and particular character of the forms of prayer will change as the monk passes through the stages of the practical and gnostic life.[97] Between the two there is no simple demarcation line. The passage from the practical life to the gnostic life is a gradual one.[98] The acquisition of imperfect impassibility opens the way for the contemplation of created beings. At the first level, called secondary natural contemplation the object is visible natures perceived in their ultimate principles or 'reasons' (*logoi*). For Evagrius, these *logoi* are both the ontological and the explicative principles of beings. To the extent that the monk is able to attain perfect impassibility he may come to enjoy the contemplation of the invisible and intelligible beings: this is called primary natural contemplation.[99] As the former is proper to human beings, so this latter mode of contemplation is proper to the angels. However, there are some human beings who will be able to come so near to complete victory

---

[94] Barsanouphios and John of Gaza, *Letter* 143 (SC 427).

[95] On the Evagrian practice of psalmody and prayer see L. Dysinger, 'The Significance of Psalmody in the Mystical Theology of Evagrius of Pontus', *Studia Patristica*, 30 (1997), 176–82; G. Bunge, '"Priez sans cesse." Aux origines de la prière hésychaste', *Studia Monastica*, 30 (1988), 7–16; id., *Das Geistgebet : Studien zum Traktat De oratione des Evagrios Pontikos*, Schriftenreihe des Zentrums Patristischer Spiritualität Koinonia im Erzbistum Köln, 25 (Cologne: Luthe, 1987), 29–43.

[96] Note the definitions of the terms in *Reflections* 26–30.

[97] Thus, for example, the prayer of intercession belongs most properly to the gnostic. Cf. *Reflections* 30. On the active and contemplative modes of Evagrian prayer see G. Bunge, 'Aktive und kontemplative Weise des Betens im Traktat *De oratione* des Evagrios Pontikos', *Studia Monastica*, 41 (1999), 211-27.

[98] See A. Guillaumont, 'La vie gnostique selon Évagre le Pontique', *Annuaire du Collège de France*, 80 (1979-80), 467-70.

[99] *KG* 2.4, 'Although the transformations are many, we have received knowledge of only four: the first, the second, the last, and the penultimate. The first, as they say, is the transition from wickedness to virtue; the second is that from impassibility to secondary natural contemplation; the third is the transition from this state to the knowledge that concerns rational beings; and the fourth is the transition from all these to the knowledge of the Holy Trinity'; *KG* 6.49 '*Egypt* signifies evil; the *desert* the practical life; the land of *Judah* the contemplation of the bodies; *Jerusalem* that of the incorporeals; and *Zion* is the symbol of the Trinity.'

over the passions of both body and soul that they may 'eat the bread of angels' (Ps. 77: 25) and thus enjoy this highest level of contemplation.[100] The contemplation by which created beings are known is that same contemplation exercised by God when he 'made all things with wisdom' (Ps. 103: 24).[101] Further, visible creation, in its *logoi*, manifests the multiform wisdom of Christ, whereas invisible creation makes known the multiform wisdom of God (Eph. 3: 10).[102]

The contemplation of beings is not an end in itself but rather directs the mind of the gnostic towards the knowledge of God.[103] This direct and unitary knowledge of God is granted to the gnostic during the rare and privileged moments of pure prayer. It presumes not only the purification of the passionate part of the soul and the attainment of impassibility, but also the voiding of the mind of all representations and all forms, both those associated with created natures and even those of God himself.[104] At this point the intellect may be granted to see itself as 'the place of God' (Exod. 24: 10). Evagrius describes this experience in *Thoughts* 39:

When the mind has put off the old self and shall put on the one born of grace (cf. Col. 3: 9–10), then it will see its own state in the time of prayer resembling sapphire or the colour of heaven; this state scripture calls the place of God that was seen by the elders on Mount Sinai (cf. Exod. 24: 9–11).[105]

---

[100] S3-Ps. 23: 6 (12. 1268C), '*This is the generation of those who seek him, of those who seek the face of the God of Jacob.* If it belongs to the angels to behold the face of God continuously, and if this is the face that human beings as well seek to see, then human beings also seek the knowledge proper to the angels, if indeed it is possible for a human being to "eat the bread of angels" (Ps. 77: 25)'; S10-Ps. 77: 25 (12. 1541BC), '*Man ate the bread of angels.* The Saviour says, "I am the bread of life who has come down from heaven" (John 6: 35). Formerly, therefore, the angels ate this bread but now human beings too eat of it. "Eating" then means "knowing", for the mind "eats" that which it knows and it does not eat that which it does not know.'

[101] Cf. *KG* 3. 24, 'The knowledge of the first nature is the spiritual contemplation which the Creator used in making the minds alone which are receptive of his nature'; *KG* 3. 26, 'The knowledge which concerns the second nature is the spiritual contemplation which Christ used in creating the nature of the bodies and the worlds derived from it'; *KG* 5. 51, 'He who sees the Creator on the basis of the harmony of beings does not know what his nature is, but he knows his wisdom with which he made everything; but I do not mean the substantial wisdom, but that which is manifest in beings, that which those who are experienced in it are accustomed to call natural contemplation. And if this is so, what is the folly of those who say that they know the nature of God?'

[102] Cf. *KG* 2. 1, 'Those things which in the beginning became something out of nothing are the mirror of the goodness of God, of his power and of his wisdom.'

[103] *KG* 2. 21, 'All that has come into being proclaims "the manifold wisdom of God" (Eph. 3: 10), but there is none among all the beings that makes known (anything) concerning his nature.'   [104] Cf. *Prayer* 66, 114, and 117.   [105] Cf. *Reflections* 2.

The intellect is said to be 'the place of God' when it is illumined by the divine light and thus appears in its true state.

The mind could not see the place of God within itself, unless it has transcended all the mental representations associated with objects. Nor will it transcend them, if it has not put off the passions that bind it to sensible objects through mental representations. And it will lay aside the passions through the virtues, and simple thoughts through spiritual contemplation; and this in turn it will lay aside when there appears to it that light which at the time of prayer leaves an impress of the place of God.[106]

In these special moments of prayer then the mind sees itself as luminous, and this light that allows it to see itself is none other than the light of the Holy Trinity.

The gnostic who has been granted such gifts is now expected to exercise these gifts in the service of others, teaching and guiding them in their progress in the spiritual life. Evagrius describes these duties and responsibilities in the *Gnostikos*. It is incumbent upon the gnostic teacher to dispense that teaching which is most suited to each individual at his particular stage of spiritual advancement. The higher teachings are to be reserved for those properly prepared to receive them; if communicated at the wrong moment, they could be misunderstood and become the source of a fall for the individuals in question.[107] This accounts for Evagrius' practice of encoding the more advanced teachings in obscure scriptural symbols that would be transparent only to others who had progressed to the gnostic life and received the appropriate teachings.

The monk who has entered upon the gnostic life does not leave the practical life behind. Far from it, he must labour all the more vigorously to overcome the passions of the soul, especially those of anger, vainglory and pride, and he is by no means exempt from the passions of the body, for such a fall is always a possibility. Irascibility in all its forms is the great obstacle to pure prayer, while vainglory will tempt the monk to assume he has reached a stage of advancement that is still beyond him. Pride takes over where vainglory leaves off, leading the monk to think that he has acquired the virtues and progressed to the highest contemplation, not with the assistance and grace of God, but by his own efforts: he is suddenly taken with the blasphemous notion that he has no need of God.[108] The gnostic, however, struggles no longer in the night of the practical

---

[106] *Thoughts* 40.

[107] *Gnostikos* 12–15, 23–5.

[108] Other blasphemous thoughts might include a denial of Christ or the relegation of the Trinity to the created order (*Monks* 134); or one might question the judgement and providence of God or the possibility of attaining virtue (S190-Prov. 19: 5); considering the

life, for he now knows 'the reasons of the warfare' and can discern more clearly the tricks and stratagems of the demons.[109] Above all, the gnostic must fortify his mind and heart by the cultivation of the virtues of faith, hope and love.

One who has acquired the virtues of love holds captive the wickedness of the passions; and he who holds from the Holy Trinity these three, namely, faith, hope and love, shall be a triple-walled city fortified by the towers of the virtues.[110]

As the pinnacle of the virtues, 'love is the door to natural knowledge, which is followed by theology and ultimate blessedness.'[111]

Evagrian Doctrine on the Origin, Fall, and Final Destiny of Rational Beings

The spiritual knowledge attained by the monk in the gnostic life enables him to decode the *logoi* of the created natures, whose true signification had till now escaped him. It also leads him to a new and more profound understanding of the scriptures, allowing him to discern there the hidden teachings regarding the practical life, natural contemplation, and theology or the knowledge of God.[112] This is the knowledge that Evagrius expounded in his biblical commentaries. Secondary natural contemplation not only guides the gnostic to discover the ultimate principles of the rational natures, it also bestows a knowledge of the reasons of providence and judgement, by which Evagrius means the reasons that presided over the origin, fall, and final destiny of rational beings as well as the role of this material world.[113] This is the teaching that Evagrius delivered primarily in his *Kephalaia Gnostika*.[114]

In his cosmology Evagrius posits a double creation, as Origen had done. In the beginning God created the rational minds for the sole end of knowing him by their union with 'substantial knowledge', that is, the knowledge of God in Unity and Trinity. They were created equal among themselves, thereby constituting a primal *henad*, which in turn was one

body to be an evil creation (*KG* 4. 60); denying free will and thus also the justice of God (*Antirrhetikos* 8. 16, F538); or considering the demons to be gods (*Antirrhetikos* 8. 47, F542).

[109] *Praktikos* 83.
[110] *Eulogios* 11. 10. 1108A.
[111] *Praktikos,* Prologue 8.
[112] *Gnostikos* 18–21, 34.
[113] *Gnostikos* 48 (where Evagrius reports a counsel of Didymus the Blind); *Monks* 132, 135.
[114] See A. Guillaumont, 'La métaphysique évagrienne', *Annuaire du Collège de France,* 81 (1980–1), 407–11.

with the divine unity or *monad*.[115] As a result of an original negligence, a movement arose among them, distancing them from substantial knowledge and creating a disparity among them, for not all fell away from knowledge to the same degree; thus there appeared the three orders of angels, humans, and demons, each assigned to their own world. In their fall, the intellects became souls, and in a second creation God provided for them material bodies, differing in the quality and proportion of the elements for each of the orders.[116] Evagrius is quite insistent that this material creation is good and is the work of a providential Deity, offering an opportunity of salvation to his rational creation.[117] The three orders of beings, in the bodies and worlds assigned to them, each possess a knowledge or contemplation proper to their state: 'thick' or obscure contemplation for the demons, secondary natural contemplation for human beings, and primary natural contemplation for the angels.[118] By the exercise of the contemplation proper to its order, a rational being is able to ascend to a contemplation of a higher order and through an eventual transformation attain the state and world of that order and ultimately

[115] On the use of these two terms in the *Kephalaia Gnostika* see G. Bunge, 'Hénade ou monade? Au sujet de deux notions centrales de la terminologie évagrienne', *Le Muséon,* 102 (1989), 69–91.

[116] Cf. *KG* 3. 28, 'The soul is the mind, which, in its negligence, has fallen from the Unity and, due to its lack of vigilance, has descended to the rank of *praktikē*'; *KG* 1. 68, 'In the angels there is a predominance of mind and fire, but in humans a predominance of earth and desire, while in the demons there is a predominance of irascibility and air.'

[117] *KG* 3. 59 (HNF 230), 'If all evil derives from the rational, the concupiscible or the irascible part, and it is possible to use these powers either for good or for evil, evils come upon us clearly according to our usage of these parts. And if this is so, nothing created by God is evil'; *KG* 4. 60 'Who will show those who blaspheme against the Creator and speak ill of this body of our soul the goodness which they have received though they are passible in that they were joined to an *organon* such as this. They bear witness to my words, who in the hallucinations of dreams are terrified by the demons and flee to wakefulness as though to the side of the angels when the body suddenly awakens'; *KG* 4. 62, 'It is necessary for the mind to be instructed, be it concerning the incorporeals or concerning bodies or to see objects simply, for these comprise its life. But it will not see the incorporeals when it is defiled in its will, nor bodies when it is deprived of the *organon* which shows it sensible things. What then will those who despise and also impugn this body of ours give to the dead soul for contemplation?'

[118] Cf. *KG* 6. 2, 'The contemplation of this world is twofold: one is manifest and thick and the other is intelligible and spiritual. Wicked men and demons attain the first contemplation, righteous men and the angels of God the second. Just as the angels have a greater knowledge of spiritual contemplation than righteous men, so do the demons have a greater knowledge of thick contemplation than wicked men. They are thought to give this also to those who belong to them. We have learned from the divine Book that also the holy angels do the same.'

return to its first state of union with the substantial knowledge of God.[119] Salvation is thus understood as progressive transformation from one order of being to another; each transformation is decided by a judgement presided over by Christ.[120]

According to Evagrian christology, Christ is an intellect like all the others, except that it remained united to substantial knowledge, who is the Word himself.[121] It is Christ who presides over the salvation of the fallen rational beings, first through the second creation that was made through him and then through the economy which subsequently came into being; through him each rational being received a body both in the beginning and at each transformation; he himself assumed a human body that he might reveal the means of salvation and guide rational beings in their return to the knowledge of God. Evagrius calls the age of the transformations 'the seventh day' or 'the reign of Christ', which lasts until all fallen rational beings, including the demons, have attained the angelic state. This will inaugurate 'the eighth day' when all will be subject to Christ and his reign will come to an end, as he submits himself to the Father, that 'God may be all in all' (1 Cor. 15: 28).[122] The intellects will then return to their original state, partaking equally with Christ in substantial knowledge. Although

---

[119] *KG* 2.4 (see n. 99 above); *KG* 3. 7, 'Each of the changes is established in order to nourish the rational beings; and those who accept nourishment attain to a change for the better, but those who refuse nourishment attain to a change for the worse'; *KG* 3. 47, 'Unique is the change that takes place "in the blink of an eye" (1 Cor. 15: 52), which will come to each according to his rank following the judgement and will establish the body of each according to the rank of its order. For the fact that someone may say that there is a change in the parts beyond that which is common means that this is one who does not know the intellections of judgement'; *KG* 3. 48, 'The change of the just is a transition from *practic* and clairvoyant bodies to clairvoyant and supremely clairvoyant bodies. [cf. S-Ps. 1: 5, 12. 1097D, 'The transformation from a *practic* body to angelic bodies constitutes the judgement of the just; the change from a *practic* body to darkling and dim bodies constitutes that of the impious, for the impious will not be raised in the prior judgement but in the second.]'; *KG* 3. 51, 'All the changes that have taken place before the world to come have joined some to good bodies and others to evil ones. But those that will take place after that which is to come will join all to gnostic *organa*.'

[120] Cf. *KG* 1. 82, 2. 75, 3. 38, 6. 57.

[121] Cf. *KG* 4. 18, 'The intelligible anointing is the spiritual knowledge of the holy Unity, and Christ is the one who is united to this knowledge. And if this is so, Christ is not the Word in the beginning inasmuch as the one who was anointed was not God in the beginning, but this one is Christ because of the former (the Word) and because of him (the Word) he (Christ) is God'; *KG* 6. 79, 'The body of Christ is connatural with our body, and his soul belongs to the nature of our souls; but the Word which is in him substantially is consubstantial with the Father.'

[122] On the seventh and eighth days see *KG* 5. 83, 'We have discovered that all the

the intellects neither lose their individuality nor their created nature, they are divinized by this union with Christ and through him with the Word and the divine Unity and Trinity itself. Reunited with one another in the *henad*, they will have entirely laid aside their number, names, and location along with the corporeal matter associated with these.[123]

Certain of Evagrius' doctrinal statements on christology, on the pre-existence of souls, and on the *apokatastasis* were condemned at the Second Council of Constantinople in 553 and this led subsequently to the disappearance of his *Kephalaia Gnostika* from the Greek theological tradition.[124] However, the majority of his ascetic works were preserved, read, and highly regarded by the Byzantine monastic tradition either under his own name or under that of Nilus of Ancyra.

---

circumcisions are seven; four of them belong to the sixth day, one of them to the seventh day and the rest to the eighth day'; *KG* 6. 7, 'If the eighth day is an allegory (symbol) for the resurrection and Christ is the resurrection, then those who are circumcised on the eighth day are circumcised in Christ'; *KG* 5. 8, 'Those who have cultivated their land during the six years of *praktikē* will nourish the orphans and the widows, not in the eighth year but in the seventh, for in the eighth year there are no orphans and widows (Exod. 23: 10–11).'

[123] On the state of final incorporeality see *KG* 1. 26, 'If the human body is part of this world and "the form of this world is passing away" (1 Cor. 7: 31), it is evident that also the form of the body will pass away'; *KG* 2. 17, 'The destruction of the worlds, the dissolution of bodies, and the abolition of names belong to the knowledge which concerns the rational beings, while the equality of knowledge perdures as does the equality of substances'; *KG* 2. 62, 'When the minds have received the contemplation that concerns them, then the entire nature of bodies shall also be removed, and thus the contemplation that concerns it shall become immaterial'; *KG* 2. 77, 'The last judgement will not make manifest the transformation of bodies, but it will make known their destruction'; *KG* 3. 66, 'Just as the first trumpet made known the generation of bodies, so too the last trumpet will make known the destruction of bodies.'

[124] For the 6th-cent. Origenist controversy see A. Guillaumont, *Les 'Kephalaia Gnostica' d'Évagre le Pontique et l'histoire de l'origénisme chez les grecs et chez les syriens,* Patristica Sorbonensia, 5 (Paris: Seuil, 1962), 124–70.

I

The Foundations of the Monastic Life: A Presentation of the Practice of Stillness

Introduction

Evagrius wrote two treatises concerned primarily with the earliest stages of monastic training, the *Foundations* and *Eulogios*. This first text takes as its central theme the practice of stillness or *hesychia*.[1] As Evagrius uses the term, *hesychia* refers to both the exterior and interior stillness that the monk must continually cultivate, for it can so easily be disrupted or lost. Both in his choice of physical space and in his regulation of his own interior space, the monk seeks for the state of perfect tranquillity that will allow him to devote himself single-mindedly to the practice of contemplation. For Evagrius, being a monk and living in true *hesychia* are virtually the same thing. The text of the *Foundations* therefore is devoted to a discussion of the necessary conditions for the cultivation of stillness and the hazards to be avoided in preserving it.

The first prerequisite is to withdraw from society in order to take up the solitary life (1–3).[2] This involves the renunciation of marriage with its attendant worries and distractions. Through an allegorical reading of a citation from Jeremiah (16: 1–4), Evagrius aligns the Pauline anxieties and cares of the world suffered by the married (1 Cor. 7: 32–4) with the thoughts and desires of the flesh. Anyone who remains bound to these cannot attain eternal life. The monk therefore abstains from marriage, renounces the thoughts and desires of the flesh, and leaves behind all material concerns of this world. Evagrius here associates the practice of monastic *hesychia* with the long-established tradition of ascetic virginity.

---

[1] See the discussion of *hesychia* and *Foundations* in A. Guillaumont, 'Les fondements de la vie monastique selon Évagre le Pontique', *Annuaire du Collège de France*, 78 (1977–8), 467–77; 'Un philosophe au désert: Évagre le Pontique', *Revue de l'Histoire des Religions*, 181 (1972), 29–56 [*Origines* 12: 185–212].

[2] The numbers in brackets refer to the sections of the text.

Even the biblical verses he cites have an established history in this context.[3]

Secondly, the monk must adopt a style of life that is simple and free of all unnecessary distractions. This means a plain and frugal diet, even taking into account the obligations of hospitality (3). Possessions and physical comforts must be reduced to the essentials required for basic subsistence (4–5). Almsgiving is not an excuse for the accumulation of wealth. Clothing is to be kept to the minimum necessary, with any surplus to be given to others in need. Servants should be considered an unnecessary distraction and a possible source of scandal in the case of a serving-boy.

Thirdly, the monk should exercise great caution in his human relationships. To preserve stillness, the monk will choose to live alone or only with like-minded brothers, avoiding any associations with people who are material-minded and involved in business affairs. Family bonds present their own dangers. Meetings with relatives should be avoided, and the monk needs to free himself from any preoccupation with his affection or worry for parents and relatives (5). Taking careful stock of his circumstances the monk must decide whether or not they are conducive to stillness and, if not, he should accept voluntary exile. The city is a dangerous place and is to be shunned as offering nothing of value to the monk's way of life. The remoteness of the desert is presented as the ideal location for the cultivation of stillness (6). But there too the monk needs to be careful about frequent encounters with the brothers, and he must choose friends carefully, spiritual friends who will aid him in his progress. Invitations to eat with a brother may be accepted on occasion, but the monk should never be away from his cell for long (7–8). Manual labour is an essential practice in the monastic life, undertaken so that the monk will not be a burden to anyone and may have some surplus to assist others in need. In thus eschewing laziness, the monk averts the danger of acedia and overcomes desires. But at some point the monk must sell the produce of his manual labour, thus involving him in the commerce of the nearby villages or towns. In the course of selling his produce or buying necessities, the monk might get caught up in the haggling over prices and the disputes that might follow. It was considered preferable to have someone else go to market on the monk's behalf (8).

Finally, Evagrius turns his attention to the ascetic exercises that will establish stillness in the monk's heart. Above all the monk must cultivate

---

[3] 1 Cor. 7 in particular was a well-known *locus classicus* for patristic writers wishing to argue the merits of celibacy. See Elizabeth A. Clark, *Reading Renunciation: Asceticism and Scripture in Early Christianity* (Princeton, NJ: Princeton University Press, 1999), 106–7, 259–329.

an interior attitude of compunction through meditation on death, judgement, heaven and hell, calling to mind the good things that lie in store for the just and the punishments that will be meted out to sinners (9). Fasting is recommended as a central ascetic practice that will purify the soul and drive away the demons, but fasting may be relaxed in giving or receiving hospitality or in the case of sickness (10). Prayer should be offered always with an attitude of vigilance and humility, remembering that the demons will make every effort to render prayer ineffectual (11).

There is very little in this short introductory pamphlet on the monastic life that can be recognized as teaching specific to Evagrius. The astute reader might perhaps recognize the reference to 'the kingdom of heaven and the righteousness of God' at the end of *Foundations* 4 as a veiled allusion to the practical and the gnostic life, for Evagrius himself offers that interpretation in *Prayer* 39.[4] The seven references in the treatise to the importance of being free from all attachments to 'materiality' of any kind[5] may suggest the Evagrian concern that the ascetic progressively divest himself, insofar as possible, of all material attachments in order that he might attain impassibility and prepare himself for pure or immaterial prayer.[6] Apart from these well-concealed references to his teaching, Evagrius presents in this treatise the common teaching of the desert tradition. This same teaching would again enter the written record within the next century in the first collections of the *Apophthegmata Patrum*.[7]

---

[4] 'In your prayer seek only righteousness and the kingdom, that is, virtue and knowledge, and all the rest "will be added unto you"' (Matt. 6: 33).'

[5] *Foundations* 2.1253B5—As a soldier of Christ the monk must be 'freed from matter and from anxieties'; 2. 1253B10, 'He has abandoned all material concerns of the world'; 3. 1253C7—He is told to 'stand free of material concerns and the passions, beyond all desire'; 5. 1256D10–1157A5. He is to avoid living with people who are 'material-minded' and should either live alone or 'with brothers who are free of material concerns'. The one who chooses to live 'with material-minded people' risks, among other things, 'madness over material things'.

[6] *Prayer* 66, 'Approach the Immaterial immaterially and you will attain understanding'; 119, 'Blessed is the mind which becomes immaterial and free from all things during the time of prayer'; 145, 'One still entangled in sins and occasions of anger, who shamelessly dares to aspire to the knowledge of more divine things or who even embarks on immaterial prayer, let him receive the rebuke of the Apostle.'

[7] See e.g. the teaching on *hesychia* in the *Apophthegmata Patrum, Alphabetical Collection*, A10, 11, 34 (Antony 10, 11, 34); A40, 63, 82 (Arsenios 2, 25, 44); A100 (Agathon 18); A138 (Anoub 1); A154 (Ammonathas); A194 (Doulas 1); A311 (Theodora 3); A340 (John Kolobos 25); A423 (Isaac the Theban 2); A471 (Makarios of Alexandria 18); A475 (Makarios of Egypt 22); A564 (Netras); A729 (Poimen 155); A793 (Paul Kosmetes 2); A801 (Rufus 1); A923 (Chairemon). For voluntary exile (*xeniteia*) see A83 (Agathon 1); A152 (Andreas); A449 (Longinus 1); A636 (Poimen 62); A776 (Pistos); A911 (Tithoes 2).

The text translated below is that of PG 40. 1252–64 with occasional reference to that of the *Philokalia* 1. 38–43 and the manuscript Lavra Γ 93.[8] The PG references are given in square brackets. The Evagrian authorship can be considered secure, for the text is attributed to Evagrius in the Greek and Syriac manuscript traditions as well in the excerpts found in the *Apophthegmata*.[9] I have added topical headings to assist in the reading of the text.

THE FOUNDATIONS OF THE MONASTIC LIFE: A PRESENTATION OF THE PRACTICE OF STILLNESS

Anachoresis

1. In Jeremiah it is said: 'And you shall not take a wife in this place, for thus says the Lord concerning the sons and daughters who are born [1253A] in this place: they shall die of a deadly disease' (Jer. 16: 1–4). This text shows that, according to the Apostle, 'The married man is anxious about the cares of the world, how to please his wife, and his interests are divided; and the married woman is anxious about the cares of the world, how to please her husband' (1 Cor. 7: 33–4). It is clear that the statement in the Prophet, 'they shall die of a deadly disease', refers not only to the sons and daughters that will issue from the married life but also to the sons and daughters born in the heart, namely, thoughts and desires of the flesh; they too shall die in the diseased, sickly and dissolute attitude of this world, and they shall not attain heavenly and eternal life. But the Apostle says: 'The unmarried man is anxious about the affairs of the Lord, how to please the Lord' (1 Cor. 7: 32); he will produce the ever-fresh [1253B] and immortal fruits of eternal life.

2. Such is the monk and so should the monk be, abstaining from a

[8] There is another witness to the text in the Pseudo-Athanasian work, *Vitae monasticae institutio* (*CPG* 2265), PG 28. 845–9, which is composed of a series of lengthy excerpts from *Foundations*.

[9] For example, the following Greek manuscripts attribute the text to Evagrius: D, E, O, and B. See A. and C. Guillaumont, *Évagre le Pontique, Traité Pratique ou le Moine*, SC 170 (Paris: Cerf, 1971), 170, 179, 268, and 140. For the Syriac manuscripts see J. Muyldermans, *Evagriana Syriaca. Textes inédits du British Museum et de la Vaticane*, Bibliothèque du Muséon, 31 (Louvain: Publications Universitaires, 1952), 31–2. The *Apophthegmata* in question are A227–8 (Evagrius 1–2).

wife, not producing son or daughter in the place mentioned by Jeremiah. Rather, he should be a soldier of Christ, freed from matter and from anxieties, uninvolved in any business concerns and activities: as the Apostle says, 'No one serving in the army gets entangled in everyday affairs, since his aim is to please the enlisting officer' (2 Tim. 2: 4). Let the monk follow this course, especially since he has abandoned all material concerns of the world and runs towards the beauteous and noble trophies of the practice of stillness. For how beauteous and noble is the ascesis that leads to stillness, how truly beauteous and noble! 'For its yoke is easy, and [1253C] the burden light' (Matt. 11: 30). Sweet is this life, the practice of it a delight!

3. Do you want therefore, beloved, to take up the solitary life for what it is, and to race after the trophies of stillness? Leave behind the concerns of the world, the principalities and powers set over them (Eph. 6: 12); that is, stand free of material concerns and the passions, beyond all desire, so that as you become a stranger to the conditions deriving from these you may be able to cultivate stillness properly. For if one were not to extricate himself from these, he would not be able to live this way of life successfully.

Food

Adhere to a frugal and measly diet, without great quantities and the sorts that easily cause distractions. And if the thought of expensive foods should arise for reasons of hospitality, leave it there and give it no credence at all, for the adversary is thereby setting a snare for you; [1253D] he is setting a trap to dislodge you from your stillness. You know how the Lord Jesus blames the soul that busies itself with such things, namely Martha: 'Why are you concerned and troubled about many things? There is need for one thing,' namely, he says, to listen to the divine word, and after that everything follows along easily. And so he adds immediately: 'For Mary has chosen the better part, which will not be taken away from her' (Luke 10: 41–2). You also have the example of the widow of Sarepta—what was the hospitality she offered the prophet (3 Kgs. 17: 10–16)? Even if you have only bread, salt, and [1256A] water, you can with these gain the reward of hospitality. And if you have not even this but receive the guest with a good disposition and offer him a helpful word, in this way you will be able to obtain the reward of hospitality, for scripture says, 'A word surpasses a good gift' (Ecclus. 18: 17).

Possessions

4. This should be your attitude towards almsgiving. Therefore do not desire to possess riches in order to make donations to the poor, for this is a deception of the evil one that often leads to vainglory and casts the mind into occasions for idle preoccupations. You have in the Gospel the widow mentioned by the Lord Jesus: with two small coins she surpassed the intention and the value afforded by the rich. [1256B] 'For they,' he says, 'contributed to the treasury out of their abundance, but she has put in all she had to live on' (Mark 12: 44).

In the case of clothes, entertain no desire for extra clothing; make provision for those sufficient to meet the needs of the body. Rather, 'Cast your cares upon the Lord and he will provide for you' (Ps. 54: 23), for scripture says 'He cares about us' (1 Pet. 5: 7). If you need food or clothing, do not be ashamed of accepting what others bring you, for this is a form of pride. But if you possess a surplus of these things, give to one who needs them. It is in this way that God wants his children to administer their property among themselves. For this reason the Apostle, in writing to the Corinthians, said regarding the needy: 'Your abundance should go to meet their need, so that their abundance [1256C] may be for your need, that there may be equality. As it is written, "The one who had much did not have too much, and the one who had little did not have too little (Exod. 16: 18)"' (2 Cor. 8: 14–15). Having therefore what you need for the present time, do not worry about the future, whether that be a day, a week, or some months. When tomorrow has arrived, that time will provide what is needed, as long as you are seeking above all for the kingdom of heaven and the righteousness of God. For the Lord says: 'Seek the kingdom of God and his righteousness, and all these things will be given to you as well' (Matt. 6: 33).[1]

5. Do not acquire a serving-boy, lest the adversary provoke a scandal against you through him and trouble your thoughts with concerns over expensive foods, [1256D] for you could no longer be concerned only for yourself.[2] And if the thought of bodily rest comes to you, consider rather that which is better, namely, spiritual rest.[3] For truly, spiritual rest is better than that of the body. Even if your intention is to benefit your serving-boy, do not let yourself be persuaded. This is not our work: it is the work of others, of the holy fathers living in community. Think only of your own benefit and preserve the way of stillness.

Human relationships and voluntary exile

Show no love for living with people who are material-minded and involved in business affairs. Either live alone or with brothers who are free of material concerns and think as you do. [1257A] The person who lives with those who are material-minded and involved in business affairs himself shares completely in their circumstances and becomes enslaved to human impositions, idle conversations, and all sorts of other dangers —anger, sadness, madness over material things, fear, and scandal.

Do not let yourself be carried away by worries for your parents or by affection for your relatives. Rather, avoid frequent meetings with them, lest they rob you of the stillness in your cell and lead you to involvement in their own circumstances. 'Leave the dead to bury their own dead, but you come follow me,' says the Lord (Matt. 8: 22). If even the cell in which you live is too easily accessible, flee and do not spare it; do not grow slack because you are attached to it. Do anything and everything so you can cultivate stillness and devote your time [1257B] to diligent application to the will of God and to the struggle with the invisible ones.

6. If you are unable to cultivate stillness with ease in your regions, direct your purpose towards voluntary exile and apply your thinking to this with diligence.[4] Be like a very good businessman, evaluating everything with regard to the cultivation of stillness and always retaining those things that are peaceful and useful in this regard (cf. 1 Thess. 5: 21).[5] Indeed, I tell you, love voluntary exile, for it separates you from the circumstances of your own country and allows you to enjoy the unique benefit of practising stillness. Avoid stays in the city, persevere with your stay in the desert. For the holy one (viz. King David) said: 'Behold, I have fled far away, and taken lodging in the desert' (Ps. 54: 8). If possible, do not enter a city at all, [1257C] for you will behold there nothing of value, nothing useful, nothing beneficial to your way of life. For again the holy one says: 'I have seen lawlessness and contestation in the city' (Ps. 54: 10). Therefore, go after places that are secluded and free from distractions. Do not be afraid of the noises there. If you see there fantasies of demons, do not be scared and do not flee the stadium of our profit.[6] Endure patiently without fear and you will see the marvels of God (cf. Deut. 11: 2, Acts 2: 11), the assistance, the solicitude, and every other assurance of salvation. For the blessed man says: 'I waited for the one who saves me from discouragement and the tempest' (Ps. 54: 9). Do not let a desire for roving overcome your purpose, for 'roving desire perverts the innocent mind' (Wisd. 4:

12). On this account temptations are many. Fear for a fall [1257D] and be steadfast in your cell.

7. If you have friends, avoid frequent encounters with them, for if you meet with them at long intervals you will be truly helpful to them. But if you think that harm may come to you through them, do not go near them at all, for you should have helpful friends who contribute to your way of life.[7] Avoid also encounters with evil and quarrelsome people and do not dwell with any of them. Rather, shun their wicked purposes, for they have no relationship with God, [1260A] nor do they abide with him. Have peaceful men as your friends, spiritual brothers, and holy fathers. For the Lord spoke of them in this way when he said: 'These are my mother, my brothers, and my fathers—those who do the will of my Father in heaven' (Matt. 12: 49–50). Have no dealings with distracted people and do not frequent their table, lest they drag you into the midst of their own deceits and lead you astray from the science of stillness, for this is the passion within them. Do not bend your ear to their words and give no reception to the thoughts of their heart, for they are harmful indeed. Let your labour be directed towards the faithful of the land and the longing of your heart be to envy their sorrow. For scripture says: 'My eyes are on the faithful [1260B] of the land, so that they may live with me' (Ps. 100: 6). But if one of those who walk according to the love of God comes to invite you to eat with him and you want to go, go then but return quickly to your cell. If possible, never sleep outside of it, so that the grace of stillness may abide with you always and you will serve your purpose there unhindered.

8. Do not become a lover of fine foods or the deceits of an indulgent lifestyle. For 'she who is indulgent is dead even while she lives,' as the Apostle says (1 Tim. 5: 6). Do not fill your belly with foods favoured by worldly people, lest you acquire a craving for these and that in turn instil within you a craving to eat at their tables. For it is said: 'Do not be deceived by the filling of the belly' (Prov. 24: 15). If you see yourself frequently invited outside your cell, decline the invitations. [1260C] A prolonged stay outside your cell is harmful: it deprives you of grace, darkens your thinking, extinguishes your longing. Note how a jar of wine left in its place for awhile to lie unmoved renders the wine clear, settled, and perfumed. But if it is carried about here and there, it leaves the wine troubled, cloudy, and showing evidence at the same time of the unpleasantness of all the badness coming from the lees.[8] Compare yourself then to this example and draw benefit from the experience. Break off relationships with a multitude of people, lest your mind be distracted and disturb the way of stillness.[9]

Manual labour

Give thought to working with your hands, if possible both night and day, so that you will not be a burden to anyone, and further that you may be able to offer donations, [1260D] as the holy apostle Paul advised (1 Thess. 2: 9; 2 Thess. 3: 8).[10] In this way you can also overcome the demon of acedia and eliminate all the other desires inspired by the enemy. The demon of acedia lies in wait for laziness and 'is full of desires,' as scripture says (Prov. 13: 4).

In the giving and receiving of payment you cannot avoid sin. So, whether you are selling or buying, take a small loss on the just price, lest you get caught up by meticulousness in the ways of greed regarding the price and fall into dealings that cause harm to the soul, such as disputes, oaths, [1261A] and perjuries, and in such things you cast dishonour on our honourable purpose and you shame its dignity.[11] Bearing this in mind, guard yourself from buying and selling. If you choose the better option and this possibility is available to you, cast this concern of yours onto some other trustworthy person, so that with an even temperament you can possess good and joyous hopes.[12]

Compunction

9. Such are the valuable counsels that the way of stillness is able to offer you. And now I will set before you the meaning of the rest of the lessons that are to be found in it. Listen to me and do what I enjoin upon you. Seated in your cell, gather together your mind, give heed to the day of your death, and then look at the dying of your body.[13] Consider the situation, accept the suffering, condemn the vanity that is in this world, [1261B] and show no weakness in virtue and zeal so that you can abide always in the same purpose of practising stillness. Call to mind also the present state of things in hell; consider how it is with the souls who are there, in what sort of utterly bitter silence, in what most terrible groaning, in what great fear and anguish, what waiting, the unceasing pain and the endless weeping of souls. But also call to mind the day of resurrection and presentation before God. Imagine that fearful and frightening judgement, bring into the open what is in store for sinners—shame before God and his Christ, the angels, archangels, powers, and all humanity; then, all the forms of punishment—the eternal fire, the worm that does not die (cf. Isa. 66: 24,

Mark 9: 48), the netherworld, the darkness, [1261C] the gnashing of teeth over all these things, the terrors and the torments. But bring forward also the good things in store for the just—intimacy with God the Father and his Christ, the angels, archangels, powers, and all the people, the kingdom and its gifts, the joy and the gladness. Bring before yourself the remembrance of both these possibilities. And at the judgement of sinners, groan, weep, and put on the form of mourning, for fear lest you find yourself among them. But at the good things in store for the just, rejoice and be glad and happy. Seek eagerly to enjoy these latter and to distance yourself from the former. Watch out lest you ever forget these, whether you happen to be within your cell or somewhere without. Do not detach your thinking from the recollection of these things, [1261D] so that through these you may escape defiling and harmful thoughts.[14]

Fasting

10. Fast as much as you are able before the Lord. Fasting completely purifies your transgressions and sins; it exults the soul, sanctifies your way of thinking, drives away demons and prepares you to be close to God. Eating once a day, do not desire to eat a second meal lest you become extravagant and trouble your thinking. Thus you will be able to accumulate an abundance for the purpose of works of beneficence, and you will be able to put to death the passions of the body. But if a visit from brothers should occur and there is need for you to eat a second and third time, do not be sullen or downcast; rejoice rather that you are obedient to necessity and, eating a second or third meal, give thanks to God that you have fulfilled the law of love [1264A] and that you have God himself as the one who disposes for your life. There will also be times when sickness of the body comes along and makes it necessary for you to eat a second and third time or even more often: so do not let your thoughts be saddened by this. It is not necessary to keep to the bodily ascetic works[15] of our way of life even in times of sickness; rather, it is necessary to give way a little in some matters in order that one may practise these same ascetic works of our way of life. With regard to abstinence from foods, the divine word did not forbid us to eat anything, but said: 'Behold, I have given you all things as I have the green plants; eat of them without distinction' (Gen. 9: 3, 1 Cor. 10: 25); and, 'It is not what goes into the mouth that defiles a person' (Matt. 15: 11). Therefore, abstinence from foods should be a matter of our own free choice and an ascetic labour of the soul.

Prayer

11. Bear gladly with sleep deprivation and sleeping on the ground [1264B] and all the other austerities by looking forward to the future glory to be revealed to you with all the saints. For scripture says: 'The sufferings of this present time are not worth comparing with the glory about to be revealed to us' (Rom. 8: 18). If you are disheartened, pray as scripture says (cf. Jas. 5: 13). Pray with fear and trembling, with effort, with vigilance and wakefulness. This is the way you should pray, especially because of our malicious and mischievous invisible enemies who would treat us insolently. When they see us engaged in prayer, then do they oppose us vigorously, insinuating into our mind things which one ought not to entertain or think about during the time of prayer, in order that they may lead our mind away captive and render [1264C] the petition and supplication of our prayer useless, empty, and profitless. Prayer, petition, and supplication become truly empty and profitless when they are not carried out, as we said, in fear and trembling, with vigilance and wakefulness. If then someone approaches a human king with fear, trembling, and vigilance and presents a petition in this way, all the more should one not present himself in similar fashion to God the Lord of all and to Christ the King of kings and Prince of princes and so make his petition and supplication? For to God be the glory forever. Amen.[16]

2

To Eulogios. On the Confession of Thoughts and Counsel in their Regard

Introduction

The *Treatise to Eulogios* is one of the least familiar works of Evagrius, even though it is one of the longest texts in the Greek ascetic corpus.[1] Its attribution to Evagrius is now generally accepted on the basis of the evidence of both the Greek manuscript tradition and the translations into Syriac. It is attributed to him in four of the principal Greek manuscripts, and in the manuscripts where it is attributed to Nilus of Ancyra it is closely associated with other genuine works of the Evagrian corpus.[2] Further, all the Syriac manuscripts inventoried by J. Muyldermans assign the treatise to Evagrius.[3]

The text of PG 79. 1093–1149 was taken from the edition published by Suaresius: *Sancti Patris nostri Nili Abbatis Tractatus seu Opuscula*, ed. Josephus Maria Suaresius, (Rome 1673), 408-50. Suaresius used for his edition a manuscript of Cypriote provenance dated to A.D. 1564 and now located in the Vatican: Ottobonianus graecus 25, fols. 165v–184r.[4] The

---

[1] It is roughly the same length as *Thoughts*.

[2] It is attributed to Evagrius in Athos, Protaton 26 and Lavra Γ 93 (Athous 333), Paris gr. 1056, and Coislin 109. See A. and C. Guillaumont, SC 170, 166–75, 175–82, 136–42, 129–35. For manuscripts of the works of Nilus of Ancyra, where *Eulogios* is associated with other genuine Evagrian works, see e.g.: Athos, Karakallou 74 (Athous 1587); Jerusalem, Saba 157; Venice, Marc. gr. 131 (471). See Guillaumont, SC 170, 262–6, 252–60; Elpidio Mioni, *Codices graeci manuscripti Bibliothecae Divi Marci Venetiarum Codices graeci manuscripti,* Istituto poligrafico e zecca dello Stato, Indici e cataloghi, nuova serie, 6 (Rome: Libreria dello Stato, 1981), 142–52.

[3] J. Muyldermans, *Evagriana Syriaca. Textes inédits du British Museum et de la Vaticane,* Bibliothèque du Muséon, 31 (Louvain: Publications Universitaires, 1952), 46–54. It is also attributed to Evagrius in the Arabo-Coptic tradition. See Kh. Samir, 'Évagre le Pontique dans la tradition arabo-copte', in Marguerite Rassart-Derbergh and Julien Ries (eds.), *Actes du IV*ᵉ *Congrès Copte. Louvain-la-Neuve, 5–10 septembre 1988*, Publications de l'Institut Orientaliste de Louvain, 41 (Louvain-la-Neuve: Institut Orientaliste, 1992), 2.130–1.

[4] On the edition of Suaresius and the manuscript Ottob. gr. 25 see J. Gribomont, 'L'édition

chapter divisions were introduced by Suaresius and do not represent any manuscript tradition. Unfortunately, this text, at least as reproduced in Migne, is seriously deficient and also misleadingly punctuated. Further, as Muyldermans surmised, it probably does not represent the original text of Evagrius.[5] The PG text is in fact a short recension (A) of the treatise, distinct from a long recension (B), found in the Syriac and Armenian translations and in a small number of the Greek manuscripts.[6] The translation presented below is that of the long recension, for which I have followed the text of Lavra Γ 93. To assist in the reading of the text, I have introduced new chapter divisions that correspond more rationally to the topical arrangement of the discussion. A comparison of the two recensions and their differences is rendered difficult by the fact that the Migne text is a poor representative of the short recension.[7] In general, the differences are most pronounced in the section corresponding to the first fourteen chapters of the Migne text. The two most significant additional sections of the B text are found in *Eulogios* 9.9 and 13.12; they are marked with square brackets in the translation below. The first expands the discussion of the activity of the demon of acedia during the practice of psalmody and the second adds to the exposition of the warfare of the thoughts a discursus on the demon of lust (*aselgeia*).

A title for the work is absent from many manuscripts, while others give various titles such as *Ascetic Treatise* or simply *To Eulogios the Monk*.[8] The Lavra manuscript offers a fuller title, *To Eulogios on the Confession of Thoughts and Counsel in their Regard*. The majority of the Syriac manuscripts have the title *To Eulogios the Monk*. There can thus be no certainty what title was given to the work by Evagrius, if indeed he gave it any.

Among the works of Evagrius, the *Eulogios* is distinctive in several respects. It is a lengthy, discursive presentation of the 'practical' or ascetic life, giving a detailed account of the experiences of the monk from the earliest stages of ascetic training onwards. The treatise begins with a letter of dedication, indicating that Evagrius wrote the work in response to a

---

romaine (1673) des Tractatus de S. Nil et l'Ottobonianus gr. 25', *Texte und Untersuchungen*, 133 (1987), 187–202, especially 193–200.

⁵ J. Muyldermans, 'Evagriana de la Vaticane', *Le Muséon*, 54 (1941), 5–9.

⁶ The long recension is found in Athos, Lavra Γ 93 (Athous 333), fols. 272r–295v and in Paris gr. 1188, fols. 103v–125v. Muyldermans also identified an excerpt from B in Vat. gr. 703, fol. 260r. See *Le Muséon*, 54 (1941), 6.

⁷ Venice, Marc. gr. 131 (471), fols. 1r–24r appears to be a good representative of the A text.

⁸ Athos, Karakallou 74 (Athous 1587) and Paris gr. 1188 for the former, and Ottobonianus 25 (and the Suarès-Migne text) for the latter.

request for guidance on the part of Eulogios.⁹ Several other Evagrian treatises have similar dedications, namely, the *Praktikos* (Letter to Anatolios),
Prayer (probably Rufinus), and the *Antirrhetikos* (Loukios). Eulogios is
designated a 'mystic initiate in the virtues,' familiar with ascetic 'labours
against the flesh,' which constitutes the matter that feeds the thoughts. In
other words, Eulogios already has some basic familiarity with the ascetic
life and seeks further counsel on the subject. Although there are several
figures named Eulogios in the monastic literature, there is little likelihood
of identifying any of them with the Eulogios of this Evagrian treatise.¹⁰

Evagrius believed that it was important for the gnostic teacher to
reveal to the student only those teachings appropriate to his particular
stage of progress.¹¹ As the *Eulogios* is concerned with the fundamentals
of the 'practical life', with only brief references to more advanced teachings, it is reasonable to suggest that this reflects the addressee's own stage
of progress. On three separate occasions in the text Evagrius treats the
circumstances of the novice monk. Immediately following the prologue,
he begins with a discussion of voluntary exile (*xeniteia*), a topic which
he also treats in *Foundations* 6, another text on the initial stages of the
monastic life. Voluntary exile is the abandonment of homeland, family,
and possessions—everything that represents the ties of worldly society.
Although Evagrius himself left his native country, he sees the fundamental option as the pursuit of the life of virtue within worldly society or apart
from worldly society, and by his time the latter had become the clearly
preferred option (2).¹² Evagrius later makes explicit reference to the
monastic novice, warning him to be wary of the esteem bestowed upon
him by his family and counselling him on how the demons will attempt to
frighten him into a cowardly retreat from his monastic commitment (22).
Lastly in *Eulogios* 30, Evagrius advises that the novice monk must first
refine the life of virtue within the setting of a community before being
allowed to pursue the solitary life: 'The elders approve highly of an anachoresis that is undertaken by degrees, if indeed one has come to this after
attaining a level of accomplishment in the virtues in community.' Even
after the adoption of a more anchoretic life, the monk must continue to

⁹ *Eulogios* 1. 1. 1093D–1096B.
¹⁰ *Apophthegmata Patrum* A217 mentions a Eulogios who was a disciple of John Chrysostom
(living in Constantinople according to the parallel in Bu I 322) and visited Abba Joseph at
Panepho in Egypt. N541 mentions an Abba Eulogios of the Enaton monastery. Palladius tells
the story (HL 21) of the Alexandrian solitary Eulogios and a cripple, who visited Antony. The
HM 16 mentions a priest named Eulogios who served a monastic community.
¹¹ See *Gnostikos* 15 and 44; also Guillaumont, SC 356, 30–3.
¹² References are to the new paragraph divisions of *Eulogios*.

prove himself and, if he should fall short of virtue, he must return to the community (29).

The relationship between the inexperienced monk and his spiritual guide was accorded great importance in the desert settlements.[13] The spiritual guide or 'father' is one 'who has yoked the gnostic life to the practical life so that from both springs he might water unto virtue the land of the soul'.[14] Evagrius' great concern is that the monk will be tempted to abandon his submission to an Abba and pursue the ascetic life on his own. The demons will move the monk to take a critical view of his father's ascetic practice or they will try to convince him that the impositions of his spiritual father are unjust and too austere. More insidiously, the demons may suggest that personal freedom in one's asceticism is just as beneficial as submission to an Abba. In this way, the demons will separate the inexperienced monk from the guidance of his spiritual father, and after allowing him some initial success in ascetic progress they will gradually lead him astray and bring about his downfall (15 and 26).

Lengthy sections of the *Eulogios* are devoted to the proper attitude that the monk must have towards ascetic exercises in themselves. Evagrius repeatedly insists that virtue, above all, must not be pursued with the intention or expectation of being honoured and respected by others. The purpose of the life of virtue is not to confer social status. The pursuit of social status reflects an attitude that is still closely allied with the values of worldly society, which the ascetic must reject. Evagrius views the quest for worldly esteem as another manifestation of attachment to the flesh, when the goal of the ascetic is to dissolve the passions of the flesh (3).

As the monk makes progress in the ascetic life, he must be constantly vigilant lest any trace of pride or vainglory enter his mind or heart. The monk 'performs' his ascetic exercises neither before himself nor before others. The former might lead him to think that his accomplishments are his own; the latter to seek the esteem of others and a consequent elevation of his social status. The temptations can be very subtle. The enthusiastic monk might engage in rigorous ascetic practices such as extended fasts, night vigils, bodily mortifications, and so forth, but there is the danger that these may become goals in themselves or may be undertaken with a hidden desire to attract the attention and esteem of others. The ascetic must be fully aware of his motives. The zealous monk might attract notice quite unwillingly and, flattered by the new-found attention, be tempted to relax his ascetic efforts. Or, having acquired a reputation and affected

[13] See Graham Gould, *The Desert Fathers on Monastic Community* (Oxford: Oxford University Press, 1993), 26–87.   [14] *Eulogios* 15. 15. 1112D.

by a consequent pride, the monk might be totally unprepared to tolerate offences or endure an unjust disgrace. If the principal motivating factor in the monk's ascetic zeal was repentance for past sins, he might be tempted at some point to think that his efforts have outweighed his previous condition or attracted God's forgiveness, and thus abandon the intensity of his commitment. In order to ward off the dangers of pride, the monk must maintain an attitude of perduring humility and repentance for sin. Vainglory can best be avoided by keeping one's ascetic exercises out of public sight and by never speaking of them. Evagrius insists that ultimately any progress in the ascetic life derives not from the monk's own dedication and effort but from the grace and the assistance of God who is the cause of all good things (14).

In the struggle for self-mastery and the construction of the new self, it is vital never to allow the ego to lapse into an attitude of self-satisfaction. The temptation to think that some progress has been made or even that some spiritual goals have been attained ever accompanies the monk's ascetic practice. Evagrius recognizes that there is the further temptation to focus on one's external practice as the measure of success—the number of years passed in the desert, the rigour of one's abstention from wine, oil, and food, and so forth. To illustrate the proper attitude of egolessness, Evagrius recounts the story of the old monk who refused to leave his desert retreat and relax his ascesis even at the end of his life, for he recognized that he was still not free of the taint of evil and had not yet been called back from his self-imposed exile (19).

In the pursuit of his ascetic commitment the monk is likely to be confronted at different times with two types of demonic deception. The demons will either move the monk's thoughts to overvalue his ascetic efforts, leading him to pride and mental imbalance, or they will belittle ascetic works as accomplishing nothing, thus leaving the monk in despair. The first is to be countered by lowliness and the second by reliance on the mercies of Christ. Evagrius, however, quickly moves his reply to another level, indicating that the basic problem here lies in the belief that ascetic austerities can of themselves produce the virtues. This clearly could lead to presumption, but it could also drive the monk to despair, if he fell prey to the demonic suggestion that his ascetic efforts were getting him nowhere. For Evagrius, all progress in virtue and knowledge derives from grace. The ascetic who believes he can rely on his own ascetic efforts runs the risk of suffering fearful demonic delusions and eventually going mad. This point is illustrated by the story of the monk who experienced frightening visions. His response was to turn to God in prayer and to remember his sins, picturing for himself the fire of judgement. Discovering humility through this practice, the monk received help from God and his demonic illusions were dispelled (27).

Evagrius concludes the treatise by repeating his earlier warnings that a dedicated commitment to the ascetic enterprise can easily be diverted from its true purpose, if the monk becomes conceited about his own efforts and their apparent success. The demons can then easily move the monk to a kind of competitive ascetic athleticism, where he values the esteem and reputation to be gained from ever more rigorous ascetic exercises. He begins to compare himself with others, envious and jealous of their attainments and any popular recognition they may receive. The ultimate conceit is for the ascetic to think that his accomplishments are due to his own efforts. Such an attitude is the ultimate demonic deception because it is blasphemous in denying the grace of God and assuming that human nature is self-sufficient and without need of God. This deception, according to Evagrius, can lead to mental imbalance and madness (31). This extended treatment of the proper attitude towards ascetic practice is indicative of the central focus of the treatise, namely, the earlier stages of monastic progress. It is also especially noteworthy that Evagrius is insistent throughout that it is not the monk's own efforts, but the grace of God that leads to any advancement in the life of virtue.[15]

The *Eulogios* is also distinctive for its extensive treatment of problems in human relations. This same emphasis is also an important characteristic of the *Apophthegmata* literature.[16] As already noted, aspiring to human esteem for one's ascetic achievements can readily lead to jealousies and petty rivalries among the brothers, thus rupturing fraternal relationships. Valuing personal esteem based on ascetic achievement also makes the monk intolerant of insults or offences of any kind and prompts him to respond either overtly through violent disputes that can embitter the brothers in a community and separate them from charity or through a harboured interior resentment (3–5). In a manner characteristic of his teaching, Evagrius insists that irascibility is to be directed against the devil and the demons and not against one's own brothers. Although the monk takes an agonistic and even militaristic stance against evil and its agents, he must always manifest gentleness towards those of his own kind. This

---

[15] In addition to the instances cited above, there are three further references to grace: *Eulogios* 8. 8. 1104B 'the grace of assistance'; 28. 30. 1133A 'grace from above'; 29. 31. 1136A 'grace more and more grants him strength'; see also 6. 6. 1101C 'drowning by the cross the resistance of the devil'.

[16] This topic has been very ably treated in Gould, *The Desert Fathers,* passim.

gentleness is expressed above all in charity, even in the midst of suffering and unjust treatment. Charity in turn is accompanied by forbearance, endurance, kindness, and patience. If wrongly directed, the irascible part of the soul gives birth to sadness and anger, but charity can bring remedy to all three (11).[17]

Malicious gossip (*katalalia*) always posed a serious threat to the harmony of monastic society, and Evagrius recognizes this in his careful treatment of the subject (16). Basil also treated this danger in his monastic teaching: 'One ought to say nothing against an absent brother for the purpose of slandering him, even though what is said may be true, for that is detraction.'[18] The problem is mentioned frequently in the *Apophthegmata*.[19] When Abba Isaias was asked to define malicious gossip, he replied 'Failure to recognize the glory of God and jealousy towards one's neighbour.'[20] Abba Poimen commented: 'Abba Poimen said: Fornication and malicious talk are two thoughts that should never be discussed or pondered in the heart; for if one wants to discern them in the heart, there is no benefit. Rather, if you avoid them forcefully, you will find rest.'[21] As Evagrius explained, malicious talk was especially serious because it involved two people in the passion, the one engaging in the gossip and the one who listened to it. He went so far as to describe the malicious detractor as stealing the souls of his listeners. There is a very similar idea in the *Apophthegmata*: 'By whispering the serpent drove Eve from paradise. Similar to the serpent then is the one who speaks maliciously against his neighbour, for he both loses the soul of the one who listens and does not save his own.'[22] At the same time the monk is counselled never to listen to gossip, which is like a deadly venom or noxious drug. The lives, foibles, and ascetic practices of others, whether living or dead, should never become the subject of curiosity or judgement for the monk, who must direct all his attention towards the reformation of his own self. Above all, the ascetic's commitment must be sincere and

---

[17] The treatise makes frequent reference to the terms charity (*agapē*), patience (*makrothumia*), and perseverance (*hupomonē*) as virtues governing the quality of human relationships.

[18] Basil, *Letter* 22. 3. 8, ed. M. Forlin Patrucco, *Basilio di Cesarea, Le Lettere*, vol. 1 (Turin: Società Editrice Internazionale, 1983); also *Great Asceticon (Regulae brevius tractatae)* 25, PG 31.1100D, 'He who makes a statement against someone in order to slander or disparage him is a detractor, even though the statement be true.' [19] Gould, *The Desert Fathers*, 121–3.

[20] A257 (Isaias 10). This Isaias is probably identical to the 5th-cent. author of the *Ascetic Discourses (CPG* 5555).

[21] A728 (Poimen 154). For the association of fornication and malicious talk see also A516 and 520. There are numerous other references: e.g., A87, 436, 642, 921, 922, 948.

[22] A923 (Hyperechios 6).

ordered toward the proper goal. Unconcerned with others, the monk attends to himself; he eschews jealousy and never disparages his brothers; he seeks the company of zealous ascetics as exemplars and teachers, and not so that he may falsely share in the esteem accorded them.

In the new society that the monk is entering, the harmonious bonds of human relationships must be closely guarded against the dangers arising from jealousy. In forming friendships the monk must be discerning about the choices he makes. An association with a brother who has a notable reputation but one unfounded in genuine ascetic virtue would be inappropriate and dangerous. A proper friend would be impervious to jealousy and free of any inclinations to malign a companion to enhance his own esteem before others. Evagrius knows that monastic companions will be tempted to jealousy, to harsh words, and thus to ruptured relationships. The cycle, however, can be broken by a charitable deed by one of the two parties.[23] Evagrius thus recommends showing respect for the other person and even inviting him to share a meal. The detailed treatment of the problem in this text suggests its seriousness for Evagrius. He describes a variety of the manifestations of jealousy. Malicious criticism may be reported to a brother as coming from a third party, leaving the one doing such reporting seemingly blameless. Criticizing a brother for his faults is also described as a way of exercising power over another, the critic thus demonstrating his superiority over his fellow. One who has committed a fault may seek to distract attention from himself by pointing out similar faults in others. Once again the monk is reminded to attend to his own interior state, ensuring the presence of a proper attitude of humility and repentance for his own failings (17).

Towards the end of the treatise, Evagrius returns once again to speak of the importance of the fraternal bonds in the monastic society (24). Care must be exercised over one's words lest the harmony of relationships be compromised in one way or another. Evagrius alludes to his notion that the community of brothers seeking the knowledge of God constitutes a special group set apart: all its members belong to 'the same race' (*homophyloi*), while those outside the community are of 'an alien race'.[24] He elaborates on this general principle through his treatment of the particular topic of hospitality (*philoxenia*). In the desert communities

---

[23] See A751 (Poimen 177), 'Wickedness in no way wipes out wickedness. Rather, if someone wrongs you, do good to him, so that by the good deed you may wipe out the wickedness.' See also Evagrius, *Virgin* 41 and *Praktikos* 26

[24] *Eulogios* 11.10.1105C and 24.25.1125C. Cf. *Letter* 53, F602.1, 'I call our seed not those who are near us by nature, but those who are near us by their state.'.

the visits of the brothers to one another were considered as privileged moments of charity and grace. Evagrius cites the instance of Abraham who with open hospitality welcomed strangers and discovered later that he had entertained angels (Gen. 18: 1–5; Heb. 13: 2). Lot's hospitality to angelic visitors is also noted by Evagrius. There is a close parallel here to a saying of Abba Apollo recorded in the *Historia monachorum*:

And he frequently spoke about the reception of the brothers: 'You must welcome the brothers respectfully when they come for a visit, for it is not them but God that you welcome. "Have you seen your brother?", it is said; "you have seen the Lord your God." ' 'This,' he said, 'we have received from Abraham (Gen. 18: 1–5). And that one must press the brothers to refresh themselves, we have learned from Lot who pressed the angels in this way (Gen. 19: 2–3).'[25]

Visits were varied in nature. The most common purposes were to consult an elder for spiritual counsel or for travelling monks to request hospitality on the road. Evagrius has in mind here only visits from other members of the monastic community, not from lay people. One of the principal questions addressed in many texts was the issue of whether or not to relax one's ascetic discipline in order to receive a visitor, especially when it was the custom to share food with a guest. Evagrius is quite clear that fraternal visitations take priority, for they strengthen the communal bonds which in turn form a defence against the devil. To reinforce this point, Evagrius cites the opinion of an anonymous monk, experienced in the gnostic life, who maintained that the humble generosity of hospitality had the power to dissipate demonic fantasies, provided only that one were already free of material concerns to some extent. Fraternal visits also provided an opportunity for any gain from one's manual labour to be turned towards the charitable end of hospitality.

Not only does Evagrius share his interest in human relationships with the later *Apophthegmata* literature, but the *Eulogios* itself witnesses to an early stage in the recording of apophthegmatic sayings and stories. Eight times in the text Evagrius illustrates his teaching with a reference to a story or saying from the oral tradition. In each case there is a formulaic introduction to the reference.[26] One such story is given a named reference and attributed to Epiphanius of Salamis, and another story found

---

[25] *HM* 8. 55–6; also quoted in *Apophthegmata* A151 (Apollo 3).
[26] 'One of the brothers'—*Eulogios* 4. 4. 1100B, 7. 7. 1101D, 19. 20. 1120A, 27. 29. 1132B; 'one of the steadfast'—19. 20. 1120B; 'one of those who partake more gnostically in the practical life'—24. 26. 1128C; 'one of the most experienced brothers'—25. 26. 1128D. For other short collections of *apophthegmata* incorporated in other works of Evagrius, see *Praktikos* 91–100 and *Prayer* 106–12.

its way into a later collection.[27] This represents clear and compelling evidence of Evagrius' reliance on the oral teaching of the desert tradition for the development of his own ascetic ideology.

The interior problematic of the thoughts is the other primary focus of the *Eulogios*. For Evagrius, the 'thoughts' stand as the symbol of the old self formed by the world of the dominant society and imbued with the sin of Adam. The monk takes an agonistic stance towards the thoughts: he must struggle with them and against them in order to effect a profound reformation of the inner self and the construction of a new subjectivity. This interior struggle requires a profound acuity in the discernment of the interior emotions, attitudes, and dispositions, in order to determine their association with either the old or the new reality. Further, the monk must be aware of the workings of the mysterious forces of the demons that lurk in the shadows of all his thoughts.

The systematic presentation of the eight principal thoughts, typical of other Evagrian texts, is not found in this treatise, although there is at least some reference to each of the thoughts. Gluttony (*gastrimargia*) is left unmentioned, although there are frequent references to fasting, especially as a remedy for fornication.[28] The association of gluttony with fornication and the recommendation of fasting as a means of warding off lustful thoughts are typical for Evagrius.[29]

Fornication (*porneia*) is treated on three occasions, first in a discussion of the strategies of the thoughts (13), then in its interior dimensions (18) and later in association with vainglory (21). The first discussion, in a passage unique to the B text, is concerned with the basic strategies deployed by the demon of lust. This demon will propose either waking or dream fantasies of sexual activities to see if the monk will be moved to pleasure and will thus be susceptible to attack on this front. The demons will also attempt to predispose the unwitting monk to sexual pleasures by tempting

---

[27] *Eulogios* 25. 27. 1128D–1129B—'this account (*logos*) was given by the holy bishop Epiphanius'; *Eulogios* 25.26.1128D = *Apophthegmata, Anonymous Collection* N 298 (165).

[28] Fasting: *Eulogios* 1. 1. 1093C, 19. 20. 1120A, 24. 25. 1125D, 26. 28. 1129D, 30. 32. 1136D–1137A, 31. 33. 1137C. Food abstinence and fornication: *Eulogios* 18. 19. 1117CD, 'torture the thoughts with abstinence from food that they may speak not out of fornication . . .'; 'a surfeit of food feeds thoughts, and a drunkard waters his sleep with fantasies.'

[29] See *Thoughts* 1. 6–8, 'it is not possible to fall into the hands of the spirit of fornication, unless one has fallen under the influence of gluttony'; *Monks* 102, 'Weigh your bread in a balance and drink your water by measure (cf. Ezek. 4: 10–11); then the spirit of fornication will flee from you.'; *Eight Thoughts* 1. 2 and 5, 'He who controls the stomach diminishes the passions; he who is overcome by food gives increase to pleasures. . . . an abundance of food nourishes desire'; 2. 1, 'Gluttony is the mother of licentiousness.'

him to gluttony first. Thus if he is lazy and negligent in his ascetic practice, the demons will the more easily gain control of the rational mind.

In the second case Evagrius carries the treatment of fornication further. The realm of concern is the heart, the soul, and the thoughts (18); the body and its natural appetites, although they may be the source of sexual desires, are of secondary importance. It is the heart then that must maintain an interior vigilance through its faculty of reason, lest when sexual desire is aroused in the body the mind be caught off guard and succumb to licentious thoughts. In this text the terms 'heart', 'mind', and 'spirit' are used as close equivalents.[30] Acknowledging that there are two types of fornication, one of the body, the other of the spirit, Evagrius devotes his attention to the latter. Fornication is presented as a kind of idolatry. Sexual thoughts produce in the spirit a 'representation of error', usually manifested as a female form that draws the soul to have intercourse with it. Evagrius describes this as 'bowing down to an insubstantial form (*eidoleion*)'. Sexual thoughts are countered not only by the vigilance of the mind and heart, but also through the important exercise of restricting food and drink, which is fundamental for Evagrius in controlling sexual appetites. When afflicted with such desires, the monk must avoid accepting invitations to meals and even continue his own fast when offering the hospitality of food to a visitor. This probably constitutes a special circumstance and an exception to the usual practice of forgoing one's fast for the sake of charity when entertaining visitors.[31] The monk is called to 'wither the flower of the flesh' with ascetic exercises and to 'practise daily his own death in the flesh'. Although the ascetic is expected to engage his or her own efforts to achieve this goal, Evagrius makes it clear that such 'interior adulteries' are only driven away by the Cross, and the monk must pray with tears of repentance at the night vigils in order to receive help.

A little later, Evagrius continues his treatment of the subject, while briefly comparing the differing operations of the spirits of fornication and vainglory (21). At this point, more attention is paid to the varying modalities of temptation deployed by the spirit of fornication. The demon of licentiousness will attack differently in different circumstances. If the monk is faithful to ascetic practice, the demon attacks with suddenness and speed, presumably hoping to catch the monk by surprise. However, if self-discipline is lax and the ascetic is already attracted by pleasure, the

---

[30] In the *Treatise to Eulogios* the word 'heart' appears 42 times, 'mind' 21 times, and 'soul' 73 times.

[31] See A427, 518. Some monks would share a meal with visitors, but then increase their fast after the visitors departed (A818).

demon can invade the heart gradually, accustoming it to vice, until it has forgotten its hatred of sin. Here too, the remedy is to waste the flesh with fasting and bodily mortifications so as to eliminate pleasure and impure fantasies from the heart.

Evagrius emphasizes the grave danger of succumbing to the attraction of sexual pleasure. Sexual pleasure is addictive, and great effort is required to break a habit of pleasure. Too much attention to the attraction of sexual pleasure may hook the ascetic into thinking that it is too difficult to control the natural appetites; perpetual discipline of the body comes to seem impossible. The ascetic is then plagued with sexual fantasies from his dreams. The demon suggests that if he cannot avoid sin today he can always repent tomorrow; after all, many great ascetics have sinned and then found repentance. Evagrius is quick to point out the deceit of this demonic temptation. There is no guarantee that one will have the opportunity to repent, and the addiction to pleasure may prove to be too powerful to overcome. Remembrance of death and the terror of divine judgement must be deployed to break the hold of sexual pleasure on the flesh. This in turn must be supplemented by ascetic exercises to control the passions of the body. These passions originate in the natural appetites and are effectively managed with self-discipline of the body. The passions of the soul, in turn, arise from the appetites of the soul and are treated by charity. It is ultimately love that will lead to impassibility and the elimination of the passions.[32]

The term avarice (*philargyria*) is not found in the treatise, but Evagrius does devote a section to poverty and freedom from possessions (12).[33] One of the defining characteristics of monastic society was its negative attitude towards the acquisition of material goods, just as the acquisition and possession of property was a fundamental characteristic of worldly society and one's social status within it. Attachment to possessions was recognized as a source of worries and anxieties directed either towards the acquisition of goods or fear for their loss. This distracted the monk from his single-hearted commitment to God. Not only was the external renunciation of material goods required, but this had to be accompanied by an interior renunciation. The thoughts would remind the monk of the inevitability of old age, the possibility of famine and sickness, tempting

[32] For further references to fornication see *Eulogios* 15. 15. 1113A and 31. 33. 1137BC.

[33] There are also brief references to freedom from possessions in 1. 1. 1093C, 'Those who hold the land of heaven as their own by means of ascetic labours do not fix their gaze on the stomach, nor on concern for perishable goods'; and 2. 2. 1096B, 'The first of the illustrious contests is voluntary exile, especially when to this end one should go abroad alone, like an athlete stripped of homeland, family, and possessions.'

him to prepare for such circumstances when he might not be able to care or provide for himself. The monk would be tempted to think of himself not only as destitute but without honour, that is, without social status. Evagrius presents both the external and internal renunciations as beneficial opportunities for the ascetic, because it is through these struggles that he will in the end receive the crown of victory.

The problem of anger is especially prominent in this work primarily because of its interest in human relationships both for the harmony of monastic society and for their impact on the individual's interior practice of stillness (*hesychia*). Thus, attachments to social status and human honours can lead to ascetic rivalries and petty jealousies, as well as the inability to bear personal offences and the tendency to fall into harboured resentments (3–5).[34] In addition to such references found throughout the treatise, Evagrius devotes an entire section to an examination of the proper, natural roles of irascibility (*thumos*) and gentleness (11). The proper uses of anger are to counter the pleasure of thoughts and to fight the devil and his demons.[35] Although the monk takes an agonistic and even militaristic stance against evil and its agents, he must always manifest gentleness towards those of his own kind. This gentleness is expressed above all in charity, even in the midst of suffering and unjust treatment. Charity in turn is accompanied by patience, forbearance, kindness, and perseverance. If wrongly directed, irascibility gives birth to hatred, jealousy, and wrath, but charity counters all three.

Anger is initially treated in the context of human relationships (3–5). This is followed by a discussion of peace and joy as the ideal characteristics not only of the harmony of monastic society, but even more so of the interior state of the soul (6). Evagrius then directs his attention to the topic of sadness (7) and follows this with a treatment of acedia (8–9). Here at least the progression of the discussion is following the common Evagrian sequence of the thoughts: anger, sadness, acedia.

Because the demons possess a power of deception that enables them to take the form of spiritual charisms, a careful discernment must be exercised in distinguishing a true charism and a demonic deception. For this reason, in his treatment of sadness Evagrius distinguishes between godly sadness and demonic sadness, drawing the distinction, no doubt,

---

[34] Further references to anger can be found at 6. 6. 1101B, 7. 7. 1104A, 20. 21. 1121A, 22. 22. 1121B, 26. 27. 1129B, 30. 30. 1133C, 30. 32. 1136D.

[35] *Thoughts* 5. 1–3, 'Our irascible power cooperates very much with the goal of the demons when it is moved contrary to nature, and it renders itself most useful to their every wicked design'; *Praktikos* 24, 'The nature of the irascible part is to fight against the demons and to struggle over any sort of pleasure.'

from 2 Cor. 7: 10: 'For godly sadness produces a repentance that leads to salvation and brings no regret, but worldly sadness produces death.'[36] Demonic sadness darkens the soul and may arise either with no apparent cause or from some unusual cause. Godly sadness, in contrast, calls the soul to repentance in tears, reminding it of death and subsequent judgement. The repentance of godly sadness eventually gives way to spiritual joy with its acceptance of death and judgement.

Pursuing the subject of sadness further, Evagrius notes briefly that sadness is a product of frustrated desires. Elsewhere, in *Praktikos* 10, he elaborates further on this, explaining that the thoughts will remind the monk of the family and society he has left behind, and the realization that these are no more a part of his life will plunge him into sadness. These memories with all their associations are further defined as 'thoughts of pleasure'. *Praktikos* 19 adds to the definition: 'sadness involves the frustration of a pleasure, whether actually present or only hoped for.' Thus attachment to any kind of earthly object or intentional objective can become the occasion for demonic sadness: for example, food, sexual pleasures, vengeance, human esteem, and material possessions.[37] As Evagrius also noted in *Praktikos* 10, sadness often follows closely upon anger, and it is treated in *Eight Thoughts* immediately after the subject of anger. In this case, sadness would result from the frustrated desire for revenge.[38] In *Eulogios* 7, sadness is said to arise as an intermediary between angry people; anger begets sadness. If sadness arises from the frustration of a desire for a perceived good, and if conflicts of anger arise between people over such frustrated desires, it is possible to see how sadness is so closely associated with anger. Thus Evagrius naturally recommends the patience of charity and the joy of innocence as the appropriate remedies for both sadness and anger.[39]

As the monk settles into his life of ascetic commitment, he will inevitably encounter the problem of acedia. Acedia is basically the temptation to relax one's ascetic efforts or even abandon them entirely. Hence, Evagrius emphasizes the importance of a steadfast and unrelenting

[36] Evagrius quotes this verse in *Antirrhetikos* 4. 74 (F512. 18–21) in his treatment of sadness.

[37] These possibilities are enumerated in *Eight Thoughts* 5. See also *Antirrhetikos*, loc. cit., 'Against the thoughts of sadness that come to us concerning passing things and that plunge the mind into great distress and kill it: 'Godly sadness produces a repentance that leads to salvation, and brings no regret, but worldly sadness produces death' (2 Cor. 7: 10).'

[38] *Eight Thoughts* 5.

[39] Beyond the treatment in *Eulogios* 7, there are references to the term sadness (*lupē*) in 4. 4. 1100B, 5. 5. 1100D, 6. 6. 1101B, 6. 6. 1101C, 11. 10. 1105D.

commitment to the ascetic training (8). If the monk has persevered with some measure of success against the demon of acedia, the next attack is that of presumption and then of vainglory, which is closely associated with it. Evagrius then addresses the more particular problem of the impact of acedia on the monk's concentration during the daily offices performed in the cell (9). The daily monastic office or synaxis in the desert settlements of Nitria, Sketis, and Kellia consisted of two principal prayer times, one in the morning and one in the evening. The latter took place sometime after the evening meal at 3 p.m. and before sunset. After several hours of rest the monk would rise for the morning office, completing it before sunrise. The office consisted of psalms, silent prayer, and sometimes readings.[40] According to Evagrius, it is the spirit of acedia that tempts the monk to laziness by proposing that the psalmody is a burden. Since the morning office takes place in the middle of the night, there is the natural tendency for the monk to relax his concentration. This is a moment of great danger, for the demons will immediately take this opportunity to introduce a variety of distracting thoughts. The *Historia monachorum* records the story of how Makarios of Alexandria saw the demons tempting the brothers during the psalmody of a night vigil. This experience left him with the following insight:

And then he understood that all vain and superfluous thoughts that anyone conceived during either the psalms or the prayers came from the illusions of the demons. Those who were able to keep control of their hearts were able to resist the black Ethiopians. He who joins his heart to God and remains intent at the time of prayer, can receive into himself nothing that is alien or superfluous.[41]

To avoid the distraction of thoughts provoked by acedia during the synaxis, Evagrius recommends that upon rising from sleep the monk should turn his thoughts toward the vision of things on high and practise 'thoughts of light'. To maintain one's attention, one can either read the psalms out loud in a low rhythmic voice or simply practise perseverance[42] during the readings, whichever technique should prove most effective in the particular circumstances. If inappropriate thoughts do impose themselves, it is important not to attempt to replace them with other thoughts; the preferred response is to resort to tears. Tears represent an attitude of humble acknowledgement of one's weakness and sinfulness, accompanied by reliance on God's help.[43]

[40] Robert Taft, *The Liturgy of the Hours in East and West* (Collegeville, Minn.: Liturgical Press), 57–66.   [41] *HM* 23. 1 (Rufinus).

[42] Or possibly, 'practise meditation'—the text is uncertain.

[43] Tears are also the recommended remedy for acedia in *Praktikos* 27. In addition to

The longer version of the B text at this point expands the discussion with further elaboration of the same points. The demon of acedia will attack either by overwhelming the monk with laziness when he is about to rise for the synaxis or he will introduce the agitation of thoughts during the time of prayer if the monk has not prepared his soul in advance with more sublime thoughts. The demon seeks to relax the intensity of the soul's commitment and render it blind to contemplation.

The topics of vainglory and pride are most fully treated in those sections of the treatise devoted to discussion of the proper attitude of the monk towards ascetic practice.[44] As he deepens his commitment to ascetic practice and makes progress in the life of virtue, the monk's dedication may be noticed by others and he will be tempted by the esteem he is accorded by his fellow monks or even by outsiders. This is the temptation of vainglory. Vainglory in turn readily gives way to pride, which will ultimately suggest to the monk that his accomplishments are his own and he has no need of God.

Although the treatment of the eight thoughts or vices is not as ordered or systematic in the *Eulogios* as it is in other Evagrian works, it would be hazardous to assume that this text belongs to a period prior to the development of the systematic presentation. The best piece of evidence against this assumption is the other treatise addressed to Eulogios, the *Vices Opposed to the Virtues*, which does present the thoughts in their usual order, although with the curious insertion of jealousy between vainglory and pride.[45] Further there are traces of the systematic presentation in *Eulogios*, where anger, sadness, and acedia are treated in sequence.[46] Vainglory is said to follow upon acedia, and is closely associated with pride. Evagrius' intention in the *Eulogios* is to examine the difficulties and pitfalls of the initial stages of the ascetic life, focusing on the proper attitude of the monk towards ascetic practice, the exterior and interior dimensions of fraternal relationships, and the problematic of the thoughts. These concerns govern the order and nature of his presentation.

Because of the basic, elementary character of the treatise, Evagrius

---

Eulogios 8–9, there are brief references to acedia elsewhere in the text: 6. 6. 1101B, 6. 6. 1101C, 13. 12. 1109B, 26. 28. 1129D.

[44] *Eulogios* 3, 14, 19, 21, 27, and 31. The term vainglory is found at *Eulogios* 8. 8. 1104C, 14. 14. 1112A, 17. 18. 1116C, 21. 22. 1121B–C, 23. 24. 1125A, 26. 28. 1129C. Pride is mentioned at *Eulogios* 3. 3. 1097C, 3. 4. 1097D, 14. 14. 1112A, 21. 23. 1124C, 24. 25. 1128A, 31. 33. 1137C.

[45] And as we have seen, the vice of jealousy is given some prominence in *Eulogios*.

[46] This ordering is found also in *Eight Thoughts*; elsewhere Evagrius places sadness before anger.

says little of the more advanced teachings of his system. Impassibility, which is the blossom of the practical life, is mentioned only twice and without any significant commentary.[47] Similarly, the division of spiritual progress into the two fundamental dimensions of the practical and the gnostic life is examined only in cursory fashion. In introducing the topic of spiritual direction in *Eulogios* 15, Evagrius advocates the close association of the gnostic and the practical life. The purpose of the practical life is to sever all one's bodily and earthly ties, whereas the gnostic life directs one's intellectual substance to the contemplation of the superior goods. Evagrius also insists that the two processes must go hand in hand, rather than being separable into two distinct stages of progress. Even one who has reached the attainment of the gnostic life still requires the guidance of an experienced teacher. The practical life and the gnostic life must not be separated; they must be practised in harmony. It is the gift and vocation of the gnostic Christian to maintain this balance in exercising the function of spiritual guidance. When Evagrius returns to the subject later in the treatise (23), he emphasizes that the path to the gnostic life is constituted by experience itself and it is the practical life of ascetic effort that guides one to such experience and forms the foundation for the gnostic life. The practical life leads the ascetic to self-knowledge; the gnostic life leads to the knowledge of God. The gnostic teacher is warned to be wary of any boasting about his attainments.

Eulogios 28 refers briefly to pure prayer, but only to say that the attainment of this highest stage of prayer will at times seem to be beyond the monk's grasp in spite of all his efforts, while at other times it can be reached with no effort of one's own. This is a clear indication to Evagrius that the work of prayer belongs ultimately to God alone, the giver of the gift. Thus the monk must seek the gift with tears and supplication to God. The remainder of the discussion is devoted to a particular kind of distraction that the monk might experience. The term 'contemplation' is used only five times in the text, but without any significant treatment of the subject.[48] Since, then, the work focuses on the fundamental issues of the practical life, digressing only occasionally and very briefly into matters of the gnostic life, we can consider this Evagrian treatise as primarily introductory in character.

---

[47] *Eulogios* 2. 3. 1097B, 'Impassible is the person who through very many battles has conquered passion'; 21. 23. 1124C, 'Love is the bond of impassibility.'

[48] *Eulogios* 6. 6. 1101B, 9. 9. 1105A⁺, 10. 9. 1105C, 17. 18. 1117A, 29. 31. 1136A.

TO EULOGIOS. ON THE CONFESSION OF THOUGHTS AND COUNSEL IN THEIR REGARD

1. Prologue

1. Those who hold the land of heaven as their own by means of ascetic labours[1] do not fix their gaze on the stomach, nor on concern for perishable goods, [1096A] like those who offer prayers for the sake of their own personal profit, 'thinking that piety is a means of gain' (1 Tim. 6: 5). On the contrary, by means of an intellectual vision they participate in a nourishing light from the highest realities, like the incorporeal beings who are surrounded by the radiance of the light of the divine glory.[2] Therefore, you too, Eulogios, mystic initiate in the virtues, in nourishing your intellectual substance[3] on the brilliance of the supreme realities, strip off the weight of the flesh by collecting your thoughts, for you know that the matter of the flesh constitutes the nourishment of thoughts. Having restrained the wiles of the flesh with the sharp instrument of ascetic labours, you choose me to be the voice of your works against the flesh, and if it were not foolhardy to break an injunction of charity, I would refuse to sail on this voyage. But since it is all the more incumbent on me to be persuaded by those of like mind, rather than to oppose them, help me in those things which pertain to God that [1096B] speech may be given me when I open my mouth (cf. Eph. 6: 19), and for my part I will assist you in the matters of obedience that it may be given to you to harvest the fruits of what you have sown.

2. Voluntary exile

2. The first of the illustrious contests is voluntary exile, especially when to this end one should go abroad alone, like an athlete stripped of homeland, family, and possessions.[4] For if in this way someone should find himself engaged in the most demanding competitions, preserving this exile safe and sound by the goal of perseverance, with the gilded wing of virtue he will take flight from his own familiar haunts and make haste to fly away towards heaven itself (cf. Ps. 54: 7).[5] But the author of evil contrives to cut off the wings of this way of life [1096C] and attempts to cast it down by means of various contrivances, and in the beginning he restrains it for

a little while, until he observes the soul overcome by nausea at his afflictions; then the dark owl brings on the night of thoughts and casts darkness upon the soul by robbing it of the ray of the superior goods.[6]

But if all alone one should stand ready in the wrestling school of the
desert and if the body should in some way happen to be impaired by illness, then does the devil present voluntary exile to the soul as especially
difficult, suggesting that the tasks of virtue can be performed not (merely)
in a particular place, but by a manner of life, and that at home with the
consolation of family it could attain the prizes of freedom from possessions with less weariness; there it would have a pleasant service [1096D]
for its weakness, and not misery and painful despondency as it now has,
because the zeal for hospitality is especially lacking in the brotherhood.
Therefore, he quickly says, 'Go away, carry yourself off, you who are the
joy and glory of your family!—to these you have without compassion
left behind an unbearable sorrow, for most people have lighted upon the
virtues in the midst of their family, without having fled their homeland.'[7]

But he who is clothed in the purple of afflictions, that is, in perseverance, in the battle line of voluntary exile, and is surrounded with faith
in regard to hopes in ascetic labours, will with unceasing thanksgiving
[1097A] shake off the raindrops of these thoughts from his inner self; and
the more they should compel the heart to turn back, all the more shall we
still flee and chant against them: 'Behold, I have fled far away, and taken
lodging in the desert; I waited for God, who saves me from fainthearted-
ness and tempest' (Ps. 54: 8). For the thoughts bring on temptations,
they coax (the heart) into turning back and they afflict it with reproaches
so as to drain it of its resolution and to cut it off from its perseverance
in thanksgiving; and so they then set their snares abroad with complete
freedom beyond what is seemly. [1097B]

3. Virtue and human honours

3. On this account, let him who is beginning to attain to such virtue consider the warfare that is launched against it, lest, caught without training,
he be easily dragged down as one unprepared. Therefore, the practice of
ascetic labours is praiseworthy when there is peace, but bravery in these
is eminently praiseworthy when warfare arises. Genuine virtue consists
in bringing forth perseverance as one's weapon, not only for those circumstances in the course of which one is engaged in ascetic labours, but
also for those evils in the course of which one is engaged in warfare; for

impassible is the person who through very many battles has conquered passion, but caught in the passions is the one who says he has acquired virtue without warfare. For the evil of the opposing forces is ranged against the battle line of the virtuous army of ascetic labours. The heart that does not have experience of warfare is deprived of the state of virtue, for 'virtue' (*aretē*) is the name of the action that comes from the word 'deeds of valour' (*aristeia*).

Virtue does not seek people's plaudits, [1097C] for it takes no delight in honour, the mother of evils. Human esteem then is the beginning of honour and its end is pride, for the person who demands honours exalts himself and such a one does not know how to bear contempt. Desire for honour is a fantasy leading to pride, for he who is in love with it imagines for himself even an office.[8] Let the ascetic labour of the virtues be an honour for you and praise according to your will a dishonour. Do not seek the glory that comes from the flesh, you who dissolve the passions of the flesh; seek after the good, and it will be your glory.[9]

He who wishes to be honoured envies the one who surpasses him in fame and by this jealousy he piles up hatred towards his neighbours; overcome by too many honours, he wishes no one to be honoured above himself and he snatches away the first prize, for fear that he appear inferior. He does not tolerate an esteemed man who is honoured when he is absent, and even in the ascetic labours of the latter he seeks to ridicule [1097D] his lowly esteem. An offence is a truly mortal wound for the person who loves esteem and he can find no escape at all from the wrath that comes of it. 4. Such a person is the slave of a barbarian mistress and has been sold to many masters—pride, jealousy, envy, and the aforementioned elite among the spirits, but he who thrashes the spirit of honour with humility will destroy the entire legion of the demons (cf. Mark 5: 9; Luke 8: 30); he who by humility presents himself to all as a servant will become like to the one who humbled himself and [1100A] took the form of a servant (Phil. 2: 7).

If you measure yourself by the lowest measure, you will not compare your measure to another. The person who discloses the weakness of his soul by his lamentations will not hold a high opinion of the ascetic labours he undertakes for himself, nor will he even give his attention to the faults of others; rather, such a person must find assurance in a different way. The demons bring degradation and offence upon the humble so that they will flee from humility, unable to bear the contempt, but the person who nobly bears dishonours with humility is all the more impelled by them towards the height of philosophy.

4. Acceptance of personal offences

When David was offended he did not respond in kind, but he restrained Abishai's power (2 Kgs. 16: 5-14). And you, when you are offended, do not give offence in return; rather, appease the person who takes vengeance on you. And if you act in this way, you block the irascibility of the beast; bear the offence, as your means of progress, and with your lips shut in the beast of irascibility.[10] Give no reply at all to those who make threats, that by your silence you may stifle the fiery lips. [1100B] Then, when you put a curb on your mouth, you will have influence over those who threaten you and give offence. For if you remain silent, you will not be eaten up by the offence, but the other person is all the more bitten by your silence when you bear patiently with the insults of the arrogant man. Shake off the praise of people from your inner self that you may also get rid of the thought of ostentation that precedes it. Watch out also for the thought of self-satisfaction, especially in your practice of stillness, lest once it has exalted you above the arrogant person it should spurn him.

No one then is able to deny that there are many different exhortations from the divine scriptures regarding the prohibition of vengeance, but for the sake of more precise instruction I will also set forth an example. One of the brothers, having endured insult and injustice from a pious person, went away divided between joy and sadness: in the case of the former, because he experienced injustice and insult and returned not opposition; in the case of the latter, because the pious person was deceived and in causing his deceit he felt joy at his expense. But consider that the Deceiver[11] also experienced the two feelings: [1100C] because on the one hand he certainly troubled the one who was experiencing joy and because on the other hand he did not trouble also the one who was sorely grieved.

5. Resentment

5. When the demons see that we have not been inflamed to the boiling point of offences, then rising up in a moment of stillness they pry open the ruling faculty so that we may treat impudently in their absence those whom we treated irenically in their presence. Therefore, whenever you have issued a rebuttal or offence in response to your brother, consider yourself as the one completely at fault, lest even in your stillness you dis-

cover a battle of thoughts in your heart: one thought reproaches you for the manner of the offences, another [1100D] in turn reproaches you for not having replied with terrible offences.

Whenever a violent dispute embitters the brothers in a community, then the thoughts suggest considering the solitary blessed in order to exhaust their patience and separate them from charity. He who overturns anger with patience and sadness with charity overturns by two forms of valour two evil beasts that fight with ferocity. He who entreats on bended knee the one who caused the irritation in order to drive away the anger drives away both beasts, because he who brings peace to those who are angry makes war on the spirit of anger. And this spirit will be wrathful with him, emboldening the anger of his fellows against him, because he took upon himself the fight of his neighbours. [1101A] He who tolerates the person with an audacious heart for the sake of peace constrains himself to become a son of peace (cf. Luke 10: 6).

6. Peace and joy

But it is not only among people that the bond of peace (Eph. 4: 3) is to be sought, but also in your body and in your spirit, and in your soul.[12] 6. When you unify the bond of this trinity of yours by means of peace, then, unified by the commandment of the divine Trinity, you will hear: 'Blessed are the peacemakers for they shall be called sons of God' (Matt. 5: 9). For if you pacify with ascetic labours the flesh which lusts against the spirit (cf. Gal. 5: 17), you will possess the glory of the Beatitudes for eternity, because you have won the war which is waged in your body against the law of your mind and which holds you captive [1101B] by the law of sin which is in your members (Rom. 7: 23). Great is the bond of peace in which has also been united the joy that enlightens the eye of the intellect for the contemplation of the superior goods.

If indeed we acquire a peaceful joy in ascetic labours, we will thereby drive away subsequent difficulties with thanksgiving and we will not grant admittance to the bellowing demon of anger, who causes mutilations in the course of afflictions and attacks the soul especially and prepares the ground for the spirit of acedia so that they may (both) darken the soul and at the same time gather up its ascetic labours. Therefore, let the joy of peace be the law written on our heart, rooting out sadness, driving away hatred and destroying wrath, dissolving acedia; for hiding in peaceful forbearance [1101C] and thanksgiving and overflowing in perseverance, the joy of peace is a sea of virtues, drowning by the cross the resistance of the devil.

7. Two types of joy and sadness

But note well that the contrary joy stands nearby with its troubling influence, lest, befuddled, you be deceived into mistaking one for the other. For the demons often take the form of spiritual charisms in order to lead the mind astray by obfuscation and make you lose your mindfulness. For demonic joy comes upon the heart when nothing stands in the way because it finds the guide to godly sadness distracted, and then it hands the soul over to the spirit of sadness because it has made it a captive of spiritual joy. [1101D]

7. I say this as well, namely, as the experience of what we seek suggested to one of the brothers, that the destroyer introduces his own joy in place of joy in the Lord; and in place of godly sadness he tempts the mind with the contrary form of sadness in order to darken the soul with changes opposed to concern for superior goods.[13] There are two types of sadness arising from evil, which can be separated in each activity: one appears in the heart without any apparent cause for sadness, the other is forcefully begotten of unusual causes. [1104A] Godly sadness calls the soul back with tears, refusing the joy and sadness of the opposing side, and it worries over approaching death and judgement; little by little it opens to accept this.

Frustrated desires produce plantings of sadness, but prayers and thanksgivings cause these to wither away.[14] Sadness gets stirred up as an intermediary between angry persons. Therefore, if the first to regain sobriety recovers from the passion, he also gives his hand to the other in an apology, driving away the bitter sadness.[15] Sadness is a disease of the soul and the flesh; it takes the former captive and it withers the latter on the spot. Sadness is begotten of opposing forces; from sadness comes wrath, and from these is born madness and insults. If you want to trample under foot sadness and wrath, embrace perseverance in charity and wrap yourself in the joy of innocence. Let your joy [1104B] not be sadness for another. He who rejoices in injustice will lament in good will,[16] and he who endures sadness in suffering unjustly will experience a radiant gladness, for the future will be the opposite of the present.

8. Acedia

8. In afflictions be especially thankful, because through them you will perceive more clearly the grace of assistance; for by thus shaking off with thanksgiving the afflictions that come upon you, you will not darken the most radiant beauty of perseverance. When the demon has cracked the whip against your flesh, it will be found to provide you with the greatest reward [1104C] if you accept the blow as a pretext for thanksgiving. For in this way it will banish the demon himself from you. In order that your reward may rain upon you more abundantly through perseverance, let your perseverance serve as the commander through the course of all your counter-efforts of asceticism, because through every evil there is also acedia that commands the army opposing you, and spying out all your ascetic efforts it puts them to the test. And if it finds one that is not securely fixed to perseverance, it bears down upon it and overthrows it. But if the demon of acedia relents before the perseverance of your ascetic labours, then in turn the wild beast of presumption bites into your achievement. If therefore, apprehensive for your safety, you drive this away, you will drive away also the spirit of vainglory along with it.[17]

9. Acedia during psalmody

At the time of the office,[18] whenever the spirit of acedia should fall upon you, it suggests to the soul that psalmody is burdensome, and it sets laziness as an antagonist against the soul, [1104D] so that with unmatchable speed it gives the flesh over to the memory as though apparently wearied for some reason. Therefore, when we have been wakeful during the night, let us not give the office over to acedia, lest the demons come upon us and gather the weeds of the thoughts and at the same time sow them in the heart (cf. Matt. 13: 25). For whenever we ruin the assembly for hymns, then we bring together the congregation of the thoughts. Therefore, after waking from sleep before the office, let us practise thoughts of light[19] beforehand within our heart, that we may be well-prepared and assist at the psalmody with wakeful mind. [1105A]

9. On some occasions one should read the psalm at the office in a low rhythmic voice,[20] but on other occasions one should employ the approved method of persevering during the psalmody.[21] We too must adopt the appropriate form in accordance with the trickery of the

adversary, because sometimes he drives the tongue to babbling when acedia envelops the soul, sometimes he encourages the chanting of the readings, [when self-satisfaction interferes with the soul. The demon of acedia instils laziness when one rises for prayer, and in turn, when one is praying or doing psalmody, he hastens to cause agitation. Thence our souls become blind to contemplation and are rendered torpid, especially when we rise together with the captivity of our thoughts and stand with them in supplication. But he who trains the soul in advance to be illumined with the most sublime thoughts cleanses beforehand the radiant monument of prayer. He who strikes the heart with inappropriate thoughts stones the grape cluster of prayer with captivity. He who the more assiduously reflects the radiance of prayers takes captive the lower thoughts by means of the highest vision],[22] as is the case when the intellectual eye receives as strength its nourishment from the light. For one who reaches out towards the vision of things on high will receive a more sharp-sighted eye, as Elisha the Prophet recounted (4 Kgs. 2: 9–12). Whenever a hostile thought comes upon your heart, do not seek to replace one thing with another through prayer, but rather, turn the sharpened sword of tears against your enemies, so that by rushing vigorously into battle you may the more quickly force him to withdraw from you.

10. Manual labour and prayer

Cherish [1105B] also in a special way alongside your manual labour the remembrance of prayer; for the former does not always have available a means of achieving the activity, but the latter offers a means continuously available. Do not delay in paying the debt of prayer when you hear a thought (that arises) by reason of the approach of work and do not make loud noises, troubling your body, during manual labour, lest you trouble as well the eye of the soul. Just as our outward person works with its hands so as not to burden anyone (cf. 1 Thess. 2: 9; 2 Thess. 3: 8), so have the inner person do its work with its mental faculties so that the mind may not be burdened. For the thoughts bring to the soul their opposing activity whenever they catch it unoccupied with godly considerations. Therefore, do the work of manual tasks for the love of humanity and the work of the rational mind for the sake of the love of wisdom, in order that on the one hand there may be hospitality for guests [1105C] and a consuming fire for laziness, and on the other hand a guide to contemplation and a winnowing of thoughts.

11. Irascibility and gentleness

Let us courageously rebuke the pleasures of flattering thoughts, turning upon them all our anger, lest in receiving with pleasure what arises from them we become on the contrary gentle towards them.[23]   10. Prepare yourself to be gentle and also a fighter, the first with respect to one of your own race[24] and the second with respect to the enemy; for the usage of irascibility lies in this, namely, in fighting against the serpent with enmity (cf. Gen. 3: 15), but with gentleness and mildness exercising a charitable patience with one's brother while doing battle with the thought. Let the gentle person then be a fighter, with his gentleness divorced from murderous [1105D] thoughts, just as his fighting is separated from those of his natural kindred. Do not turn the usage of irascibility instead to one that is contrary to nature, so as to become irascible with your brother by imitating the serpent (cf. Ps. 57: 5) on the one hand and on the other hand to form a friendship with the serpent by consenting to thoughts. The gentle person, even if he suffers terrible things, does not abandon charity, for it is because of this that he exercises patience and forbearance, kindness and perseverance (cf. 1 Cor. 13: 3–7). If indeed the exercise of patience belongs to charity, angry contention has nothing to do with charity; for irascibility rouses hatred, jealousy, and wrath, but charity hates the three of them. If you have a firm foundation in charity, pay more attention to this than to the person who trips you up. Serve God with fear and love: in the first case as master and judge, [1108A] in the second as one who loves and nurtures human beings. One who has acquired the virtues of love holds captive the wickedness of the passions; and he who holds from the Holy Trinity these three, namely, faith, hope, and love, shall be a triple-walled city fortified by the towers of the virtues.

12. Poverty

You will be proclaimed charitable, not simply because you have refused to accept something from another person, but rather you will be recognized as a renunciant because you have given without stinting.[25] When you distribute material goods, strive to cast pure seeds, lest instead of wheat you have nettles come forth (Matt. 13: 24–30). In what you offer, remember God who is both the giver and the receiver (cf. 1 Cor. 4: 7; Matt. 25: 40), so that with praises he may reckon to your account the rewards of renunciation. [1108B]

11. The person without possessions enjoys the pleasure of a life free from cares, but the one attached to possessions has the distress of the rich person as his constant concern. When you do not give your heart to considerations of material things, at that moment you may drive away captive the crowd of thoughts. When you deny the desire of acquisitiveness, at that moment you will bear also the cross without distraction. But the thought of material things will forebode for you old age, famines, and sicknesses in order to divide your hope in God among financial concerns.[26] Let him who has chosen to practise the ascesis of renunciation make for himself a wall of faith, a fortification of hope, and a secure grounding in love. For faith is not the abandonment but the substance of superior goods in the hope of perseverance and the love of life (cf. Heb. 11: 1).

When, having renounced [1108C] external material goods in freedom from passion, you walk in the path of the superior goods, then the sword-like thoughts will watch out for an opportunity to make poverty and destitution reproachful to you, presenting you with degradation and dishonour, in order that the murderers may work with murderous cunning a change of mind from such a radiant virtue. If then you give intelligent attention to victory in the contest, you will then discover rather that through the things that present you with reproaches a crown is being plaited for you; for in practising renunciation, you do so through those contests for which you receive reproaches. Therefore, do not surrender in the battle with the interior thoughts, because it is not at the beginning of renunciation that the end is praised, but rather at the end of perseverance the beginnings receive the crown. It is not only for bodily exercise that the contests receive applause, but the goal of the crown is also sought in the battle with the thoughts. [1108D]

13. Thoughts

12. Judge the thoughts in the tribunal of your heart so that, when the thieves are done away with, the chief thief may take fright; for one who is a rigorous examiner of his thoughts will also be truly a lover of the commandments. Thus, whenever there arises in the heart a thought that is difficult to discern, then ignite all the more against it intense ascetic labours;

for either it will depart, unable to bear the heat of its opposite, or else it will persevere because it belongs to the straight path.

But sometimes the demons suggest to the heart a thought that is apparently good and, immediately transforming themselves, they pretend to oppose it, so that from this opposition you may think that they know even the ideas of your heart.[27] That is not their only purpose, but their intention is also to argue the case [1109A] that with your conscience you passed judgement as one defeated by evil's opposition to the good. And again, sometimes they give you hints of their trickery so that you might of your own accord think you are smart.

[The demon of lust sometimes suggests to the intellect licentious intertwinings with a virgin, and sometimes it offers dream fantasies of intertwining with young girls, so that if one should incline towards pleasure at the memory of the scene that was fantasized, the demon could make use of the thoughts for warfare; but if one should not so incline but rather fight back, even when one feels the passion remembered by one's nature, the thoughts of shame cannot join battle before they gain a foothold to converse with the soul; nor in turn would the soul be moved to engage in warfare before it learns that it is ranging itself against the opposing thoughts. Whenever the demons attempt to dislodge one's thinking with shameful pleasures, then they introduce the warfare of gluttony, so that once they have fired the stomach beforehand they can the more effortlessly cast the soul into the pit of lust. In the laziness of the soul the demons are able to get hold of our rational mind and in the thoughts they disgorge the pleasures of evil. Sometimes the thoughts attract the passions and sometimes the passions the thoughts, and then the thoughts through the passions make war on the soul.][28]

When thoughts transport us to places which they have suggested we will like, then they in turn make us feel regret in order that they may render us completely unstable and unproductive. Therefore, let us not disperse ourselves from place to place, but rather let us bend ourselves to the practice of stillness and ascetic toils, because from our laziness the thoughts get power against us. He who knows the experience of warfare in the place where he was called remains there with God, but the person who does not know the experience proceeds as one still untried. Let those who change locations from one place to another proceed towards those more conducive to spiritual attainments and not to those more conducive to rest. For perseverance, patience, [1109B] and love are ever offering occasions of thanksgiving in the midst of afflictions, but acedia, levity, and selfishness rejoice in occasions of rest. He who does not preserve stillness brings warfare to his soul from the senses associated with sight, but the person who loves stillness guards the senses and makes war on thoughts.

13. Therefore, let your ruling faculty assemble the ranks of the senses under the edict of the law, lest by sight and by hearing you bring the scourges of the vices down upon your soul. [1109C] Since you consist of two substances, be careful to allot to each its rank, in order that the one may prevail and the other not rebel. And do not give tribute to the tyrant, because when this one has been given over to the fire you will pay the last penny (Matt. 5: 26).

14. Ascetic achievement and pride

When you fight against the causes of the passions to put them to flight, do not at that moment let a thought exalt you in its treachery, lest perchance you put your confidence in a spirit of deceit and lose your mindfulness. Seek to scrutinize the suggested reasons for which you labour at ascesis, lest the goals of your attainments become corrupted through interior thoughts. Some people, lauded for their achievements, in time neglected ascetic labours, and their fame passed away and their ascetic labours were undone. Others endured hardship on account of the burden of the vices and were highly regarded; their soul's conscience was torn apart, the disease of fame spread abroad, the thoughts led the soul astray [1109D] from its wounds and bore away its ascetic labours in the midst of praises. When those most practised in ascetic labours receive a wealth of human honours, then the demons devise and introduce dishonours, so that, distanced from honours, they cannot bear dishonours nor can they tolerate offences.

Whenever you offer a great repentance for sins, then the thoughts, by magnifying the struggles of your ascetic efforts, make light of your sins and often conceal them with forgetfulness, or else they indicate that they are forgiven, so that, giving up on your ascetic labours, you do not take account of your failings so as to lament all the more over them. 14. He who fights to cut off the passions that attack him [1112A] will bring to the battle armed soldiers more numerous than the passions. Do not forget that you have fallen, even if you have repented, but hold onto the memory of your sin as an occasion of compunction that leads to your humility, so that thus humbled you will by necessity disgorge your pride.

If a person who has committed crimes should wish to change his life for the better, let him stand against his adversarial actions by exchanging them for better ones. For indeed, he who in each deed of wickedness sets against it the opposite action shoots the dragon with arrows from the intelligible quiver of the virtues. But the sharpest weapon of the beast is vainglory, which shoots down ascetic labours; he who has seized this vice in advance by means of the hidden military resources of his works has got close enough to bring down the head of the devil completely.

Set the seal of silence on the spices of your ascetic labours, lest unfastened by your tongue they be stolen by esteem. Conceal your tongue [1112B] in the practical means of ascesis, for by keeping silence you may have your ascetic labours as trustworthy companions to witness for your life. He who is unable to have testimony given as to whoever he may be on the basis of his present ascetic labours, let him not bear witness for himself by his tongue. Some people who have removed themselves from the austerity of their ascetic labours put forward their actions of time past as a cover for their laziness, producing an unreliable presentation of foreign witnesses for works that do not now exist.

As you conceal your sins from people, so too hide your ascetic labours from them; for when it comes to a counter-scheme for the secrets of your heart, hidden snares, and renewed struggles, you may offer resistance against them. But if we securely hide our offences, but perilously reveal our labours against them, [1112C] we accomplish the opposite in both cases. Rather be ashamed of the public revelation of your shameful deeds, lest you make the misfortunes of your soul into a matter of disgrace and humiliation. Do you not fear also the display of your ascetic labours, lest by a fawning accusation you bring about the ruin of your soul? But if you show to God alone your shameful transgressions, do not show to men your struggles against them lest they think they already constitute the crowns of victory.

15. As for those who have received from grace the strength for ascetic labours, [1112D] let them not think that they possess this from their own power, for the word of the commandments is for us the cause of all good things, just as the Deceiver is for evil suggestions. For the good things you accomplish, therefore, offer thanksgiving to the cause of good things; as for the evil things that torment you, throw them back at their author. At the conclusion of every work dedicate your thanksgiving to the Good so that, with your offering made according to the law, evil may be put to shame. For he who has joined thanksgiving to action will possess inviolate the treasure of his heart, having fortified with towers its double wall against evil.

15. Spiritual direction

Praiseworthy is the person who has yoked the gnostic life to the practical life so that from both springs he might water unto virtue the land of the soul. For the gnostic life gives wings to the intellectual substance [1113A] by the contemplation of the superior goods, and the practical life 'puts to death the members that are upon earth: fornication, impurity, passion, vice, evil desire' (Col. 3: 5). Therefore, those who through these two have put on the protection of full armour (cf. Eph. 6: 11, 13) will then easily overcome the wickedness of the demons.

The demons make war on the soul by means of thoughts and they are countered in turn with a more difficult warfare by means of perseverance; and in fear they then go to battle, regarding with suspicion the mighty commander of the match. If you wish to lead your army against the phalanx of the demons, bar the gates of your soul with stillness, listen acutely to the words of your spiritual father in order that you may then set fire to the thorns of the passions even more than those of the thoughts (cf. Luke 8: 14).

Whenever you listen to the counsel of your father, be not a judge of his works, but an examiner of his words. [1113B]   16. It is usual for such thoughts to divert you to the practical asceticism of your counsellor in order to set you up as a severe judge of this man and distance you from his beneficial counsel. Do not refuse to receive counsel, even if you are a gnostic. For if the practical life is separated from the gnostic life, there is need for one who can join the harmony of the virtues to the terrifying penalty of judgement. He who shakes his father's command from his ear will be disobedient also to the command of the law.

Do not speak with delight only of the accomplishments of the fathers, but also require yourself to achieve these through the greatest ascetic effort. He who applies great ascetic effort to seeking which thought is countered by which ascetic labour [1113C] finds himself an expert in the struggle against error. Among all your intellectual ascetic labours, if one is lacking, the one who plundered it slips into its place. Remember to watch over the heart with the understanding of ascetic labours, lest forgetfulness, having plundered it of its care for the superior goods, hand it over to the captivity of thoughts. Forgetfulness of captivity lunges towards vice in order that, with the mind purloined by forgetfulness, vice might readily slip in. A mind stolen away and alienated from God in its memory sins with indifference through the external senses, for such a person is unable to guide his hearing and speech because he has let go of the charm of external ascetic labours.

16. Malicious gossip

When one likes to listen to a person finding fault with someone, the two individuals are collaborating with two collaborator spirits; [1113D] for listening to slander is to be a collaborator with speaking slander, and they are in love with one another for the ruin of the heart.   17. Block your ears from hearing malicious talk lest you commit a twofold transgression against the law with them: namely, accustoming yourself to a terrible passion and not stopping them from prattling their gossip. The person who loves to ridicule steals the soul of better people, ruining an unsound hearing with calumnies. He who escapes a tongue abusive of his neighbour chases away his own abusive behaviour as well. He who lends an open ear to an abuser draws the venom of the beast into his ears. Let your ear not partake [1116A] of such a bitter drug, lest perchance you impart such a mixture to another. Do not bewitch your ear with malicious gossip, lest, sold out to a passion, you become the slave of a multitude of passions, for once a single passion among many has found a place in you, it brings others along to the same sheep-fold. Then the ruling mind is enslaved to a multitude of vices when it has been yoked to a passion and has unyoked its ascetic labours.

The person who tries to inquire into other people's mockeries makes no real inquiry into his own actions. Do not deride a person who has passed away for having lived his life in negligence lest you become as though by habit a bitter judge of the living and of the dead. To those who commit faults pay no attention with an arrogant thought that holds you up as a judge, but attend to yourself (cf. Deut. 15: 9) with a watchful thought to scrutinize your actions. Lament when you commit a fault and do not get puffed up when you succeed in not being despised. Do not boast lest you put on evil [1116B] as your adornment.[29]

Some people, in fact, who were unable to make themselves known for their piety strove eagerly to be so known even if it was for their vice. Others, exalted by jealousy, throw pretexts from on high and disparage to their fellows those who are stable in the virtues. Some people, babbling over petty matters, dress themselves in a godly life not so as to mourn their faults with ascetic labours but to obscure the rumours of their censure. On the contrary, do not make a display of yourself for the one who

deceives you, nor rejoice at being deceived; for if you join yourself to the
zealous for the sake of simple reputation, you practise your works not for
God but for other people.

17. Jealousy

Do not associate freely with one who lives without ascetic labours, even
if a great reputation ostentatiously escorts him; he is a friend for the sake
of appearances, and time will become his accuser. [1116C]   18. Acquire
a friend who is afraid of a scoffer in order that you may find shelter from
your failings, but hide what is to be envied in you especially from one
who is envious. When your friend is made to feel inferior because of the
praises you receive for your ascetic labours and is diverted into jealousy to
the point of hurling words motivated by vainglory at your ascetic labours,
even before those about him, so that with jests at your expense he may
obscure the esteem circulating in your regard, then do not get stung by
paying attention to his envy lest you draw a bitter venom into your soul.
For it is the work of Satan to inflame him with jealousy and to consume
you with bitterness. Instead, let us humble ourselves and let us be the first
to render honour to such people, mollifying even through a meal their
attitude which was driven wild [1116D] by jealousy.[30]

Out of jealousy do not blame your friend as though your blame of him
were apparently coming from another's mouth, in order to leave yourself
innocent and hold yourself up as blameless. For this was the disguise of
Satan who in the person of the serpent blamed the Most High in order to
attribute his own jealousy to God by pretending it came from the mouth
of another and to be considered free of jealousy himself (Gen. 3: 1–5).

Do not attempt to seize upon the faults of your brother, as though you
wished to have him as your underling, lest you find yourself as Satan's collaborator. Let him who has committed a fault not attempt to blame others
or cause them to stumble in order that he might not be the only one to fall
[1117A] into evil: this was also the work at the origin of the devil's fall. Let
him be repentant for the inappropriate works he committed, undertaking
a lamentation of sorrow against them, and he will draw to himself the stillness that presides over ascetic labours and reveals to him the many-eyed
contemplation of the virtues. Let the person who practises stillness with
his tongue act courageously against the thoughts, for courage of soul is
demonstrated not in stillness of body alone, but also in bravery regarding
thoughts and constancy in the face of insults and injustices. Thus are the

terrible lashes of the devil applied indiscriminately in the midst of social contacts. [1117B]

18. Fornication

19. Let not only the mouth but also the heart maintain its guard. For the eye of the soul is blinded by the spirit of complaisance at the moment when the mind is sprinkled with dust.[31] Let your mind be blind to the most shameful things,—for 'the Lord endows such blind people with wisdom' (Ps. 145: 8)—and let it be clear-sighted in the finest things, in order that it may be blind with regard to the most wicked things.

Now consider that there are two types of fornication, coupled together yet distinct, that of the body and that of the spirit, as the virgin too, 'that she may be holy both in body and in spirit' (1 Cor. 7: 34).[32] Whenever a thought of fornication mingles with your soul, then your soul has concourse with a representation of error. The demon assumes a female form in order to bewitch your soul into having intercourse with it. The fleshless apparition bears the outline of a form in order to have the soul commit fornication with a lustful thought. [1117C] Therefore, do not bow down to an insubstantial little figure lest you do the same also in the flesh. Such people who do not drive away with the cross the interior adulteries of the spirits have been led astray by a spirit of fornication.

Torture the thoughts with abstinence from food that they may speak not out of fornication but out of hunger for prayer. Hold a vigil of tears that you may receive help for the warfare at hand. At the time of the warfare of fornication, refuse the invitations of dinner hosts; and if a guest arrives, you shall offer him refreshment while serving him, but yourself you shall secretly fortify with abstinence. May your reward be double for both works when you assign to each one its practical exercise for the sake of virtue. Do not eat with your brother for the sake of the belly, but for the sake of Christ dwell together with charity. A surfeit of foods feeds thoughts, and a drunkard waters his sleep with fantasies. [1117D] The pleasure of indulgence is dead after it has passed the throat and the lecheries of the stomach sleep in the grave. The ascetic works of austerity end in rest, but the ways of sensuality end in the fire. He who withers the flower of the flesh with ascesis daily practises his own death in the flesh. Let the accounting of the heart take the measure of the body, lest when the latter is struck the former too may grow weary. Let the flesh be satisfied with restraining the natural appetites. Let your bodily exercise be managed in

the context of your morals in order that you may learn to work the heart
and work the soul together in the labours of asceticism.

19. Self-satisfaction

20. Those who in their ascesis have made the pallor of their faces shine,
let them cast away people's praise even before [1120A] it comes, throwing
it off from their interior thought even prior to social contact. Whenever
you abstain for some time from wine, oil, and superfluous foods, then
the thoughts make you take into account the periods of time along with
the praises; they harass you into giving way a little in the ascetic exercises
you do for the sake of the body. Rightly then do you contradict the evil-
minded calculators with counter-arguments to overturn their treachery.

One of the brothers, when he was praised by the demons within for
his ascetic labours, spoke the psalm verse: 'Let them straightaway turn to
flight in shame, those who say to me, "Well done, well done!"' (Ps. 69: 4).
Do not tolerate the thoughts that bring to you a cycle of many years in the
solitary life, lest they make your ascetic works depend on their length of
time, or lest you be captured and boast of your perseverance in the desert.
Rather, in perseverance in your lowly estate [1120B] remember that you
are a useless servant (Luke 17: 10).

Because of his advanced old age, someone used force to remove from
the solitary life one of the steadfast, a solitary elder. But he said to him,
'Stop forcing me, for, evil as I am, I have not yet been called back from
exile.' While I was seeking to learn the meaning of this teaching, he said:
'First, seek arduously for the fear that is innate, and then you will find the
word of fire within that teaches man knowledge.' And when the same
man was asked also about fear, he replied: 'He who ever has a care for the
remembrance of death is led also to the fear of judgement.'

Out of fear become conversant with the divine scriptures on a daily
basis, for by association with these you will drive away converse with
thoughts. He who by meditation treasures the divine scriptures in his
heart easily expels thoughts from it. [1120C] In listening to the divine
scriptures in the night-time reading at vigils, let us not render our hearing
moribund by means of sleep, nor hand over our soul to the captivity of
thoughts; rather, with the goad of the scriptures let us prod the heart, so
that with the goading of diligence we may pierce through the opposing
negligence.

20. Miscellaneous counsels

21. Some people make friends with the pious for the sake of their own good repute and not for the sake of the care of their soul, in order to procure credit for themselves without ascetic effort.

The person who burns with charity through the remembrance of heavenly things purges the allurement of earthly things from his consideration.

Your conscience bears witness for you [1120D]: do not give it up to a thought that treats your fault lightly and coats it with honeyed words.

Do not maintain a relationship with one who loves contention, in order that you may not wage war against passion with a passion and be found inferior in virtue.

Do not exalt yourself with an arrogant thought that blows against the wind of an opposing spirit.

There is no praise for the tongue that speaks hurriedly, but there is honour for the lips that move with calm.

When you listen to a discourse, question your mind and then with discernment you will cast your vote.

Do not mislead your mind with ill-advised words, lest your Canaanite tongue should be thrown into the abyss.[33]

Do not let a garrulous spirit (cf. Job 8: 2) lead you astray, for treacherous deceit lurks within it. [Rather, arm yourself with a true word of wisdom in order that you may make war on greatly inventive deceit.][34]

The person stung by the insults of others, [1121A] who does not hurl these at the devil, rouses the mob of his own thoughts against himself and provokes himself all the more to ready weapons, because his soul happens to have been wounded through such as these.

If you travel abroad for the sake of your office,[35] do not expect to be hospitably entertained by everyone, reckoning yourself to be unworthy of the welcome so that you may in this way chase away the thought of insult, even if you think it speaks the truth.

When charity is absent and you are insulted or wronged in the worst ways, you should not bear resentment but offer blessings instead. For he who bears resentment towards demons does not do so towards men, but the one who bears resentment towards his brother is at peace with the demons.

The wrath of a quarrel is a conflagration of the heart, but souls that are free of resentment are covered with a spiritual dew.

Coals give off sparks of fire, [1121B] and so resentful souls give off evil thoughts.

Just as the strike of a scorpion produces a very sharp pain, so too the resentful soul produces a most bitter venom.

21. Fornication and vainglory

22. Bring your resentment to bear against the spirit of fornication and vainglory, two bitter demons opposed to one another; for the one flees from people, but the other rejoices in people. The demon of lust, after suddenly hurling its filth at the champion of ascesis, springs quickly away from the fiery torch of his ascetic labours, unable to bear the heat. [1121C] For little by little the demon plots against the person who has relaxed his abstinence due to the flattery of pleasures, in order to become the familiar of his heart, so that once ignited by converse with vice it may be captured and its hatred of sin come to an end. The deceiver in vainglory, being addicted to popularity, surreptitiously lights upon the soul of those devoted to ascetic efforts, pursuing for himself the esteem which they earn through their ascetic labours.[36] If therefore one should wish to prevail over these (two demons) with God's help, let him waste the flesh to counter fornication and let him humble the soul to counter vainglory, for thus will we easily drive out the empty esteem of the one and be pleasing to God; and we shall blow away the impure fantasies of the other and render our heart pure of pleasures.

It is a very serious matter [1121D] for the heart to be bound to a habit of pleasures, and much effort is needed to cut off completely the spread of evils. Therefore, do not accustom your thinking to a familiarity with the pleasures of the thoughts, for in the assemblage of evils there burns a fire. Giving you warmth in this way, they have you reckon that it is an effort to master the fire of one's nature, and the time of perseverance is lengthy and the life of abstinence is burdensome; and they bring back to you memories of the shameful fantasies that they suggested during the night, forming before you burning images of error. Then, having ignited in your flesh an even more intense burning, they introduce within you by means of the law of sin the notion that so far as you do not have the strength to restrain the force of your nature, even if you sin today by necessity, tomorrow you will repent for the sake of the commandment (cf. Rom. 7: 23-5); for the law is humanitarian and forgives the iniquities of those who repent. And they present you with the example of certain people [1124A] who fell off in their abstinence and in turn repented, in order from these examples to render credible the counsel of their own deceit. Thus, after restoring the soul by a reverse repentance, they make the temple of chastity into a place of fornication. In this way, the double-tongued serpents of the thoughts hiss within the troubled workplace of the heart.

23. You, man of abstinence, [1124B] do not get hooked on the bait of uncertain hopes under the pretext of a new repentance, for many have fallen and were immediately snatched away, and others were unable to recover, for they were bound by the habit of pleasures as though they were under a law. How do you know, fellow, whether you will live to repent, that you ascribe years of life to yourself? And here, in committing a fault, you indulge your flesh; rather grant yourself the remembrance of death and depict for your heart the terrifying penalty of judgement, (to see) if you should be able at all to extinguish the feverish mind of the flesh (cf. Rom. 8: 6).

Indeed you cannot otherwise extinguish the passions until you mingle with the flesh ascetic labours to overcome it; nor indeed, the passions of the soul until you rain the fruits of charity down upon your heart. The passions of the body take their origin from the natural appetites of the flesh, against which [1124C] abstinence is effective; the passions of the soul have their conception from the appetites of the soul, against which charity is effective.[37] Love is the bond of impassibility and the expunging of the passions; it brings patience to the fore and it has a cooling effect on boiling irascibility; it promotes humility and topples pride. Love possesses nothing of its own apart from God, for God is love itself (1 John 4: 8).

22. The monastic novice

As for one who has been recently admitted to the radiant assembly of monks, let him drive away the thoughts coming to him from his family that hold out praise as bait, in order that he might not seek people's praise but the beatitude that comes from the commandments. Let him show courage against the demons who introduce their cowardice, 'for you have not received a spirit of cowardice to fall again into fear' (Rom. 8: 15). On this account let him not cower with fear because of the spirit of cowardice, nor tremble at the nocturnal racket [1124D] of the demons, when they do not even have authority over swine (Luke 8: 32). Thus when he has left his cell in the late evening hours, let him not cry out with fear and leap back in fright, as if the demons were running after him; rather, with knees bent in the spot where he takes fright, let him make a prayer, for they will not fall upon you even though they terrorize you in this way. And when you get up, encourage and exhort your heart with the psalm verse, saying: 'You shall not fear the terror that comes by night nor the arrow that flies by day nor a thing that moves in the darkness, nor a chance event or the noonday demon' (Ps. 90: 5-6). For having acted thus once and for all, you shall more quickly drive from you the demon of cowardice. When they are unable to cause harm in deed, they terrify the soul with fantasies [1125A] so that we will think that the weak and the feeble are strong and mighty.

23. The practical life

24. Do not dress yourself in the finest clothes lest you quite blatantly put on the demon of vainglory, for the virtues are not born in the beauty of one's clothes, but in the beauty of the soul ascetic works are worn as golden embroideries. Put on the fear of God for the punishments of judgement so that out of fear of the inextinguishable fire you may put on the indivisible robe of ascetic works (cf. John 19: 23) and be more quickly endowed with wisdom against the evil artifice of the thoughts, for 'fear is the beginning of wisdom' (Ecclus. 1: 14).

He who through his experience makes known the error of the thoughts will not be recognized by all, except for those with experience, [1125B] for experience constitutes the path towards the gnostic life at this stage. The ground for both of them is the practical life; and if we lay hold of this with greater ascetic effort, we will come to know ourselves, we will pass judgement on thoughts and we will come to know God. As for the person experienced in the emigration of the practical life and the homecoming of the gnostic life (cf. 2 Cor. 5: 8-9),[38] who anoints the simple with the skill of the thoughts[39]—let him watch out, let him not boast about the gnostic life to make a show for his own glory. But if a thought steals in to exalt him, let him take for his assistance the newcomer Jethro who gave to Moses, the great prophet, a wise counsel and discerning judgement inspired by grace (Exod. 18: 13-27).

Let the power of your words be constituted by your works. For acts to be done are dearer to wisdom than words to be said, as they also involve greater ascetic effort. Just as, when the practical life is present, words are dazzling bright, [1125C] so when works are absent, words do not flash forth with the power of works. (They are no more than) a complaint of grey-haired men, a youthful word and bragging lips trembling with laughter. He who troubles and is troubled at random will be excluded from tranquillity and even when there is no rough sea he is battered by storms.

24. Fraternal relations

25. Do not hunt for a saying that is untimely, lest you endure the same thing from those you would rather not. Avoid goading the tongue of your neighbour, in order that you too may escape the goading of the devil. Avoid rebuking your brother's faults lest you be deprived of compassion as one of an alien race.[40]

One who does not possess kindness and love towards his brother, how could he be a member of Christ-bearing love? [1125D] When a brother visits you during your intense fast and practice of stillness, do not accept the odiousness of thoughts that suggest disturbance of your stillness and interruption of your fast. They do this so that when you see your brother you will not see him as God. Let us not speak of the frequent visits of the brothers as disturbances, but rather let us trust their community as a helpful alliance against the phalanx of the adversary; for thus united by the charm of charity, we shall expel wickedness and transfer the works of manual labour into the treasury of hospitality. [1128A]

Let us not welcome our brothers as though we were doing them a favour, but rather, let us treat them hospitably with supplication as though we were indebted to them by a loan, as Lot set the example (Gen. 19: 2–3). Some people flatter themselves in a strange way with the role of the host, and whenever they invite a distinguished guest they do not implore him at all, but they amplify the message of invitation with their pride, and when an invitee refuses the invitation they censure him as they would one who had given insult. Great conceit is thus enkindled by this, for the thoughts blind the eye of the soul by piercing it so that we will employ the finest of the commandments in the most wicked way.

26. When a thought hinders you from constraining [1128B] your brother over-much to share your table, through him it then makes a mockery of you because you did not have the impulse of your charity under control.[41] For perhaps it suggests to you that your brother is one of the vagabonds—'Let him come and get his fill of bread!'; but to your brother it gives the notion that he had found no hospitality at all with you. For with an eye to effecting a change in his practical life, it (viz. the thought) gives to each heart a particular notion in order to undercut

hospitality in one case and to produce insults in another.

If Abraham, seated in front of his tent, saw someone passing by he welcomed him by his deed and for those who lived in impiety he spread a table, and by receiving foreigners he did not miss the opportunity of meeting angels (Gen. 18: 1-5; Heb. 13: 2).[42] All those who have lived abroad know the sweetness of hospitality and have been entertained by it as guests, when also a gentle word [1128C] prepares a sweet table for the heart. With great zeal then let us practise the kindness of hospitality that we may welcome not only angels but also God. For the Lord says, 'As you did it to one of the least of these my brothers, you did it to me' (Matt. 25: 40).

One of those who partake more gnostically in the practical life[43] answered thus: 'The zeal of hospitality and a generous service rendered with enthusiasm usually destroy the fantasies of the demons that resound in the heart, if indeed one is free in some way at least of material concerns. When these things are done with humility and contrition of heart, they usually deliver more quickly one who suffers from fantasies.'

25. Humility

The demons have a very great fear of humility, for they know that this was the garment of the Lord. One of the most experienced brothers offered a word about humility [1128D] and made this point. 'A father,' he said, 'among the very experienced was struck on the cheek by a possessed man, who was also deprived of his wits in a terrible way, and he immediately presented in exchange the other one ready to be struck. But the demon, struck in turn by the lightning-bolt of humility, cried out and suddenly leapt from the creature.'[44]

27. This account was given by the holy bishop Epiphanius.[45] 'It happened,' he said, 'that the son of a faithful widow was possessed by [1129A] the demon of Python and after some time in the affliction could not submit to healing.[46] With his mother rendered humble by mourning, thanksgiving cooled the passion, and having suspended his soul from the cross, it cast the demon out of the child by means of her prayers. While the youth was wandering in the parts round about and his mother was at home praying, the demon crying out the woman's name was plagued with torments. But when the woman heard of this, she did not run to the scene, binding the battle of nature to humility; but, drawn by others, she was led there against her will, and henceforth, the demon too was driven mad to

the point of taking flight. Standing by, then, she embraced her child in tears and cast forth her thanksgiving and humility against the demon; and after she had wept bitterly, imploring Christ [1129B] and making the sign of the cross, the demon quickly ran away from her child before so many lashes of the whip.'

26. Spiritual submission

The demons are jealous of those who are dazzling bright in their submission to a (spiritual) father and they gnash their teeth against them, because to their submission they have yoked a renunciation free of cares. Formulating an accurate list of pretexts against them, they concoct violent disputes and they engrave the memory with the resulting anger; then, little by little, they will bring to a boil hatred towards the father, as if he were punishing unjustly and showing partiality, in order to cause the soul agitation on all sides and in different ways and so separate it from the paternal embrace. Therefore, let him who is in submission to a (spiritual) father not be defeated by insults, let him gain the victory by humility, let him be tempered by patience, [1129C] and when the thoughts murmur surreptitiously let him not resist the austerity of his father[47] and the burden of works and the insolence of the brothers.

28. For beyond this the demons insinuate in a special way that freedom is equivalent to wretched servitude so that by rendering the submissive person self-willed they can easily entangle him in material concerns.[48] Some they are eager to separate from the direction of a spiritual father through these means, while for others they use other means. 'Work, acquire possessions, entertain guests', they chant within, 'in order that you may acquire for yourself a fine reputation.' For from these seeming good things, they sow bit by bit the weeds of wickedness (cf. Matt. 13: 25).

In the beginning they allow the brother to enjoy the sweetness of vainglory, [1129D] to be vigilant in continuous fasting, to rise enthusiastically for the prayers and offices, so that he will figure to himself that when he was in submission he was not such. For in the former situation there were insults, sorrows, and troubles, but here there is peace, tranquillity, and joy; in the former situation, the severity of a (spiritual) father, fear, and punishment, but here freedom from cares, fear, and punishment. And then, they steal and snatch away his mind in circumstances like these: emerging suddenly during excessive sleep, they sprinkle the soul with fear and hinder the offices with negligence and acedia; they remind him that the reception of guests is an annoyance; they introduce all the magic tricks of wickedness in order to cast acedia upon him and make life hateful for him, and after thus stripping him naked [1132A] of the virtues they will make a show of him to the angels.

27. Demonic deceptions

Sometimes the demons, through the thoughts, exalt ascetic efforts, but sometimes they belittle them for accomplishing nothing, in order to inspire presumption[49] on the one hand and to sow despair on the other. For they exalt those who do not stoop to relax their ascetic efforts so as to inspire presumption, while on the other hand the demonic chants hint that those who are not persuaded to stoop to presumption accomplish nothing more besides their ascetic works, so that when they have caused them to become lax they can sow despair.   29. Therefore, when the thoughts exaggerate the value of ascetic efforts, spurning such thoughts, let us keep the soul in lowliness; but when [1132B] in turn the thoughts make light of ascetic efforts for accomplishing nothing, let us, as far as we are able, exalt the mercies of Christ.

For the more you treat your body harshly, penetrate all the more your conscience. Learn to know yourself by perceiving the secret plunderings of the thoughts, lest perhaps, swept away unawares regarding their hidden thieveries, we find ourselves in darkness to reap the virtues by austerity alone. For some people, afflicted in their imaginations in this way, have had their wits shaken loose, like locusts, when the demons deluded their imaginations and led their faculties of sight astray, sometimes even ravaging the soul with fear.

While one of the brothers was keeping vigil at night, the demons formed for him terrifying fantasies, not only in his outward eye but also in his inner sight [1132C] so that during the following night, struggling with anxiety, he ran the risk of losing his wits, and for several nights the battle was waged against the soul. But the one at risk forced himself to restrain interiorly the ruling faculty of his mind, while having his soul depend on the giver of prayer; bringing forward against himself the actions of his faults, he struggled to gaze within himself. Then, diverting the soul's attention to the fire of judgement, he instilled it with fear so that by striking fear with fear he might drive away his cowardice. And so it came about, just as the one who had experienced the warfare said. For while the demons were terrifying his soul in many ways, the sufferer besought God in prayer; and while they were distracting his soul with fantasies, he gathered up the mass of his faults and disclosed them to God who sees all. [1132D] And in turn, when they tried to draw his eye from prayer, he countered with the fear of judgement and wiped out his fear of phantasms. For when one dimension of fear exceeded the other, it overcame error with the help of God. When the soul was humbled by the remembrance of its sins and awakened from sleep by the fear of judgement, it exhaled from its inward parts the terrors of the demons. But everything came from grace from above: driving away the terrors of the demons and sustaining the soul that was falling, for 'The Lord upholds all those who are falling and sets aright all those who are cast down' (Ps. 144: 14). [1133A]

28. Pure prayer

30. Sometimes we exert ourselves to make our prayer pure, and we may perhaps be unable. But in turn it also happens that pure prayer arises in the soul when we are making no effort; for our weakness on the one hand and grace from above on the other call on us to ascend to purity of the soul, while at the same time through both means training us not to attribute the work to ourselves in the practice of pure prayer, but to acknowledge the one who bestows the gift: 'For we do not know how to pray as we ought' (Rom. 8: 26). Whenever then we make an effort to have our prayer purified and are unable, but find ourselves in the darkness, then, having drenched our cheeks with tears, let us beseech God for the night of warfare to be brought to an end and for the radiance of the soul to be illumined.

When for the sake of his office [1133B] the brother who lives with you goes on a trip, renew his memory according to the custom of your prayers, but do not hold him in your imagination beyond measure, lest perhaps the demons seize from you the beginning of disquiet and sharpen it to an ever finer point, covering this brother with their darkness in your chanting of the psalms and forming images in the time of godly disquiet,[50] in order to counter disquiet with disquiet and as captives to lead us away from the superior goods so we will not take into account the verse: 'Cast your disquiet upon the Lord' (Ps. 54: 23).

They know in fact that out of excessive concern about one's brother they can shape feelings of sadness and so trouble the ruling faculty. Further, they quietly enkindle complaints of tardiness, as if the brother was neglectful regarding the urgency of his office, [1133C] so that the much-disquieted yearning might perhaps even turn into hatred. In worries concerning the traveller it is the custom of the demons to do this: on the day when they see him arriving, they show his image in a dream so that, when the dream has gone away, they may make of us on the occasion of absent travellers interpreters of dreams and have us accept once again those whom we must rather abandon and avoid at all costs for fear lest they divert the soul from these into other errors as well.   31. In fact, the demons know nothing in advance, but what they see happening, [1133D] this they make known and represent in the imagination. Often when we are practising in stillness and they see a brother coming to us, they foretell this through thoughts, which one must not trust even if they seem to be telling the truth. For through this supposed truth they are introducing deceit so that from these partial truths they may weave a patchwork of snares on the paths before us.

29. Community and anachoresis

Just as unrefined gold cast in a smelting-furnace becomes more pure, so too a novice monk who refines his morals in a community is restored radiant in his practices of persevering abstinence. For through the brothers' imposition of commands he works at learning obedience, and through the one who reprimands him he prepares his nature [1136A] to possess patience. Therefore, whenever he accepts insults with joy and greets humiliation with lowliness, rising above the opposing passions, he struggles thenceforth to shine brightly with the virtues, as grace more and more grants him the strength. As those who go down to the roots of the earth dig up gold, so those who descend to golden humility bring back the virtues. Then the mind perceives rest, when, having cut off the causes of the passions, it occupies itself with contemplation, but before these are severed it perceives toil and misery, for in weakness it engages in battle with the adversaries. [1136B]

32. The elders approve highly of an anachoresis that is undertaken by degrees, if indeed one has come to this after attaining a level of accomplishment in the virtues in community. If one is able to make progress in anachoresis, let him prove himself; but if because of his inability he falls short of virtue, let him return to the community for fear that, being unable to counter the devices of the thoughts, he lose his wits.

30. True understanding

Just as sons are a consolation when a widow is in mourning, so too ascetic works are an encouragement when the soul has fallen, for they disperse the despair of thoughts, sow confidence in repentance, proclaim the mercies of Christ, and denounce the sins committed. Therefore, we ought not to labour at ascetic works as merely habitual, but rather [1136C] with an understanding of thanksgiving, in order that the soul might not be found stripped of such philosophy. If for each action we are aware of the one who brings ascetic efforts to their completion, we set the seal of thanksgiving on it. Just as a puppy almost from birth watches out for bread to snatch it, so an evil thought seeks to snatch understanding from the heart. Therefore let us not be silent while they deploy the evil of adverse works, lest we hand over the soul to be plundered by them. Just as the torch-bearing dance of the stars lights up the sky, so the lamp-bearing truth of words lights up the human person in order that we may bear the way of the truth upon the tongue because 'the Lord gives the single-minded a house to dwell in' (Ps. 67: 7).[51] Just as violent lightning-flashes darting forth herald thunder, so too words delivered with precision proclaim faith. [1136D]

Let us hasten then to be faithful in the truth that we may advance in love towards the metropolis of the virtues. As the sun smiles upon the entire earth with its gleaming golden rays, so love with its luminescent actions gives joy to the entire soul. If we have indeed acquired love, we have extinguished the passions and have let our light shine into the heavens. You shall undertake every ascetic work until you attain holy love, because if this is absent there is no value in your present activities. For in fact anger is provoked, morals are aggravated, and ascetic works executed with presumption are mingled with glory. Through humility of soul David fasted with mourning (2 Kgs. 12: 16), [1137A] and through fasting let us bring the soul to humility.

31. Demonic conceit

33. He who engages in the training of bodily ascetic works with greater harshness, let him not engage in such work for reasons of praise nor let him put on airs for reasons of glory. For if the demons can make the soul conceited in these matters, they can fortify both the harshness and the

ascesis of the body with glory and draw the soul on to the attainment of greater ascetic works with the result that it puts on even greater airs. They speak interiorly through the thoughts, introducing such notions as these: 'Just as so-and-so undertook a very rigorous ascetic regime and so-and-so attained a great reputation and after he died was still talked about, so you too, mount to the height of ascetic achievement [1137B] so you can bring glory on yourself and have your great reputation spread abroad so that even after your death people will speak of you profusely!' Through the deceits worked in this manner, not only do they make war on your bodily ascetic efforts, but they also invite you to become their ally, because through these means they make contact with the soul in the greater hardships.

And indeed, they elevate the monk even to the throne of the teaching office, so that on this account he might be acclaimed as holding first place among the great ascetics and gnostics. They incite him to be envious and jealous of those acclaimed for their achievements and whose ascetic practice is most admirable and whose gnosis is similar. Sometimes they deceptively put to sleep the burning of his flesh, hiding impure thoughts from his interior self, [1137C] so that he might think that he has overcome the spirit of fornication by means of his austerity and sanctified his heart in the radiance of the saints (cf. Ps. 109: 3) and has ascended to the highest rank of holiness.

Both in these ascetic works and also in his abstention from foods and his prolonged fasts, they confirm for him their durations, in which he ought to take pride as one who stands out and to be arrogant towards the brotherhood as if it were of no account. And so they have him recount his struggles as if they had been accomplished by his strength alone: 'I did this, I accomplished such and such ascetic works, I was maltreated', while they stop his mouth from saying further—'It was not I, but the assistance that was in me.' For they do not allow him to acknowledge God as his helper in the works they made him boast of, so that he might demand all the praises [1137D] due him for his contests as if he had accomplished the entirety of the struggles by his own supposed strength, with the result that he should be plunged into the depth of blasphemy, as he suggests through his insensibility that he can provide for his own assistance.[52]

34. So then, when the heart resounds with the glory of the thoughts and there is no resistance, he will not escape madness in the secret of his mental faculties, for his ruling faculty risks being shaken loose from its senses, either through dreams which are given credence, or through forms that take shape during vigils, or through visions seen in a change

of light. [1140A] For 'Satan himself takes on the form of an angel of light' (2 Cor. 11: 14) to deceive us: he indicates perhaps that he will grant charisms so you will fall down and worship him (cf. Matt. 4: 9); or he proclaims that he will take you up as a saint; or he promises to sanctify some of those who having received the faith missed the mark regarding the truth and became mentally deranged.

32. Conclusion

As for you, then, suppliant of the Holy Trinity, as you know these matters for which you make painstaking efforts, preserve your heart with every care for fear that in attending to outward ascetic efforts alone you may choke on interior baits. My words were therefore addressed to you, and may your heart preserve what I said. Remember Christ who has kept guard over you and do not forget the worshipful and Holy Trinity.[53]

3

[To Eulogios.] On the Vices
Opposed to the Virtues

Introduction

This short treatise often follows *Eulogios* in the Greek manuscript tradition and some manuscripts at least indicate that it is addressed to the same person.[1] Although usually attributed to Nilus of Ancyra, certain important manuscripts recognize its Evagrian authorship.[2] Similarly, both the Syriac and Arabic traditions assign the work to Evagrius, and it is now generally accepted as such.[3] The text published in PG is missing a section near the end, which treats freedom from jealousy, pride, and humility.[4]

In the prologue to the treatise Evagrius describes the intention and form of the text and attributes the teaching not to himself but to the 'sound discourses' that he has heard from the fathers and the example they have given by their deeds. The work is a rhetorical *tour de force*, detail-

---

[1] For example: (Ma) Venice, Marc. gr. 131 (471), fol. 24r; Vat. gr. 703, fol. 176v.

[2] For example: (E) Athos, Lavra Γ 93 (Athous 333), fol. 295v, where it has the ascription *tou autou* and immediately follows *Eulogios* which is ascribed to Evagrius; Vat. gr. 703 also places the text under the name of Evagrius the monk.

[3] J. Muyldermans, *Evagriana Syriaca. Textes inédits du British Museum et de la Vaticane*, Bibliothèque du Muséon, 31 (Louvain: Publications Universitaires, 1952), 59–60. However, the short excerpt from the Syriac version edited by Muyldermans (p. 60) shows no relationship to the Greek text: '*On Freedom from Jealousy*: Freedom from jealousy is an innocent eye, a good thought, the perfection of charity, the stability of brotherly love, the destruction of evil, the beginning of all praises, the assembly of the virtues, the support of the soul, sweetness of the tongue, the handmaid of obedience, the enemy of sadness, the dissipating of distress, the destroyer of deceit, joy without end, the likeness of God, the helpmate of Christ, the neighbour of the angels, the heavenly life.' For the Arabo-Coptic tradition see Kh. Samir, 'Évagre le Pontique dans la tradition arabo-copte', in Marguerite Rassart-Derbergh and Julien Ries (eds.), *Actes du IVe Congrès Copte. Louvain-la-Neuve, 5-10 septembre 1988*, Publications de l'Institut Orientaliste de Louvain, 41 (Louvain-la-Neuve: Institut Orientaliste, 1992), ii. 131–2.

[4] PG 79. 1140B–1144D. The missing section was published by J. Muyldermans, 'Evagriana de la Vaticane', *Le Muséon*, 54 (1941), 5.

ing the nature of the vices and their opposing virtues by attributing to each one a series of brief and pithy descriptors. As with the works divided into brief 'chapters', the intention here is probably that the monk would meditate at some length over each descriptor to elicit the fullness of the teaching that it has to offer on the particular vice or virtue. This, however, would seemingly be impossible unless the reader already had some familiarity with Evagrian teaching or at least with the oral tradition of the desert.

One unusual feature of the treatise is the addition of a ninth vice to the usual list of eight: jealousy is inserted between vainglory and pride. According to *Vices* 7, Evagrius holds these three to be intimately related. Such a list of nine vices is not found elsewhere in Evagrius, although he does discuss jealousy at various points, and with some prominence in the treatise *Eulogios*, where he closely associates it with the vice of vainglory.[5]

The text translated below is that of PG 79. 1140B–1144D along with the missing section edited by Muyldermans. In addition, I have collated the text against the manuscripts Athos, Lavra *Γ* 93 and Venice, Marc. gr. 131 (471).

ON THE VICES OPPOSED TO THE VIRTUES

Prologue

1. [1140B] It is necessary, I think, to submit in brief to your industriousness also the vices that are opposed to the virtues, until, having so ploughed the intellect, we remove the thorns of the thoughts from the sown land. We have not come to this task because of works that we have done (cf. Titus 3: 5), but having as our model the sound discourses which we have heard from the fathers, we have been equally a witness to some of their deeds. All is grace from above, which shows even to sinners the schemes of the deceivers and which also offers assurance, saying 'For what do you have that you did not receive' (1 Cor. 4: 7), so that in having received, on the one hand, we may give thanks to the one who granted the gift, and in having possession, on the other hand, we may not attribute to ourselves any boasting of honour, as though denying the gift. Wherefore

---

[5] *Eulogios* 17.

scripture says, 'And if [1140C] you received it, why do you boast, as if you did not receive it? Already you have become rich' (1 Cor. 4: 7–8), it says, you who were poor in works, already you have been filled, now that you have begun to receive teaching. In these matters the error has now passed over to to my account, for the reason that I, on the one hand, am in debt becasue I disguise the poverty of my works and, on the other hand, because of the opinion I recommended, whereas now I am reversing my instruction that one should receive teaching.

But nevertheless [1141A] if any allowance has been made on your part, render it to me as well that we may make a brief submission on the vices opposed to the virtues, indicating what is gluttony against which abstinence is opposed, what is fornication and chastity, what is avarice and freedom from possessions, sorrow against which there is joy, what is anger and patience, acedia and perseverance, what is vainglory and freedom from it, jealousy and freedom from it, pride and humility. In what follows we have set these down in brief as opposed, contrary, and antithetical to one another.

1. Gluttony and abstinence

2. There is gluttony then, the mother of fornication, nourishing [1141B] the thoughts with words, the relaxation of fasting, the muzzling of ascesis, terror over one's moral purpose, imagining of foods, picturer of condiments, a dissolute fawn,[1] unbridled madness, a receptacle of disease, envy of health, an obstruction of the throat, a groaning of the innards, the extremity of insults, a fellow initiate in fornication, pollution of the intellect, weakness of the body, wearisome sleep, gloomy death.

Abstinence is a bridle for the stomach, a scourge of immoderation, a balance of due proportion, a muzzle for gourmandise, renunciation of rest, the undertaking of austerity, a place of chastisement for thoughts, an eye for vigilance, deliverance from lustful burning, pedagogue of the body, a tower of ascetic works and a wall for our ways, reserve in morals and repression of the passions, mortification of one's (bodily) members, revivification of souls, imitation of the resurrection, a life of sanctification.

2. Fornication and chastity

Fornication is a conception of gluttony, that which softens the heart in advance, [1141C] a furnace of lustful burning, an arranger of marriages with idols, unnatural activity, a form covered in shadows, an (sexual) intertwining wrought in the imagination, a bed of dreams, unfeeling sexual congress, bait for the eyes, immodesty of sight, dishonouring of prayer, shame of the heart, guide to ignorance.

Chastity is a robe of truth, an axe for wantonness, a charioteer for the eyes, an overseer for one's thinking, a circumcision of thoughts, excision of licentiousness, a planting opposed to nature and a counter to lustful burning, an assistant to our works and a collaborator with abstinence, a lantern for the heart and an inclination for prayer. [1141D]

3. Avarice and freedom from possessions

3. Avarice is the parsimony of idols, the prophecy of the crowd, a vote for stinginess, a hoarding mentality, a wealth of captivity, a race of injustice, an abundance of illnesses, a diviner of many years, an enchanter for industriousness, a counsellor of sleeplessness, poverty of the belly, meagreness of foods, insatiable madness, a wickedness of many cares.

Freedom from possessions is the uprooting of avarice and the rooting of freedom from it, a fruit of love and a cross of life, a life free of suffering, a treasure free of envy, a heaven free of care, a sun without distraction, immeasurable matter, incomprehensible wealth, a scythe for cares, the practice of the Gospels, the world readily abandoned, a fast-running contestant.

4. Sadness and joy

Sadness is one who dwells over loss, who is familiar with frustrated acquisition, a forerunner of exile, remembrance of family, a deputy of want, a kinsman of acedia, a complaint of exasperation, a reminder of insult, and a darkening of the soul, dejection in morals, drunkenness of prudence, a soporific remedy, [1144A] a cloud of form, a worm in the flesh,[2] sadness of thoughts, a people in captivity.

Joy is the destruction of sorrow and thanksgiving for misfortunes, a vision that comes from prayers and gladness that comes from ascetic works, happiness from doing good, an ornament of renunciation, a receptacle of hospitality, a refuge of hopes, nourishment of ascetics, an encouragement for mourners, a consolation for tears, a help for affliction, a supporter of love, a partner in patience.

5. Anger and patience

Anger is a plundering of prudence, a destruction of one's state, a confusion of nature, a form turned savage, a furnace for the heart, an eruption of flames, a law of irascibility, a wrath of insults, a mother of wild beasts, a silent battle, an impediment to prayer.

Patience is a shield for prudence, a tribunal for anger, a surgery for the heart, admonition of the over-confident, calm for the troubled, a harbour from storms, beneficence towards those in sorrow, [1144B] gentleness towards all; it blesses when slandered, rejoices when insulted; a consolation for those in difficult circumstances, a mirror of things hoped for, a prize of those mistreated.

6. Acedia and perseverance

4. Acedia is an ethereal friendship, one who leads our steps astray,[3] hatred of industriousness, a battle against stillness, stormy weather for psalmody, laziness in prayer, a slackening of ascesis, untimely drowsiness, revolving sleep, the oppressiveness of solitude, [1144C] hatred of one's cell, an adversary of ascetic works, an opponent of perseverance, a muzzling of meditation, ignorance of the scriptures, a partaker in sorrow, a clock for hunger.

Perseverance is the severing of acedia, the cutting down of thoughts, concern for death, meditation on the cross, fear firmly affixed, beaten gold, legislation for afflictions, a book of thanksgiving, a breastplate of stillness, an armour of ascetic works, a fervent work of excellence, an example of the virtues.

7. Vainglory and freedom from vainglory

Vainglory involves fantasizing about social encounters, a pretence of industriousness, the contrary of the truth, author of heresies, desire for privilege, the ultimate title, slavery to praises, a spirit with many forms, a beast with many teeth; the mean of vainglory is entwined with pride and jealousy, which are found within one another and which make war through one another, the three-strand chain of vices,[4] the threefold poisonous mixture [1144D] of passions, the threefold tongue of heretics.

Freedom from vainglory is the working of humility, a defection from obsequiousness, blindness to praises, contemplation of knowledge, a counter to the world, keen perception of the soul, a teaching of lowliness, a hiding place for ascetic works, hostility to fame, a hidden treasure in a corruptible body.

8. Jealousy and freedom from jealousy

Jealousy is the garment of pride, the disrobing of humility, the root of slander, the coveting of cheerfulness, the feigning of friendship, treachery in confidence, hatred of love, envy of people highly esteemed, tumult of the steadfast, disparagement of the famous, alteration of the eyes, [friend of curiosity.

Freedom from jealousy is a guide to humility, hatred of slander, friend of cheerfulness, sincerity in friendship, purity in confidence, harmony with love, gladness for people highly esteemed, reversal of wicked deeds, support of steadfastness.

9. Pride and humility

Pride is opposition to God, demonic fantasy, wicked jealousy, obscuring blindness, insolence in one's attitude, conceit of the flesh, false love of esteem, servitude to wicked thoughts, friendship with the demons, an eminent soul, an obvious siege by the adversary, an admonition to destruction.

Humility is a thankful acknowledgement of God, a true recognition of one's nature, a forceful confession of one's weakness, a fortress for love, a refuge from hatred, an unfallen acropolis, a parting of the diabolic waves, flight over the snares of the enemy, the natural overthrowing of Satan, a pleasing life, praise of enemies, a philosophy provided by God, and true friendship with wisdom.

10. Conclusion

Knowledge of these things and their practical investigation purifies the heart.][5] Who is the person pure in heart who does not find fault with himself for rejecting, or falling short of, or neglecting God's commandment?

4

On the Eight Thoughts

Introduction

The treatise *On the Eight Thoughts* survives in two Greek versions, one shorter (recension A) and one longer (recension B). Recension A usually bears the title *On the Eight Spirits of Wickedness*, whereas recension B most commonly reports the title as *On the Eight Thoughts*. The text in Migne, PG 79. 1145–64, taken from the edition of J. M. Suarès, is that of recension A. In 1939 J. Muyldermans published the principal variants and additions found in recension B.[1] The long recension is also represented in the Syriac, Ethiopic, Armenian, and Coptic versions, and at least partially in the Latin.[2] The translation presented below is that of recension B, based on the collations of Muyldermans and a fresh collation of the following manuscripts: Paris, Bibliothèque Nationale, Coislin 109, Coislin 123, Paris gr. 1188; Athos, Lavra *Γ* 93 (Athous 333); Jerusalem, Stavrou 55; Venice, BNSM, Antico 131 (471).[3] In the Syriac manuscript tradition *Eight Thoughts* is preceded by another text, attributed to Evagrius, which is given various titles such as *On the Signs of Stillness*. Because of its close association with *Eight Thoughts*, Muyldermans originally suggested that this text serves as a sort of preface to the work, and Gabriel Bunge included it in his German translation.[4] However, there is no evidence of a preface in the Greek transmission of *Eight Thoughts*, and the corresponding Greek text *On the Signs of Stillness*, in three different recensions, is attributed to

[1] J. Muyldermans, 'Une nouvelle recension du *De octo spiritibus malitiae* de S. Nil', *Le Muséon*, 52 (1939), 235–74. Muyldermans offers detailed information on the early editions of the Greek text, the manuscripts that were used, as well as information on the Latin, Syriac, Ethiopic, and Armenian versions of the text.

[2] On the Latin, Ethiopic, and Armenian versions see Muyldermans, ibid., 259–61, 263–4, and 264–73. For the Syriac version see J. Muyldermans, *Evagriana Syriaca. Textes inédits du British Museum et de la Vaticane,* Bibliothèque du Muséon, 31. (Louvain: Publications Universitaires, 1952), 55–9.

[3] The list of principal variants and additions can be found in Appendix 1.

[4] J. Muyldermans, *Evagriana Syriaca*, 84–6, 120–22, 154–5; G. Bunge (trans.), *Evagrios Pontikos: Über die acht Gedanken* (Würzburg: Echter, 1992), 26–7, 31–3.

John of Lycopolis, Epiphanius of Salamis, and Makarios of Egypt, as Muyldermans subsequently discovered.[5] It is thus unlikely that the text *On the Signs of Stillness* belongs to Evagrius.

There are over eighty extant Greek manuscripts of the text, most of them assigning authorship to Nilus of Ancyra. However, two important manuscript witnesses attribute the text to Evagrius, namely, Protaton 26 and Lavra *Γ* 93.[6] In his publication of the Berlin Evagrius ostrakon, H.-M. Schenke showed that the text was translated into Sahidic Coptic at an early period and maintained its ascription to Evagrius.[7] Further, the Coptic ostrakon is a witness to the long recension, as it provides the text of 8. 22. The Syriac, Arabic, and Ethiopic versions also place the treatise under the name of Evagrius.[8] Evagrian authorship is thus now generally accepted by modern scholarship.[9]

This Evagrian text takes the literary form of a series of wisdom sayings or proverbs concerning the eight thoughts or vices. Many of these are characterized by a *parallelismus membrorum*, where the first phrase introduces a metaphor and the second elucidates it in relation to the particular thought in question. Interspersed among these short aphorisms there are also longer pieces of admonitory discourse. In the translation I have followed the lead of Gabriel Bunge's German translation in dividing and numbering the text so as to indicate these literary structures.[10] The Greek manuscripts divide the text into sections corresponding to the eight thoughts, providing a title for each. I have added numbers to the titles, while retaining the 'chapter' divisions of the Migne/Suarès text (which are not found in the manuscripts) in round brackets. Recension

---

[5] J. Muyldermans, 'Un texte grec inédit attribué à Jean de Lycopolis', *Recherches de Science Religieuse*, 41 (1953), 525–30; and 'À propos d'un texte grec attribué a Jean de Lycopolis', ibid., 43 (1955), 395–401. Cf. *CPG* 2. 2469.

[6] For the description of the manuscripts, see A. Guillaumont, SC 170, 166–82.

[7] H.-M. Schenke, 'Ein koptischer Evagrius', in P. Nagel (ed.), *Graeco-Coptica: Griechen und Kopten im byzantinischen Ägypten,* Wissenschaftliche Beiträge der Martin-Luther-Universität (Halle–Wittenberg, 1984), 219–30; id., 'Das Berliner Evagrius-Ostrakon (P. Berol. 14 700)', *Zeitschrift für ägyptische Sprache und Altertumskunde*, 116 (1989), 90–107

[8] A. and C. Guillaumont, 'Évagre le Pontique', *Dictionnaire de spiritualité*, 4 (1961), 1737. For the Ethiopic version see O. Spies, 'Die äthiopische überlieferung der Abhandlung des Evagrius περὶ ὀκτὼ λογισμῶν', *Oriens Christianus,* 3rd ser., 7 (1932), 203–28; and on the Arabic see Kh. Samir, 'Évagre le Pontique dans la tradition arabo-copte', in Marguerite Rassart-Derbergh and Julien Ries (eds.), *Actes du IVe Congrès Copte. Louvain-la-Neuve, 5–10 septembre 1988* Publications de l'Institut Orientaliste de Louvain, 41 (Louvain-la-Neuve: Institut Orientaliste, 1992), 2:135–6.

[9] A. Guillaumont, 'Evagrius Ponticus. Leben, Werk, Nachwirkung, Quellen/Literatur', *Theologische Realenzyklopädie,* 10 (1982), 566.

[10] *Evagrios Pontikos: Über die acht Gedanken* (Würzburg: Echter, 1992).

B frequently offers a better, more comprehensible text than the A text of Migne and, more significantly, it provides 18 additions to the text, with 11 of them appearing at the end. The additions are fully in accord with the rest of the text both with respect to their style and the Evagrian character of their content. There is thus every likelihood that they genuinely belong to the original text of Evagrius or one revised by him.

The nature of the exposition of the eight thoughts in the treatise suggests that the work was intended as an introduction to the subject for a reader or audience still engaged in the initial stages of the struggle against the passions or the 'practical life', as Evagrius called it. Even the instructions on the practical life are elementary and lacking the sophisticated analysis of temptation and its remedies, found in the treatise *On Thoughts*. There are only passing references and veiled allusions to the stages that lie beyond the attainment of impassibility.

The struggle with gluttony stands at the beginning and the foundation of the practical life. The immoderate appetite for food and drink fuels desire and the attraction to pleasures in a general sense, but more specifically, gluttony and an excessively moist diet lead to an increase of sexual desire. An immoderate consumption of food also gives rise to lethargy, blunting the intellect, and darkening the mind, and thus making prayer and attainment of knowledge impossible. The remedy applied to gluttony is abstinence, which in turn is the starting point of what Evagrius here calls 'practical contemplation'. By this he presumably means the intelligent consideration of the nature of the struggle against the thoughts and the application of the appropriate therapeutic to each. In this sense *On the Eight Thoughts* itself represents just such a 'practical contemplation'. Perhaps, at another level, the term may refer also to the meditative reading of the scriptures to elicit from them the insights required for the conduct of the practical life. Abstinence requires a strict (but not destructive) dietary regimen oriented towards 'dry' foods as well as a restricted intake of water. Above all, eating to satiety had to be avoided. In accord with the prescriptions of the known physiology and health practices of his time, Evagrius understood that the prevention of excessive build-up of fluids in the body would limit the production of semen and hence curb sexual desires.[11] Further, abstinence left the monk more attentive, more awake for the practice of the nightly vigils. Abstinence is thus understood to be the first step in the disciplined control of the body and its appetites

---

[11] For the background on the subject see Teresa M. Shaw, *The Burden of the Flesh. Fasting and Sexuality in Early Christianity* (Minneapolis, Minn.: Fortress, 1998), 53–64.

[12] Cf. also *KG* 5. 6 and 5. 88.

and the first step towards the 'state of peace' that Evagrius elsewhere calls impassibility.

This presentation of the temptation of gluttony is quite straightforward and treats largely of the external, bodily ascetic practices. In section 1. 24–5, however, there are the two aphorisms of the slow and the speedy traveller: the latter quickly gains the city as the abstinent monk attains the state of peace, while the former camps in the desert as the gluttonous monk fails to attain impassibility. Later, in 7. 13 on vainglory, Evagrius contrasts the 'road full of thieves' with the 'city of peace' and then cautions against boasting while on the road but announces the enjoyment of all good things upon entering the city. The city in all these cases is clearly a symbol for the attainment of impassibility and probably also for the entry into natural contemplation, especially if the 'city of peace' in 7. 14 is understood as an allusion to Jerusalem. Evagrius elaborated this symbolism in *KG* 6. 49, '*Egypt* signifies evil; the *desert* the practical life; the land of *Judah*, the contemplation of bodies; *Jerusalem*, that of the incorporeals; and *Zion* is the symbol of the Trinity.'[12] The 'slow traveller' camped in the desert then is one who is stuck in the struggles of the practical life.

Fornication is the label given in the monastic tradition to all temptations of a sexual nature, whether completed in act or only entertained in thought. Evagrius has three basic counsels to offer: avoid satiety in food and drink, avoid all encounters with women, and practise vigilance over one's thoughts, memories, and fantasies. Thus, there is again here the emphasis on abstinence as the absolute prerequisite for the preservation of chastity. More particularly, Evagrius is insistent about the great risks involved in the mere sight of a woman, let alone any actual conversation or familiarity with one. The sight of a woman is an arrow poisoned with the venom of wild beasts or a raging fire or a mighty wave of a storm at sea—all lead to inevitable ruin and destruction. Thus, public occasions such as local festivals or even feast days of the church must be shunned for the risk of encountering women who will almost inevitably lead the monk into temptation. This is the same sense of the danger of women found in the *Apophthegmata patrum*.[13] Vigilance must also be exercised over one's inner life lest the image of a woman be entertained overlong in the mind and ignite sexual desire. In the statements of 2. 18–19 Evagrius relates sexual desire to the state of impassibility in two contrasting circum-

---

[13] Cf. *Apophthegmata* A66 (Arsenios 28), 'Do you not know that you are a woman, and that through women the enemy makes war against the saints'; A184 (Daniel 2), 'Never put your hand to a dish with a woman and eat with her, and in this you will escape from the demon of fornication for a little while.'

stances. On the one hand, the monk must be cautious about presuming too quickly that he has reached impassibility, if encounters with women do not stir the passion. On the other hand, it is a sign of impassibility if the memory of a woman no longer rouses any sexual desire, especially if the ascetic is able to interpret the woman's members allegorically as symbols of the faculties of the soul. Evagrius here alludes to a method for countering temptations which he discusses at greater length in *Thoughts* 24. The practice relies on the principle that the mind cannot be occupied with two mental representations simultaneously. Therefore it is possible to use one thought or mental representation to drive out another, but this technique is more appropriate for the gnostic.[14] Even then, Evagrius will caution, as he does here, that the form of a woman should not be retained in the intellect for very long because of the risk of rousing desire.[15]

Avarice in the first instance is an attachment to possessions, but in the end it represents all ties to material realities. Evagrius describes this most graphically in his portrayal of the person near death, who even in that moment cannot let go of the goods of this world and so dies in utter misery. Possessions are treated as burdens that can only cause anxieties and worries, and in their absence one succumbs to a sense of loss and frustration that Evagrius calls sadness. An attachment to possessions, whether actual goods retained or even the memories of goods forgone, is ultimately an imperfect anachoresis, an incomplete renunciation of the world. The sensible monk looks after the basic needs of the body for food, clothing, and shelter, but nothing more. In so doing he achieves a freedom of mind and heart that can then be devoted to prayer, reading, and the other ascetic exercises that will assist him in 'laying up treasure in heaven' (Matt. 6: 20). Evagrius' presentation of avarice here is very basic; he leaves the subject without discussing the various ways in which an attachment to possessions and the material world can manifest itself in the life of the monk.

[14] Cf. *Praktikos* 58, 'And if you should be able (to dispel a thought of fornication with one of vainglory or vice versa), know that you are near the frontiers of impassibility, for your mind found the strength to annihilate the thoughts of the demons by means of human thoughts. The ability to drive away the thought of vainglory by means of humility or the thought of fornication by means of chastity would be proof of the most profound impassibility.'

[15] Whether or not one should confront thoughts directly and enter into a struggle with them was a matter of some dispute in the desert tradition. See *Apophthegmata* A728 (Poimen 154), 'Abba Poimen said: On the subject of fornication and slander, no one should speak of these two thoughts, nor should one consider them at all in the heart. For if one is absolutely determined to discern them in the heart, he derives no benefit. Rather, if one is turned to anger against them, he will find rest.'

The significance that Evagrius attributes to the vice of anger and its opposite, the virtue of gentleness, is indicated immediately by the role allotted to them in the individual's spiritual progress. A 'soul free of anger' is a temple of the Holy Spirit; a gentle person is remembered by God; 'Christ reclines his head on a patient spirit'; and 'an intellect at peace' is 'a shelter for the Holy Trinity'; patience and freedom from resentment open the way for visions of the holy angels, the contemplation of spiritual reasons, and the answers to mysteries. In other words, freedom from anger and the virtues of gentleness and patience are directly related to the summit of the spiritual life, while irascibility and all manifestations of anger will 'darken the mind', 'thicken the intellect', and render prayer itself an abomination to God. Anger and irascibility dehumanize the individual caught in their grasp, turning him more and more towards an animal, bestial nature, and for Evagrius, anger is the dominant characteristic of the demonic.[16] The person consumed by anger gradually loses his humanity also in the sense of a gradual but inevitable descent into a kind of madness and a loss of one's wits, manifested in hallucinations and terrifying nightmares.

In this treatise Evagrius reverses his usual ordering of the thoughts in which anger follows sadness.[17] However, he is not absolutely rigid about his schema, because he realizes that there are variations in the ascetic experience of different individuals and personalities. Thus, in *Praktikos* 10, he admits that sadness may arise from a frustration of one's desires, especially those desires which still bind the individual to the goods which he has renounced, or it may follow closely upon anger. Even within this chapter in *Eight Thoughts*, Evagrius allows for both possibilities. The first aphorism finds sadness arising from thoughts of anger, but later it is said to be constituted by 'the frustration of an appetite', just as in *Praktikos* 10. Evagrius then offers a more detailed list of such 'frustrated appetites': for food, for sexual pleasure, for vengeance, for human esteem, and for possessions—or in sum the frustration of any worldly pleasure. This indicates very clearly that the Evagrian schematic order is not intended to be rigidly applied to everyone's ascetic experience, even though Evagrius does maintain that the schema does have a general validity that is useful in discerning the workings of the thoughts. The remedy for sadness is absolute detachment from all the pleasures of the world, for when one desires nothing from the material world sadness can find no foothold. This is 'worldly sadness', but Evagrius also allows for a 'godly sadness',

---

[16] Cf. *Praktikos* 5; *KG* 1. 68, 3. 34, 5. 11.

[17] The usual ordering is found in *Antirrhetikos, Praktikos,* and *Vices.*

which purifies the soul from sins. This is a reference to the compunction (*katanuxis*) and mourning (*penthos*) that constitute the work of repentance.[18] The counsels that Evagrius offers concerning sadness are again mostly elementary in nature, with only passing references to the obstacles posed by sadness for contemplation and pure prayer.

Evagrius defines acedia as a relaxation or loss of the soul's 'tension'. By this he means a loss of a sense of commitment or dedication to the goal of the ascetic life and the exercises necessary to reach that goal. This loss of heart for the ascetic life manifests itself in numerous ways, ranging from the abandonment of the cell to distractions while reading. The monk afflicted with acedia will turn anywhere to avoid the task at hand. He will visit the sick, undertake a service for others, fantasize about a taking a trip somewhere, change his usual manual labour, or move to another location which he imagines to be more conducive to the monastic life. Then there is the wonderful picture that Evagrius paints of the monk who is unable to apply himself to his reading (6. 15). Perseverance, patience, and the attentive application to every task until its completion are given here as the remedies for acedia.

The description of vainglory is presented in very simple terms: any desire for human esteem can interfere with and destroy all the virtues and practices of the ascetic life, whether they be abstinence, almsgiving, prayer, or others. The necessary recourse is to be diligent in hiding one's virtue while still on the road of the practical life. Only with the arrival in the City, the symbol of the attainment of impassibility and spiritual knowledge, will the dangers posed by vainglory cease, and one can then enjoy 'all good things'.[19]

For Evagrius, pride is fundamentally the failure to acknowledge God as the source of all virtue and goodness in one's life; there is no ascetic victory or accomplishment that stands apart from God's help. In pride, then, the individual distances himself from God by placing all his trust in his own strength. For a human being to follow such a direction is to step outside the bounds of nature and reject the Creator. As a result, the proud person is abandoned by God and given over to the demons who then plague the poor fellow with terrifying fantasies and hallucinations until he is overcome by a kind of cowardly paranoia.

The additional chapters placed at the end by recension B form a mis-

---

[18] See *Eulogios* 7. 6–7.

[19] Cf. *Praktikos* 32, 'The person who has attained knowledge and enjoys the pleasant fruit that derives from it will no longer allow himself to be persuaded by the demon of vainglory.'

cellany dealing with a variety of topics already treated earlier (8. 21–31). The first two aphorisms continue the discussion of practising hidden virtue as a counter to pride; the next four treat the practical life under the symbol of the staff; three aphorisms are devoted to chastity and the danger of pleasure; and the last two close the treatise with a further reference to vainglory and pride.

Finally, it is worth noting that in this treatise Evagrius refers to the eight types of temptation almost exclusively with the term 'thought(s)'. Only four times does he designate a vice by the formula 'the spirit of x' (2. 4; 6. 3, 5, 18) and not once does he use the formula 'the demon of x'. There is in fact only one reference to the term 'demon' in the entire treatise, in 8. 10: 'The soul of the proud person is abandoned by God and becomes a plaything of the demons.' This is in stark contrast with other treatises where the terms 'demon' and 'demonic' are ubiquitous, appearing for example, 55 times in *Eulogios*, 72 times in the *Praktikos*, and 98 times in *Thoughts*.

ON THE EIGHT THOUGHTS

1. Gluttony

1. (1) [1145A] Abstinence is the origin of fruitfulness, the blossom and beginning of the practical life.

2. He who controls the stomach diminishes the passions; he who is overcome by food gives increase to pleasures.[1]

3. 'Amalek was the first of the nations' (Num. 24: 20); and gluttony is the first of the passions.[2]

4. Wood is the matter used by fire, and food is the matter used by gluttony.[3]

5. A lot of wood raises a large flame; an abundance of food nourishes desire.

6. A flame grows dim when matter is wanting; a lack of food extinguishes desire.

7. He who seized the jawbone destroyed the foreign nations and easily tore asunder the bonds of his hands (Judg. 15: 9–20).[4]

8. The (place called) Destruction of the Jawbone begat a spring of water;[5] and when gluttony was wiped out, it gave birth to practical contemplation.[6]

9. A tent peg, passing unnoticed destroyed an enemy's jawbone (Judg. 4: 21); and the principle of abstinence [1145B] has put passion to death.[7]

10. Desire for food gave birth to disobedience and a sweet taste expelled from paradise (Gen. 3: 6, 23).

11. Extravagance in foods pleases the throat, but it nourishes the unsleeping worm of licentiousness.[8]

12. A stomach in want is prepared to spend vigils in prayers, but a full stomach induces a lengthy sleep.

13. Vigilant thinking is found in the driest regimen; a life of moist diet plunges the mind into the deep.[9]

14. The prayer of one who fasts is like a young eagle[10] soaring upwards, whereas that of a drunkard is born downwards under the weight of satiety.

15. The mind of one who fasts is like a radiant star in the clear night air; that of a drunkard is concealed in a moonless night.

16. Fog conceals the sun's rays; and heavy consumption of food darkens the mind. [1145C]

17. (2) A soiled mirror does not produce a clear image of the form that falls upon it; when the intellect is blunted by satiety, it does not receive the knowledge of God.[11]

18. Land that has become barren produces thorns; and the mind of a glutton grows shameful thoughts.

19. It is not possible to find spices in the mud, nor the fragrance of contemplation in a glutton.

20. A glutton's eye is busy looking for dinner parties; the eye of the abstinent person is busy looking for meetings of the wise.

21. A glutton's soul rejoices at the commemorations of the martyrs;[12] that of the abstinent person imitates their lives.

22. A cowardly soldier shudders at the trumpet that announces the battle; the glutton shudders at the proclamation of abstinence.

23. The gluttonous monk, under the burden and scourge of his belly, [1148A] demands a daily share of the spoils.

24. The speedy traveller will quickly gain the city, and the abstinent monk a state of peace.[13]

25. The slow traveller will have to make camp in the desert[14] under the sky, and the gluttonous monk will not attain the abode of impassibility.

26. The smoke of incense sweetens the air, and the prayer of the abstinent person presents a sweet odour to God (cf. Rev. 8: 4).

27. If you give yourself over to the desire for food, nothing will suffice to fulfil your pleasure, for the desire for food is a fire that ever takes in and is ever in flames.

28. A sufficient measure fills a vessel; a full stomach[15] does not say, 'Enough!'

29. An extension of hands put Amalek to flight (Exod. 17: 11), and the raising of practical works subdues the passions of the flesh. [1148B]

30. (3) Exterminate from yourself every breath of wickedness and forcefully mortify the members of your flesh (cf. Col. 3: 5). In the same way that an enemy destroyed can cause you no fear, so the mortified body will not trouble the soul.

31. A dead body does not experience the pain caused by fire, nor does the abstinent person experience the pleasure of desire that is dead.

32. If you strike an Egyptian, hide him in the sand (Exod. 2: 11–12); and do not fatten the body with a vanquished passion, for as the hidden plant grows on fertile land, so does passion sprout afresh in a fat body.[16]

33. An extinguished flame lights again if it is given firewood; and a pleasure that has been extinguished is rekindled in a satiety of food.

34. Do not pity a body that is debilitated and in mourning,[17] nor fatten it up with rich foods, for if [1148C] it gains strength it will rebel against you and wage unrelenting war upon you, until it takes your soul captive and delivers you as a slave to the passion of fornication.

35. A docile horse, lean in body, never throws its rider, for the horse that is restrained yields to the bit and is compelled by the hand of the one holding the reins; the body is subdued with hunger and vigil and does not jump when a thought mounts upon it, nor does it snort when it is moved by an impassioned impulse.

2. Fornication

1. (4) Abstinence gives birth to chastity; gluttony [1148D] is the mother of licentiousness.

2. Oil feeds the light of a lamp; encounters with women ignite the fire of pleasure.[18]

3. The force of the waves batters a ship without ballast in a storm; the thought of fornication will act similarly on the intemperate mind.

4. He who wars against the spirit of fornication will not bring along satiety as an ally, for satiety will leave him and stand with his adversaries and fight to the end with his enemies.

5. The one who loves stillness ever remains unwounded by the enemies' arrows; the one who mingles with a crowd receives continuous blows.

6. The sight of a woman is a poisoned arrow; it wounds the soul and injects the poison, and for as long a time as it stays there it causes an ever greater festering.

7. The one who guards against [1149A] these arrows does not frequent public festivals, nor will he go around agape on feast days, for it is better to stay at home, passing time at one's prayers, than to become an accomplice in the work of one's enemies by thinking that one is reverently observing the feast days.

8. Flee encounters with women if you want to be chaste, and never allow them the familiarity to be bold with you. For in the beginning they will have or pretend to have pious reverence, but later they will dare anything without shame. At the first encounter they keep the eyes lowered, they speak softly, cry emotionally, dress modestly, and moan bitterly; they inquire about chastity and listen earnestly. At the second meeting you notice her looking up a little bit. A third time, they look directly at you without shame, you smile, and they laugh heartily. Then they adorn themselves and make an open display of themselves for you; they look at you [1149B] in a way that shows the promise of their passion. They raise their eyebrows and bat their eyelashes; they bare the neck and use the entire body in an enticing manner; they speak words that caress the passion and they practise a voice that is enchanting to hear, until they besiege the soul by every means. These are the hooks laid out to catch you in death and

the entangling nets that drag you to destruction. May they not lead you astray with their nice words, for the evil poison of beasts is concealed in these women.[19] [1149C]

9. (5) Better you should approach a raging fire than a young woman, if you yourself are young. For when you have approached a fire and felt pain, you will quickly draw back; but if you have been weakened by a woman's words, you will not easily withdraw.

10. A plant flourishes when it stands near water; the passion of licentiousness flourishes in encounters with women. *

11. The one who fills his stomach and then announces that he is chaste is like one who says he can hold in check the action of fire in a reed. In the same way that it is impossible to restrain the momentum of fire rushing through a reed, so is it impossible to stop the licentious impulse that is fired by satiety.

12. A pillar is erected on a base; the passion of fornication comes to rest on satiety.

13. A ship caught in a storm hastens toward a harbour; a chaste soul seeks solitude. The former flees the waves [1149D] of the sea that threaten danger, while the latter flees the forms of women which give birth to ruin.

14. A prettily adorned form overwhelms worse than a wave, for it is possible to plunge through the latter out of desire for life, but the deceitful form of a woman persuades one to disregard life itself.

15. A desert bush escapes the flames of a fire without harm; the chaste person who stays away from women will not be burned by the passion of licentiousness. For just as the memory of fire does not burn the intellect, so too a passion has no strength when matter is not present (for it to work on).[20]

16. (6) If you show mercy to an adversary in war, he will be your enemy; if you spare a passion it will revolt against you.

17. The sight of a woman arouses the licentious person to pleasure, but the chaste person it moves [1152A] to offer glory to God.

18. If the passion stays calm during encounters with women, do not believe it when it proclaims your impassibility.[21] For at one time a dog wags its tail when left in a crowd, but at another time when it goes outside it shows its bad character.[22]

19. When the memory of a woman arises without passion,[23] then consider that you have arrived at the boundaries of chastity; and when her image rouses you to consider it and you are able to compare her members to the faculties of your soul, then you can be convinced that you have the habit of virtue.[24] But do not spend so much time in such thoughts, nor hold converse with the form of a woman in your intellect for a long while, for this passion loves to cause backsliding, and danger is close at hand. As moderate smelting refines silver but an overlong process burns and easily ruins it, so does [1152B] prolonged fantasizing about a woman destroy the habit of chastity.

20. Do not give your mind over to the fantasy of a woman, nor converse overlong with it, lest you ignite the flame of pleasure within you and burn the threshing floor of your soul, for as a spark that alights for awhile on chaff raises a flame, so the prolonged memory of a woman kindles desire.

3. Avarice

1. (7) Avarice is the root of all evils (1 Tim. 6: 10), and it nourishes the remaining passions like evil branches.[25] If you cut off a branch, it immediately puts forth another and does not allow the blossoms that sprout from it to wither.

2. One who wishes to cut off the passions should cut out their root; for while avarice remains, there is no benefit in trimming the branches: whenever they are cut off they will immediately sprout again. [1152C]

3. A monk with many possessions is like a heavily laden boat that easily sinks in a sea storm. Just as a very leaky ship is submerged by each wave, so the person with many possessions is awash with his concerns.

4. The monk free of possessions is a well-prepared traveller who finds shelter in any place.

5. The monk free of possessions is like a high-soaring eagle who swoops down upon food whenever need requires.

6. This sort of person is above every temptation and scorns present realities; he rises above them, withdraws from earthly things, and associates with the things above, for he is light on the wings, not weighed down by concerns. Affliction comes and with no sadness he leaves that place.

Death approaches and he departs with a good heart, for he does not bind his soul with any earthly fetter.

7. But the monk with many possessions has bound himself with the fetters of his worries, as [1152D] a dog is tied to a leash, even when he is forced to move off elsewhere. He carries around the memories of possessions as a heavy burden and a useless weight; he is stung with sadness and is mightily pained in his thoughts. He has abandoned his possessions and is lashed with sadness.[26] Even if death should approach, he is miserable in leaving behind present things and giving up his soul; he cannot take his eyes away from (material) things. He is dragged away unwillingly like a runaway slave: he is separated from the body but he is not separated from his possessions; the passion (for possessions) has a greater hold on him than those dragging him (towards death). [1153A]

8. (8) The sea is never filled up even though it takes in a multitude of rivers (cf. Eccles. 1: 7); the desire of the avaricious person cannot get its fill of riches. He doubled his wealth and wants to double it again, and he does not stop doubling it until death puts a stop to his endless zeal.

9. The monk who possesses understanding will attend to the needs of the body and will fill the want of his stomach with bread and water; he will not flatter the rich for the sake of the pleasure of his stomach, nor will he enslave his free mind to many masters. For his hands are sufficient to serve the body and fulfil physical necessity in every circumstance.

10. The monk free of possessions is like an athlete who cannot be thrown and a light runner who speedily attains 'the prize of his higher calling' (Phil. 3: 14).

11. The monk with many possessions rejoices [1153B] over many profits, but the monk free of possessions rejoices over the crowns of his accomplishments.

12. The avaricious monk works very hard; the one free of possessions spends his time in prayers and readings.

13. The avaricious person fills his storerooms with gold; the one without possessions 'lays up treasure in heaven' (cf. Matt. 6: 20).

14. 'Cursed be the one who makes an image and puts it in hiding' (Deut. 27: 15). The same is true for the one who has the passion of avarice, for the former worships a useless piece of base metal; the latter carries around in his mind the fantasy of wealth.[27] [1153C]

4. Anger

1. (9) Anger is a passion that leads to madness and easily drives those who possess it out of their senses; it makes the soul wild[28] and moves it to shun all (human) encounter.[29]

2. A fierce wind will not move a tower; irascibility cannot carry off a soul free from anger.

3. Water is driven by the force of the winds; the irascible person is troubled by senseless thoughts.

4. The angry monk, like a solitary wild boar, saw some people and gnashed his teeth.[30]

5. The forming of a mist thickens the air; the movement of irascibility thickens the intellect of the angry person.[31]

6. A passing cloud darkens the sun; a thought of resentment darkens the mind.[32]

7. A lion in a cage continuously rattles the hinges; the irascible monk in his cell rattles thoughts of anger.

8. A calm sea is a delight to contemplate, but there is nothing more delightful than a state of peace.[33] For dolphins go diving in a sea that is calm; thoughts worthy of God swim in a state of peace. [1153D]

9. A patient monk is like a still spring offering a gentle drink to all, but the intellect of an angry person is always disturbed and provides no water[34] to the thirsty, and if it does offer water it is muddy and useless.

10. The eyes of an angry person are irritated and bloodshot and are indicative of a troubled heart; the face of a patient person is composed, with gentle eyes looking downwards.

11. (10) The gentleness of a man is remembered by God (cf. Ps. 131: 1),[35] and a soul without anger becomes a temple of the Holy Spirit. [1156A]

12. Christ reclines his head on a patient spirit (cf. Matt. 8: 20), and an intellect at peace becomes a shelter for the Holy Trinity.[36]

13. Foxes find shelter in the resentful soul,[37] and beasts make their lairs in a troubled heart.

14. A distinguished person avoids a shameful inn, and God avoids a resentful heart.

15. When a stone falls into water it troubles it; an evil word troubles a man's heart.

16. Remove thoughts of anger from your soul, and let not irascibility lodge in your heart, and you will not be troubled at the time of prayer. In the same way as the smoke from chaff irritates the eyes, so does resentment irritate the mind in the time of prayer.

17. The thoughts of the irascible person are a viper's offspring (cf. Matt. 3: 7); they consume the heart that gave them birth.

18. The prayer of the irascible person is an abominable incense offering (cf. Isa. 1: 13); the psalmody of an angry person is an irritating noise.

19. The gift of a resentful person is a blemished sacrifice (cf. Lev. 22: 22) [1156B] and does not approach the consecrated altar.

20. The irascible person sees disturbing nightmares, and an angry person imagines attacks of wild beasts.[38]

21. A patient person has visions of encounters with holy angels, and one free from resentment discourses on spiritual matters[39] and receives in the night the answers to mysteries.

5. Sadness

1. (11) Sadness is a dejection of the soul and is constituted from thoughts of anger,[40] for irascibility is a longing for revenge, [1156C] and the frustration of revenge produces sadness.[41]

2. Sadness is the maw of a lion and readily devours one afflicted by it.

3. Sadness is a worm in the heart,[42] and consumes the mother who gives it birth.

4. A mother experiences pain in giving birth to a child; when she gives birth, she is freed from the pain (cf. John 16: 21). But when sadness is begotten, it provokes much toil, and since it stays on even after the birth pains, it causes not a little suffering.

5. A monk afflicted by sadness knows no spiritual pleasure, nor can someone with a very high fever taste honey.

6. A monk afflicted by sadness cannot move the mind towards contemplation or offer up pure prayer, for sadness poses an obstacle to all that is good.

7. Fetters on the feet are an impediment to running; sadness is an impediment to contemplation.

8. A prisoner of barbarians is bound in irons; a prisoner of the passions is bound with sadness.

9. Sadness has no strength [1156D] unless the other passions are present, as a fetter is without strength unless there is someone to attach it.

10. The person who is bound by sadness has been vanquished by the passions and he carries the fetters as proof of his defeat, for sadness is constituted by the frustration of an appetite [of the flesh][43], and an appetite is joined to every passion.

11. One who has overcome his appetites has overcome the passions; one who has overcome the passions will not be dominated by sadness.

12. An abstinent person does not experience sadness in the absence of food, nor does the chaste person experience sadness in the lack of a licentious pleasure; similarly, the person free of anger in not attaining vengeance, or the humble person when deprived of human esteem, or the person free of avarice when he suffers a loss—for such people have decisively turned away from the appetite for these things. Just as one who wears armour [1157A] is not affected by an arrow, so the person who has attained impassibility will not be wounded by sadness.

13. (12) A shield is a soldier's safety, and a wall a city's, but for the monk impassibility offers a greater safety than both these. For often a whizzing arrow passes through a shield and a throng of attackers demolishes a wall, but sadness cannot overcome impassibility.

14. He who has gained control of the passions [1157B] has gained control of sadness, but one who has been defeated by pleasure will not escape the fetters of this vice.

15. One who is continuously afflicted by sadness but pretends to impassibility is like a sick person who feigns health. As a sick person is shown up by the colour of his complexion, so one who is caught in the passions is exposed by his sadness.

16. The person who loves the world (cf. 1 John 2: 15) will experience a

lot of sadness, but one who disdains the things of the world will always know gladness.

17. An avaricious person who has suffered a loss will be bitterly saddened, but he who disdains riches will be free of sadness.

18. One who values esteem will experience sadness when dishonour comes upon him, but the humble person will welcome it as a familiar friend.

19. A smelting-furnace purifies base silver; a godly sadness (cf. 2 Cor. 7: 10) purifies a soul caught in sins.[44]

20. Continuous smelting reduces lead; worldly sadness diminishes the mind.[45]

21. Darkness obstructs the activity of the eyes; [1157C] sadness dulls the mind's capacity for contemplation.

22. Sunlight does not penetrate a great depth of water; the light of contemplation does not illumine a heart overcome by sadness.

23. The sunrise is pleasant for all people, but the soul caught in sadness takes scant pleasure even in this.

[24. He who loves the Lord will be free of sadness since the fullness of love drives out sadness.][46]

25. Jaundice takes away the sense of taste; sadness takes away the perception of the soul. One who disdains the pleasures of the world will not be vexed by thoughts of sadness.

6. Acedia

1. (13) Acedia is a relaxation of the soul, and a relaxation of soul which is not [1157D] in accord with nature does not resist temptations nobly. For what is food for the healthy body constitutes a temptation for the noble soul.

2. A north wind nourishes young plants; temptations strengthen the endurance of a soul.

3. A waterless cloud is chased away by a wind, a mind without perseverance by the spirit of acedia.

4. A springtime dew will increase a field's fruit; a spiritual word uplifts the state of the soul.

5. The spirit of acedia drives the monk out of his cell, but the monk who possesses perseverance will ever cultivate stillness.

6. A person afflicted with acedia proposes visiting the sick, but is fulfilling his own purpose.

7. A monk given to acedia is quick to undertake a service, but considers his own satisfaction to be a precept.

8. A light breeze bends a feeble plant; a fantasy about a trip away drags off the person overcome with acedia.

9. The force of the wind does not shake a well-rooted tree; [1160A] acedia does not bend the soul that is firmly established.

10. A wandering monk is like a dry twig in the desert; he is still for a little while and then is carried off unwillingly.

11. A plant that is transplanted will not bear fruit; a wandering monk will not produce the fruit of virtue.

12. A sick person is not satisfied with a single type of food; the monk caught in acedia[47] with a single type of work.

13. One wife is not enough for a man given to pleasure; a single cell is not enough for the monk given to acedia.[48]

14. (14) The eye of the person afflicted with acedia stares at the doors[49] continuously, and his intellect imagines people coming to visit. [1160B] The door creaks and he jumps up; he hears a sound, and he leans out the window and does not leave it until he gets stiff from sitting there.

15. When he reads, the one afflicted with acedia yawns a lot and readily drifts off into sleep; he rubs his eyes and stretches his arms; turning his eyes away from the book, he stares at the wall and again goes back to reading for awhile; leafing through the pages, he looks curiously for the end of texts, he counts the folios and calculates the number of gatherings.[50] Later, he closes the book and puts it under his head and falls asleep, but not a very deep sleep, for hunger then rouses his soul and has him show concern for its needs.[51]

16. The monk afflicted with acedia is lazy in prayer and will not even say the words [1160C] of a prayer. As a sick person cannot carry about a heavy

burden, so the person afflicted by acedia will not perform a work of God [with diligence].[52] The former has lost the strength of his body and the latter has dissipated the exertions of his soul.

17. Perseverance is the cure for acedia, along with the execution of all tasks with great attention [and the fear of God].[53]

18. Set a measure for yourself in every work and do not let up until you have completed it. Pray with understanding and intensity, and the spirit of acedia will flee from you.

7. Vainglory

1. (15) Vainglory is an irrational passion and it readily gets tangled up with any work of virtue.[54] [1160D]

2. A bindweed vine entangles itself round a tree and when it reaches the upper part it dries out the roots; vainglory grows alongside the virtues and does not withdraw until it eradicates their power.

3. A grape bunch that trails on the ground quickly goes rotten, and virtue is ruined when it leans on vainglory.

4. The monk afflicted with vainglory is an unpaid workman; he undertakes the work but gets no pay.

5. A perforated bag does not hold what is put into it, and vainglory destroys the rewards of the virtues.

6. The abstinence of the vainglorious person is like smoke from a stove; both will get dispersed in the air.

7. The wind wipes out a man's footprint, and vainglory almsgiving.

8. A thrown stone [1161A] does not reach the sky, and the prayer of one who loves popularity will not rise up to God.

9. (16) Vainglory is an underwater rock; if you run against it you lose your cargo.

10. The prudent person hides a treasure, and the sensible monk the labours of virtue.[55]

11. A clever monk imitates the bee; he plunders the flowers outside while inside he produces the honeycomb.[56]

12. Vainglory advises you to pray in the streets, but he who wars against it prays in his chamber (cf. Matt. 6: 5–6).

13. The foolish man makes a public show of his wealth and motivates many to plot against him. Hide what is yours, for you are on a road full of thieves, until you reach the city of peace (cf. Heb. 7: 2)[57] and can safely make use of what is yours.

14. Think of the present life as a road full of brigands and a city well-ordered with respect to the future age.

15. Do not boast on the road, for that is foolish and easily provokes people to plot against you; but if you manage to enter the city, you will enjoy all good things without danger and no one will take your works from you.[58]

16. The virtue of a vainglorious person is like a flawed sacrificial victim (cf. Lev. 22: 22): it cannot be brought [1161B] to the altar of God.

17. A line written in water is obliterated; so also a work of virtue in a soul affected by vainglory.[59]

18. In the night eat the meat of Passover (Exod. 12: 8) and do not make public your secret abstinence, nor reveal it to many witnesses as in the light, that 'the Father who sees in secret may give you your reward in the open' (Matt. 6: 6).[60]

19. A hand becomes white if it is hidden in the breast (Exod. 4: 6), and a deed that is hidden shines more brilliantly than light.

20. Acedia loosens the tension of the soul, and vainglory strengthens the mind that has fallen away from God; it makes the sick person healthy and the older stronger than the younger, only if there are many witnesses present. Then fasting, vigils, and prayer are light matters, for the praise of the multitude rouses the enthusiasm.

21. Do not sell your labours for people's esteem, nor hand over the future glory for the sake of paltry fame, for human esteem settles in the dust (cf. Ps. 7: 6) and its reputation is extinguished on earth, but the glory of virtue abides for eternity. [1161C]

8. Pride

1. (17) Pride is a tumour of the soul filled with pus; when it has ripened, it will rupture and create a great disgusting mess.

2. A flash of lightning foretells the sound of thunder; vainglory announces the presence of pride.

3. The soul of a proud person mounts a great height, and casts him down from there into an abyss.

4. A rock broken off from a mountain descends in a quick rush; the person who has withdrawn from God quickly falls.[61]

5. The one who has distanced himself from God suffers the disease of pride in ascribing his accomplishments to his own strength.

6. As he who mounts a spider web falls through and is born downwards, so he falls who is confident of his own strength.

7. A lot of fruit bends a tree's new branches; an abundance of virtue humbles a person's thinking.

8. Rotten fruit is useless to the farmer; the virtue of the proud person will be of no use to God.

9. The vine-prop supports the young branch weighed down with fruit; the fear of God the virtuous soul. As the weight of fruit knocks down [1161D] the young branch, so does pride cast down the virtuous soul.

10. Do not give your soul to pride, and you will not see terrifying fantasies, for the soul of the proud person is abandoned by God and becomes a plaything of the demons: at night he imagines a multitude of wild beasts approaching and by day he is troubled by thoughts of cowardice; when he falls asleep he is continually jumping up and when he is awake he cowers at a bird's shadow; the sound of a leaf frightens the proud man and the noise of water breaks down his soul. He who a little while before set himself against God and rejected his help is later frightened by paltry fantasies. [1164A]

11. (18) Pride cast the archangel from heaven and made him fall to earth like lightning (cf. Isa. 14: 12; Luke 10: 18). Humility leads a person up to heaven and prepares him to dance with the angels.

12. Why do you put on airs, fellow, if you are mud and rot (cf. Job 4: 19;

25: 6)? Why do you puff yourself up and exalt yourself above the clouds? Consider your nature, that you are earth and ashes (cf. Gen. 18: 27), and in a little while will dissolve into dust—a swaggerer now, but in a while a worm (cf. Ps. 21: 7). Why do you raise your neck which in a while will turn to rot? A great thing is the human being who is helped by God; he is abandoned and then he realizes the weakness of his nature. You have nothing good which you have not received from God (cf. 1 Cor. 4: 7). Why then do you glory in another's (good) as if it were your own? Why do you pride yourself in the grace of God as if it were your own possession? Acknowledge the one who gave it and do not exalt yourself so much. [1164B] You are a creature of God; do not reject the Creator. You receive help from God; do not deny your benefactor. You have mounted to the height of this way of life, but he has guided you. You have attained the accomplishments of virtue, but he has wrought this together with you. Confess the one who exalted you that you may remain secure on the heights. You are a human being; remain within the bounds of your nature.[62] Acknowledge one of your own kind because he is of the same substance as you; do not deny the relationship because of vain boasting.[63]

19. Though he is humble and you are haughty, still the same Creator formed you both. Do not despise the humble person, for he stands more secure than you. He walks on the earth and does not quickly fall, but the haughty person [1164C] will get bruised if he falls.

13. Pride is an unsound vehicle, and he who gets into it is quickly thrown. The humble person always stands firm and the foot of pride (Ps. 35: 12) will never trip him.

14. The proud monk is a tree without roots; he will not bear the rush of the wind.

15. An attitude that is not puffed up is a walled city; he who lives in it will be unharmed.

16. A breath of wind sends straw into the air; an attack of presumption exalts the proud man.

17. When a bubble bursts it will disappear; the memory of the proud person perishes after his death.

18. The word of a humble person is a soothing ointment for the soul, but that of a proud person is filled with boasting.

19. The prayer of a humble person gets God's attention, but the supplication of the proud vexes God.

20. A precious stone is striking in a gold setting; a person's humility is resplendent among many virtues.[64]

21. One celebrating Passover eats unleavened bread often (cf. Exod. 12: 18–20); a virtuous soul is nourished on freedom from arrogance. For as leavened bread rises from the moment it is first near a fire, but unleavened bread remains in a lowly form, so virtue exalts the proud person but it does not puff up the humble person with presumption.[65]

22. If you are fleeing Laban the Syrian, flee in secret and do not trust his promise to escort you, for through those means whereby he said he would escort you, he shall restrain you. For in escorting you with musicians, flutes, and drums, he contrives to pull back the fleeing mind by beguiling it with the sound of music and by dissipating its moral resolve with the harmony of the melody (Gen. 31: 20–7).[66]

23. A staff is a symbol of instruction;[67] he who holds it crosses the Jordan of life (cf. Gen. 32: 10).

24. A staff in the hand of a traveller is useful for every purpose; instruction in the practical life directs a person's life.

25. A staff cast away becomes a serpent (Exod. 4: 3); instruction that departs from the practical life becomes pleasure.[68]

26. Do not let the serpent that crawls on the ground frighten you;[69] nor the passion of pleasure that creeps among earthly material concerns. For if you grab it by the tail, it will again be a staff in your hand (Exod. 4: 4); if you gain control of a passion it will again become instruction.

27. In the desert a serpent bites and kills the soul (cf. Num. 21: 6); pleasure wounds and destroys the mind with ease.

28. He who looks at the bronze serpent escapes death (Num. 21: 9); he who gazes upon the rewards of chastity shall live forever.

29. A serpent bites a horse's hoof (Gen. 49: 17–18); the reason of chastity touches passion.[70]

30. A long-standing infection is cured with a cautery; a habit of vainglory by dishonour and sadness.

31. The scalpel and cautery cause a great deal of pain, but they restrict the spreading of the wound; on the one hand, dishonour pains the one being treated, but on the other, it puts a stop to the grievous passions, namely vainglory and pride.

32. Humility is the parapet of a housetop, and it keeps safe the one who gets up upon it (Deut. 22: 8).[71] When you ascend to the height of the virtues, then you will have much need of security. He who falls at ground level gets up quickly, but he who falls from a high place is in danger of death.

5

The Monk: A Treatise on the Practical Life

Introduction

This treatise was the first to receive a magisterial critical edition at the hands of A. and C. Guillaumont.[1] Apart from the Prologue and Epilogue at the beginning and end, the text is divided into a series of 100 numbered chapters. In a note, very probably from the hand of Evagrius himself, directions are given to the copyist to preserve the numbering of the chapters and to begin each new chapter on a separate line. From their research, the Guillaumonts concluded that the treatise was probably composed in two separate redactions, separated by a considerable length of time.[2] The primitive form of the text was constituted by the first 90 chapters, without the Prologue, Epilogue, and the series of apophthegmata at the end. This first redaction was probably written prior to the *Gnostikos* and the *Kephalaia Gnostika*, mentioned in the Prologue. It is also prior to the composition of the *Scholia on the Psalms* and the *Antirrhetikos*, both of which make reference to the earlier work. Guillaumont also places the writing of the *Scholia on the Psalms* before the *Kephalaia Gnostika*.[3]

If four works, three of them very lengthy, were written between the two redactions, a considerable length of time must be allowed for their production.[4] By the time that Evagrius assembled the second redaction of the *Praktikos* there may have been growing suspicion of the Origenist monks at Kellia.[5] The *Apophthegmata patrum* report several sayings in

---

[1] A. and C. Guillaumont (eds.), *Évagre le Pontique, Traité Pratique ou Le Moine*, SC 170–1 (Paris: Cerf, 1971).

[2] SC 170, 381–6.

[3] S1-Ps. 143: 1, ed. M.-J. Rondeau, *Les commentaires patristiques du Psautier (IIIe–Ve siècles)*, Vol. 1, Orientalia Christiana Analecta, 219 (Rome: Pont. Institutum Studiorum Orientalium, 1982), 289; *Antirrhetikos*, Prologue, F474. 13–14.

[4] Rondeau, 387–8.

[5] On the subject see A. Guillaumont, *Les 'Kephalaia Gnostica' d'Évagre le Pontique et l'histoire de l'origénisme chez les grecs et chez les syriens,* Patristica Sorbonensia, 5 (Paris: Seuil, 1962), pp. 47–59.

which Evagrius is criticized for his dedication to learning and his pre-occupation with books.[6] In addition, Palladius cites the monk Heron as a critic of Evagrius' teaching.[7] Perhaps it was to counter such suspicions and criticisms that Evagrius is careful in the second redaction of the *Praktikos* to emphasize his faithfulness to the teaching of the holy fathers who preceded him in the desert. He three times assures Anatolios that his explanation of the symbolism of the monastic habit is drawn from what he learned from the desert elders.[8] Further, he insists that the teaching he is about to present on the practical and the gnostic life is based, not on his own observations and experience, but on what he was taught by the fathers.[9] At the end of the work, Evagrius once again acknowledges his indebtedness both to the holy fathers and to his earlier teacher, Gregory Nazianzen.[10] The addition of the 'Sayings of the Holy Monks' in the last ten chapters serves a similar function. The collection is introduced by an assertion of the importance of enquiry into 'the upright ways of the monks who have gone before us' and the necessity of regulating our lives according to their example.[11] Then in the last chapter Evagrius declares his respect for the priests and elders of the community. All these assurances of a teaching faithful to the received tradition of the desert monks suggests at the very least that Evagrius felt some need for caution in disseminating his writings.

Anatolios had addressed to Evagrius from 'the Holy Mountain' a request for an explanation of the symbolism of the monastic habit. There is unfortunately little that can be said about the identity of Anatolios, beyond a few conjectures. The 'Holy Mountain' is very likely a reference to Jerusalem and the monastic community founded by Melania the Elder and Rufinus on the Mount of Olives. Evagrius, who had been welcomed in this monastery before moving on to Egypt, maintained a correspondence with Melania, Rufinus, and their entourage.[12] The Anatolios of the Prologue may be identical with the Anatolios mentioned in the Coptic version of the Lausiac History as a wealthy notary, originally from Spain, who later became a monk and visited Abba Pambo. With his wealth, he may have undertaken to have copied and disseminated the three

---

[6] *Apophthegmata patrum* A233 (Evagrius 7), A224 (Euprepios 7, *re vera* 'Evagrius'), A43 (Arsenius 5).

[7] *HL* 26. 1 (81. 1–7).

[8] *Praktikos*, Prologue 6–7, 46–7, and 52–3.   [9] Prologue 53–5.

[10] Epilogue 7–9.   [11] *Praktikos* 91.

[12] Guillaumont, SC 170, 390. See also Gabriel Bunge, *Evagrios Pontikos: Briefe aus der Wüste*, Sophia, 24 (Trier: Paulinus, 1986), pp. 176–93.

works that Evagrius sent to him: the Praktikos, the Gnostikos, and the Kephalaia Gnostika.[13]

The symbolism of the habit proposed in the Prologue is not known earlier in monastic literature and may have been developed by Evagrius himself on analogy with the symbolic description of the garments of the High Priest proposed by Philo of Alexandria. The symbolism was adopted and further elaborated by John Cassian in his *Institutes*, as well as enjoying a subsequent history in the East.[14]

The 90 chapters that constitute the core of the *Praktikos* divide roughly into two principal sections, 6–53 treating the eight thoughts, the passions, and the demons, and 54–90 on the subject of impassibility. The structure can best be displayed in the following analysis:[15]

Prologue (1–9
A. Part 1 (1–53)
   I. Introduction (1–5)
   II. Thoughts, Passions, Demons (6–53)
      i. *On the Eight Thoughts* (6)
        1. Gluttony (7)
        2. Fornication (8)
        3. Avarice (9)
        4. Sadness (10)
        5. Anger (11)
        6. Acedia (12)
        7. Vainglory (13)
        8. Pride (14)
      ii. *Remedies Against the Eight Thoughts* (15)
        1. Gluttony (16)
        2. Fornication (17)
        3. Avarice (18)
        4. Sadness (19)
        5. Anger (20–6)
        6. Acedia (27–9)

---

[13] On Anatolios see Bunge, 32–7. For the Coptic *Life of Pambo* see G. Bunge and Adalbert de Vogüé, *Quatre ermites égyptiens d'après les fragments coptes de l'Histoire Lausiaque*. Spiritualité Orientale, 60 (Bégrolles-en-Mauges: Abbaye de Bellefontaine, 1994), 99–100.

[14] For further details see Guillaumont, SC 171, 484–5.

[15] In the analysis the titles internal to the work and preserved in the manuscript tradition are given in italics. In the translation titles or parts of titles not in the manuscript tradition are given in square brackets.

Epilogue

As an introduction to the whole work, the first five chapters describe the division of the ascetic life into the practical life that engages the monk in the struggle for virtue and the control of the passions, followed by the attainment of natural contemplation, also called the contemplation of beings, and finally, theological contemplation or the knowledge of the Holy Trinity. Chapters 4–5 introduce more specifically the discussion of the practical life that will follow.

In terms of its content and detail of exposition of the practical life, the *Praktikos* stands between *On the Eight Thoughts* and *On Thoughts. Eight Thoughts* is more hortatory in character; its gnomic sayings are intended to spur the monk to undertake the struggle against the vices through the practice of the corresponding virtues, but they provide only a general and introductory account of their nature. The *Praktikos*, on the other hand, adopts a more instructional style, now giving some details on the nature and workings of the individual vices along with an account of the principal remedies to be used against them. This is accompanied by a discussion of the nature of the passions and how they are set in motion by the demons and are in turn countered by certain ascetic exercises. The second part of the treatise moves to the frontiers of the practical life as it treats the state of impassibility and the signs that indicate its approach, as well as going into some detail on the practices of asceticism at this stage. The treatise *On Thoughts* drops the systematic exposition of the eight vices to offer a more extensive treatment of particular temptations and the interrelationship of certain vices. At the same time there is a more developed analysis of the nature of the passions and the activities of the demons, especially as these influence the inner life of the monk through mental representations by day and dream fantasies by night. If *Eight Thoughts* takes the perspective of the monk entering the struggle of the practical life, the *Praktikos* addresses those who are further along in their progress, some of whom at least may be approaching the boundaries of impassibility. *On Thoughts*, however, is written more for the perspective of the gnostic who has won through to impassibility but must still struggle in particular ways with new manifestations of the vices.

THE MONK: A TREATISE ON THE PRACTICAL LIFE

[Prologue—Letter to Anatolios]

1. Beloved brother Anatolios, from the Holy Mountain you have recently made known to me in residence at Sketis your request for an explanation of the symbolism of the habit of the monks in Egypt. For you have considered that it is not by chance or superfluously that it is so different from the clothing of other people. Now then we will recount all that we have learned from the holy fathers about it.[1]

2. The *koukoullion* is a symbol of the grace of God our Saviour, which protects their ruling faculty and keeps fervent their youth in Christ, with a view to those who are always trying to batter and wound them. Therefore, those who wear this on the head sing these words with vigour: 'Unless the Lord build the house and guard the city, the one who does the building and the one who tries to maintain the guard labours in vain' (Ps. 126: 1). Such words instil humility and root out pride, the ancient evil which cast to earth Lucifer 'who rises near dawn' (Isa. 14: 12).[2]

3. Having the hands bare shows a way of life without dissimulation, for vainglory is clever at shrouding and obscuring the virtues and is ever seek-

ing after people's esteem and chasing away faith. For scripture says: 'How can you believe when you accept glory from one another and do not seek the glory that comes from the only God?' (John 5: 44). The good must be chosen, not for something else, but rather for itself. For if that is not granted, what moves us to do the good will appear of far greater value than the good that is realized. This absurdity would mean conceiving and speaking of something as superior to God.[3]

4. The *analabos*, which is in the form of a cross and is folded over their shoulders, is a symbol of faith in Christ which upholds the gentle (cf. Ps. 146: 6) and ever restrains what hinders them and provides them with an activity that is free of obstacles.[4]

5. The belt that is tightened around their kidneys wards off all impurity and proclaims: 'It is well for a man not to touch a woman' (1 Cor. 7: 1).[5]

6. They wear the *melote* who 'always carry in the body the death of Jesus' (2 Cor. 4: 10) in muzzling all the irrational passions of the body and in cutting off the evils of the soul by participation in the good; they love poverty, while fleeing greed as the mother of idolatry (cf. Col. 3: 5).[6]

7. The staff is 'a tree of life to those who lay hold of it and a strong support for those who lean upon it as upon the Lord' (Prov. 3: 18).[7]

8. In short, these are the things of which the habit is a symbol, and these are the words which the fathers are ever saying to them. The fear of God, my child, strengthens faith, and abstinence in turn strengthens fear of God, and perseverance and hope render abstinence unwavering, and from these is born impassibility of which love is the offspring; love is the door to natural knowledge, which is followed by theology and ultimate blessedness.[8]

9. For the present that is enough said about the holy habit and the teaching of the elders. We are now going to discuss the practical and the gnostic life, not as much as we have seen or heard, but what we have learned from them to say to others. We have condensed and divided up the teaching on the practical life in one hundred chapters and on the gnostic life in fifty in addition to the six hundred.[9] We have kept some things hidden and have obscured others, so as 'not to give what is holy to dogs and throw pearls before swine' (Matt. 7: 6). But these things will be clear to those who have embarked upon the same path.[10]

One hundred chapters

[I pray the brothers who come upon this book and wish to copy it not to join one chapter to another, nor to place on the same line the end of the chapter just written and the beginning of the one about to be written, but to have each chapter begin with its own beginning according to the divisions which we have marked also by numbers. In this way the ordering of the chapters can be preserved and what is said will be clear. We begin then by the first chapter with what Christianity is and we have proposed defining it as the teaching of Christ our Saviour, comprised of the practical, the natural, and the theological.[11]]

1. Christianity is the doctrine of Christ our Saviour. It is comprised of the practical, the natural, and the theological.[12]

2. The kingdom of heaven is impassibility of the soul accompanied by true knowledge of beings.[13]

3. The kingdom of God is knowledge of the Holy Trinity co-extensive with the substance of the mind and surpassing its incorruptibility.[14]

4. Whatever a person loves he desires above all; and what he desires he struggles to attain. Now desire is the source of every pleasure, and sensation gives birth to desire. For that which has no part in sensation is also free from passion.[15]

5. The demons fight directly against anchorites; but in the case of those who practise virtue in monasteries or in communities they equip the most negligent among the brethren with their weapons. Now this second warfare is much lighter than the first, for there is not to be found on earth any human beings more embittered than the demons or who could undertake all at once the totality of their malevolence.[16]

On the eight thoughts

6. All the generic types of thoughts fall into eight categories in which every sort of thought is included. First is that of gluttony, then fornication, third avarice, fourth sadness, fifth anger, sixth acedia, seventh vainglory, eighth pride. Whether or not all these thoughts trouble the soul is not within our

power; but it is for us to decide if they are to linger within us or not and whether or not they stir up the passions.

[I. Gluttony]

7. The thought of gluttony suggests to the monk the rapid demise of his asceticism. It describes for him his stomach, his liver and spleen, dropsy and lengthy illness, the scarcity of necessities and the absence of doctors. Frequently it brings him to recall certain of the brethren who have fallen prey to these sufferings. Sometimes it even persuades those who have suffered such maladies to visit those who are practising abstinence and to tell them of their misfortunes and how they came about as a result of their asceticism.[17]

[II. Fornication]

8. The demon of fornication compels one to desire various bodies. It attacks more violently those who practise abstinence in order that they give it up, convinced that they are accomplishing nothing. In defiling the soul, the demon inclines it to shameful deeds, has it speak and hear certain things, almost as if the object were visible and present.

[III. Avarice]

9. Avarice suggests a lengthy old age, inability to perform manual labour, famines that will come along, diseases that will arise, the bitter realities of poverty, and the shame there is in accepting goods from others to meet one's needs.[18]

[IV. Sadness]

10. Sadness sometimes occurs through the frustration of one's desires, or sometimes it follows closely upon anger. When it is through the frustration of one's desires, it occurs in this way. When certain thoughts gain the advantage, they bring the soul to remember home and parents and one's former life. And when they observe that the soul does not resist but rather follows right along and disperses itself among thoughts of pleasures, then with a hold on it they plunge it into sadness with the realization that former things are no more and cannot be again because of the present way of life. And the miserable soul, the more it allowed itself to be dispersed among the former thoughts, the more it has now become hemmed in and humiliated by these latter ones.

[V. Anger]

11. Anger is a passion that arises very quickly. Indeed, it is referred to as a boiling over of the irascible part and a movement directed against one who has done injury or is thought to have done so.[19] It renders the soul furious all day long, but especially during prayers it seizes the mind and represents to it the face of the one who has hurt it. Sometimes when this goes on for awhile and turns into resentment, it provokes disturbances at night accompanied by wasting and pallor of the body, as well as the attacks of venomous wild beasts. One could find these four signs that follow upon resentment accompanying numerous thoughts.

[VI. Acedia]

12. The demon of acedia, also called the noonday demon (cf. Ps. 90: 6), is the most oppressive of all the demons.[20] He attacks the monk about the fourth hour [viz. 10 a.m.] and besieges his soul until the eighth hour [2 p.m.]. First of all, he makes it appear that the sun moves slowly or not at all, and that the day seems to be fifty hours long. Then he compels the monk to look constantly towards the windows, to jump out of the cell, to watch the sun to see how far it is from the ninth hour [3 p.m.], to look this way and that lest one of the brothers . . .[21] And further, he instils in him a dislike for the place and for his state of life itself, for manual labour, and also the idea that love has disappeared from among the brothers and there is no one to console him. And should there be someone during those days who has offended the monk, this too the demon uses to add further to his dislike (of the place). He leads him on to a desire for other places where he can easily find the wherewithal to meet his needs and pursue a trade that is easier and more productive; he adds that pleasing the Lord is not a question of being in a particular place: for scripture says that the divinity can be worshipped everywhere (cf. John 4: 21–4). He joins to these suggestions the memory of his close relations and of his former life; he depicts for him the long course of his lifetime, while bringing the burdens of asceticism before his eyes; and, as the saying has it, he deploys every device in order to have the monk leave his cell and flee the stadium. No other demon follows immediately after this one: a state of peace and ineffable joy ensues in the soul after this struggle.[22]

[VII. Vainglory]

13. The thought of vainglory is a most subtle one and readily insinu-
ates itself within the virtuous person with the intention of publishing
his struggles and hunting after the esteem that comes from people (cf.
1 Thess. 2: 6). It invents demons crying out, women being healed and a
crowd touching his garments (cf. Matt. 9: 20–1; Mark 5: 27); it even predicts
to him that he will eventually attain the priesthood;[23] it has people come
to seek him at his door, and if he should be unwilling he will be taken away
in bonds. When this thought has thus raised him aloft on empty hopes,
it flies off abandoning him to be tempted either by the demon of pride or
by that of sadness, who brings upon him further thoughts opposed to his
hopes. Sometimes it delivers him over to the demon of fornication, he
who a little earlier was a holy priest carried off in bonds.

[VIII. Pride]

14. The demon of pride brings the soul to the very worst sort of fall. It
induces the soul to refuse to acknowledge that God is its helper and to
think that it is itself the cause of its good actions, and to take a haughty
view of its brothers as being unintelligent because they do not all hold the
same opinion of it. Anger and sadness follow closely upon this as well
as the ultimate evil, derangement of mind, madness, and the vision of a
multitude of demons in the air.[24]

[Remedies] against the eight thoughts

15. When the mind wanders, reading, vigils, and prayer bring it to a
standstill.[25] When desire bursts into flame, hunger, toil, and anachoresis extinguish it. When the irascible part becomes agitated, psalmody,
patience, and mercy calm it.[26] But these practices are to be engaged in at
the appropriate times and in due measure, for what is done without due
measure or not at the opportune moment lasts but a little while; and what
is short-lived is more harmful than it is profitable.[27]

[I. Gluttony]

16. When our soul yearns for a variety of foods, then let it reduce its ration
of bread and water that it may be grateful even for a small morsel. For
satiety desires foods of all sorts, while hunger thinks of satiety of bread
as beatitude.

[II. Fornication]

17. The restrained use of water contributes greatly to chastity. You should be so persuaded by the three hundred Israelites in Gideon's company who subdued Midian (Judg. 7: 5–7).[28]

[III. Avarice]

18. As it is inadmissible for life and death to coexist in the same person at the same time, so is it impossible for charity to exist alongside riches in a given individual. For not only is charity destructive of riches, but also of our transitory life itself.

[IV. Sadness]

19. One who flees all worldly pleasures is a citadel inaccessible to the demon of sadness. For sadness involves the frustration of a pleasure, whether actually present or only hoped for. And so if we have an attachment to some earthly object, it is impossible to repel this enemy, for he sets his snare and produces sadness precisely where he sees we are particularly inclined.

[V. Anger]

20. Anger and hatred increase irascibility, but compassion and gentleness diminish even that which is present.[29]

21. 'Let the sun not go down upon our anger' (Eph. 4: 26), lest by night the demons come upon us to strike fear in our souls and render our minds more cowardly for the fight on the morrow. For frightful apparitions usually arise from the disturbance of the irascible part. Indeed nothing else so inclines the mind to desertion like a disturbance in the irascible part.[30]

22. When, having seized on a pretext, the irascible part of our soul is troubled, then at the same moment the demons suggest to us that anachoresis is a fine thing, lest we resolve the causes of our sadness and free ourselves from the disturbance. But when the concupiscible part becomes heated, then in turn they try to make us sociable, calling us austere and uncivil, so that out of desire for bodies we seek encounters with bodies. We must not obey them, but rather do the opposite.[31]

23. Do not give yourself to the thought of anger, fighting in your intellect with the person who hurt you, nor to the thought of fornication by

continually imagining the pleasure. The first brings darkness to the soul,[32] the second invites it to experience the fires of passion: both leave your mind defiled. And when you entertain such images during the time of prayer and do not offer your prayer to God purely,[33] you immediately fall prey to the demon of acedia, who leaps upon dispositions especially such as these and rips the soul apart as a dog would kill a fawn.

24. The nature of the irascible part is to fight against the demons and to struggle over any sort of pleasure. And so the angels, on the one hand, suggest to us spiritual pleasure and the blessedness that will come from it, and they urge us to turn our irascibility against the demons. These latter, on the other hand, drag us toward worldly desires and compel the irascible part, contrary to its nature, to fight with people, so that with the mind darkened and fallen from knowledge it may become the traitor of the virtues.[34]

25. Be attentive lest you ever provoke the departure of one of the brothers because you drove him to anger; as a result, you will not be able to escape in your lifetime the demon of sadness, which will always be an obstacle to you during the time of prayer.

26. Gifts extinguish resentment: let the example of Jacob convince you of this, for he beguiled Esau with gifts when he was coming out to meet him with four hundred men (Gen. 32: 7). But since we are poor, let us make up for our poverty by the hospitality of the table.[35]

[VI. Acedia]

27. When we come up against the demon of acedia, then with tears let us divide the soul and have one part offer consolation and the other receive consolation. And sowing within ourselves goodly hopes, let us chant with holy David this incantation: 'Why are you saddened, O my soul, and why do you trouble me? Hope in God; for I shall confess him, the salvation of my face and my God' (Ps. 41: 6).[36]

28. You must not abandon the cell in the time of temptations, fashioning excuses seemingly reasonable. Rather, you must remain seated inside, exercise perseverance, and valiantly welcome all attackers, especially the demon of acedia, who is the most oppressive of all but leaves the soul proven to the highest degree. Fleeing and circumventing such struggles teaches the mind to be unskilled, cowardly, and evasive.[37]

29. Our saintly teacher with his great experience in the practical life used

to say: The monk must ever hold himself ready as though he were to die tomorrow, and in turn must treat the body as though he would have to live with it for many years. The first practice, he would say, cuts off the thoughts of acedia and makes the monk more zealous; the latter keeps the body healthy and always maintains its abstinence in balance.[38]

[*VII. Vainglory*]

30. It is difficult to escape the thought of vainglory, for what you do to rid yourself of it becomes for you a new source of vainglory. It is not always the demons who oppose every upright thought of ours, but rather, in some cases, the vices that have influenced our conduct are also involved.

31. I have noted that the demon of vainglory is pursued by almost all the demons and with the fall of its pursuers it shamelessly comes forward and displays for the monk the grandeur of his virtues.[39]

32. The person who has attained knowledge and enjoys the pleasant fruit that derives from it will no longer be persuaded by the demon of vainglory, even if it should bring before him all the pleasures of the world. For what greater than spiritual contemplation could it promise? To the extent that we have not tasted knowledge let us work devotedly at the practical life, demonstrating to God our goal of doing all things for the sake of his knowledge.[40]

[*VIII. Pride*]

33. Remember your former life and your transgressions of old, and how, while you were caught in the passions, you made the transition to impassibility by the mercy of Christ, and how in turn you left the world that had inflicted upon you many and frequent humiliations. Consider this for me. Who was it that protected you in the desert? And who was it that drove away the demons who gnashed their teeth against you? Such thoughts instil humility and deny admittance to the demon of pride.[41]

On the passions

34. When we have impassioned memories of certain things, it is because we previously entertained the objects with passion; and in turn, when we entertain objects with passion, we will have the impassioned memories associated with these. Wherefore the person who has overcome the operations of the demons despises the operations wrought by them.[42]

For the immaterial warfare is more difficult than the material.[43]

35. The passions of the soul have their origin in human beings; those of the body have their origin in the body. Abstinence cuts away the passions of the body; spiritual love cuts away those of the soul.[44]

36. Those (viz. the demons) who preside over the passions of the soul hold out until death; those that preside over those of the body withdraw more quickly. Whereas the other demons are like the sun which rises and sets, touching only one part of the soul, the noonday demon is accustomed to enveloping the entire soul and strangling the mind. And so anachoresis is sweet after the elimination of the passions, for then the memories are only simple ones and the struggle no longer disposes the monk to combat but to the contemplation of it.[45]

37. One should pay attention to whether it is the representation that sets the passions in motion, or the passions that set the representation in motion. Some people have held the first opinion, others the second.[46]

38. The passions are naturally set in motion by the senses. When love and abstinence are present, they will not be set in motion; when they are absent, they will be set in motion. The irascible requires more remedies than the concupiscible, and for this reason love is said to be great (1 Cor. 13: 13), for it is the bridle of anger. Moses, that holy man, in his treatise on nature gave it the symbolic name of serpent-fighter (Lev. 11: 22).[47]

39. The soul usually flares up against thoughts at the bad smell that prevails among the demons, when it perceives their approach upon being affected by the passion of the one who torments it.[48]

Instructions

40. It is not possible on every occasion to fulfil the habitual rule, but it is necessary to pay attention to the occasion and to try to carry out as best one can the precepts that are possible. For the demons themselves are not unaware of these occasions and circumstances, and thus will make their move against us, hindering what can be done and forcing us to do what cannot be done. And so they prevent the sick from giving thanks for their sufferings and acting patiently towards those who are looking after them; in turn, they encourage them to practise abstinence even while they are weak and to say the psalms standing even when they feel weighed down.[49]

41. When we have to stay for a while in cities or villages, then especially we should hold vigorously to the practice of abstinence while in the company of seculars, lest, with our mind grown thick[50] and without taking the usual care in the occasion at hand, it do something ill-considered and become a fugitive under the blows of the demons.

42. When you experience temptation, do not pray before you have directed some words of anger against the one causing the affliction. For when your soul is affected by thoughts, it follows that your prayer is not pure. But if you speak some angry word against them, you confound and dispel the mental representations coming from your adversaries. This is the natural function of anger, even in the case of good mental representations.

43. It is necessary to recognize also the differences among demons and to make note of their attendant circumstances. We shall know them on the basis of the thoughts, and the thoughts on the basis of the objects, that is, with regard to which of the demons are uncommon and more oppressive, what sort are persistent but easier to bear, and which ones burst upon us suddenly and carry the mind away into blasphemy. It is necessary to know these things, so that when the thoughts begin to set their proper matter[51] in motion and before we are cast out of our own state we may pronounce some word against them and denounce the one at hand. In this way we may readily make progress with God's help and set them to flight in amazement and consternation over us.[52]

44. When the demons appear powerless in their struggle against the monks, then they withdraw a little and observe which of the virtues has been neglected in the mean time, and through that means they gain sudden entrance and rend asunder the miserable soul.

45. The wicked demons draw to their aid demons even more wicked, and if they are opposed to one another in their dispositions they agree on one thing alone, the destruction of the soul.

46. Let us not allow ourselves to be troubled by the demon that carries the mind off to blaspheme God and to imagine those forbidden things which I dare not confide to writing; and let us not allow this demon to sunder our commitment. For the Lord 'knows people's hearts' (Acts 1: 24) and he knows that not even when we were in the world were we afflicted with such folly. This demon's goal is to stop us from praying so that we may not stand before the Lord our God and dare not extend our hands to him, against whom we have conceived such thoughts.[53]

47. Some word proffered or a movement arising in the body is an indication of the affections present within the soul. Through these the enemies perceive whether we hold and nourish their thoughts, or cast them aside and devote our concern to our salvation. For only the God who made us knows our mind and has no need of indications to know what is hidden in the heart.[54]

48. The demons war with seculars more through objects, but with monks they do so especially through thoughts, for they are deprived of objects because of the solitude. Further, to the extent that it is easier to sin in thought than in action, so is the warfare in thought more difficult than that which is conducted through objects. For the mind is a thing easily set in motion and difficult to check in its tendency towards unlawful fantasies.

49. We have not been commanded to work, to keep vigil, and to fast at all times, but the law of unceasing prayer (1 Thess. 5: 17) has been handed down to us. In fact, those things which heal the passionate part of the soul require also the body to put them into practice, and the latter because of its weakness is not sufficient for these labours. Prayer, on the other hand, invigorates and purifies the mind for the struggle, since it is naturally constituted for prayer, even without this body,[55] and for fighting the demons on behalf of all the powers of the soul.

50. If one of the monks should wish to acquire experience with the cruel demons and become familiar with their skill, let him observe the thoughts and let him note their intensity and their relaxation, their interrelationships, their occasions, which of the demons do this or that particular thing, what sort of demon follows upon another and which does not follow another; and let him seek from Christ the reasons for these things.[56] For the demons become quite infuriated with those who partake more gnostically in the practical life,[57] and they are willing 'to shoot in the dark at the upright in heart' (Ps. 10: 2).

51. By observation you will discover two of the demons to be especially quick and almost able to overtake the movement of our mind: namely, the demon of fornication and the one that snatches us away into blaspheming God. But the second is short-lived, and the former, unless it should set the thoughts in motion with passion, poses us no hindrance to the knowledge of God.[58]

52. Separating body from soul belongs solely to the one who joined them

confer social status and social position. Within local monastic societies one or more elders gradually acquired reputations as teachers, counsellors, effective intercessors, healers, and miracle workers. For example, from the papyri documentation, we have seven letters from an assortment of lay people addressed to the monk Paphnoutios who was renowned for his 'noble way of life', for being an intercessor whose prayers offered resolutions of difficulties, deliverance from temptation, and even healing from illnesses. See V. L. Wimbush (ed.), *Ascetic Behaviour in Greco-Roman Antiquity: A Sourcebook* (Minneapolis, Minn.: Fortress Press, 1990), 459–62. These reputations did not long remain limited to their local communities, but extended beyond to the nearby villages and towns, to Alexandria, and soon across the Mediterranean. By the late 4th cent. pious tourism with its incessant stream of visitors had become a serious problem for the desert communities of Nitria, Sketis, Kellia, and elsewhere in Egypt. It was not uncommon for local churches to seek candidates for the clergy and episcopacy from among the monastic elders with a reputation for holiness. In 394 Bishop Theophilos made Dioskoros, one of the Tall Brothers, bishop of Hermopolis, and ordained two others, Eusebios and Euthymios, as clerics to assist him in Alexandria. The fourth brother, Ammonios, apparently escaped by cutting off his ear (Socrates, *HE* 6. 7; Sozomen, *HE* 8. 12; Palladius, *HL* 11. 1–2). For other examples see *Apophthegmata Patrum*, A120 (Ammonas 8); A122 (Ammonas 10); A140 (Apphy); A534 (Motios 2), 'And after these events he (Motios) became a bishop, for he was a miracle worker.' Even Evagrius, according to the *Apophthegmata*, was subject to temptations of worldly honour (A233, Evagrius 7).

10 *the beast of irascibility.* Evagrius frequently refers to the demons as wild animals or beasts, and associates the wild savagery of the animal state with the demonic nature. Cf. S9-Ps. 73: 19 (12. 1532C), '*Give not over to the wild beasts the soul that makes confession to you.* If the demons are called beasts and irascibility predominates in beasts, then irascibility predominates in the demons. And in Job it says, "The wild beasts will be at peace with you" (Job 5: 23).'

11 *the deceiver*, namely, the devil.

12 *in your body, in your spirit, and in your soul.* These are the three elements (body, soul, and spirit or mind) that constitute the present reality of the human person in Evagrian anthropology.

13 *godly sadness . . . the contrary form of sadness.* The two types of sadness are mentioned in 2 Cor. 7: 10, 'For godly sadness produces a repentance that leads to salvation and brings no regret, but worldly sadness produces death.' Evagrius quotes this verse in *Antirrhetikos* 4. 74 (F512. 18–21) in his treatment of sadness. See also S313-Prov. 25: 20, '*As a moth in a garment and a worm in wood, so does sadness do harm to a man's heart.* Sadness is blameworthy when it comes from the frustration of a corruptible pleasure, but it is praiseworthy when it comes from the frustration of the virtues and of the knowledge of God.'

14 *Frustrated desires produce plantings of sadness.* In *Praktikos* 10, Evagrius elaborates
further on sadness as a product of frustrated desires, explaining that the
thoughts will remind the monk of the family and society he has left behind,
and the realization that these are no more a part of his life will plunge him
into sadness. These memories with all their associations are further defined
as 'thoughts of pleasure'. *Praktikos* 19 adds to the definition: 'sadness involves
the frustration of a pleasure, whether actually present or only hoped for.' Thus
attachment to any kind of earthly object or intentional objective can become
the occasion for demonic sadness: for example, food, sexual pleasures,
vengeance, human esteem, and material possessions. These possibilities are
enumerated in *Eight Thoughts* 5. See also *Antirrhetikos*, 6.74 (F 512. 18–21),
'Against the thoughts of sadness that occur to us concerning transient possessions and that plunge the mind into great distress and kill it'. Note also *Apophthegmata* A1002 (Syncletica S10).

15 *sadness . . . as an intermediary between angry persons.* As Evagrius also noted in *Praktikos* 10, sadness often follows closely upon anger, and it is treated in *Eight
Thoughts* 5 immediately after the subject of anger. In this case, sadness would
result from the frustrated desire for revenge. In *Eulogios* 7, sadness is said to
arise as an intermediary between angry people; anger begets sadness. If sadness arises from the frustration of a desire for a perceived good, and if conflicts
of anger arise between people over such frustrated desires, it is possible to
see how sadness is so closely associated with anger. Thus Evagrius naturally
recommends perseverance in charity and the joy of innocence as the appropriate remedies for both sadness and anger. Cf. *Eight Thoughts* 5.1, 'Sadness is a
dejection of the soul and is constituted from thoughts of anger, for irascibility
is a longing for revenge, and the frustration of revenge produces sadness.'

16 *injustice . . . good will.* Evagrius here resorts to a play on words (*adikia–eudokia*)
which cannot easily be translated. One who rejoices in injustice (*adikia*) now
will experience only lamentation in the time of the promised future beatitude
of God's gracious good will (*eudokia*).

17 *acedia . . . presumption . . . vainglory.* These and the following comments of Evagrius
—all subjects that he elaborates on elsewhere—bear an interesting similarity
to a teaching reported in the *Apophthegmata, Anonymous Collection* N 374, 'The
elders used to say that the monk ought to struggle unto death against the
demon of *acedia* and despondency, especially at the time of the *offices* (*sunaxeis*).
And if with God's help you are successful in this, pay attention to the thought
of self-satisfaction and *presumption*, and say to the thought: "If the Lord should
not build the house, in vain have the builders laboured" (Ps. 126: 1), "for a
human being is nought but earth and dust" (Ecclus. 17: 31), and remember
that "the Lord resists the proud and gives grace to the humble" (Jas. 4: 6).'

18 *at the time of the office (sunaxis).* The term *synaxis* is ambiguous, for it can refer to
the weekend liturgical assembly in the desert communities where the monks
gathered together in the central church (or liturgical assemblies in a monastery

church), or it may designate the office of psalms said by the monk privately in his cell. Here and in what immediately follows, Evagrius appears to be talking about the daily or nightly office performed by the monk in his cell. For the private office of the cell see *Apophthegmata* A62, A311, A360, A390, A742, A875, N395, N435; for public liturgical assemblies see A54, A423, A439, A533, A585, A606, A797.

19 *let us practise thoughts of light.* Since Evagrius is here talking about the preparation for prayer, he seems to be advising the reader to direct his thoughts immediately towards the immaterial, supernatural realm and not let them be dragged down to material, mundane concerns that would be a hindrance to prayer.

20 *a low rhythmic voice.* The reference here is to reading or reciting in a low voice, effectively a soft, rhythmic, lightly voiced whisper.

21 *persevering during the psalmody.* The Pg reading, ἀδολεσχεῖν, 'to meditate during the psalmody', appears to make more sense but is not supported by the manuscripts CEMa.

22 *[when self-satisfaction... highest vision].* The passage delineated by square brackets is unique to recension B and is found also in Paris gr. 1188, Vat. gr. 703 (partially), as well as in the Syriac and Armenian translations. See J. Muyldermans, 'Evagriana de la Vaticane', *Le Muséon*, 54 (1941), 5–9.

23 *turning upon them all our anger.* Ordinarily, Evagrius opposes the virtue of gentleness to the vice of anger, but when anger is directed against the passions it becomes virtuous, and similarly gentleness towards the passions become vicious. See *Praktikos* 24.

24 *one of your own race.* For Evagrius, the term 'one of the same race' refers to someone committed to seeking the knowledge of God. Cf. *Letter* 53, F602.1, 'I call our seed not those who are near us by nature, but those who are near us by their state.'

25 *because you have given without stinting.* Cf. *Foundations* 8. 1260CD, 'Give thought to working with your hands, if possible both night and day, so that you will not be a burden to anyone, and further that you may be able to offer donations, as the holy apostle Paul advised (1 Thess 2: 9; 2 Thess 3: 8).'

26 *old age, famines, and sicknesses.* Cf. *Praktikos* 9.

27 *they (viz. the demons) know even the ideas of your heart.* Cf. *Thoughts* 37.

28 *[The demon of lust... war on the soul.]* The passage delineated by square brackets is unique to recension B, as found in Lavra Γ 93, but it is absent from Paris gr. 1188.

29 *malicious gossip (katalalia).* This always posed a serious threat to the harmony of monastic society. Basil also treated this danger in his monastic teaching. Cf. Basil, *Letter* 22. 3. 8, ed. M. Forlin Patrucco, *Basilio di Cesarea, Le lettere,* Vol. 1 (Turin: Società editrice internazionale, 1983), 'One ought to say nothing against an absent brother for the purpose of slandering him, even though what

is said may be true, for that is detraction.' See also *Great Asceticon (Regulae brevius tractatae)* 25, PG 31. 1100D, 'He who makes a statement against someone in order to slander or disparage him is a detractor, even though the statement be true.' For the frequent mention of the problem in the *Apophthegmata* see Graham Gould, *The Desert Fathers on Monastic Community* (Oxford: Oxford University Press, 1993), 121–3.

30 *mollifying even through a meal.* Cf. *Praktikos* 26, 'Gifts extinguish resentment: let the example of Jacob convince you of this, for he beguiled Esau with gifts when he was coming out to meet him with four hundred men (Gen. 32: 7). But since we are poor, let us make up for our poverty by the hospitality of the table.' See also *Monks* 15, 'If your brother annoys you, invite him to your place or do not hesitate to go to him, but eat your portion with him, for in so doing you will save your soul and there will be no obstacle for you in the time of prayer'; *Virgin* 41: 'Love turns away anger and irascibility; gifts overcome resentment.'

31 *when the mind is sprinkled with dust.* That is, the mind's vision is obscured when the dust of thoughts is thrown at it, and in consequence the eye of the soul is blinded. The alternative reading of PgA (*pausomenou*), 'held in check', seems less likely.

32 *two types of fornication.* Note here the reading of the Syriac version: 'Know and take note that fornication is found in two forms joined together, namely, in body and in spirit, as was said by the Apostle concerning the virgin, "that she may be holy in body and in spirit" (1 Cor. 7: 34).' See J. Muyldermans, *Evagriana Syriaca,* 52.

33 *your Canaanite tongue.* Cf. Isa. 19: 18, 'In that day there will be five cities in Egypt which speak the Canaanite tongue and swear by the name of the Lord.' In a critical note on this passage, Pierre Augustin takes the expression 'Canaanite tongue' in Evagrius' text as a reference to this verse of Isaiah: 'Note critique sur deux traités d'Évagre', *Revue des Études Augustiniennes,* 39 (1993), 207–12. From an examination of the patristic commentaries on this scripture verse, Augustin concludes that the term 'Canaanite tongue' evokes for Evagrius the incomprehensible language of his correspondent (a dialect of Aramaic?) or it may refer to the Syrian origin of Eulogios. However, Origen in his *Homilies on Joshua* interprets the Canaanites and other peoples of Palestine to be the 'diabolic races of hostile powers against which we are engaged in battle with much effort during this life' (e.g. *Homily* 1. 6, SC 71. 108). Uncharitable speech of any kind is thus characterized here as 'Canaanite' or diabolic in inspiration. I believe this interpretation to be more plausible and I consider the reference to the Isaian verse to be unlikely.

34 *[Rather, arm yourself . . . inventive deceit.]* An addition (?) from Paris gr. 1188.

35 *for the sake of your office.* An 'office' (*diakonia*) is a duty assigned to a monk.

36 *the deceiver in vainglory.* Cf. *Praktikos* 13.

37 *The passions of the body . . . the passions of the soul . . . .* Cf. *Praktikos* 35, 'The passions of the soul have their origin in human beings; those of the body have their origin in the body. Abstinence cuts away the passions of the body; spiritual love cuts away those of the soul.'

38 *the emigration of the practical life and the homecoming of the gnostic life.* Note the contrast *ekdēmia / endēmia*, 'emigration' / 'homecoming' and its different usage in *Eulogios* 2. 2. 1096C4; cf. *Prayer* 46.

39 *anoints the simple with the skill of the thoughts.* That is, the gnostic teacher who instructs the novice ascetic aspirants in the skill of discerning and countering the thoughts.

40 *one of an alien race.* Since for Evagrius, the term 'one of the same race' (see above, *Eulogios* 11. 10. 1105C) refers to someone committed to seeking the knowledge of God (i.e. a true monk), 'one of an alien race' would be someone outside of that community.

41 *because you did not have the impulse of your charity under control.* Pg has the reading 'because you did not have a tongue compelled by the constraint of charity', but this is not supported by the manuscripts CEMa.

42 *the opportunity of meeting angels.* Note the parallel to this use of the examples of Abraham and Lot in *HM* 8. 55–56; also quoted in *Apophthegmata* A151 (Apollo 3), 'And he frequently spoke about the reception of the brothers: "You must welcome the brothers respectfully when they come for a visit, for it is not them but God that you welcome." "Have you seen your brother?", it is said; "you have seen the Lord your God." "This," he said, "we have received from Abraham" (Gen. 18: 1–5). And that one must press the brothers to refresh themselves, we have learned from Lot who pressed the angels in this way (Gen. 19: 2–3).'

43 *one of those who partake more gnostically in the practical life.* The same expression appears in *Praktikos* 50. 7–8.

44 *One of the most experienced brothers offered a word about humility . . . .* The same story appears almost verbatim in *Apophthegmata* N 298 (165), 'A man possessed by the devil, who was foaming terribly at the mouth, struck a hermit monk on the cheek. The elder in exchange offered the other cheek as well. The demon, unable to bear the burning of humility, immediately leapt away.'

45 *the holy bishop Epiphanius.* Presumably, Epiphanius, Bishop of Salamis in Cyprus 365–403. This story does not appear to be known from any other source.

46 *the demon of Python.* Cf. Acts 16: 16, where Paul on his way to prayer was met by a slave girl who had a spirit of divination (*pneuma puthōna*). The Python was the serpent or dragon that guarded the Delphic oracle (Strabo 9.3.12), but later the term was used to refer to a sort of divinational ventriloquism whereby the spirit or demon spoke from the possessed person's belly (cf. Plutarch, *On the Delphic Oracle* 9.414E).

47 *of his father.* This phrase is not found in the Lavra manuscript (E), probably through an error, but is present in ACMa.

48 *rendering the submissive person self-willed.* Evagrius is having the demons suggest to the monk that freedom is just as good as wretched servitude, and a lot more pleasant, with the resulting implication that he should abandon submission to spiritual authority.

49 *in order to inspire presumption.* Evagrius seems here to be playing on the double meaning of the Greek word *aponoia,* which can refer either to an overweening arrogance or to mental imbalance and madness.

50 *in the time of godly disquiet.* i.e. a disquiet that is entrusted to God, according to Ps. 54: 23. The demons will try to dispel this 'godly disquiet' with their own.

51 *a house to dwell in.* Cf. Evagrius, S5-Ps. 67: 7 (*AS* 3. 82–3), '*God is in his holy place. God grants the single-minded a house to dwell in.* The place of God is a pure soul, wherefore he adds, 'God grants the single-minded a house to dwell in': namely, those who dedicate to him alone their own life, having removed from it all duplicity and worldly desire. Thus he promises to grant these a dwelling in his house, that is, in the heavenly city.'

52 *through his insensibility.* On the demon of insensibility see *Thoughts* 11.

53 *My words . . . Holy Trinity.* These two sentences are virtually identical with the closing sentence of *Virgin* 56.

VICES

1 *a dissolute fawn.* In Evagrian exegesis the fawn is a symbol of impassibility and the completion of the life of the virtues. A dissolute fawn would therefore represent a disordered life of the virtues. See S65-Prov. 5: 19.

2 *a worm of the flesh.* Cf. *Eight Thoughts* 5. 3, 'Sadness is a worm in the heart'; S313-Prov. 25: 20.

3 *one who leads our steps astray.* Or possibly, 'a tourguide of churches'.

4 *the three-strand chain of vices.* Cf. John Climacus, *Ladder* 25, PG 88. 989D, 'This all-holy three-strand chain'—mourning, penitence, and humility.

5 *[friend of curiosity . . . purifies the heart.]* The section enclosed by square brackets is the portion of the text missing from the edition in Migne and supplied by J. Muyldermans, 'Evagriana de la Vaticane', *Le Muséon,* 54 (1941), 5. It is also present in the manuscript E.

EIGHT THOUGHTS

1 *he who controls the stomach.* Cf. *Praktikos* 7 and 16.

2 *Amalek.* After the exodus from Egypt Amalek was the first of the nations to attack Israel. According to Origen's allegorical reading, Amalek was called 'first of the nations' because he was a hostile power, the first to turn people to paganism. See Origen, *Homily on Numbers* 19.2, ed. W. A. Baehrens, *GCS* 30: Origenes 7, 181. The Greek term *ta ethnē*, 'nations, peoples', came to have the connotation 'foreigners', 'gentiles', and 'pagans'.

3 *the matter used by gluttony.* The passions use sensible objects or the memories of such as the 'matter' or material to tempt human beings. The different passions have a greater or lesser range of material to draw upon for this purpose. See the comments of Evagrius on the subject in *Reflections* 14 and *Thoughts* 36.

4 *he who seized the jawbone.* When Samson took revenge on the Philistines, they in turn attacked Judah. The men of Judah then captured Samson, bound his hands with ropes and handed him over to the Philistines. The Spirit of the Lord came upon Samson and the bonds caught fire and dropped from his hands. Samson then took the jawbone of an ass and slew a thousand Philistines. Throwing the jawbone away, he called that place 'Destruction of the Jawbone'. Since Samson was thirsty, God opened the wound of the jawbone (according to the LXX text) and water came forth from it.

5 *a spring of water.* Evagrius usually understands springs of water as the virtues from which flow gnosis. Cf. S51-Prov. 4: 21, '*So that your springs may not abandon you, guard them in your heart.* He calls the virtues 'springs', from which is begotten the 'living water' (John 4: 11), which is the knowledge of Christ.'; cf. also S9-Ps. 17: 16 (12. 1232A), 'He calls springs the virtues from which there issues knowledge.'

6 *practical contemplation.* The term may refer to the contemplation of the *logoi* or ultimate principles of the practical life, what Evagrius elsewhere calls the 'reasons of the warfare' (*Praktikos* 83); it could also refer to the 'contemplation' or consideration of the scriptures for their insights into the practical life.

7 *a tent peg.* Jael killed Sisera by approaching quietly while he slept and driving a tent peg into his head.

8 *the unsleeping worm.* Cf. *Foundations* 9. 1261B15 ('undying worm'). The 'unsleeping worm' is mentioned in the *Apocalypse of Ezra* 4.21; also by Gregory Nazianzen, *On Holy Baptism* 40. 36, PG 36. 412A12–13. Cf. also the 'undying worm' of Mark 9: 48 (Isa. 66: 24).

9 *the driest regimen.* Cf. *Praktikos* 17 and *Monks* 102.

10 *like a young eagle.* Cf. *Ad Prov.* 30: 17, n. 18 in SC 340. 489, 'The young of eagles are the holy powers entrusted with casting down the impure beings.' The same text is also found in *Chapters 33.* 33, PG 40. 1268B.

11 *a soiled mirror.* Cf. *Exhortation* 2. 5, 'Just as it is not possible to see one's own image in water that has been disturbed, so too the mind will not be able to see the Lord as in a mirror without having set right its interior state and without having purified the soul of passionate attachments to material things.'

12 *the commemorations of the martyrs.* Funeral banquets were held to commemorate the death of the martyrs. Such celebrations were often occasions for excesses in eating and drinking.

13 *a state of peace.* This is a synonym for *apatheia*, 'impassibility': see *Reflections* 3.

14 *make camp in the desert.* In S6-Ps. 28: 8 (12. 1292A) Evagrius interprets the desert as a symbol for 'the rational soul deprived of God'. Cf. also *KG* 6. 49, '*Egypt* signifies evil; the *desert* the practical life; the land of *Judah*, the contemplation of the bodies; *Jerusalem*, that of the incorporeals; and *Zion* is the symbol of the Trinity.'

15 *a full stomach.* Or 'a bursting stomach' according to some manuscripts.

16 *If you strike an Egyptian, hide him in the sand.* For Evagrius Egypt is the symbol of all evil (*KG* 5. 88, 6. 49) and the Egyptians a symbol for the disposition of evil (S19-Ps. 67: 32, 12. 1509C). So the Egyptian buried in the sand is the evil passion buried in sterile soil where it will wither and die.

17 *that is debilitated and in mourning.* Or 'that laments its debility' according to some manuscripts.

18 *encounters with women.* Cf. *Praktikos* 8 and 17.

19 *the evil poison of beasts.* Bunge in his translation unnecessarily separates this last sentence from the foregoing, giving it a separate numbering. For wild beasts as a symbol for the demons see S9-Ps. 73: 19 (12. 1532C), '*Do not give over to wild beasts the soul that makes confession for you.* If the demons are called wild beasts and irascibility dominates in wild beasts, then irascibility dominates in the demons.'

20 *when matter is not present.* Cf. *Thoughts* 20.

21 *If the passion stays calm* . . . Elsewhere Evagrius discusses in greater detail the reasons why a temptation may have little strength and can be easily overcome. Cf. *Thoughts* 20 and 34.

22 *a dog . . . shows its bad character.* For the association of the dog with the passions see *Thoughts* 5. 14, 27; S324-Prov. 26: 11.

23 *arises without passion.* Some manuscripts add at this point 'and the fantasy of her does not stimulate the passion'.

24 *compare her members to the faculties of your soul . . . habit of virtue.* This is the reading of the B text. Cf. *Praktikos* 67. The practice described here is that of using good thoughts to drive out bad thoughts, relying on the principle that the mind cannot hold two mental representations simultaneously. It is described in detail in *Thoughts* 24. This, however, is a practice best reserved for the gnostic,

rather than one still struggling in the practical life, hence the caution added by Evagrius here. In S4-Ps. 140: 7 (*AS* 3.349) the powers or faculties of the soul are referred to as the 'bones of the soul'. These powers are enumerated in S1-Ps. 102: 1 (12. 1560A), '*Bless the Lord, my soul, and all that is within me his holy name.* The interior realities of the inner self are the powers of intellection, discursive thought, observation, interpretation, imagination, and memory.'

25 *Avarice is the root of all evils* . . . Cf. *Praktikos* 9 and 18.

26 *lashed with sadness.* Cf. *Praktikos* 10.

27 *Eight Thoughts* 4. 14. This is the first of the three sentences on the Coptic ostrakon published by H.-M. Schenke, 'Das Berliner Evagrius-Ostrakon (P. Berol. 14 700)', *Zeitschrift für ägyptische Sprache und Altertumskunde,* 116 (1989), 90–107.

28 *makes the soul wild.* Cf. S9-Ps. 73: 19 (12. 1532C), cited above, n. 19.

29 *anger.* Cf. *Praktikos* 11 and 20–26.

30 *a solitary wild boar.* The 'wild boar' is a reference to Satan. Cf. S7-Ps. 79: 14 (*AS* 3. 134); *Reflections* S3, 'The demon of fornication is a filthy pig, that of anger a wild boar; he who breaks their teeth by the power of God, shatters their power.'

31 *the movement of irascibility thickens the intellect.* For the 'thickening' of the mind through the passions and the obstacle this poses for prayer see *Prayer* 50 and commentary note.

32 *darkens the mind.* Cf. S7-Ps. 30: 10 (12. 1301A) '*My eye was troubled with anger.* Nothing so darkens the intellect as troubling irascibility'; also *Prayer* 128.

33 *a state of peace.* viz. impassibility.

34 *provides no water.* According to some manuscripts 'pure water'.

35 *The gentleness of a man is remembered by God.* Cf. S1-Ps. 131: 1 (12. 1649C), '*Remember, Lord, David and all his gentleness.* The Lord remembers the one in whom he resides, and he remembers not the one in whom he does not reside. And if the Lord of gentleness is to remember, there is required great freedom from anger in order that one may receive the Lord. For gentleness is the freedom from disturbance in the irascible part, which arises with the suppression of corruptible pleasures.'

36 *a shelter for the Holy Trinity.* Cf. *Reflections* 34, 'The mind is the temple of the Holy Trinity.' *Eight Thoughts* 4. 11–12 are given as the second text on the Coptic ostrakon: see Schenke, 'Das Berliner Evagrius-Ostrakon'.

37 *Foxes find shelter in the resentful soul.* 'Foxes', like 'beasts', is a symbolic designation for the demons. Cf. *Letters* 3. 3, F566. 37 and 48, F596. 35.

38 *disturbing nightmares* . . . *attacks of wild beasts.* Cf. *Praktikos* 54.

39 *discourses on spiritual matters* (γυμνάζει λόγους πνευματικοὺς). Note the similar expression in *Praktikos* 94. 4–5 (λόγους . . . γυμνάζοντος).

40 *Eight Thoughts* 5. 1. The text of recension A begins this new section with the sentence, 'A monk afflicted with sadness knows no spiritual pleasure,' which is

repeated verbatim only a few lines later. Recension B omits the first instance, thus beginning the section with a definition, as we find at the beginning of all but the first two sections.

41 *the frustration of revenge produces sadness.* Cf. *Praktikos* 10 and 19; *Eulogios* 7. 6–7.

42 *a worm in the heart.* Cf. *Vices* 4, 'a worm in the flesh'; S313-Prov. 25: 20.

43 *of the flesh.* This phrase is absent in the manuscripts ESt.

44 *a smelting-furnace purifies base silver.* The same imagery of purification is also found in *Eulogios* 29. 31. 1133D8 (gold in a smelting furnace). Cf. *Monks* 60.

45 *godly sadness . . . worldly sadness.* Evagrius discusses the two types of sadness in *Eulogios* 7. 6–7.

46 *Eight Thoughts* 5.24. This sentence is added by the manuscript A.

47 *the monk caught in acedia.* CESt add here the phrase 'will not be contented'.

48 *Eight Thoughts* 6. 13. This sentence is omitted in ESt.

49 *the doors.* Or 'the windows' in some manuscripts.

50 *calculates the number of gatherings.* Some manuscripts add the phrase 'finds fault with the writing and the ornamentation'.

51 *Eight Thoughts* 6.15. Evagrius examines the temptation of distraction in reading in *Thoughts* 33.

52 *with diligence.* Most long recension manuscripts omit this phrase.

53 *and the fear of God.* Most long recension manuscripts omit this phrase.

54 *vainglory.* Cf. *Praktikos* 13 and 30–2. The B text here transposes two sentences of the A text to a new position at 7. 17 and 19.

55 *The prudent person . . .* The manuscript St expands this aphorism: 'The prudent person hides a treasure, guarding it carefully and spending it on those in want according as one has need; the sensible monk hides the labours of virtue, fleeing popularity, but helping those who approach him with his counsel.'

56 *Eight Thoughts* 7. 11. This sentence is unique to the B text. On the symbolism see S72-Prov. 6: 8, 'Go to the bee then . . . Kings and ordinary people bring their labours for their health. By the 'ant' Solomon is seemingly describing for us the practical path, and by the bee he indicates the contemplation of creatures and of the Creator himself . . . It also appears to me that the honeycomb corresponds to the realities themselves, whereas the honey that it contains is the symbol of their contemplation'; S270-Prov. 24: 13, '*Eat honey, my son, for the honeycomb is good, that your throat may enjoy its sweetness.* He who draws profit from the divine scriptures eats honey; he who extracts their doctrines of realities themselves—both the holy Prophets and Apostles took from these—eats the honeycomb. Eating honey is accessible to all who wish, but eating the honeycomb belongs only to the pure.'

57 *the city of peace.* This mention of a city and the one in the next aphorism should

probably be read as a reference to Jerusalem, which Evagrius takes as a symbol for natural contemplation (*KG* 5. 6, 5. 88, 6. 49).

58 *Eight Thoughts* 7. 14–15 are unique to the B text.

59 *Eight Thoughts* 7. 17 and 19 are transposed here in the B text.

60 *Eight Thoughts* 7. 18 is unique to the B text.

61 *Eight Thoughts* 8. 4 is unique to the B text.

62 *You are a human being; remain within the bounds of your nature.* This sentence is unique to the B text.

63 *do not deny the relationship because of vain boasting.* Note the similarities with *Praktikos* 14.

64 *Eight Thoughts* 8. 20–32. The A text concludes with sentences 19, 32, and 20 in that order.

65 *Eight Thoughts* 8. 21–31 are inserted here by the B text in the manuscripts ACc. The manuscript St inserts the same sentences (with some further additions) after 32. Unfortunately, the manuscript E is missing a folio at this point. For the text see J. Muyldermans, 'Une nouvelle recension du *De octo spiritibus malitiae* de S. Nil', *Le Muséon*, 52 (1939), 251–2.

66 *Eight Thoughts* 8. 22 is the third sentence on the Coptic ostrakon: see Schenke 'Das Berliner Evagrius-Ostrakon', 94. The Coptic text thus witnesses to the long recension.

67 *A staff is a symbol of instruction.* Cf. *Reflections* 11, 'Instruction is the rejection of impiety and worldly desires.' In other words 'instruction' is equivalent to the practical life, as the following aphorisms indicate. See also S4-Ps. 2: 12 (*AS* 2. 449), '*Lay hold of instruction, lest the Lord become angry.* Instruction is a moderation of the passions, which naturally derives from the practical life. The practical life is a spiritual teaching which purifies the passionate part of the soul'; S3-Ps. 22: 4 (12. 1261C), 'As a staff gives instruction, so does the practical life teach restraint over the passions.' On the relationship of 'instruction' and 'wisdom' in Evagrius see S3-Prov. 1: 2 (with Géhin's commentary).

68 *Eight Thoughts* 8. 24–25. Bunge's translation fails to note the homoioteleuton omission in the manuscript A (Coislin 109), which resulted in the conflation of the two sentences 24–25. The missing text is found in Muyldermans' apparatus in 'Une nouvelle recension', 252.

69 *the serpent that crawls on the ground.* Cf. Plato, *Timaeus* 92A.

70 *the reason of chastity.* The *logos* of chastity may refer either to a 'word' of counsel about chastity or the 'reason', the ultimate principle, of chastity that dissolves passion. One manuscript (St) extends the scriptural allusion: 'When the horse was bitten by a serpent, the horseman fell backwards (Gen. 49: 17); the mind of one who loves pleasure inclined to evil when passion caught hold. The rider who fell backwards when the horse broke off waits for salvation from the Lord

(Gen. 49: 18); when the mind has fallen away it calls upon the help of God. An extension of hands put Amalek to flight (Exod. 17: 11); actions directed upwards in truth mortify the passions.'

71 *the parapet of a housetop.* Deut. 22: 8, 'If you build a new house, you shall make a parapet on the housetop, and you will not be responsible for a death in your house if someone falls from it.'

PRAKTIKOS

1 *the Holy Mountain.* The location in question is likely to be Jerusalem (cf. Isa. 27: 13), where Anatolios may perhaps have lived in the monastery founded on the Mount of Olives by Melania and Rufinus. For the benefit of his addressee, Evagrius used Sketis as a general term for the desert settlements of Nitria, Sketis, and Kellia; Evagrius actually lived in the latter.

2 *koukoullion.* Evagrius appears to be the first to develop the symbolism of the monastic habit. Cassian relied on Evagrius in his own treatment of the symbolism in the *Institutes* 1. 1–11. The *koukoullion* was a sort of hood or cowl extending to the shoulders and covering the head and neck. Palladius (*HL* 32. 3, 90. 1–3), Sozomen (*HE* 3. 14) and Dorotheos of Gaza (*Instruction* 1. 18) note that it was worn by small children.

3 *having the hands bare.* The hands and forearms were left bare because the monks wore a garment called the *kolobion* which had no sleeves and was distinct from the long-sleeved tunic favoured during the fourth century. Evagrius also understands the hands as a symbol of the practical life. See S26-Eccles. 4: 5, *'The fool covers his hands and consumes his flesh.* If the hands are a symbol of practical activity, anyone who does not do the work of justice covers his hands'; S203-Prov. 19: 24, *'He who conceals his hands in his breast unjustly will certainly not bring them to his mouth.* He who does not live uprightly hides his hands in his soul unjustly, because he is unwilling to cultivate his own land and take his fill of bread (cf. Prov. 12: 11, 28: 19). For the virtues of the practical life correspond to the hands that present to our mouth the bread that came down from heaven and gave life to the world (cf. John 6: 33).' The good chosen for itself is an Aristotelian principle (cf. *Rhetoric* 1. 7, 1363b13–14, 'we call good that which is desirable for its own sake and not for anything else, and that which all things aim at and which they would choose if they possessed reason and practical wisdom . . .'; see also *Nicomachean Ethics* 1. 5, 1097a33–4).

4 *analabos.* This was a band of woollen cloth worn round the neck and crossing at the chest. Its purpose was to keep the tunic out of the way and leave the arms to move freely.

5 *the belt . . . tightened around their kidneys.* Evagrius understood the kidneys to be the seat of the passions. See S14-Ps. 72: 21 (12. 1528BC), *'For my heart was enkindled*

and my kidneys were changed. By the heart he refers to the rational faculty and by the kidneys he refers to the passionate part, from which is begotten the concupiscible and the irascible'; S1-Ps. 25: 2 (12. 1273A), *'Test my kidneys and my heart in the fire.* The kidneys are a symbol of the passionate part of the soul, that is, of the irascible and the concupiscible, as the heart is of the rational.' 'Having the loins girded' (cf. Exod. 12: 11) is more particularly a symbol for the life of chastity. See Origen, *Homily on Luke*, fr. 80 (SC 87. 536–7), 'Those who live in chastity have their loins girded.'

6 *melote.* This was a sheep or goatskin mantel.

7 *the staff is 'a tree of life'.* Evagrius identifies the 'tree of life' (Gen 2: 9) with the wisdom of God in S32-Prov. 3: 18 and with Christ in *KG* 5. 69. Elsewhere he associates the term 'staff' with the practical life (S3-Ps. 22: 4, 12. 1261C); see also *Eight Thoughts* 8. 23–5.

8 *faith, fear of God, abstinence, perseverance, hope.* This fundamental schema of the succession of the virtues with some variants appears frequently in Evagrius' writings. See especially *Praktikos* 81, *Monks* 3–5 and 67–9. A. Guillaumont has shown that Evagrius is indebted to Clement of Alexandria for this schema (*Stromateis* 2. 31. 1, ed. Staehlin, 129). See SC 170, 52–5.

9 *the practical and the gnostic life.* These are the two great divisions of spiritual progress in Evagrian teaching. Evagrius refers in this paragraph to three of his treatises: namely, *Praktikos* (100), *Gnostikos* (50), and the *Kephalaia Gnostika* (600). Only the first work survives complete in Greek.

10 *those who have embarked upon the same path.* Throughout the *Gnostikos* (e.g. 12–15, 23–4, 35–6), Evagrius cautions against revealing certain teachings to those who are not yet ready for them; each stage of the spiritual life has a set of teachings appropriate to it. The advanced teachings must therefore be concealed from those in the earlier stages of progress.

11 *Copyist's note.* Some manuscripts introduce at this point this note to the copyist, which is almost certainly by Evagrius himself.

12 *the practical, the natural, and the theological.* This threefold division of the spiritual life is found throughout the works of Evagrius. See for example *Letter on Faith* 8. 4. 19–22, 'He (Christ) called flesh and blood his entire mystic sojourn and revealed the teaching that consists of practical, natural, and theological elements, through which the soul is nourished and prepared even now for the contemplation of realities'; and *Monks* 118–20.

13 *the kingdom of heaven . . . the kingdom of God.* In 2–3, Evagrius makes a distinction between the kingdom of heaven (or of Christ) and the kingdom of God, basing the distinction upon the type of contemplation engaged in by the believer. The kingdom of heaven corresponds to natural knowledge or the knowledge of beings; the kingdom of God is then theology or the knowledge of God. See *Letter on Faith* 8. 7. 22–4, 'For they say that the kingdom of Christ is the entirety of material knowledge, but the kingdom of our God and Father is immaterial

knowledge, that is, as one might say, the contemplation of the naked Godhead itself.'

14 *surpassing its incorruptibility.* In *KG* 3.33 Evagrius makes reference to 1 Cor. 15: 54 ('For this corruptible nature must put on the incorruptible, and this mortal nature must put on immortality.'), and then relates the term 'incorruptible' to natural contemplation and the term 'immortal' to knowledge of the Trinity. The latter 'surpasses' the former as a higher knowledge. The knowledge of the Trinity is 'coextensive with the substance of the mind' because it fulfils and completes the mind's ultimate destiny, for the 'natural unity' of the mind (also known as the 'image of God') is that which is receptive of the divine Unity (cf. *KG* 3. 32).

15 *sensation gives birth to desire.* Sensation is at the root of desire and all the passions. Thus, to attain impassibility, which is the goal of the practical life, the ascetic must remove himself as far as possible from sensations by the practice of anachoresis, a physical separation from worldly society.

16 *The demons fight directly (literally, 'naked') against anchorites.* i.e. in the sense that they act directly on the individual's thoughts, moving them towards passion. In the communal setting of the monasteries, the demons can rely on ordinary social frictions to provide sources of temptation. For Evagrius the great characteristic of the demonic nature was the overweening anger expressed in their wickedness (Cf. *KG* 1. 68, 3. 34, 5. 11.).

17 *the thought of gluttony.* Gluttony thus refers here to the temptation to reduce the rigour of one's ascetic practices for fear of injury to health. Various stomach and intestinal tract ailments seem to have been fairly common in the desert. Evagrius himself suffered in this way. See Palladius, *HL* 38. 13 (122. 10–15).

18 *accepting goods from others to meet one's needs.* Cf. *Foundations* 4, 'If you need food or clothing, do not be ashamed of accepting what others bring you, for this is a form of pride.'

19 *a boiling over of the irascible part.* For similar terms applied to a discussion of definitions of anger see Aristotle, *De anima* 403a29–b1. Note also the definition in Chrysippus: 'Anger then is a desire for vengeance on one who is thought to have committed a wrong' (*Stoicorum veterum fragmenta,* ed. H. von Arnim (Stuttgart: Teubner, 1964), 3. 397). In the *Praktikos, Antirrhetikos,* and *Vices* Evagrius places sadness before anger on the assumption that the latter often arises from some prior personal hurt or injury (*lupē*). Cf. *Praktikos* 11. 4 and 23. 2; he cites scriptural justification (Prov. 15: 1) in *Reflections* 43.

20 *Praktikos* 12. Cassian's treatment of acedia in *Institute* 10 is closely dependent on this chapter.

21 *look constantly towards the windows . . . jump out of the cell . . . lest one of the brothers.* Note the similarity of this description with the one in *Eight Thoughts* 6. 14.

22 *acedia.* Note the discussion of acedia in S1-Ps. 139: 3 (12. 1664B), '*Who considered*

wickedness in their heart; all day long they waged battles. Through the thoughts the demons range themselves for battle, sometimes moving desires, sometimes anger, and at other times in the same moment irascibility and desire, through which arises the thought that is called complex. But this happens only during a time of acedia, whereas the other thoughts follow one another in succession at intervals. No consideration follows the thought of acedia on that day, first of all, because it persists for a time, and then it contains within itself almost all the thoughts'; see also S13-Ps. 118: 28 (12. 1593AB), *'My soul was half asleep from acedia; strengthen me in your words.* Acedia is a prolonged movement of irascibility and desire at the same time: the former displays anger over what is present and the latter shows longing for what is not. It is a drowsiness of the rational soul, neglect of the virtues and of the knowledge of God; it is a sleep of the rational soul and a wilful separation from true life. Wherefore the wise Solomon exhorts one "not to give sleep to the eyes nor drowsiness to the eyelids" (Prov. 6: 4).'

23 *The thought of vainglory . . . predicts to him that he will eventually attain the priesthood.* For the description of another development of this same temptation see *Thoughts* 21.

24 *derangement of mind, madness, and the vision of a multitude of demons in the air.* Cf. *Eight Thoughts* 8. 10.

25 *When the mind wanders, reading, vigils, and prayer bring it to a standstill.* This sentence is cited in a slightly different form in *Exhortation* 1. 3, 'When the mind wanders, reading the words of God along with vigil accompanied by prayer restrains it.'

26 *psalmody, patience, and mercy calm it.* Evagrius frequently recommends psalmody for its calming effect on anger: cf. *Prayer* 83, *Monks* 98, *Praktikos* 71, *Exhortation* 1. 4. This effect was generally recognized by Christian writers of the time. See for example Basil, *Homilies on the Psalms* 1. 2, PG 29. 212C, 'Psalmody is a calming of souls, an arbiter of peace, which restrains the tumult and agitation of thoughts; it calms the part prone to irascibility and tempers the part given to indiscipline.' For further references see A. Guillaumont, SC 171, 537–8. For acts of mercy or charity as a means of dissolving anger, Evagrius recommends such simple things as a small gift or the offering of a meal. See *Eulogios* 17. 18. 1116C, *Praktikos* 26, *Virgin* 41.

27 *at the appropriate times and in due measure.* Cassian provides an extensive discussion of discernment of due measure and appropriate times in *Conference* 2.

28 *the three hundred Israelites in Gideon's company who subdued Midian (Judg. 7: 5–7).* In choosing the Israelites to do battle with the Midianites, Gideon was instructed by the Lord to lead the people to the water and pick the ones who drank from their hands rather than those that knelt to drink directly from the water. Restriction of water as a remedy for fornication was a frequent recommendation of Evagrius. See for example *Monks* 102.

29 *Praktikos* 20–6. The prominence given here to the problem of anger is an indication of its importance in the teaching of Evagrius.

30 *frightful apparitions usually arise from the disturbance of the irascible part.* A similar observation was made by Plato, *Republic* 9. 572A3–B1, 'When he has in like manner calmed the irascible part, and falls asleep without having succumbed to anger against someone, . . . then the visions of his dreams are least likely to be lawless.'

31 *the demons suggest to us that anachoresis is a fine thing.* Cf. *Eulogios* 5. 5. 1100D, 'Whenever a violent dispute embitters the brothers in a community, then the thoughts suggest considering the solitary blessed in order to exhaust their patience and separate them from charity.'

32 *The first brings darkness to the soul.* Cf. S7-Ps. 30: 10 (12. 1301A), '*My eye was disturbed with anger.* Nothing so darkens the intellect as a disturbance in the irascible part.'

33 *when you entertain such images during the time of prayer.* Cf. *Virgin* 6, 'Avoid encounters with men, lest images arise in your soul; they will be an obstacle for you in the time of prayer.'

34 *compel the irascible part, contrary to its nature, to fight with people.* Cf. *Eulogios* 11. 10. 1105D, 'Do not turn the usage of irascibility instead to one that is contrary to nature, so as to become irascible with your brother by imitating the serpent (cf. Ps. 57: 5) on the one hand and on the other hand to form a friendship with the serpent by consenting to thoughts.'

35 *let us make up for our poverty by the hospitality of the table.* Evagrius probably has in mind Prov. 21: 14, 'A gift in secret averts anger.' Cf. *Monks* 15, 'If your brother annoys you, invite him to your house or do not hesitate to go to him, but eat your morsel with him, for in so doing you will deliver your soul and there will be no obstacle for you in the time of prayer'; also *Virgin* 41 'Charity drives away anger and wrath; gifts overcome resentment.'

36 *with tears let us divide the soul.* The remedy of tears applied to the problem of acedia is mentioned frequently by Evagrius: see *Virgin* 39, *Monks* 56. The recommended use of the Psalm verse here reflects the method for combating the passions advocated by Evagrius in the *Antirrhetikos*.

37 *You must not abandon the cell . . . you must remain seated inside.* Remaining seated in the cell indicates a single-hearted commitment to the practice of stillness (*hesychia*). See *Monks* 55.

38 *Our saintly teacher.* In all probability the teacher in question is Makarios the Egyptian (mentioned explicitly in ch. 93). The counsel of the daily remembrance of death can be found in the *Letter of Makarios to his Sons* 17, ed. Werner Strothmann, *Die syrische Überlieferung der Schriften des Makarios*, 2 vols., Göttinger Orientforshungen, series 1, Syriaca vol. 21 (Wiesbaden: Harrasowitz, 1981), 2.xxii. John Cassian attributes the teaching of this chapter to Makarios in *Institute* 5. 41.

39 *the demon of vainglory is pursued by almost all the demons.* Since vainglory plays on the monk's self-esteem it is incompatible with the presence of the other thoughts or passions, with the exception of pride. See *Reflections* 57, 'Alone among the thoughts, the thoughts of vainglory and pride arise after the defeat of the remaining thoughts.'

40 *The person who has attained knowledge and enjoys the pleasant fruit that derives from it will no longer be persuaded by the demon of vainglory.* The danger posed by vainglory ceases with the attainment of spiritual knowledge or contemplation. Cf. S7-Ps. 24: 16 (12. 1272C), '*Look upon me and have mercy on me, for I am all alone and poor.* He who does and says everything for the sake of the knowledge of God has the eyes of his soul always upon the Lord'; also S5-Ps. 129: 8 (12.1648D–1649A), '*And he himself will redeem Israel from all its iniquities.* The mind is delivered from sins or iniquities of thought at the moment when it is deemed worthy of knowledge. For the practical life does not remove mental representations from the heart, but rather impassioned mental representations.'

41 *Such thoughts instil humility and deny admittance to the demon of pride.* For Evagrius pride is ultimately the refusal to recognize the help of God. See *Eight Thoughts* 8. 12. There is a very similar development in Cassian, *Institute* 12. 9–11, where he seems to be drawing on both the *Praktikos* and the *Eight Thoughts* of Evagrius.

42 *despises the operations wrought by them.* i.e. he disdains their attempts at activating impassioned memories.

43 *the immaterial warfare is more difficult than the material.* Passions originate either with direct contact with sensible objects or indirectly through the memories of them. Since the monks of the desert have removed themselves from objects, their warfare will be primarily immaterial, i.e. with the thoughts engendered by memories.

44 *the passions of the body . . . those of the soul.* The passions of the body are those which are born of the natural needs of the body and are characterized by Evagrius as the passions of gluttony and fornication, which find their remedy in abstinence. The passions of the soul arise in the midst of relationships between people (anger at an offence, for example) and find their remedy in the practice of charity. In this way, all the methods for combating the passions amount to the twofold practice of abstinence and charity. See *Eulogios* 21. 23. 1124B–C, 'The passions of the body take their origin from the natural appetites of the flesh, against which abstinence is effective; the passions of the soul have their conception from the appetites of the soul, against which charity is effective.'

45 *then the memories are only simple ones.* Simple memories are those which no longer have any attachments to the passions. Once delivered from the passions, the soul may then turn to contemplation of 'the reasons for the warfare' (*Praktikos* 83).

46 *whether it is the representation that sets the passions in motion, or the passions that set the*

representation in motion. A. Guillaumont has suggested that the first opinion probably belongs to the Stoics, while the second one can be found in Aristotle. See SC 171, 584–5, n. 37. Evagrius would probably hold that either position might be true, depending on the circumstances. He discusses the relation between sensible objects, the passions, and mental representations at greater length in *Thoughts.* See for example *Thoughts* 19; also S2-Ps. 145: 8 (12. 1676A ; *AS* 3. 357), '*The Lord looses those who are bound.* Neither do objects bind the mind nor do their mental representations, but rather the impassioned mental representations of objects. For the Lord created gold and he made woman, but none of the beings created by God are opposed to people's salvation, but rather fornication and greed bind the mind and force the mental representations of objects to delay in the heart. For objects hold the mind in check by means of impassioned mental representations, just as water holds the thirsty person by means of thirst, and bread the hungry person by means of hunger. Why then does the physician of souls not abolish created objects (for he is their Creator), or restrain the mind from apprehending them? It is because they came into being for the purpose of being apprehended by the mind. But by spiritual teaching and the commandments, he sets the mind free from its bonds by overthrowing the passions (which are distinct from the mental representations and the objects, as they have their origin in us). And this would be the meaning of the scripture: "The Lord looses those who are bound".'

47 *love . . . is the bridle of anger. Moses . . . gave it the symbolic name of serpent-fighter.* Cf. *KG* 3. 35, 'Spiritual knowledge purifies the mind, love heals the irascible part and abstinence halts the flowing of desire.' Looking to Ps. 57: 5 ('Their anger bears the likeness of a serpent.'), Evagrius identified the serpent with anger, and so the serpent-fighter of Leviticus with love.

48 *the bad smell that prevails among the demons.* Cf. *KG* 5. 78, 'The bodies of demons neither grow nor diminish, and a strong stench accompanies them, whereby they also set in motion our passions. They are easily recognized by those who have received from the Saviour the power of perceiving this odour.'

49 *the habitual rule.* The rule mentioned in this chapter refers to the daily routine determined by the desert tradition but occasionally modified by an elder to meet the specific needs of his disciple. It was the common practise to relax the regimen of abstinence either on the occasion of sickness or to practise the charity of hospitality.

50 *with our mind grown thick.* Evagrius applies the metaphor of 'thickening' to the intellect that relaxes its vigilance, falling away from knowledge into forgetfulness.

51 *set their proper matter in motion.* The 'matter' in question comprises the sensible objects, social circumstances, or appetitive and emotional weaknesses of the individual.

52 *On Thoughts* is devoted to a detailed exploration of the subject outlined in this chapter.

53 *the demon that carries the mind off to blaspheme God.* Such blasphemous thoughts might include a denial of Christ or the relegation of the Trinity to the created order (*Monks* 134); or questioning the judgement and providence of God or the possibility of attaining virtue (S190-Prov. 19: 5); considering the body to be an evil creation (*KG* 4. 60); denying free will and thus also the justice of God (*Antirrhetikos* 8. 16, F538); or considering the demons to be gods (*Antirrhetikos* 8. 47, F542). For other examples see A. Guillaumont, SC 171, 604–5.

54 *Through these (words or bodily gestures) the enemies perceive whether we hold and nourish their thoughts.* Evagrius treats this subject at greater length in *Thoughts* 37. In one of his letters Evagrius offers a detailed list of examples: *Letter* 16, G2. 66–7, 'Each of the demons guards his own boundaries and observes the monk who passes by to see whether he inclines to the right or to the left or walks the Royal Road (Num. 20: 17; 21: 22). For example, the demon of gluttony wants to see if the monk in his fast appears radiant or has affected a sullen attitude, accusing his deprivation, or by a word has hinted at some such thing in an encounter so that he might hear those present say: "He is very pale and thin!" In the same way the demon of fornication guards its boundaries to see whether the monk who encounters a woman did so out of necessity or fabricated a reasonable excuse, or if he pronounced a word that provoked laughter or that invited an apparent reverence; and he observes his eye to see if it is not curious and his walk to see if it is not relaxed and his mantle to see if it is his everyday one. In the same way, the demon of avarice observes how we are when rich people meet with us and if we say or do something to receive (gifts), for example, if we lament over our poverty and if we welcome the rich gladly, but turn away the poor. The demon of vainglory imitates these demons and concerns itself with all our affairs to see whether we have said or done something that contributes to the glory of praises, or if when recalled from some difficult work we groaned that we might be praised for our labours; or further, if for the sake of esteem we have brought forward something that happened to us in the cell either from the part of the holy angels or from the demons. But why is it necessary to go on at length about all their maliciousness? In this regard the Lord says, "Be prudent as serpents and innocent as doves" (Matt. 10: 16).'

55 *it (the mind) is naturally constituted for prayer, even without this body.* Cf. S5-Ps. 141: 8 (12. 1668B) '*Lead my soul out of prison.* It is not for everyone to say, "Cast my soul out of prison", but it belongs to those who are able because of their purity to attain the contemplation of beings even without this body.' The same text is found in *KG* 4. 70.

56 *the reasons for these things.* After the monk has attained a basic empirical knowledge of the demonic thoughts and acquired at least some level of impassibility, he is then able to contemplate the *logoi*, the 'reasons' or 'ultimate principles' of the warfare. The gnostic fights no longer in the dark but with knowledge (cf. *Praktikos* 83). Cf. S1-Ps. 143: 1 (ed. M.-J. Rondeau, *Les commentaires patristiques du Psautier (IIIe–Ve siècles),* i, Orientalia Christiana Analecta, 219 (Rome:

Pontificium Institutum Studiorum Orientalium, 1982), 289), '*Blessed be the Lord my God, who instructs my hands for battle and my fingers for war.* The one instructed by the Lord for the warfare with the opposing power knows the reasons of the virtues and the vices, the differences among the thoughts, the indicators of impassibility and its boundaries; further, he knows also the reasons of nocturnal phantasms and dreams—some of which come from the rational part of the soul when the memory is set in motion, and some come from the irascible part, while others come from the concupiscible part—but we have dealt with these matters more precisely in the *Monachos* (for such a discernment of the reasons belongs to the ethical treatise), but now we are moved by our intention to present the warfare taught by the Lord.'

57 *those who partake more gnostically in the practical life.* Note the use of this expression also in *Eulogios* 24. 26. 1128C6 (B Text).

58 *the movement of the mind.* Here this expression refers to the process by which the mind becomes conscious of an attack and determines to defend itself.

59 *separating soul from body . . . a meditation on death.* The notion of separating soul from body through a purification effected by the practice of the virtues is found in Plato, *Phaedo* 67C, where purification is defined as 'separating the soul from the body as far as possible'. The notion of the 'practice of death' is taken from *Phaedo* 67DE and 80E–81A. The meditation on death had become a common notion by the end of the fourth century. See e.g. Athanasius, *Life of Antony* 19, ed. G. J. M. Bartelink, SC 400. 185–7. For other patristic references see A. Guillaumont, SC 141, 620–1. Evagrius discusses the meditation on death in more detail in *Foundations* 9.

60 *those who have attained impassibility of the soul through this body.* For Evagrius the body plays a positive role in that it was given to the fallen minds for their good in order to assist them towards salvation. The body makes possible the exercise of the practical life and thereby the attainment of impassibility of the soul. By means of the body and the sensible knowledge obtained through it the fallen mind can attain to spiritual knowledge and the contemplation of beings.

61 *with our ready consent.* Literally, 'and we run towards'.

62 *Praktikos* 54–6 treat the subject of dreams as a way of determining the soul's state of health and progress towards impassibility. Evagrius also discusses dreams at some length in *Thoughts* 4 and 27–9. See the analysis of the subject in F. Refoulé, 'Rêves et vie spirituelle d'après Évagre le Pontique', *Supplément de la Vie Spirituelle*, 59 (1961), 470–516.

63 *the natural movements of the body.* i.e. seminal emissions during sleep. See the discussion of the subject in David Brakke, 'The Problematization of Nocturnal Emissions in Early Christian Syria, Egypt, and Gaul', *Journal of Early Christian Studies*, 3 (1995), 419–60. Cassian discusses nocturnal emissions and erotic dreams in *Institute* 6. 10 and *Conferences* 12. 7 and 22.

64 *knowledge, which alone is wont to unite us to the holy powers.* Spiritual knowledge unites

us to the incorporeal angels and, according to the Platonic principle of similitude (*Theaetetus* 176B), this implies that we are like the angels in their perfect impassibility. Union with the holy powers means a transformation from the human to the angelic condition.

65 *two peaceful states of the soul, one arising from natural seeds, the other resulting from the retreat of the demons.* Impassibility is the defining characteristic of the peaceful state of the soul. See *Reflections* 3, 'Impassibility is the tranquil state of the rational soul, constituted by gentleness and chastity.' The natural seeds are the virtues. See *KG* 1. 39, 'We were constituted as possessing the seeds of virtue, but not those of evil.' The theme of original goodness and virtue can be found also in Athanasius, *Life of Antony* 20 (SC 400. 188–90), 'Virtue therefore has need only of our will, since it is within us and springs from us. Virtue is maintained when the soul holds to the spiritual side of its nature. It maintains its natural state when it remains as it came into being; and it came into being beautiful and perfectly straight . . . The soul is said to be straight when the spiritual side of its nature is in the same state as when it was created.'

66 *it is impossible for them to attack the soul at the same time.* Evagrius discusses other reasons for this in *Thoughts* 24.

67 *to knock out one nail with another.* For the proverb cf. Palladius, *HL* 26. 4 (82. 6).

68 *the successive demons.* This phenomenon of the succession of the demons is discussed in greater detail in *Thoughts* 34.

69 *the demons that oppose the practical life . . . the demon still fighting against it.* The demons opposing the practical life, who attack the passionate part of the soul, are distinguished from those that oppose the activity of the gnostic, namely, contemplation.

70 *Praktikos* 61. Note the near verbatim similarities in S377-Prov. 31: 21, '*Her husband shows no concern for those in the household, when he tarries somewhere, for all who are with her are clothed.* The mind could not advance nor attain the contemplation of the incorporeals, without having set right what is within, for domestic trouble usually turns it back to where it has come from. But when it has acquired impassibility, it tarries in contemplation and is unconcerned with those in the household, for its irascible part is clothed in gentleness and humility and its concupiscible part in chastity and abstinence.'

71 *to practise prayer without distraction.* Cf. *Prayer* 35, 'Undistracted prayer is the mind's highest act of intellection.' The greatest temptation for the gnostic is irascibility.

72 *when the mind has begun to see its own light.* Cf. *Reflections* 2, 'If someone should want to behold the state of the mind, let him deprive himself of all mental representations, and then he shall behold himself resembling sapphire or the colour of heaven (cf. Exod. 24: 9–11). It is impossible to accomplish this without impassibility, for he will need God to collaborate with him and breathe into him the connatural light.'

73 *possesses little or no awareness at all of the irrational part of the soul.* Note the very similar statement in *Thoughts* 29 and *KG* 2.6.

74 *Praktikos* 69. This saying passed into the *Apophthegmata patrum*, A229 (Evagrius 3). Cf. S1-Ps. 137: 1 (*AS* 3. 340), '*I will confess to you, O Lord, with all my heart, and before the angels I will sing psalms to you, for you have heard all the words of my mouth.* To chant the psalms in the presence of the angels refers to psalmody without distraction, where either our ruling faculty is impressed solely with the objects indicated by the psalm, or it receives no impression'; also *Prayer* 85, 'Psalmody belongs to the realm of multiform wisdom; prayer is the prelude to the realm of immaterial and uniform knowledge.' Multiform wisdom is a term taken from Eph 3: 10. It designates the first stage of contemplation which is directed towards the *logoi* of created beings.

75 *no longer remembers the law or the commandments or punishment.* Cf. *KG* 6. 21, 'Virtue is the excellent state of the rational soul, in which it is moved to evil only with difficulty.'

76 *demonic songs.* That is, certain types of secular songs or songs associated with pagan cults. Cf. *Virgin* 48; S5-Ps. 101: 10 (12. 1557D), '*For I ate ashes as bread and mingled my drink with weeping.* This verse is useful for those who take enjoyment in flute-playing and songs while drinking.'

77 *being assailed and assailing in return.* In all the struggles with the demons associated with the practical life, sometimes the battle turns to their favour and sometimes to ours. With the attainment of impassibility, however, the victory is decisive, though not necessarily irrevocable. Cf. S21/22-Ps. 17: 38 (12. 1237C), 'He pursues the enemies who does not allow impassioned thoughts to arise within himself, for from these we acquire sins. Impassibility brings about a cessation of enemies.'

78 *Rest is linked with wisdom, but ascetic labour with prudence.* The contrast between rest and ascetic labour and between wisdom and prudence is ultimately the contrast between the gnostic and the practical life.

79 *Sin for a monk.* Since Evagrius defines the temptation and sin of the gnostic in *Gnostikos* 42–3, it can be assumed that the monk here in *Praktikos* 74–5 refers to one who is still engaged in the level of the practical life. Cf. S5-Ps. 143: 7 (*AS* 3.352–3), '*Send forth your hand from the heights, draw me forth and save me from the many waters, from the hand of foreigners' sons, whose mouth has spoken vanity and whose right hand is a hand of iniquity.* The 'foreign hand' is the thought that arises in the company of the passionate part of the soul and which restrains the mind; but this hand attacks those in the practical life, while the hand that attacks those in the contemplative life is the false knowledge of objects themselves or the contemplation of them, insinuating that the Creator is unjust or deprived of wisdom.'

80 *Praktikos* 78. Cf. S4-Ps. 2: 12 (*AS* 2. 449), '*Lay hold of discipline, lest the Lord become angry.* Discipline is a moderation of the passions, which naturally derives from

the practical life. The practical life is a spiritual teaching which purifies the passionate part of the soul.'

81 *The actions of the commandments . . . the corresponding contemplations.* Perfect impassibility is achieved, not simply by perfect virtuous practice in an external or formal sense, but rather, only when the mind comes to a knowledge of the ultimate principles (the *logoi*) of the practical life. Cf. S5-Ps129: 8 (1648D–1649A) '*And he himself will redeem Israel from all its iniquities.* The mind is delivered from sins or iniquities of thought at the moment when it is deemed worthy of knowledge. For the practical life does not remove mental representations from the heart, but rather impassioned mental representations.'

82 *It is not possible to oppose all the thoughts inspired in us by the angels.* Human nature cannot resist angelic thoughts absolutely because of the natural goodness, the 'seeds of virtue', inherent in human nature from its creation (*KG* 1. 39). And further, when the soul has been purified, there is no longer anything within it to oppose the thoughts inspired by angels.

83 *Praktikos* 81. For the more complete genealogy of the virtues see *Praktikos,* Prologue 8.

84 *the mind in acting with its proper activity.* The proper activity of the mind is contemplation. At this level, the gnostic can diagnose any disturbance experienced in his own powers (the concupiscible and irascible) and prescribe the appropriate remedies.

85 *the reasons of the warfare.* Cf. S14-Ps. 118: 32 (*AS* 3. 265), '*I ran the way of your commandments, when you opened wide my heart.* The reasons (*logoi*) of the commandments open wide the heart and render the way of the practical life easy for it.'

86 *Those demons . . . opposed to the practical life; . . . those that cause great vexation to the rational part are called . . . adversaries of contemplation.* On the two types of warfare see S2-Ps. 117: 10 (12. 1580D), '*All the nations have surrounded me and with the name of the Lord I have defended myself against them.* Among the demons some made war against him as engaged in the practical life, others as engaged in the contemplative life. He defended himself against the former by means of justice and against the latter by means of wisdom.'

87 *the virtues both purify the soul and remain with it once it has been purified.* The 'seeds of virtue' are inherent in the soul from the beginning and always abide with it (*KG* 1. 39–40).

88 *For the passions there will one day be complete destruction, but in the case of ignorance they say one form will have an end, the other will not.* The passions cease their activity when the passionate part of the soul becomes completely conformed to nature. The two forms of ignorance correspond to the two forms of knowledge, namely, knowledge of beings and knowledge of God or theology. Full knowledge of beings is attained with perfect impassibility, but the knowledge of God is without limit and can never be exhausted. Cf. S2-Ps. 144: 3 (*AS* 3. 354, PG 12. 1673A), '*Great is the Lord and greatly to be praised, and of his greatness there is no limit.*

The contemplation of all beings is limited; only the knowledge of the Holy Trinity is without limit, for it is essential wisdom.'

89 *Things which are good or bad according to their usage.* Evagrius is speaking of the good and bad usage of the parts of the soul (the rational, concupiscible, and irascible), which are meant to be directed according to their nature. Cf. *KG* 3. 59, 'If all evil derives from the rational, the concupiscible or the irascible part, and it is possible for us to use these powers either for good or for evil, evils come upon us clearly according to our usage of these parts. And if this is so, nothing created by God is evil.'

90 *our wise teacher.* The teacher in question is most likely Gregory Nazianzen. Dorotheos of Gaza specifies Gregory in a reference to this chapter: *Instruction* 17. 176 (SC 92. 478. 19). See also *Gnostikos* 44 and *KG* 6. 51.

91 *Praktikos* 89. For this chapter Evagrius drew upon some text of the school tradition, such as the anonymous treatise *On the Virtues and the Vices* 1–2 (or another treatise very much like it), adapting it to his own doctrine: 'If according to Plato the soul is taken to be tripartite, prudence is the virtue of the rational part, gentleness and courage that of the irascible part, temperance and abstinence that of the concupiscible part, and justice, liberality, and magnanimity that of the entire soul. The vice of the rational part is folly, that of the irascible irascibility and cowardice, that of the concupiscible licentiousness and intemperance, that of the entire soul injustice, servility, and pusillanimity. Prudence is the virtue of the rational part, which prepares those who are striving for happiness. Gentleness is the virtue of the irascible part, according to which they are moved with difficulty by anger. Courage is the virtue of the irascible part, according to which they can hardly be terrified by fears concerning death. Temperance is the virtue of the concupiscible part, according to which they are without desires for the enjoyments of base pleasures. Abstinence is the virtue of the concupiscible part, according to which they restrain by reason the desire that impels them to base pleasures. Justice is the virtue of the soul that distributes proportionately. Liberality is the virtue of the soul that is lavish unto the good. Magnanimity is the virtue of the soul, according to which one is able to bear good and bad fortune, honour and dishonour' (ed. F. Susemihl, *Aristotelis Ethica Eudemia* (Leipzig, 1884), 82–3). Note, however, that Evagrius adds virtues with a strong scriptural background: understanding and wisdom (cf. Col 1: 9), charity and abstinence (cf. 1 Tim. 2: 15; 2 Pet. 1: 6), and perseverance (e.g. Rom 5: 3).

92 *as tears accompany the sowing, so does joy accompany the sheaves.* Cf. S3-Ps. 125: 5 (12.1641AB), '*Those who sow in tears will reap in rejoicing.* Those who practise the practical life with ascetic labour and tears 'sow in tears', but those who partake in knowledge without labouring 'will reap in rejoicing'.'

93 *Praktikos* 91. 1–6. This saying passed into the *Apophthegmata patrum*, A232 (Evagrius 6).

94 *'My book, philosopher, is the nature of beings, and it is there when I want to read of the words of God.'* Cf. *Life of Antony* 72–80 (SC 400, 320–40). Cf. S8-Ps. 138: 16 (*AS* 3. 344, PG 12. 1661C–D), *'And in your book they shall all be written.* The contemplation of bodies and incorporeals is the book of God in which the pure mind is inscribed through knowledge.'

95 *Praktikos* 93. A similar saying is found attributed to Makarios in the *Apophthegmata patrum*, A489 (Makarios 36).

96 *the holy father Makarios.* Probably Makarios of Alexandria, who was the priest at Kellia in the time of Evagrius. See A. Guillaumont, SC 171, 699–700.

97 *Stop blaspheming, my Father is immortal!* Palladius attributed this saying to Evagrius himself in *HL* 38.13 (123.1–3).

98 *Praktikos* 96. This saying passed into at least some versions of the *Apophthegmata patrum* (A952, Evagrius S3), though under different names (Eulogios, Epiphanius, Helladios). See. J.-C. Guy, *Recherches sur la tradition grecque des Apophthegmata Patrum*, Subsidia Hagiographica, 36 (Brussels: Société des Bollandistes, 1962), 50.

99 *Praktikos* 97. This story of the little Gospel book was retold many times in slightly different versions. See e.g. Palladius, *HL* 116, PG 34. 1220C–D. It is cited in the *Apophthegmata patrum*, N392.

100 *the lake called Maria.* i.e. lake Mareotis, present-day Mariut.

101 *Praktikos* 99.1–4. Cf. *Apophthegmata patrum* (A951, Evagrius S2).

102 *We should honour our elders like the angels, for it is they who anoint us for the struggles and who heal the wounds inflicted by the wild beasts.* The 'wild beasts' are the demons. Cf. *KG* 6.90, 'All who have attained spiritual knowledge shall assist the holy angels and return rational beings from evil to virtue and from ignorance to knowledge'; *KG* 3.46, 'The judgement of the angels is the knowledge of the illnesses of souls, which returns to health those who have been wounded.'

103 *Gregory the just.* i.e. Gregory Nazianzen. Cf. *Gnostikos* 44.

MONKS

1 *Monks* 3–5 present an example of the chain of the virtues. See *Praktikos* 8 and 81.

2 *invite him to your place . . . eat your portion with him.* Cf. *Eulogios* 17. 18. 1116C, *Praktikos* 26, and *Virgin* 41.

3 *The wealthy person will not attain knowledge.* The scripture text paraphrased here refers to the difficulty that the rich person will have in entering the 'kingdom of heaven' and the 'kingdom of God'. According to *Praktikos* 1–2, these two references to the kingdom can be taken as the two stages in the attainment of knowledge, namely, true knowledge of beings and knowledge of the Holy Trinity.

4 *your going forth will be like the going forth of a star.* The 'going forth' or 'exodus' of the soul is its departure from evil (cf. S12-Prov. 1: 20–1). The stars are sometimes taken as a symbol for the second natural contemplation (*KG* 3.84). In *KG* 5.19, 22, 25, Evagrius elucidates the three dimensions of the resurrection: that of the body's transformation from an inferior to a superior state, that of the soul's progress from passibility to impassibility, and that of the mind's passage from ignorance to true knowledge. The sun is usually understood as a reference to the 'sun of righteousness' (Mal. 3: 20), namely, Christ. Cf. S2-Ps. 18: 6 (12.1142D–1144A), '*In the sun he has placed his dwelling.* Our Lord is the sun of righteousness and in him does the Father dwell, according to the verse, "I am in the Father and the Father is in me" (John 14: 10); and again, "The Father who dwells in me does his works" (John 14: 10); also the Apostle, "God was in Christ reconciling the world to himself" (2 Cor. 5: 19).'

5 *the artisans of good deeds.* If *Monks* 32 is read as an allusion to Prov. 14: 22, then the good artisans are those who have the qualities of mercy and compassion; both are virtues which counter irascibility.

6 *Today is the Feast.* In *Monks* 39 and in 41–2 the designation 'feast' is set in parallel with 'Pentecost', while in 40 'Passover of the Lord' is the parallel member for 'Pentecost'. It thus seems reasonable to assume that the 'feast' in question is intended to be Easter, the 'Feast of Feasts' (Gregory Nazianzen, Or. 45. 2, *On Holy Easter*, PG 36. 624B).

7 *Feast of God, amnesty for evil deeds.* The reference again is to Easter, the feast of God's forgiveness of the sins of humanity. Evagrius very likely intends here also the monk's imitation of God's forgiveness.

8 *One who eradicates evil thoughts from his heart.* Cf. S5-Ps. 136: 9 (12. 1660A), '*Blessed is the one who will seize and dash your infants against the rock.* All those who according to the teaching of Christ eradicate wicked mental representations from the soul dash the infants of Babylon against the rock.'

9 *the vigilant one (viz. monk) will be like a sparrow.* Cf. S4-Ps. 101: 8 (12. 1557D), '*I was vigilant and became like a solitary sparrow on a rooftop.* Nothing else renders the mind nimble like vigilance.'

10 *Do not give yourself to empty stories during vigil.* In *Thoughts* 28 Evagrius warns about the demons 'telling some stories so as to have us neglect the hours of the office.'

11 *Monks* 54. This is quoted in the *Apophthegmata patrum* A230 (Evagrius 4). On the practice of remembrance of death see *Foundations* 9. 1161A–C, *Praktikos* 29.

12 *nor a wicked thought in your heart.* Cf. S68-Prov. 5: 20, 'It is impossible, so long as one is human, to avoid wicked thoughts, but it is however possible not to linger with them.'

13 *As fire tests silver and gold.* For other examples of this imagery see *Eight Thoughts* 5. 19, *Eulogios* 29. 31. 1133D8.

14 *the enemies will terrify you through the air and frightful nights will come to you.* For the apparitions in the air of the cell and terrifying nightmares induced by the demon of pride see *Thoughts* 21 and 23.

15 *one who descends from knowledge falls prey to thieves.* Cf. *Eight Thoughts* 7.13, 'The foolish man makes a public show of his wealth and motivates many to plot against him. Hide what is yours, for you are on a road full of thieves, until you reach the city of peace (cf. Heb. 7: 2) and can safely make use of what is yours.' Here the movement is in the opposite direction, from the 'road full of thieves' up to the 'city of peace' (Jerusalem).

16 *the pure soul.* On the Evagrian notion of purity see *Letter* 56, G1.139–40, 'Just as it is impossible to apprehend sensible objects without the body, so is it impossible to see the incorporeal without the incorporeal mind, and it is not as such that the mind sees God, but as a pure mind, for scripture says, "Blessed are the pure of heart, for they shall see God" (Matt. 5: 8). Note also that he declared them blessed not because of their purity, but because of their vision of God, since purity is impassibility of the rational soul and the vision of God is true knowledge of the worshipful and Holy Trinity; this vision they will see who here below have become accomplished in the practical life and have purified themselves through the commandments.' See further Jeremy Driscoll, 'Apatheia and Purity of Heart in Evagrius Ponticus', in Harriet A. Luckman and Linda Kulzer (eds.), *Purity of Heart in Early Ascetic and Monastic Literature* (Collegeville, Minn.: The Liturgical Press, 1999), 141–59.

17 *Without milk a child cannot be fed.* Milk is an image for the practical life. Cf. S153–Prov. 17: 2 (cited below, n. 21).

18 *Wisdom . . . prudence.* Cf. *Praktikos* 89, 'The work of prudence is to lead in the war against the opposing powers and to defend the virtues and to draw the battle lines against the vices and to manage indifferent matters according to the circumstances. . . . The work of wisdom is the contemplation of the reasons of bodies and incorporeals'; on wisdom see also S3–Prov. 1: 2, '*To know wisdom and instruction.* In this regard he says, "He became king in Israel so as to know instruction and wisdom." And wisdom is the knowledge of bodies and of incorporeals and of the judgement and providence considered in these. Instruction is the moderation of the passions which are observed around the passionate or irrational part of the soul.'

19 *A flaming arrow ignites the soul.* Cf. *KG* 6. 53, 'The intelligible arrow is the evil thought which is constituted by the passible part of the soul'; *Exhortation* 2.29, 'As it is impossible for a person struck by an arrow not to be injured, so it is impossible for the monk who has accepted a wicked thought not to be wounded.'

20 *Pleasant is honey and sweet the honeycomb.* Cf. *KG* 3. 64, 'If among the things which have taste there is nothing sweeter than "honey and the honeycomb" (Ps. 18: 11), and if the knowledge of God is said to be superior to these things (cf. Ps.

118: 103), it is clear that there is nothing among all the things on earth which gives pleasure like the knowledge of God.'

21 *An unjust steward . . . the just one.* Evagrius understands stewardship not just in the sense of managing the material affairs of the community but also in the spiritual sense of dispensing knowledge according to the need and capacity of each individual. Cf. S153-Prov. 17: 2, '*The intelligent servant will prevail over foolish masters, and he will distribute portions to his brothers.* If "everyone who commits sin is a slave to sin" (John 8: 34), everyone who has rejected evil and through the virtues has prevailed over the demons "has prevailed over foolish masters". Such a person will become also a steward of the mysteries of God, distributing spiritual knowledge to each of the brothers in proportion to his state, giving the Corinthian milk to drink (1 Cor. 3: 2) and feeding the Ephesian with more solid food (Heb. 5: 12).'

22 *The wandering monk. Eight Thoughts* 6. 10 associates the 'wandering monk' with the problem of acedia.

23 *shepherds shameful thoughts.* Cf. S344-Prov. 28: 7, '*The intelligent son keeps the law, but he who pastures debauchery dishonours his father.* He calls the mind a shepherd and the impassioned mental representations within it sheep; if he nourishes these within himself "he dishonours God through the transgression of the law" (Rom 2: 23). For debauchery of the soul consists of impassioned thoughts activated through the body; debauchery of the mind consists of the acceptance of false doctrines and considerations.'

24 *Monks* 82–3. Cf. *Letter* 16, G2. 66. 7–12, 'In the same way the demon of fornication guards its boundaries to see whether the monk who encounters a woman did so out of necessity or made up a reasonable excuse, or if he pronounced a word that provoked laughter or that invited an apparent reverence; and he observes his eye to see if it is not curious and his walk to see if it is not relaxed and his mantle to see if it is his everyday one.'

25 *The lazy monk . . . the drowsy one.* The problem addressed here is that of acedia. Cf. *Eight Thoughts* 6.10 and 16.

26 *the book of the living.* Cf. S17-Ps. 68: 29 (12. 1517AB), '*Let them be expunged from the book of the living, and let them not be enrolled in the company of the righteous.* The book of the living is the knowledge of God, from which those who possess impure hearts are fallen. For "Blessed are the pure of heart, for they shall see God" (Matt. 5: 8). "Seeing God" refers to being deemed worthy of knowledge of him.'

27 *One who has placed his trust in his own abstinence.* Cf. *Letter* 27, CG 220. 65–9, 'Let no one, I pray you, attend to abstinence alone, for it is not possible to build a house with a single stone or to construct a house with a single brick. An irascible abstinent person is a dry autumn twig without fruit, twice-dead, and uprooted. The irascible person will not see the dawning of the morning

star, but is on his way to a place from which he shall not return, to a dark and gloomy land, to a land of eternal darkness (cf. Job 10: 21–2).'

28 *the morning star in heaven and the palm tree in paradise.* The morning star in this case is probably a reference to Christ, based on such scripture texts as Rev. 22: 16, 2 Pet. 1: 19, and Luke 1: 78. This would accord with the reference to the vision of the morning star denied to the irascible person in *Letter* 27, CG 220.65–9 (quoted above). According to Evagrian christology, Christ was the pure mind that never fell, always remaining united to essential knowledge. As for the second image, the palm tree is probably a figure for 'the just' as in Ps. 91: 13, 'The just shall flourish like the palm tree.' Driscoll has made the intriguing suggestion that 'paradise' is a reference to a lesser form of knowledge (*The* Ad Monachos *of Evagrius Ponticus: Its Structure and a Select Commentary*, Studia Anselmiana, 104 (Rome: Pontificio Ateneo S. Anselmo, 1991), 270–2). Paradise is a 'place of instruction' (*paideutērion*) according to S7-Ps. 9: 18 (12. 1189D), '*Let sinners be turned back to Hades.* As Paradise is a place of instruction for the just, so Hades is a place of punishment for sinners.' This may be a reflection of Origen's notion that after death the just will remain on earth in a place called 'paradise' where they will receive instruction regarding the truths of creation (what Evagrius would call 'the reasons of providence and judgement'), after which, according to their purity of heart and mind, they will ascend to the kingdom of heaven (*On First Principles* 2. 11. 6, SC 252. 406–10).

29 *the words of God.* As elsewhere, the term *logoi* is ambiguous: the wise person, that is the gnostic, examines the words of God in scripture for their true, hidden meaning; but the sage will also examine the ultimate principles or 'reasons' that preside over God's creation and saving economy.

30 *One who loves honey eats its honeycomb.* Cf. S270-Prov. 24: 13, '*Eat honey, my son, for the honeycomb is good, that your throat may enjoy its sweetness.* He who draws profit from the divine scriptures eats honey; he who extracts their doctrines of realities themselves—both the holy Prophets and Apostles took from these— eats the honeycomb. Eating honey is accessible to all who wish, but eating the honeycomb belongs only to the pure'; S72-Prov. 6: 8, 'It also appears to me that the honeycomb corresponds to the realities themselves, whereas the honey that it contains is the symbol of their contemplation.'

31 *flesh of Christ . . . blood of Christ* (*Monks* 118–19). For a similar interpretation of the flesh and blood of Christ see S13-Eccles. 2: 25, '*For who shall eat and who shall drink besides him?* Indeed, who without Christ will be able to eat his flesh or drink his blood (cf. John 6: 51–8), which are the symbols of the virtues and of knowledge?' The same symbolism is implicit in the allegorical interpretation of the Eucharist in *Gnostikos* 14. A somewhat different interpretation is found in the *Letter on Faith* 4. 16–22, 'Christ says, "He who eats me will live because of me" (John 6: 57), for we eat his flesh and drink his blood, becoming through his incarnation and sensible life partakers in the Word and in Wisdom. For he

called flesh and blood his entire mystical sojourn and he revealed the teaching constituted by the practical life, natural contemplation, and theology, through which the soul is both nourished and prepared even now for the contemplation of beings.'

32 *Breast of the Lord.* This verse continues the allegory of the Eucharistic institution at the Last Supper, where the beloved disciple, identified by tradition with John the Evangelist, rested his head on Jesus' breast. Cf. *Letter to Melania* 13. 519–22, '... the great treasury which contains all the stores of wisdom: this is the breast of Christ to which John lay close during the Supper.' Probably before the end of the 3rd cent. and certainly by the 4th, John the Evangelist had been given the epithet of 'the Theologian': see Eusebius of Caesarea, *On Ecclesiastical Theology* 2. 12 (PG 24.925A).

33 *the holy teachings . . . the faith of your baptism . . . the spiritual seal.* In all likelikhood Evagrius is here speaking of fidelity to the doctrine of the Trinity and especially the divinity of the Holy Spirit, which had been in question in the second half of the 4th cent. Cf. S249-Prov. 22: 28, '*Do not shift the perpetual boundaries which your fathers set in place.* One who displaces the boundaries of piety turns it into superstition or impiety, and one who displaces the boundaries of courage turns it into rashness or cowardice. One should consider the same to be true also for the other virtues and for doctrines and for faith itself. But above all one should observe this precept with respect to the Holy Trinity, for one who denies the divinity of the Holy Spirit does away with baptism, and one who calls others gods introduces polytheism.'

34 *Monks* 126. Gabriel Bunge has proposed that this verse refers to Evagrius' encounter with three heretical clerics, who according to the story were in reality demons: ' Origenismus-Gnostizismus', *Vigiliae Christianae*, 40 (1986), 24–54, esp. 26–30. The text of the story is found in *HL* 38. 11 (121. 9–122. 1) along with the expansion in the Coptic version and in a Greek fragment: see Butler, *Lausiac History*, 1. 132–5; also Adalbert de Vogüé and Gabriel Bunge, 'Palladiana III. La version copte de l'Histoire Lausiaque. II. La vie d'Évagre', *Studia Monastica*, 33 (1991), 7–21. For another, related, warning against false doctrine see *Virgin* 54, especially with the longer text of the Latin and Syriac versions.

35 *the paradise of God . . . a garden of vegetables.* According to the imagery suggested by the scripture text, the 'garden of vegetables' represents Egypt, which for Evagrius is a symbol of evil (cf. *KG* 5. 88, 6. 49) and is contrasted with the 'paradise of God'; the 'river of God' is then contrasted with the Nile.

36 *The reasons of providence . . . the contemplations of judgement.* The reasons of providence and judgement mentioned here and in *Monks* 135 refer to the ultimate principles of God's creation and saving economy.

VIRGIN

1 *the mother of Christ.* Note the allusion to Mary as ascetic exemplar. This is probably to be taken as a reference to Mary's quiet obedience to the will of God. *Virgin* 20, 21, and 45 treat the unquestioning obedience owed to the 'mother' of the community.

2 *Love your sisters as the daughters of your mother.* Evagrius is clearly addressing an ascetic community of women, exhorting them to live as a familial group.

3 *Pray without ceasing.* On unceasing prayer see *Praktikos* 49.

4 *lest images arise in your soul.* On the problem of obstacles and images in the time of prayer see *Praktikos* 23.

5 This verse is found only in L.

6 *in the church of the Lord.* Members of the community visited the local church, presumably to attend the liturgical services.

7 *the soul of a virgin is difficult to heal when it has been wounded.* Cf. *Thoughts* 36, 'For it is easier to purify an impure soul than it is to bring back to health one that has been purified and wounded again'; *Exhortation* 2. 29.

8 *gifts overcome resentment.* Cf. *Praktikos* 26.

9 *The songs and pipings of demons.* Cf. *Praktikos* 71; S5-Ps. 101: 10 (12. 1557D), '*For I ate ashes as bread and mingled my drink with weeping.* This verse is useful for those who take enjoyment in flute-playing and songs while drinking'; *Praktikos* 71.

10 The passage in square brackets is found only in L and Syr.

11 *Remember Christ... consubstantial Trinity.* This sentence is virtually identical to the conclusion of *Eulogios* 32. 34. 1140A.

ON THOUGHTS

1 *Thoughts* 2. This chapter is probably not in its original place within the treatise. It appears to be designated as chapter 17 in *Thoughts* 24: 'For we said in chapter 17 that no impure thought arises within us without a sensible object.'

2 *mental representations of sensible objects.* Cf. *Reflections* 52, 'A demonic thought is a mental representation of a sensible object, which moves the irascible or the concupiscible part in a manner contrary to nature.'

3 *adultery and violence.* i.e. concupiscence and irascibility.

4 *the image of God.* The expression θεοῦ τὴν φαντασίαν refers to the 'image' of the God who gave the Law to Moses. As such it is an image stored in the memory.

5 *only with the suppression of all mental representations associated with objects.* Note the

similar statement made in *Letter* 58 (G1. 143. 5–7): 'The Holy Spirit wants the contemplative state to be without images and free of all impassioned thoughts, for just as an eye afflicted with leucoma does not apprehend sensible objects, so the mind with impassioned thoughts does not recognize intellections.'

6 *from these two passions are constituted almost all the demonic thoughts. Almost* all the thoughts come from the concupiscible and irascible parts of the soul. Elsewhere, Evagrius suggests that vainglory (and pride) have another origination. Cf. *Thoughts* 28. 1–4; also *Disciples* 130 and 177 (SC 438. 158–9 n. 3); the latter text assigns acedia, vainglory, and pride to the rational faculty.

7 *disregard for food, riches, and esteem.* As in *Thoughts* 1, Evagrius again underlines the importance of the three fundamental vices of gluttony, avarice, and vainglory.

8 *the physician of souls.* i.e. Christ.

9 *those who are pure and free from passion no longer experience such a thing (impassioned dreams).* The absence of such dreams is one of the indicators of impassibility. See *Praktikos* 56, 'We shall recognize the proofs of impassibility in the thoughts by day and in the dreams by night.'

10 *coming either from ourselves or from the holy powers.* In *Thoughts* 28 Evagrius discusses the three types of dreams, depending on their origin: demonic, human, and angelic.

11 *moved contrary to nature.* The natural object of anger is evil and the demons.

12 *'the gall-bladder and the loin are inedible to the gods'.* Menander, *Dyskolos* 451–3. Evagrius may have taken the quotation from Clement of Alexandria, *Stromateis* 7. 31. 1 (SC 423. 114).

13 *how one ought not to worry about clothes or food.* See the more detailed treatment in *Foundations* 4.

14 *we possess the seeds of virtue.* Evagrius held that the seeds of virtue implanted by God in human nature were indestructible (*KG* 1. 40; S62-Prov. 5: 14).

15 *Thoughts* 7. The complete text of this chapter appears verbatim in *Letter* 18, F578. 12–22.

16 *the reason why gold was made.* At issue here is the spiritual signification of gold: the gold scattered through the earth and subsequently rediscovered, refined, and refashioned for a holy purpose is for Evagrius a symbol of the fall of the intellects from the realm of the pre-existence and their dispersal through different worlds along with their joining to souls and bodies; subsequently, by the practice of the virtues, they are purified and delivered from the captivity of the devil ('the king of Babylon'), ultimately regaining spiritual knowledge and restoration to their original state.

17 *about the time of dawn.* i.e. during the time of the night office or *synaxis*, which the monk performs alone in his cell.

18 *the radiance of its state.* Evagrius is here referring to the mind's natural state, unmoved by the passions and receptive to spiritual knowledge and the reflection of the divine light.

19 *By means of abandonment.* Evagrius discusses abandonment also in *Gnostikos* 28. A little earlier in the Egyptian tradition the subject was treated briefly by Ammonas, *Letter* 4 (Greek in PO 11.443.10–14): 'Know that at the beginning of the spiritual life the Holy Spirit grants people joy and sweetness when he sees their hearts pure. But when the Spirit has granted joy and sweetness, he then departs and leaves them. This is a sign of his activity and he does this with every soul that seeks God in the beginning: he departs and leaves them that he may know whether they go on seeking him or not.'

20 *the greatest and primary degree of impassibility.* In *Thoughts* 35 Evagrius distinguishes between two degrees of impassibility, one which hinders sins in act and one which also restricts impassioned thoughts.

21 *thoughts that counsel the soul to make its escape or force it to flee far from its place.* i.e. the temptation to acedia. Cf. *Praktikos* 12.

22 *vainglory has an abundance of matter.* i.e. vainglory can arise from an abundance of human circumstances and so make its inroads in the life of the monk. Cf. *Reflections* 44.

23 *remaining seated.* i.e. the monk must remain in his place, his cell; he must maintain his commitment without wavering.

24 *'a verdant place and water for refreshment', 'a harp and a lyre', and 'a rod and staff . . . the mountain grass'.* The grass and water are symbols for the practical life and gnosis (S1-Ps. 22: 1–2, 12. 1260C3–5); the lyre is a symbol for the practical life and the harp for the pure mind moved by spiritual knowledge (S2-Ps. 32: 2, 12. 1304B; S2-Ps. 91: 4, 12. 1552D); the rod and staff are symbols for the chastisements that guide the sinner back to goodness (S3-Ps. 22: 4, 12. 1260D–1261A); the mountain grass is a symbol for the knowledge of the holy powers which presides over the irrational state of souls (S341-Prov. 27: 25).

25 *as a human being . . . as an irrational animal.* Cf. *Reflections* 40, 'Among thoughts, some come to us as animals, others as human beings. Those that come as animals are all those that derive from the concupiscible and the irascible; those that appear as human beings are all those that derive from sadness, vainglory and pride; those that derive from acedia are mixed, coming to us both as animals and as human beings.'

26 *crows.* Cf. *Ad Prov.* 30: 17, n16, in SC 340. 489, 'Crows are the holy powers who destroy the vices.' The same text is also found in *Chapters 33.* 31, PG 40. 1268B.

27 *circumcising this pleasure.* On spiritual circumcision see *KG* 4. 12, 'The intelligible circumcision is the voluntary rejection of the passions for the sake of the knowledge of God.'

28 *the First City.* i.e. Constantinople.

29 *we have crossed the Jordan and are near the city of the palm trees . . . beaten upon by the foreigners.* The crossing of the Jordan and the taking of Jericho ('city of the palm trees') symbolize the completion of the practical life (the sojourn in the desert) and the attainment of impassibility; the 'foreigners' in the Septuagint version of Judges are the Philistines, whom Evagrius identifies with the demons. See *Antirrhetikos*, Prol., F472. 29–39; *KG* 6. 49, 5. 30, and 5. 68.

30 *he (the demon) encompasses it (the soul) with the thoughts of avarice and hands it over to the demon of vainglory.* Cf. *Foundations* 4, 'This should be your attitude towards almsgiving. Therefore do not desire to possess riches in order to make donations to the poor, for this is a deception of the evil one that often leads to vainglory and casts the mind into occasions for idle preoccupations'; *Antirrhetikos* 7. 10, F532. 8–10, 'Against the thoughts of vainglory that cause the mind to attend to mental representations of every kind, sometimes making it a steward of the goods of God and sometimes establishing it as an overseer of the brothers.'

31 *as the mental representation of bread . . . on account of greed.* Note the near verbatim parallel text in *Letter* 39, G1. 134. 1–3.

32 *will be discussed in the Chapters on Prayer.* See e.g. *Prayer* 12, 43, 55–7, 67–8, 70, 112, 115. This reference to *Prayer* shows that it was being written or at least planned at the same time as *Thoughts*. It also indicates that both treatises are by the same author.

33 *many among the brothers who fell afoul of this shipwreck.* Evagrius may indeed be referring to an incident involving the brothers Valens and Hero, known to Palladius, *HL* 25–6 (79–82).

34 *we said in chapter 17.* The reference should in fact be to *Thoughts* 2, an indication that the current ordering of the chapters may not be original.

35 *Demonic thought . . . in succession.* An almost identical definition is found in *Reflections* 13.

36 *The mind wanders about . . . But it ceases . . . spiritual desires.* These two sentences are found verbatim in *KG* 1. 85.

37 *The first renunciation . . . the second . . . the third renunciation.* The three renunciations are cited in *KG* 1.78–80 and also transmitted by John Cassian, *Conference* 3. 6–7 (SC 42. 145–50). Later the teaching is reported by John Climacus, *Ladder* 2, PG 88. 657A.

38 *Beneficence and mercy.* On several occasions Evagrius mentions the performance of charitable works as an effective remedy for thoughts of anger. See S36-Prov. 3: 24–5 'From this text we learn that almsgiving does away with the terrifying fantasies that come to us in the night. Gentleness, absence of anger, and patience accomplish the same thing, as well as all the virtues that calm the irascible part when it is troubled. Indeed, it is from the troubling of the irascible part that terrifying apparitions usually arise.'

39 *a fantasy of the priesthood.* Cf. *Antirrhetikos* 7. 26, F534. 9–11, 'Against the demon
who during the sleep of the night makes me a shepherd of a flock and who during the day explains to me this dream saying: You will be a priest and behold
those who are seeking you are following quickly behind you.'

40 *throwing down from high ladders.* Later, the depiction of monks being cast or
pulled from the rungs of a ladder by menacing demons would become a
common theme in Byzantine art. See e.g. Kurt Weitzmann, *Byzantine Book
Illumination and Ivories* (London: Variorum, 1980), article I, 40–1 and figs. 33–4
(St Catherine's Monastery, Mount Sinai: Icon and MS Arab 343, fol. 13v); K.
Weitzmann and G. Galavaris, *The Monastery of Saint Catherine at Mount Sinai. The
Illuminated Greek Manuscripts,* i. *From the Ninth to the Twelfth Century* (Princeton:
Princeton University Press, 1990), plate CLXIV, no. 594 (MS Sinai gr. 418, fol.
15v.).

41 *telling some stories so as to have us neglect the hours of the office.* Cf. *Monks* 47 on the
danger of being distracted during vigil by 'empty stories'.

42 *Angelic dreams.* Dreams of course may be inspired not only by demons but also
by angels. Cf. *Monks* 52, 'The angelic dream rejoices the heart, but the demonic
dream troubles it.' The placement of natural contemplation ('certain reasons
of beings') after pure prayer is odd and may be an indication of a problem with
the text.

43 *For the soul . . . gives it rest.* The same text appears in *KG* 2. 6 (HNF 230).

44 *the wings of that holy Dove.* This is the dove that descended on Jesus at his baptism (Matt. 3: 16), which Evagrius interprets as a symbol either of the Word
(*Reflections* 5) or of the Holy Spirit (S1-Ps. 56: 2, 12. 1472A3–4). Cf. S2-Ps. 54: 7
(12. 1465C6–9), 'The wings of the holy dove are the contemplation of bodies
and of incorporeals, through which the mind is raised on high and finds repose
in the knowledge of the Holy Trinity.'

45 *they corrupt our intention or the way in which the commandment must be fulfilled.* A similar point is made by Paphnoutios in the presence of Evagrius, Albanius, and
Palladius in *HL* 47.7 (2. 138. 14–17): 'Sometimes the intention is sinful, as
when something is done for an evil purpose, but sometimes the act is sinful,
as when something is done in a corrupt manner or in a way in which it should
not be done.'

46 *Concerning these thoughts blessed David wrote.* Cf. S1-Ps. 141: 4 (12. 1665D6–
1668A4), '*On the road where I was proceeding they hid a snare for me.* Our enemies
lay schemes against all the virtues. In the case of courage they hide the trap of
cowardice; in the case of gentleness they instil rashness; in the case of almsgiving, it is a matter of doing it not for God but for those who see us; and in
the case of fasting, it is to fast for the sake of men. These are the cases that
relate to the practical life. But what would one say of contemplation regarding the numerous traps that the enemies lay through heresies for orthodox
teaching?'

47 *Opposed to the demonic thought . . . good seed in his field.* The text of *Thoughts* 31.1–11 appears independently in *Letter* 18, F578. 6–12.

48 *If we are capable of something . . . non-being is not a quality.* This sentence is also cited independently in *KG* 1. 39 (HNF 230).

49 *For there was a time . . . finest seed of virtue. Thoughts* 31. 15–20 appears independently in *KG* 1. 40; S62-Prov. 5: 14; *Letter* 43, F596. 4–7; *Letter* 59, F608. 23–6.

50 *its celestial state.* At the height of the experience of pure prayer the state of the mind is said to take on a 'celestial' quality. Cf. *Reflections* 4, 'The state of the mind is an intelligible height resembling the colour of heaven, to which the light of the Holy Trinity comes in the time of prayer.'

51 *they quarrel with their neighbours, often taking them to court.* Cf. the similar comment in *Gnostikos* 8, 'It is disgraceful for the gnostic to become involved in legal proceedings, whether he is the victim or the perpetrator of an injustice: if he is the victim, because he did not bear the injustice patiently; if he is the perpetrator, because he committed an injustice.'

52 *they touch the eyelids and the entire head, cooling it with their own body, for the bodies of the demons are very cold and like ice.* Cf. *KG* 6.25 (HNF 233), 'When the demons are not able to set the thoughts in motion for the gnostic, then they take possession of his eyes and, cooling them down completely, they draw them into a very deep sleep, for all the bodies of the demons are cold and like ice.'

53 *the companions of Daniel, their poor life and the grains.* Evagrius also refers to this episode of Daniel and his companions in the context of gluttony, but with a different emphasis, in *Antirrhetikos* 1. 45, F480. 13–15, 'For the soul that is not satisfied with bread for food and water for drink, but along with these seeks vegetables, and does not remember the affliction of the grains that Daniel and his companions ate.'

54 *the brothers have determined by experience that this regimen is the very best.* Cf. *Apophthegmata* A605 (Poimen 31), 'Abba Joseph asked Abba Poimen, "How ought one to fast?" Abba Poimen said to him, "I would have a person eat a little every day so as not to reach satiety." Abba Joseph said to him, "When you were younger, did you not fast for two days at a time, Abba?" And the elder replied, "Yes indeed, even three, four days, or a week at a time." The fathers conducted all these experiments to the extent they were able and they found that it is best to eat daily, but only a little, and they passed this tradition on to us as the royal road (Num. 20: 17), because it is light.'

55 *the spiritual circumcision of the hidden Jew.* Cf. *KG* 4. 12 (see above, n. 27).

56 *they are unable to extend themselves to many objects.* i.e. impure thoughts draw upon an abundance of objects in the created world as well as numerous human circumstances to tempt the ascetic. Purification gradually restricts the activities of the demons and the sources of temptation that they can deploy.

57 *they are moved in a manner that is more contrary to nature.* Evagrius may mean that

when the demons have exhausted the usual channels of temptation they resort to suggesting sinful acts against nature, specifically, homosexuality. Cf. S92-Prov. 7: 12 'Those who "roam about in the streets" have thoughts of adultery, fornication, and theft. Those who "roam beyond these" have movements contrary to nature, as they seek the bed of men and receive images of certain other forbidden things.'

58 *our holy priest.* i.e. Makarios the Alexandrian.

59 *it is inappropriate for such things to be made public and have them fall upon the ears of the profane.* i.e. pure things may not be passed on to those who are impure, hence the reference to the Levitical regulations on purity and impurity.

60 *it will see its own state in the time of prayer resembling sapphire or the colour of heaven.* Cf. *Reflections* 2, 'If someone should want to behold the state of the mind, let him deprive himself of all mental representations, and then he shall behold himself resembling sapphire or the colour of heaven (cf. Exod. 24: 9–11). It is impossible to accomplish this without impassibility, for he will need God to collaborate with him and breathe into him the connatural light.'

61 *Thoughts* 39. This text appears almost verbatim in *Letter* 39, F592. Cf. *Reflections* 25, 'From the holy David we have learned clearly what the place of God is; for he says, "His place has been established in peace and his dwelling on Sion (Ps. 75: 3)." Therefore, the place of God is the rational soul, and his dwelling the luminous mind that has renounced worldly desires and has been taught to observe the reasons of (that which is on) earth.'

62 *that light which at the time of prayer leaves an impress of the place of God.* This statement is curious because the following chapter makes it quite clear that the mental representation of God is one of those that leave no impress on the mind. The text here is almost identical to that of *Reflections* 23. G. Bunge, however, suggests a different interpretation for the final phrase which he translates as 'expresses the place of God'. In other words, the place of God becomes visible only when the light of the Holy Trinity is present. See Bunge's article, 'La montagne intelligible. De la contemplation indirecte à la connaisance immédiate de Dieu dans le traité *De oratione* d'Évagre le Pontique', *Studia Monastica*, 42 (2000), 12 n. 56.

63 *Among mental representations some leave an impress and a form . . . knowledge which leaves no impress or form in the mind.* Cf. *Reflections* 17.

64 *mental representation.* In this case the term *noēma*, 'mental representation' is being used more in the sense of 'idea' or 'concept'.

65 *leaves a form in the mind . . . leaves an impress on the mind.* The mind forms an image, a 'mental representation', of the sensible realities described in the scripture verse.

66 *'I saw the Lord seated on a high and lofty throne' (Isa. 6: 1).* Evagrius makes the distinction between the sensible imagery of God sitting on a throne, which leaves an

impression on the mind, and the spiritual signification of the verse which has no sensible association to leave any impress.

67 *Demonic thoughts . . . the contemplation of beings.* Note the identical text in *Reflections* 24.

PRAYER

1 *(our) great guide and teacher in his blessed manner.* The teacher in question was very likely Makarios the Egyptian, the great elder of Sketis, whom Evagrius also mentions in *Praktikos* 29 and 93. The use of the adverb *makariōs* is undoubtedly a veiled allusion to the name Makarios. Cf. G. Bunge, 'Évagre le Pontique et les deux Macaire', *Irénikon*, 56 (1983), 215–27; 323–60.

2 *having done good service to win Rachel and having received Leah.* Evagrius here takes Leah as a symbol for the practical life and Rachel as a symbol for the gnostic life. This allegorical interpretation seems to be unknown prior to Evagrius, although Philo took Leah and Rachel to be symbols for interior spiritual states but not in the same sense as Evagrius (cf. *De congressu eruditionis gratia* 24 and 31–2, ed. Monique Alexandre, *Les oeuvres de Philon d'Alexandrie,* no. 16 (Paris: Cerf, 1967)).

3 *the matter of number.* Evagrius is sending his recipient a collection of *kephalaia* on prayer, 153 in number. The number he takes from that of the catch of fish in John 21: 11 and he then proceeds to offer an interpretation of the symbolism of this number. Following some basic introductory text on arithmetic, such as that of Nicomachus of Gerasa, Evagrius identifies the number 153 as both triangular and hexagonal. A triangular number is one equal to the sum of all preceding successive numbers starting with 1. Thus $153 = 1+2+3+ \ldots +16+17$. If you omit every other number in the succession (i.e. the even numbers) starting with 2, you will have square numbers: thus $100 = 1+3+5+ \ldots 17+19$. If you omit two numbers after each number included in the succession, you have pentagonal numbers. If you omit three, you have hexagonal numbers: thus $153 = 1+5+9 \ldots +29+33$. The number of 153 chapters is therefore both triangular, representing symbolically the orthodox knowledge of the Trinity, and also hexagonal, representing the description of the ordering of the world (established in the *six* days of creation): in other words, the theology and the economy. Taking the analysis of the symbolism further, Evagrius notes that the number 153 is composed of a square number (100) and a triangular number (53). The number 53 in turn is the sum of a triangular number ($28 = 1+2 \ldots +7$) and a spherical number (25). A spherical number, is one which multiplied by itself produces a number with the same final digit (in effect, a number ending in 1, 5, or 6). According to Nicomachus, this should properly be called a 'cyclical' number. Evagrius takes the square number as a symbol for the four cardinal virtues (prudence, continence, courage, and justice) and the spherical number as a symbol for the cyclical nature of the temporal order of the world.

Finally, the triangular number of the chapters can also be understood as a symbol for the threefold division of spiritual progress (the practical life, natural contemplation, and theology—the subject matter of the treatise); or the three virtues of faith, hope, and love; or the gold, silver, and precious stones of 1 Cor. 3: 12.

4 *fragrant incense . . . the four primary virtues.* Cf. *Reflections* 6, 'The pure mind is an incense burner at the time of prayer when it touches upon no sensible object.' The four cardinal virtues (prudence, continence, courage, and justice) were known to Plato (*Laws* 12.964B6) and were a commonplace of Stoic teaching (cf. Plutarch, *On Stoic Self-Contradictions* 7; Musonius Rufus, *On Ascesis*, ed. Cora E. Lutz, Yale Classical Studies, (New Haven: Yale University Press, 1947), 52). Evagrius discusses them especially in *Gnostikos* 44, where he claims that he received the teaching from Gregory Nazianzen, and in *Praktikos* 89. According to the Stoic notion of the interdependence of the virtues, the four cardinal virtues would have included all the others that followed upon them. Cf. *Gnostikos* 6, '(The gnostic) should ever be attempting *to practise all the virtues equally*, so that *they follow upon one another* in him as well, because the mind is betrayed by the one that grows weak.'

5 *the full complement of the virtues.* The manuscript tradition is about equally divided between the readings 'virtues' and 'commandments'.

6 *it (the soul) stabilizes the attitude of the mind and prepares it to receive the desired state.* Note how it is the 'soul' that must be purified as the principal locus of the passions, before the mind can realize the requisite stability for the 'desired state' of pure prayer.

7 *Prayer is a communion of the mind with God.* A similar definition of prayer is found in Clement of Alexandria, *Stromateis* 7. 7. 39. 6 (SC 428. 140), 'Therefore, to speak more boldly, prayer is converse with God. So even if we speak to him silently in a whisper without moving the lips, we cry out interiorly. For God listens unceasingly to all our interior converse.' This definition of prayer appears also in Maximus of Tyre, *Lectures* 4. 7, thus indicating that it may be Greek, rather than Christian, in origin. See A. Le Boulluec, SC 428, 140 n. 3. Although Clement uses the term '*homilia*' in a way that suggests some sort of interior conversation with God, Evagrius, in this instance at least, probably excludes this notion in favour of something like a communion of constant presence, free of words and forms. This is confirmed by the qualifications attributed to the state of prayer: 'without turning back' and 'without intermediary'. Cf. S1-Ps. 140: 2 (*AS* 3. 348), 'There is one form of prayer, *the communion of the mind with God*, which preserves the mind free of impress; I call a mind without impress one which imagines nothing corporeal at the time of prayer, for only those names and words which indicate something sensible leave an impress and a form on our mind, but the mind that prays must be absolutely free of sensible things, and the intellection of God necessarily preserves the mind free of impress, for he (God) is not a body.'

8 *until he removed the sandals from his feet.* There was an exegetical tradition that interpreted Moses' sandals as the attachment to the material, corporeal life that he needed to abandon in preparation for the vision of God. See e.g. Gregory of Nyssa, *Life of Moses* 1. 20. 15–18 (SC 1. 60), 'The voice from that light prevented Moses from approaching the Mountain while he was weighed down by dead sandals, but when he loosed the sandal from his feet he was able to touch that ground which was illumined by the divine light.'; id., *Funeral Oration on Meletius, Bishop of Antioch* (*CPG* 3180, PG 46.455), 'He [Meletius] has left Egypt behind, this earthly life. He has crossed not that Red Sea, but this black and darkling sea of life. He has entered the land of the promise and holds philosophical converse with God on the Mountain. He has loosed the sandal from his soul that with the pure step of the intellect he may set foot on the holy ground where God is seen.' See also Gregory Nazianzen, *On Holy Easter* (Or. 45.19), PG 36. 649B, 'As for sandals, let one who is about to touch the holy ground trodden by God put them off, as Moses did on the Mountain, that he may bear nothing dead, nothing to come between God and human beings.'

9 *mollify the wildness.* The human soul moves between two opposite poles: the wild savagery of the animal state, which characterizes the demonic nature, and the peaceful state of *apatheia* or impassibility that is achieved only after the long battle against the passions. For the demons as wild beasts see *Prayer* 91; also S9-Ps. 73: 19 (12. 1532C), '*Give not over to the wild beasts the soul that makes confession to you.* If the demons are called beasts and irascibility predominates in beasts, then irascibility predominates in the demons. And in Job it says, "The wild beasts will be at peace with you" (Job 5: 23).'

10 *entertain absolutely no exaltation within yourself for being superior to most people.* On the danger of vainglory see *Praktikos* 30.

11 *in their madness they have gone astray.* Or 'they have lost their senses' according to some MSS witnesses. In 7 Evagrius warned that the thoughts of vainglory and pride can corrupt the gift of tears, thus turning the remedy into a passion; in 8 he issues the further warning that these vices can ultimately lead to psychological imbalance.

12 *mental representations of certain apparently necessary objects.* The reference here is to a preoccupation with supposedly necessary or important concerns: e.g. concern for one's health—having enough to eat and drink; the effects of bodily asceticism on one's health; the importance of having something to give to the poor; worry and anxiety regarding one's family. Cf. *Foundations* 3–5.

13 *Prayer* 12. The text transmission for this chapter is somewhat confused. Note the Syriac version: 'Whenever temptation or contrariness comes upon you and provokes you against the one before you, while in vengeance a passion sets wrath in motion to let loose an inappropriate word in reply, remember prayer and the judgement against it, and immediately the movement of rage in you will quiet down.'

14 *stumbling block for you at the time of prayer.* Cf. *Praktikos* 25, *Monks* 15.

15 *Go, 'sell your possessions and give to the poor'.* Cf. *KG* 1. 78 (HNF 230), 'The first
    renunciation is the abandonment of the objects of the world, which is willingly
    undertaken for the sake of the knowledge of God.'

16 *when you suffer all sorts of troubles for the sake of prayer, practise love for wisdom.* Cf. the
    Syriac translation: 'when you are suffering many evils for the sake of prayer,
    practise love for becoming wise.' For Evagrius, wisdom is associated with the
    highest knowledge of God attained in pure prayer.

17 *like people who draw water and put it into a jar full of holes.* Evagrius here draws on
    the commonplace metaphor derived from the story of the Danaids, who for
    their punishment in the underworld were made to continually pour water into
    a leaking vessel. Cf. Xenophon, *Oeconomicus* 7. 40; in *Gorgias* 493B, Plato applies
    the metaphor to insatiable appetites.

18 *make use of every means to avoid an outburst of anger.* Cf. *Eulogios* 11. 10. 1105C–D,
    Praktikos 24.

19 *in thinking you can heal another person.* It is unclear whether the problem in ques-
    tion is vainglory or anger. Cf. *Apophthegmata patrum* A470 (Makarios 17), 'The
    same Abba Makarios said: If in reproving someone you are moved to anger,
    you fulfil your own passion, for to save others you should not cause yourself
    ruin.'

20 *When an angel attends us.* On the service of the angels to those seeking contem-
    plation see *Praktikos* 76.

21 *pray rather as you were taught, saying: 'Your will be done' in me.* There exists in Cop-
    tic and Arabic a brief commentary on the Our Father attributed to Evagrius
    (*CPG* 2461). See the comments of Khalil Samir on the Arabic text in 'Évagre le
    Pontique dans la tradition arabo-copte', in Marguerite Rassart-Derbergh and
    Julien Ries (eds.), *Actes du IVᵉ Congrès Copte. Louvain-la-Neuve, 5–10 septembre 1988*,
    Publications de l'Institut Orientaliste de Louvain, no. 41, Louvain-la-Neuve:
    Institut Orientaliste, 1992, ii. 149–50. See also *Prayer* 58.

22 *What good is there besides God?* Cf. *Eight Thoughts* 8. 12, 'A great thing is the human
    being who is helped by God; he is abandoned and then he realizes the weak-
    ness of his nature. You have nothing good which you have not received from
    God (cf. 1 Cor. 4: 7).'

23 *Prayer* 34a. There remains some uncertainty regarding the location of this
    chapter in the collection.

24 *the ascent of the mind towards God.* Evagrius often refers to the state of prayer as
    an intelligible height or mountain which the mind must ascend, just as Moses
    ascended Mount Sinai to receive the vision of God (Exod. 24). Cf. *Prayer* 52
    ('intelligible height'); *Reflections* 4, 'The state of the mind is an intelligible height
    resembling the colour of heaven, to which the light of the Holy Trinity comes
    in the time of prayer'; *Letter* 58, G1. 143, 'It is impossible for the mind to be

saved without ascending this mountain, for the intelligible mountain is the knowledge of the Holy Trinity erected on a height difficult of access. When the mind has attained this, it leaves all the intellections associated with objects. It was to this mountain that the holy angels of God at that time guided Lot, saying: "Save yourself upon the mountain for fear that you be taken along with them" (Gen. 19: 17).'

25 *renounce absolutely all things, so that you may inherit the whole.* One should probably take seriously the contrast between 'all things' and 'the whole' (multiplicity/unity): in renouncing the multiplicity of the created and intelligible worlds, the monk at prayer aspires to regain the unicity of the substantial knowledge of the Trinity.

26 *the passions . . . ignorance and forgetfulness . . . temptation and abandonment.* At each of the three stages of progress, the monk makes the appropriate supplication: in the practical life he prays for the purification of the passions; in the first stage of the gnostic life, as he enters into natural contemplation, he prays for deliverance from ignorance; in the advanced stage of the gnostic life, all can still be lost through temptation (especially pride) and the gnostic may have to endure abandonment. Cf. *Gnostikos* 28. On Evagrius' teaching on abandonment see J. Driscoll, 'Evagrius and Paphnutius on the Causes for Abandonment by God', *Studia Monastica,* 39 (1997), 259–86.

27 *'seek only justice and the kingdom'.* The terms 'justice' and 'kingdom' are Evagrian code words for the practical and the gnostic life respectively. In S1-Ps. 30: 2 (12. 1297D) he defines justice as 'inclusive of all the virtues'; and in *Praktikos* 2–3 he identifies the 'kingdom of heaven' with knowledge of beings and the 'kingdom of God' with knowledge of the Holy Trinity.

28 *for your entire race.* For Evagrius, 'your entire race' refers not to all people, but specifically to those committed to seeking the knowledge of God. In reference to Isa. 58: 7, Evagrius writes in *Letter* 53, F602. 1, 'I call our seed (race) not those who are near us by nature, but those who are near us by their state.' Cf. *Letter* 12, F574. 20–3, 'But we are not such that we are able to pray for others, for we do not possess purity of heart, nor the uncovered face (cf. 2 Cor. 3: 18) which belongs to rational nature by virtue of impassibility of soul together with knowledge of the truth. For who will say, according to the word of Solomon: "My heart, you are pure" or "I am free of sins" (cf. Prov. 20: 9).' It is especially the role of the angels to make intercession for the salvation of others. Cf. *Reflections* 30, 'Intercession is an entreaty brought to God by a superior being concerning the salvation of others.'

29 *using a show of prayer as a cover.* Or according to certain MSS, 'using the prolongation of prayer as a cover'.

30 *Prayer with perception.* Or according to some text witnesses, 'the character of prayer'.

31 *adorning the outer tent.* Cf. *Prayer* 152. The expression 'adorning the outer tent' refers to a preoccupation with the body and its needs.

32 *guard your memory vigorously.* Note that the memory may play either a negative role (source of distraction via past memories) or a positive role (moving one towards a knowledge of one's presence before God).

33 *his setting out towards God.* For Evagrius' use of the expression 'setting out' or 'emigration' (*ekdēmia*) as applied to the practical life see *Eulogios* 2. 2. 1096C4 and 23. 24. 1125B5. Gregory Nazianzen, whom Evagrius revered as his teacher, makes frequent use of the expression 'the emigration of the mind unto God': e.g. *Or.* 6. 2, PG 35. 724A; also *Or.* 4. 71, 593B and *Or.* 24. 17, 1189B.

34 *When . . . the . . . demon is unable to impede the prayer of the zealous person.* Cf. *Praktikos* 44.

35 *the mind becomes thickened by them.* See *KG* 2. 62, 'When the minds have received the contemplation that concerns them, then the entire nature of bodies (S¹ 'the thickness of bodies') shall also be removed, and thus the contemplation that concerns it shall become immaterial'; *KG* 4. 36, 'The intelligible fat is the thickness that arises in the mind as a result of evil'; S4-Ps. 16: 9–10 (12. 1220CD), 'The intelligible fat is the thickness that arises in the ruling faculty as a result of evil'; *Letter on Faith* 7. 31–3 (ed. M. Forlin Patrucco), 'But since our mind, now become thick, has been joined to earth and is mixed with clay and is unable to fix its gaze in simple contemplation . . .' See also *Monks* 48, *Praktikos* 41.

36 *the virtues . . . the reasons of created beings . . . the Word.* Note the three stages: virtues—*logoi* of created beings—the *Logos* who gave them being. These represent the three stages of spiritual progress: the practical life, natural contemplation, and theology. According to Evagrian anthropology, the mind was one of the *logikoi* ('rational beings') in its original state and even now through its rational faculty (*logistikon*) it naturally seeks the *Logos*: initially through the fundamental principles or *logoi* which he has impressed as traces of himself on all created things, and then directly in himself.

37 *impassible habit . . . supreme love . . . intelligible height.* Here too Evagrius speaks of three stages: impassibility, love, and the intelligible height. The allusions to wisdom and spirit are ultimately references to the mind's relationship to the Son and the Holy Spirit. See G. Bunge, *Das Geistgebet : Studien zum Traktat De oratione des Evagrios Pontikos,* Schriftenreihe des Zentrums Patristischer Spiritualität Koinonia im Erzbistum Köln, 25 (Cologne: Luthe, 1987), 75–6.

38 *mental representation tied to the passions.* For a detailed discussion of mental representations along with the forms and impressions they leave on the mind see *Thoughts* 41.

39 *simple intellections.* Here the term '*noēmata*' is best translated as 'intellections', rather than 'mental representations' which refers more specifically to a mental

image of a sensible object. 'Simple intellections' are those concerned with the rational principles of created beings, whether corporeal or incorporeal; they belong to the domain of natural contemplation. The statements of this chapter and the subsequent ones are further clarified by Evagrius' elaboration of the subject in *Letter* 58, G1. 143, 'The Holy Spirit wants the contemplative state to be without images and free of all impassioned thoughts, for just as an eye afflicted with leucoma does not apprehend sensible objects, so the mind with impassioned thoughts does not recognize intellections. It must advance gradually through all the intellections and thus come even to the Cause and Father of the intelligibles, who will appear to the heart with the suppression of the intellections associated with objects. The contemplation of created beings provides a multiplicity of information, but that of the Holy Trinity is a uniform knowledge, for it is substantial knowledge which is manifest to a mind divested of passions and bodies.'

40   *'the place of prayer'*. Cf. *Prayer* 71, 102, 152.

41   *occupied with the knowledge of intelligible objects*. That is, the mind may be engaged in the contemplation of the reasons of incorporeal beings. For further comments on 'the place of God' see *Reflections* 20, 23, and 25.

42   *worshipped in spirit and in truth*. The reference to 'worship in spirit and truth' (John 4: 23–24) appears four times in the treatise: *Prayer* 58–9, 77, and 146. See the *Commentary on the Our Father* translated by I. Hausherr, *LeÁons,* 83: *'Que ton règne vienne.* Le règne de Dieu, c'est l'Esprit-Saint. Nous prions qu'il le fasse descendre sur nous.'

43   *honours the Creator no longer on the basis of creatures, but praises him for himself.* In the final stages of pure prayer the monk has completely abandoned all created realities and seeks God alone in and for himself.

44   *if you pray truly, you will be a theologian.* For Evagrius, the 'theologian' is one who has attained the true knowledge of God in contemplation.

45   *the flesh . . . mental representations . . . memory . . . temperament.* Note here the degrees of withdrawal that precede pure prayer: the flesh (i.e. material objects), mental representations of material objects, memories, and temperament. The last of these Evagrius will explain in greater detail in *Prayer* 68. Cf. *Reflections* 17.

46   *(God) visiting the mind directly and introducing within it knowledge of what he wishes.* Cf. *Gnostikos* 4, 'The knowledge that comes to us from outside attempts to make known material things by means of their reasons; but the knowledge that arises within us by the grace of God presents objects directly to the intellect, and when the mind looks upon them it approaches their reasons. Error opposes the former, while the latter is opposed by anger and irascibility and the things that follow upon these.'

47   *like one who wants acuity of vision but does harm to his own eyes.* Cf. *Gnostikos* 5, 'All the virtues pave the way for the gnostic, but above them all is freedom from anger.

For one who has touched upon knowledge and is easily moved to anger is like a person who gouges his own eyes with a pointed piece of iron.'

48 *the presumption of rashly localizing the Divinity.* Cf. *KG* 1. 62, 'Knowledge is said to be in a place when the one who receives it is joined to one of the secondary beings, one which truly and principally is said to be in a place.' In other words, all knowledge that localizes or locates an object in a place, belongs to knowledge of creatures. Note the version of this chapter in S¹: 'Knowledge is said to be in a place when it attends to the intellections of creatures, but it is in no place when it regards the Holy Trinity with wonder.'

49 *the temperament (krasis) of the body.* This refers to the body's physiological constitution, which the demon may influence in one way or another so as to distract the mind at prayer, especially when other means have failed. Cf. *Antirrhetikos* 4.22, F504.34–6, 'Against the thought that does not realize that the singing which accompanies the psalms alters the temperament of the body and banishes the demon that touches the back, chills the nerves, and troubles all the members.' In *Prayer* 72–3 Evagrius describes how the demon can cause palpitations in the blood vessels in the head or alter the light around the mind by touching a certain part of the brain. Cf. also *Thoughts* 33; *Reflections* 17.

50 *prayer is the laying aside of mental representations.* Cf. *Reflections* 26, 'Prayer is a state of the mind destructive of every earthly mental representation.'

51 *the demons no longer attack it on the left, but on the right.* Cf. *Thoughts* 42, 'Demonic thoughts blind the left eye of the soul, which perceives the contemplation of beings; the mental representations that leave an impress and a form on our ruling faculty cloud the right eye, which in the time of prayer contemplates the blessed light of the holy Trinity; by this eye the bride ravished the heart of the bridegroom himself in the Song of Songs (S. of S. 4: 9).'

52 *A man experienced in the gnostic life.* The MSS tradition is evenly divided between the two readings 'practical' and 'gnostic'. Hausherr, *Leçons,* 106, has suggested that the individual in question may be John of Lykopolis (Cf. *Antirrhetikos* 2.36, 5.6, 6.16, 7.19), on whom see P. Devos, 'John of Lycopolis, Saint', *Coptic Encyclopedia,* 5 (1991), 1363–6.

53 *the influence of the passion of vainglory.* See *Antirrhetikos* 7.31, F534.21–6, 'Against the thought of vainglory that manifests itself to us in the state of pure prayer and assimilates the mind to the form that it wills, while the mind itself is invisible and without form, and it represents it as praying to the Divinity. Thus it happens to the mind which is troubled by the passion of vainglory and by the demon which approaches the place at the time of prayer so as to show that it is being seen by many children and women. Whoever is able to understand, let him understand.' For other examples of the demons' ability to effect physiological changes see *KG* 6. 25 and *Thoughts* 9, 33.

54 *the divine and essential knowledge.* i.e. knowledge of the Holy Trinity.

55 *the light associated with it (the mind).* On a number of occasions Evagrius speaks of the light surrounding the mind. In *Gnostikos* 45 he speaks of 'those who in the time of prayer contemplate the proper light of the mind which illumines them'; and in *Praktikos* 64 he claims 'It is a proof of impassibility when the mind has begun to see its own light.' Ultimately, this is the divine light radiating within the human mind. The demons will try even at this point to divert the monk into giving form and location to this vision of light. See A. Guillaumont, 'La vision de l'intellect par lui-même dans la mystique évagrienne', in *Mélanges de l'Université Saint-Joseph* 50 (*Mélanges in memoriam Michel Allard et Paul Mwyia*) (Beirut: Université Saint-Joseph, 1984), 255–62 (*Études* IX. 143–50).

56 *The bowls of incense.* It is actually the incense itself that represents the prayers of the saints, as becomes clear from the next chapter.

57 *the perfect and spiritual love.* Cf. *Reflections* 6, 'The pure mind is an incense burner at the time of prayer when it touches upon no sensible object.'

58 *a young eagle soaring in the heights.* Cf. *Ad Prov.* 30: 17, n. 18 in SC 340. 489, 'The young of eagles are the holy powers entrusted with casting down the impure beings.' The same text is also found in *Chapters 33.33*, PG 40.1268B. See also *Eight Thoughts* 1. 14, 'The prayer of one who fasts is like a young eagle soaring upwards.'

59 *Psalmody . . . prayer.* As Evagrius describes it here, psalmody is an ascetic exercise proper to the practical life, for it helps to allay the passions and temptations associated with the bodily appetites. Here and in the next chapter, it is contrasted with prayer which guides the mind in the contemplative activity that is true to its original nature.

60 *Psalmody belongs to multiform wisdom.* In other words, the mind will normally be occupied with the 'objects' mentioned by the psalm, although at times Evagrius suggests that there is an even higher form of psalmody in which the mind remains free from mental impressions. S1-Ps. 137: 1 (*AS* 3. 340) 'To chant the psalms in the presence of the angels refers to psalmody without distraction (reading *aperispastōs*), where either our ruling faculty is impressed solely with the objects indicated by the psalm, or it receives no impression.'

61 *awaken the intellectual power of the mind to contemplation of divine knowledge.* The 'knowledge' that awakens the mind to divine gnosis must presumably be that bestowed by natural contemplation.

62 *swifter than the movement and vigilance of your mind.* Cf. *Praktikos* 51.

63 *like wild beasts they will come upon you and maltreat your entire body.* Evagrius frequently refers to the demons as wild animals, and he also takes seriously the physical nature of the demonic attacks. Cf. *KG* 1.53 (HNF 230), 'The demons that fight with the mind are called birds; wild animals, those that trouble the irascible part; and those that set desire in motion are named domestic animals.' For examples of the physical attacks of the demons see *Antirrhetikos* 4 (Sadness): 15, 22, 33, 36, 56.

64 *a sword drawn against you or a light rushing at your eyes . . . some unsightly and bloody figure.* Again *Antirrhetikos* 4 offers examples of these phenomena: 20, 23, 47.

65 *if you are fervent in your supplication before God.* Some MSS read: 'if you are experienced in using the staff of supplication to God'.

66 *a short and intense prayer.* This would involve the use of a short phrase or verse taken from scripture, such as those laid out in great number in the *Antirrhetikos.*

67 *Prayer* 101. Note the tripartite division: body, soul, mind.

68 *Do not pray like the Pharisee but like the tax-collector.* Cf. the similar recommendation made in *Admonition* 2, F566. 15–17, 'Take heed lest he (Satan) deceive you with praises, that he may not exalt you in your own eyes, lest you become proud of your attainments like the Pharisee. Rather, strike yourself like the Publican, beat your breast like him, saying: "O God, have mercy on me a sinner. O God, forgive me my debts."'

69 *if you do not forgive your debtor, neither will you yourself obtain forgiveness.* Cf. *KG* 4. 33 (HNF 230–1, G2. 64), 'Demons without pity will receive after their death those who are without pity, and demons even more cruel than these will receive those who are more pitiless. If this is so, then it has escaped the notice of those who take themselves from the body (viz. by suicide) what sort of demons will meet them after their departure. For it is said that none of those who go forth according to the will of God are handed over to such demons.'

70 *Abba Theodore.* i.e. the superior of the Pachomian *Koinonia* from c. 350–68.

71 *the flesh . . . the soul . . . the mind.* Note how Evagrius holds to his tripartite division of the human person: body, soul, mind.

72 *his fiery prayer.* Cf. John Cassian, *Conference* 9. 15 (*prex ignita*), 9. 26 (*oratio ignita*).

73 *equal to the angels.* The monk becomes equal to the angels in the sense that by renouncing the passions of the body and the soul he lives then according to the mind (110), and 'a predominance of mind' is characteristic of the angels (*KG* 1. 68). Cf. S163-Prov. 17: 17. 1–2, *At every moment may you have a friend; and may brothers prove useful in times of need.* If the sons of Christ are brothers of one another, and if angels and just people are sons of Christ, then angels and holy people are brothers of one another, begotten by the spirit of adoption.'

74 *lest you go completely insane.* This is the meaning of the word *phrenērēs* required by the context; the word retains this sense ('frenzied, crazed, mad, insane') in modern Greek.

75 *even to novices.* This is the reading (*kai neōterois*) of almost all the manuscript witnesses collated (PgPhAcJMaStUZ). Only a corrector hand in Coislin 109 (A²) and perhaps the Arabic version give the reading *kai en eterois*, 'elsewhere as well'. Hausherr, *Leçons,* 151, accepts the reading of A², arguing quite rightly that Evagrius would not have communicated the higher mysteries of pure prayer to those who were still beginners in the spiritual life. However, the macarism

in this chapter could be understood even at a basic level by a beginner: Do not form images in the mind when you pray! The saying itself does not necessarily reveal any higher teachings that should not be communicated to beginners. Like so much in Evagrius, it remains at the discretion of the gnostic teacher to explain the saying at a level appropriate to the individual's progress.

76 *the fruits of his every primary intellection.* The meaning of 'primary intellection' (*prōtonoia*) is not immediately clear. It could refer simply to the practice of offering to God the first thoughts of one's day. More likely, Evagrius uses the term to designate the highest level of contemplation.

77 *no cloud to obstruct your sight.* Cf. *Eight Thoughts* 4. 6, 'A passing cloud darkens the sun; a thought of resentment darkens the mind.'

78 *the promises . . . rulership.* Both refer to the attainment of contemplation.

79 *immaterial and substantial knowledge.* i.e. knowledge of the Holy Trinity.

80 *pray openly against them and to speak against them.* As in the numerous examples of the *Antirrhetikos.*

81 *the spiritual teacher.* i.e. one experienced in the gnostic life.

82 *the fullers.* i.e. the demons. Cf. *Monks* 55, 60.

83 your mind resists virtue and truth. i.e. the practical and the gnostic life.

84 *the sorrowful remembrance of his sins and the just sanction for them in the eternal fire.* Cf. *Praktikos* 33; *Foundations* 9.

85 *Unshaded and persistent staring at the sun.* Cf. *KG* 6. 63 (HNF 232), 'Just as those who have an illness of sight and stare at the sun fall to tears and see the air mingled with numerous colours, so too the pure mind when it is troubled by anger is incapable of apprehending contemplation and it sees something like clouds floating round objects.'

86 *passed beyond every other joy in your prayer.* That is, the joy of spiritual contemplation surpasses all other joys. Cf. *Praktikos* 32; *Monks* 72, 110; *Virgin* 52.

REFLECTIONS

1 *resembling sapphire or the colour of heaven.* Exod. 24: 10, 'And they saw the place where the God of Israel stood, and what was under his feet was like brick-work of sapphire and like the form of the colour of heaven in its purity.' Evagrius apparently read 'the colour of heaven' instead of 'the firmament of heaven'. Cf. *Thoughts* 39, 'When the mind has put off the old self and shall put on the one born of grace (cf. Col. 3: 9–10), then it will see its own state in the time of prayer resembling sapphire or the colour of heaven; this state scripture calls the place of God that was seen by the elders on Mount Sinai (cf. Exod. 24: 9–11).'

2 *the connatural light.* Evagrius probably intends here the light that is connatural to the mind and which 'came into existence simultaneously with the mind', as

G. Bunge translates the phrase. See his article, 'La montagne intelligible. De la contemplation indirecte à la connaisance immédiate de Dieu dans le traité *De oratione* d'Évagre le Pontique', *Studia Monastica*, 42 (2000), 12 and n. 59. On the vision of the intellect see A. Guillaumont, 'La vision de l'intellect par lui-même dans la mystique évagrienne', in *Mélanges de l'Université Saint-Joseph* 50 (*Mélanges in memoriam Michel Allard et Paul Muyia*) (Beirut: Université Saint-Joseph, 1984), 255–62 (*Études* IX. 143–50). *Reflections* 2 is cited under the name of Nilus by Gregory Palamas (*c.*1296–1357) in the work *To Xene on the Passions and the Virtues*, PG 150. 1081B8–14.

3 *an intelligible height.* Evagrius often refers to the state of prayer as an intelligible height or mountain which the mind must ascend, just as Moses ascended Mount Sinai to receive the vision of God (Exod. 24). Cf. *Prayer* 52 ('intelligible height'); *Letter* 58, G1.143, 'It is impossible for the mind to be saved without ascending this mountain, for the intelligible mountain is the knowledge of the Holy Trinity erected on a height difficult of access. When the mind has attained this, it leaves all the intellections associated with objects. It was to this mountain that the holy angels of God at that time guided Lot, saying: "Save yourself upon the mountain for fear that you be taken along with them" (Gen. 19: 17).' *Reflections* 4 was also cited by Palamas, *Xene*, PG 150. 1081B4–8.

4 *the dove that alighted upon him.* Cf. S2-Ps. 54: 7 (12. 1465C5–9), '*And I said: Who will give me wings like a dove, and I will fly away and find rest?* The wings of the holy dove are the contemplation of bodies and of incorporeals, through which the mind is raised on high and comes to rest in the knowledge of the Holy Trinity.'

5 *The pure mind is an incense burner at the time of prayer.* Cf. *Prayer* 1, 75–7.

6 *the eighth day . . . the last day.* The eighth day is the day of Christ's resurrection, which inaugurates the new life of grace, opening for humanity the possibility of attaining the fullness of purification in the practical life. Only with the 'last day', however, will it become possible to return to the fullness of essential knowledge. Cf. S1-Ps. 118: 1 (12. 1588AB).

7 *A blameworthy kiss.* Cf. S92-Prov. 7: 13, 'A demonic kiss is an impassioned mental representation that invites the soul to a shameful activity.'

8 *a power of the soul that is capable of destroying thoughts.* Indeed, Evagrius holds that this is the only proper and natural use of irascibility. Cf. *Praktikos* 24.

9 *like a dog.* References to dogs in Evagrius are usually negative and concern attachments to the passions. See *Eight Thoughts* 2. 18 and 3. 7; *Thoughts* 5. 14, 5. 27; S324-Prov. 26: 11.

10 *Instruction.* i.e. the practical life. See S4-Ps. 2: 12 (*AS* 2. 449), '*Lay hold of instruction, lest the Lord become angry.* Instruction is a moderation of the passions, which naturally derives from the practical life. The practical life is a spiritual teaching which purifies the passionate part of the soul'; S3-Ps. 22: 4 (12. 1261C), 'As a staff gives instruction, so does the practical life teach restraint over the passions.' On the relationship of 'instruction' and 'wisdom' in Evagrius see

S3-Prov. 1: 2 (with Géhin's commentary). See also *Eight Thoughts* 8. 23–5.

11 *demonic thought.* Evagrius discusses this mechanism of demonic thoughts in more detail in *Thoughts* 25, at the end of which he gives an almost identifical definition.

12 *the world constituted by his intellect.* On the intelligible world see *Reflections* 38–9; *KG* 5. 12, 5. 39, 5. 41–2; *Letter* 39, F592. 23.

13 *four ways by which the mind grasps mental representations.* Cf. *Thoughts* 4. 1–6, 'It is necessary to investigate also how the demons leave an impress and a form on our ruling faculty in the fantasies that occur during sleep. Such things appear to occur in the mind either when it sees through the eyes, or hears through hearing, or through whatever sense faculty, or else they arise from the memory, which leaves its impress on the ruling faculty, not through the body, but by putting in motion those things which it has acquired through the body.' In *Thoughts* 41 Evagrius discusses further the topic of which mental representations leave an impress on the mind and which do not. Cf. *Prayer* 61.

14 *a light without form.* A. Guillaumont has suggested the restoration of the word 'light', which is absent from the Greek, based on the reading of the Syriac text (*Pseudo-Supplement* 21, F440. 36). See *Vision*, 147, n. 3.

15 *substantial knowledge is obscure.* That is, it is impossible to apprehend in any true way the substance of God, as one can in the case of corporeals and incorporeals. As Evagrius explained in 18, there is in the Trinity only consubstantiality. Further, when God is considered under the aspect of unity, there can be no question of distinction or difference of any kind.

16 *Reflections* 22. This chapter can best be understood if we remember that the fundamental context for Evagrian prayer is psalmody. In the recitation of the psalm the mind will move among the mental representations suggested by the verses; from there it may proceed to deeper spiritual insights or 'contemplative considerations' and from there to moments of imageless prayer or pure prayer. Cf. *Prayer* 82–8; S1-Ps. 137: 1 (*AS* 3. 340) 'To chant the psalms in the presence of the angels refers to psalmody without distraction (reading *aperispastōs*), where either our ruling faculty is impressed solely with the objects indicated by the psalm, or it receives no impression.'

17 *Reflections* 23. This chapter is identical with *Thoughts* 40 apart from an addition at the end of the latter.

18 *Reflections* 24. This text is identical with the first sentence of *Thoughts* 42.

19 *the place of God . . . his dwelling.* This is stated more succinctly in S2-Ps. 75: 3 (12. 1536C5–6), 'Place of God, the pure soul; dwelling of God, the mind engaged in contemplation.'

20 *a state of the mind destructive of every earthly mental representation.* Cf. *Prayer* 70.

21 *Prayer . . . Petition . . . Intercession.* The terms defined in 27–8 and 30 are presumably taken from 1 Tim. 2: 1.

22 *Hades is a place without light.* Cf. *Chapters 33.* 25, 'Hades is the ignorance of the rational nature that arises as a result of the deprivation of the contemplation of God.'

23 For similar couplets comparing the *praktikos* and the *gnostikos* see *Gnostikos* 1–3 and *KG* 5. 65.

24 *the temple of the Holy Trinity.* Cf. *Eight Thoughts* 4. 12.

25 *Among thoughts, some come to us as animals, others as human beings.* See the parallel text in *Thoughts* 18, which elaborates further on the subject.

26 *concupiscibility.* Supported by two Greek manuscripts and the Syriac version, this reading appears preferable to the reading 'pride'.

27 *with an abundance of matter those deriving from vainglory.* Cf. *Thoughts* 14, 'Alone among the thoughts, that of vainglory has an abundance of matter; embracing nearly the whole inhabited world, it opens the gates to all the demons, like some evil traitor of a city.'

28 *Reflections* 45. The MSS Ue have a slightly different version of this chapter: 'Among thoughts, some harm a person only after a time, others after time and a sinful act. Those (that do harm) solely after time are natural; those that do so with time and action are contrary to nature, for it is common to all thoughts to do harm with time.'

29 *the demonic and that proceeding from an evil free choice.* Cf. *Praktikos* 30. 3–5.

30 *To the evil thought. . . from an angel.* Again, the MSS Ue have a slightly different text: 'To the evil thought there are opposed three thoughts: the angelic thought, that from an upright free choice, and that produced from natural seeds.' Cf. *Thoughts* 31. 1–11; *Letter* 18, F578. 6–12.

31 *Reflections* 51. Ue and Syr have a slightly expanded version of this chapter: 'While all the thoughts have their own proper pleasures, only the thoughts of sadness have no pleasures.' See the related statement in *Reflections* 61 and also *Thoughts* 12, 'All the demons teach the soul to love pleasure; only the demon of sadness refrains from doing this. Instead he corrupts the thoughts of those in the place by cutting off and drying up every pleasure of the soul by means of sadness.'

32 *the thoughts of vainglory and pride arise after the defeat of the remaining thoughts.* Cf. *Thoughts* 14, 'When all the demons have been defeated, together they augment this particular thought (viz. vainglory) and thereby they all regain their entrance into souls'; *Praktikos* 31.

33 *Causing harm with time.* The MSS Ue add 'and with consent'.

34 *that of anger a wild boar.* Cf. *Eight Thoughts* 4. 4.

EXHORTATIONS

1 *avarice, the mother of idolatry.* Cf. *Praktikos*, Prol. 41, where 'greed' (*pleonexia*) is identified as the 'mother of idolatry'.

2 *Exhortation* 1. 3. A slightly different version of this sentence is given in *Praktikos* 15.

3 *Exhortation* 1. 7. The long recension has expanded this sentence.

4 *Encounters with many people.* Cf. *Foundations* 7. 1257D; *Gnostikos* 11.

5 *will hand over.* Or 'ruin' according to the MS E.

6 *virtue is difficult to attain.* Cf. S190-Prov. 19: 5.

7 *winged with the virtues.* See *Eulogios* 2. 2. 1096B11.

8 *Exhortation* 2. 4–5. Elements of these two sentences are found also in *Praktikos* 61 and S377-Prov. 31: 21.

9 *impossible to conduct the warfare successfully without prudence.* Cf. *Praktikos* 89, 'The work of prudence is to lead in the war against the opposing powers and to defend the virtues and to draw the battle lines against the vices and to manage indifferent matters according to the circumstances.'

10 *the knowledge of God . . . progress to greater things.* This sentence is identical with *Gnostikos* 9, but note that Guillaumont there omits the phrase 'of God' based on the evidence of the versions.

THIRTY-THREE CHAPTERS

1 In a passage taken from his commentary on Psalm 4, Origen associates the same two biblical verses (Deut 32: 24, Lev. 26: 16). See *Philokalia* 26. 2. 38–42 (SC 226).

2 For an interpretation of this verse of Proverbs similar to the one found in 30 (15), 31 (16), and 33 (18) see S294-Prov. 30: 17.

MAXIMS 1–3

1 *Maxims* 1. 1. This text and many of those that follow are cited in John Damascene, *Sacra Parallela* (abbr. *SP*), PG 96. 141D2.

2 *Maxims* 1. 2. Sextus 152; Clitarchus 28; Pythagoras 7; *SP*, PG 95. 1205C6. References to the *Sentences* of Sextus, Clitarchus, and the Pythagoreans are cited from the edition of Henry Chadwick, *The Sentences of Sextus. A Contribution to the History of Early Christian Ethics* (Cambridge: Cambridge University Press, 1959).

3 *Maxims* 1. 4. Sextus 606.

4 *Maxims* 1. 5. Cf. Clitarchus 6, 'It is not the one who offers many sacrifices that is pious, but the one who commits no wrong.' The Evagrian version would appear to be more Christian.

5 *Maxims* 1. 6. Pythagoras 29; *SP*, PG 95. 1245D5–6.

6 *Maxims* 1. 7. *SP*, PG 96. 405C12.

7 *Maxims* 1. 8. *SP*, PG 95. 1357C10–11.

8 *Maxims* 1. 9. *SP*, PG 95. 1549A1.

9 *Maxims* 1. 10. Sextus 75a, 'It is a most terrible thing to be a slave to the passions'; cf. Pythagoras 21, 'It is more dangerous to be a slave to the passions than to tyrants.' Evagrius seems to have adapted both *Maxims* 1. 10 and 3. 6 to his own teaching, describing the passions as 'shameful' in the one case and 'of the flesh' in the other.

10 *Maxims* 1. 11. *SP*, PG 95. 1549A2.

11 *Maxims* 1. 12. Clitarchus 138.

12 *Maxims* 1. 15. Sextus 477. Here Evagrius has apparently added an explanatory gloss of his own.

13 *Maxims* 1. 17. Cf. Pythagoras 90, 'Wine strengthens the bond of the soul, the bones, that which is most proper to the body, but it is most inimical to the soul'; Sextus 413, 'Feed your soul with the divine word and your body with simple foods.' Here Evagrius has apparently combined two sentences into a single pithy expression.

14 *Maxims* 1. 18. *SP*, PG 95.1224B9.

15 *Maxims* 1. 19. Sextus 534.

16 *Maxims* 1. 20. Cf. Sextus 71a.

17 *Maxims* 1. Clitarchus 83.

18 *Maxims* 1. 22. Cf. Sextus 462 and Pythagoras 54, 'Accept not the outward appearance of the Cynic philosopher, but rather emulate his greatness of soul'; *SP* 4, PG 96. 429B1–2. Evagrius replaces the Cynic with a Christian, and greatness of soul with the attitude of the soul.

19 *Maxims* 1. 23. Cf. Sextus 194, 'To accuse a wise man and God is the equivalent sin'; *SP*, PG 96. 220B4 and 425A12. Here Evagrius alters the sentence in the direction of Christian charity.

20 *Maxims* 1. 24. Clitarchus 144c.

21 *Maxims* 2. 1. *SP*, PG 95. 1556C3–4.

22 *Maxims* 2. 2. Cf. Sextus 394, 577; *SP*, PG 95. 1305B1.

23 *Maxims* 2. 3. Cf. Pythagoras 34; Clitarchus 92; *SP*, PG 96. 405C13.

24 *Maxims* 2. 4. Cf. Clitarchus 61; *SP*, PG 96. 381C8.

25 *Maxims* 2. 5. *SP*, PG 96. 381C9.

26 *Maxims* 2. 6. Cf. Sextus 305 and Pythagoras 49, 'An evil demon is a guide to evil deeds'; *SP*, PG 95.1217B2. Evagrius alters this sentence in the direction of his teaching that the demons seek to move humans towards animal irrationality.

27 *Maxims* 2. 9. Cf. Sextus 46a, 'The intellect of the pious man is a holy temple of God.'

28 *Maxims* 2. 11. Cf. Sextus 171a; Clitarchus 44; *SP*, PG 95. 1205C7–8.

29 *Maxims* 2. 12. *SP*, PG 96. 405C14.

30 *Maxims* 2. 15. *SP*, PG 96. 289C2–3.

31 *chastity and gentleness of soul*. Chastity and gentleness are for Evagrius the primary virtues that characterize the impassibility of the concupiscible and irascible parts of the soul.

32 *Maxims* 2. 21. Sextus 141; Clitarchus 25.

33 *Maxims* 2. 24. Cf. Sextus 138; *SP*, PG 96. 421A6.

34 That is, charity begins with esteem for one's neighbour.

35 *Maxims* 3. 3. *SP*, PG 96. 381C8–9.

36 *Maxims* 3. 4. *SP*, PG 95. 1473D6–7.

37 *Maxims* 3. 5. *SP*, PG 95. 1400D4.

38 *Maxims* 3. 6. Cf. Sextus 75a; Pythagoras 21.

39 *Maxims* 3. 8. *SP*, PG 96. 228D2.

40 *Maxims* 3. 9. *SP*, PG 96. 89C5.

41 *Maxims* 3. 11. *SP*, PG 96. 381.C10–11.

42 *Maxims* 3. 12. *SP*, PG 96. 381C11–12.

43 *Jesus Christ is the tree of life*. In S32-Prov 3: 18, Evagrius identifies the 'tree of life' with the 'wisdom of God'. If Christ is the wisdom of God (1 Cor. 1: 24), it would then be only a small step to identify the 'tree of life' with Christ.

44 *Maxims* 3. 22. *SP*, PG 96. 405C14.

45 *Maxims* 3. 25. *SP*, PG 95. 1205C8–9.

46 *Maxims* 3. 26. *SP*, PG 95. 1093B5.

APPENDIX 1: VARIANT READINGS

SIGLA

A   Paris, Coislin 109 (11th cent.); SC 170. 129–35.

a   Vatican, Vaticanus gr. 703 (14th cent.); SC 170. 294–6.

B   Paris, Paris gr. 1056 (11th cent.); SC 170. 136–42.

b   Vatican, Barberinianus gr. 515 (AD 1244); SC 170. 290–3.

C   Paris, Paris gr. 1188 (11th cent.); SC 170. 142–52.

c   Paris, Coislin 123 (11th cent.); Robert Devreesse, *Bibliothèque Nationale, Département des manuscrits: Catalogue des manuscrits 2—Le fonds Coislin* (Paris: Imprimerie Nationale, 1945), 117–18.

D   Athos, Protaton 26 (10th cent.); SC 170. 166–75.

E   Athos, Lavra *Γ* 93 (Athous 333), 11th cent.; SC 170. 175–82.

e   El Escorial, MS Y. III. 4 (274), 13th cent.; SC 170. 301–2.

F   Athos, Panteleimon 635 (Athous 6142), 17th cent.; SC 170. 183–6.

G   Paris, Paris gr. 362 (14th cent.); SC 170. 187–94.

J   Athos, Vatopedi 57 (13th–14th cent.); SC 170. 218–26.

Ma   Venice, Marcianus gr. 131 (471), 11th cent; SC 438. 59.

O   Athos, Lavra M 54 (Athous 1745), 18th cent.; SC 170. 267–70.

St   Jerusalem, Stavrou 55 (AD 927); A. I. Papadopoulos-Kerameus, Ἱεροσολυμιτικὴ βιβλιοθήκη ἤτοι κατάλογος τῶν ἐν ταῖς βιβλιοθήκαις ὀρθοδόξου πατριαρχικοῦ θρόνου τῶν Ἱεροσολύμων καὶ πάσης Παλαιστίνης ἀποκειμένων ἑλληνικῶν κωδίκων, 5 vols. (St.-Petersburg, 1891–1915), 3. 109–11.

U   Amorgos, Chozobiotissis 10 (10th–11th cent.); SC 170. 153–8.

X   Jerusalem, Saba 157 (11th cent.); SC 170. 252–60.

Z   Sinai, Sinai gr. 462 (13th cent.); SC 170. 241–8.

Pg   *Patrologia Graeca*

Ph   *Philokalia*, i (Athens: Aster, 1974).

Column and line references are to the PG edition cited at the head of the entry, unless otherwise noted. Variant readings are provided below only for those instances that significantly affect the translation of the text.

1. FOUNDATIONS

Editions: Pg = PG 40. 1252–1264; Ph = *Philokalia* 1. 38–43.

MS Witnesses: E

E = Lavra Γ 93, fols. 240v–245v, *Title* τοῦ αὐτοῦ τὰ κατὰ μοναχοὺς αἴτια καὶ ἡ καθ᾽ ἡσυχίαν τούτων παράθεσις.

Testimonia: Ath = Pseudo-Athanasius, *Vitae monasticae institutio* (CPG 2265), PG 28. 845–9 (excerpts).

1253
B
1 τῆς αἰωνίου ζωῆς EPh: τῆς οὐρανίου ζωῆς Pg
C
1 ἡ πρᾶξις τερπνή EPh Ath: ἡ πρᾶξις στέρνη Pg
14 μὴ ὅλως πεισθῇς αὐτῷ EPh Ath: μὴ ὅλως προσθῇς αὐτῷ Pg
D
10 κἂν ἅλας post ἔχῃς add. EPh

1257
A
15 ὅπως δυνηθῇς EPh Ath: πῶς δυνηθῇς Pg
C
3 τοὺς οὖν ἰδιάζοντας EPh: τοὺς οὖν ἰδίους Pg
4 ἦχον αὐτῶν EPh Ath: εἶχον αὐτῶν Pg

1260
C
12 περισπαστικὸς EPg: περιστατικὸς Ph
D
8 κατ᾽ ἀκρίβειαν τοῖς περὶ E: κατ᾽ ἀκρίβειαν τῆς περὶ Ph; κατ᾽ ἀκρίβειαν ἢ τοῖς περὶ Pg
9 φιλοκερδίας ἐνεχθεὶς EPh: φιλοκερδίας ἐπενεχθεὶς Pg

1261
B
1 ἐπιμέλησαι deest in EPh
3 μὴ ἀσθενήσῃς EPh: μὴ ἀσθενήσας Pg

1264
A
4–5 οὕτω μὴ ἔστω σου λελυπημένος ὁ λογισμός EPh: οὕτως ἔστω σοι λελυμένος ὁ λογισμός Pg
7–9 τάχιον ἐπὶ τὴν εὐρωστίαν ἐπανελθὼν πάλιν om. EPh
10–11 ὅτι τῷ θεῷ . . . αἰῶνας. Ἀμήν. ending in EPg

2. EULOGIOS

See Appendix 2 for the text of Lavra Γ 93(E), fols. 295v–298r.

3. VICES

Editions: Pg = PG 79. 1140B–1144D.

MS Witnesses: EaMa
E = Athos, Lavra Γ 93, fols. 295v–298r, *Title* τοῦ αὐτοῦ [no further title]
a = Vat. gr. 703, fols. 176v–178r unedited section published by J. Muyldermans, 'Evagriana de la Vaticane', *Le Muséon* 54 (1941): 1–15, text on p. 5 Ma
= Venice, Marc. gr. 131 (471), fols. 24r–26r, *Title* τοῦ αὐτοῦ πρὸς τὸν αὐτὸν περὶ
τὰς ἀντιζύγους τῶν ἀρετῶν κακίας.

1140
B
4 ἀναβάλλομεν EMa
12 ἵνα διὰ μὲν τοῦ λαβεῖν εὐχαριστῶμεν τῷ δεδωκότι, διὰ δὲ τοῦ κατέχειν, μὴ
ἑαυτοῖς ἀποδιδόαμεν . . . EMa
C
1 τί καυχᾶσαι EMa

1141
A
12 λογοτρόφος λογισμῶν EMa
B
6 πορνείας σύμμυστος EMa
9 ἡδυφαγίας κημός EMa
C
4 ὀφθαλμῶν δέλος EMa
7 ἐννοίας ἐπίσκοπος, λογισμῶν περιτομή EMa
10 εὐχῆς γνώμη EMa
D
2 ἐναπόθετος λογιστεία EMa
11 εὔλυτος κόσμος EMa
14 ἀκηδίας σύμφυτος EMa

1144
B
7 μονίας βάρος Ma: μανίας βάρος Pg; deest in E
C
2 ὡρολόγιον πείνης EMa
10 ἐσχατιὰ προσηγορίας E, ἐσχάτη δὲ προσηγορίας Ma

12 κενοδοξίας PgMa: φιλοδοξίας μέση E
13–14 τρίσειρος ἄλυσις EMa
D
11 πολυπραγμοσύνης . . . καθαροποιεῖ τὴν καρδίαν add. E: deest in PgMa
11 πολυπραγμοσύνης φίλος post ἀλλοίωμα add. E
Muyldermans addition:
7 πολιορκία E: πολυορκία a
12 θεοπάρεσχος E: θεοπάροχος a

1144
D
13–15 Χριστὸς . . . Ἀμήν doxologia in Pg: deest in Ea

4. EIGHT THOUGHTS

Editions: PG 79. 1145A–1164D; J. Muyldermans, 'Une nouvelle recension du *De octo spiritibus malitiae* de s. Nil', *Le Muséon*, 52 (1939): 235–74 (variants and sections of the text unique to the long recension).

MS Witnesses: ACcEStMa (the long recension is represented by ACcESt)
A = Paris, Coislin 109, fols. 15r–23v, *Title* τοῦ αὐτοῦ Νείλου μοναχοῦ περὶ τῶν η′ λογισμῶν   C = Paris, Coislin 1188, fols. 228v–237r, *Title* τοῦ ὁσίου πατρὸς ἡμῶν Νίλου ἀσκητοῦ, περὶ λογισμῶν. εὐλόγησον   c = Paris, Coislin 123, fols. 349v–359r, *Title* τοῦ αὐτοῦ μακαρίου Νείλου περὶ τῶν ὀκτὼ λογισμῶν E = Athos, Lavra Γ 93, fols. 308r–315v, *Title* πρὸς τοὺς λογισμοὺς ὑποθῆκαι, E² in marg. περὶ τῶν η′ λογισμῶν παροιμίαι [the final folio of the last gathering is missing: the text ceases with the words . . . ταπεινὸς ἐκεῖνος (1164B9).]
St = Jerusalem, Stavrou 55, fols. 71v–85r, *Title* τοῦ αὐτοῦ Νείλου μοναχοῦ περὶ τῶν η′ λογισμῶν   Ma = Venice, Marc. gr. 131 (471), fol. 45vb–54va [A text], Ma² *Title* περὶ τῶν η′ λογισμῶν.

Versions:
Syriac: Syr = J. Muyldermans, *Evagriana Syriaca. Textes inédits du British Museum et de la Vaticane*, Bibliothèque du Muséon, 31 (Louvain: Publications Universitaires, 1952), 55–9. Muyldermans gives a series of examples where one group of Syriac manuscripts reports the long recension. Of the concluding section 8. 20–30, the Syriac gives only 8. 29–30. The translation has a tendency to abbreviate the text.

Latin: Lat = Muyldermans, ibid., 259–61. Muyldermans examined a group of Latin manuscripts that represent the long recension and reported selected passages. The Latin text, however, breaks off at 1164C1.

1145
A
7 καὶ ὕλη γαστριμαργίας CcESt: ὕλη δὲ γαστρὸς AMa

B

5 ἐν προσευχαῖς CcESt

C

9 χαίρει ESt

9 ἀριθμεῖ: χαίρει ESt

1148

A

10 γαστὴρ δὲ κορεννυμένη ESt: γαστὴρ δὲ ῥηγνυμένη ACcMa

B

13 ἀτονοῦν καὶ ὀδυρόμενον ESt [E ὀδυρώμενον] ἀτονίαν ἐποδυρόμενον AcMa [c ὀδυρόμενον]; ἀτονίαν ἐποδυρόμενον Pg

13–14 μὴ ἐλεήσῃς ... βρωμάτων om. C

C

4 καταβάλῃ AcESt: καταβάλλῃ Ma; καταβάλλει C; καταβαλεῖ Pg

5 ἐπιβάτην ACcESt

10 titulus: περὶ πορνείας: περὶ σωφροσύνης C

D

4–5 ὁ πολεμῶν πνεύματι [A πνεῦμα; C πνεύμασι] πορνείας οὐ παραλήψεται [A παραλείψεται] κόρον εἰς συμμαχίαν [c κόρον ἐπιθυμίας] ACcESt

1149

A

5 συντυχίας ACcEMaSt

D

2 ὠδινούσας ὄλεθρον AcEMaSt: ὀδινούσας ὄλεθρον Pg; ἀπηλούσας ὄλεθρον C

1152

A

6 καὶ ἡ φαντασία αὐτῆς μὴ κινήσῃ τὸ πάθος post ἀπαθῶς add. ACcESt

7–8 τὰ βέλη...ἀρετῆς: τὰ μέλη αὐτῆς δυνηθῇς ψυχῆς ἐφαρμόσαι [Cc -ώσαι] δυνάμεσι, τότε ἐν ἕξει πέπεισο εἶναι τῆς ἀρετῆς ECc; τὰ μέλη αὐτῆς μορφῶσαι μὴ δυνηθείη, τότε ἐν ἕξει πεπεῖσθαι εἶναί σε τῆς ἀρετῆς St; τὰ μέλη αὐτῆς ἡδονὴν ταῖς τῆς ψυχῆς ἐφαρμώσει δυνάμει, τότε ἐν ἕξει πέπεισο · εἰ ἐνχρονήσεις τοῖς τοιούτοις λογισμοῖς A. See Muyldermans, 253–4

14 καίει καὶ AEMaSt: καίει αὐτὸν καὶ C; καὶ solum Pg

B

1 μηδὲ ἐπὶ πολὺ...ἡδονῆς φλόγα: μηδὲ ἐπὶ πολὺ προσομιλήσῃς, ἵνα μὴ ἀνάψῃ ἐν σοὶ ἡδονῆς φλόγα A; μὴ δῷς σὴν διάνοιαν φαντασίᾳ [St -ίαις] γυναικός, μηδὲ προσομιλήσῃς ἐπὶ πολύ τῷ φανέντι προσώπῳ, ἵνα μὴ ἀνάψῃ ἐν σοὶ ἡδονῆς φλόγα CcSt; μὴ δὸς οὖν σὴν διάνοιαν φαντασίᾳ γυναικός, ἵνα μὴ ἀναστῇ ἐν σοὶ φλὸξ ἡδονῆς E

10–11 ἐὰν ἐκκόψῃς κλάδον [E -ους; c κλάδον ἕνα], ἄλλον [E -ους; c -ος] εὐθὺς [St εὐθέως] ἀναδίδωσι post πάθη add. AECcSt

11 ἀφίησι ACcESt

C

3 βασανίζεται: βαπτίζεται ACcEMaSt

D

9 πραγμάτων: κτημάτων ACcESt

1153

B

4 μοναχὸς om. CESt

C

2 γνῶσιν: αὐτὸ C, αὐτὴν c, om. ESt

3 ποιεῖ: κινεῖ AcESt

6–7 μοναχὸς ὀργίλος, σύαγρος ἐρημικός, εἶδέ τινας [EMa εἶδέ τινα] ACcEMaSt

12 γαληνιῶσα ACcEMaSt

14 γαληνιώσῃ θαλάσσῃ AMaPg: γαληνιώσης θαλάσσης CE;   ἐν θαλάσσῃ γαληνιώσῃ c; ἐν γαληνιώσῃ θαλάσσῃ St

14 ἐγκολυμβῶσι: ἐγκυβιστῶσι ACcEMaSt

D

4 ὕδωρ καθαρόν, κᾶν ἐπιδώσει AcSt

7 ὀρθὰ om. ACcEMaSt

1156

A

3 κατασκηνοῦσιν AcSt: κατασκηνώσουσιν CE; κατοικοῦσιν Pg

B

1 περιραντηρίῳ [E -ρρ-] βωμῷ ACcESt

7–8 οὐκ οἶδε πνευματικὴν ἡδονὴν λυπούμενος μοναχός om. ACcESt

8 δὲ om. ACcESt

C

8 χαρὰν: ἡδονὴν ACcEMaSt

8 ὡς om. CcESt

D

4 σαρκικῆς om. CESt

8–9 ἀφροσύνης: ἡδονῆς ACcESt

1157

A

5 διέβη ESt: διέδυ ACcPg; ἔδυ Ma

5 πολεμίων ACcESt

7 κρατήσας ACcESt

C

3 θεωρίας φῶς ACcESt

4 ὁ ἀγαπῶν τὸν κύριον ἀλυπος ἔσται· ἡ γὰρ τελεία ἀγάπη ἔξω βάλλει τὴν λύπην post ψυχή add. A

D

8 ῥεῦμα: πνεῦμα ACcEMaSt

9 ἐκ τῆς ἰδίας κέλλης E: ἐκ τοῦ κελλίου αὐτοῦ A; ἐκ τῆς οἰκίας αὐτοῦ Pg; ἐκ τοῦ

οἴκου αὐτοῦ cMa; ἐκ τοῦ ἰδίου οἴκου St; ἐκ τοῦ τόπου αὐτοῦ C
14 φυτὸν ἀσθενὲς AcEMaSt: φύλλον ἀσθενὲς C; φυτὸν ἀδρανὲς Pg
16 πνεύματος ACcEMaSt

1160

A
4 καρποφορήσει ACcESt
6 καὶ ἀκηδιαστὴς μοναχὸς ἐν ἔργῳ ἑνί PgA: καὶ ὁ ἀκηδιαστὴς μοναχὸς ἔργῳ ἑνί c; καὶ ἀκηδιαστὴς μοναχὸς οὐ στοιχήσει ἔργῳ ἑνί ESt; καὶ ἀκηδιαστὴς οὐ στοιχήσει ἐν ἔργῳ C
6–8 φιληδόνῳ . . . κέλλα om. CcESt
9 ταῖς θύραις CcESt Syr: ταῖς θυρίσιν AMa
B
3 ἕως ἂν ναρκήσῃ ACcEMaSt
11 ψέγει . . . κόσμησιν AMa: om. CcESt Syr
14 τὰ [om. c] ἑαυτῆς φροντίζειν [C φροντίζει] ACcESt
C
2 ἐπιμελῶς om. CcESt
6 καὶ φόβου θεοῦ om. CcESt; A καὶ φόφου θεοῦ καὶ ὑπομονῆς
8–9 συνεχῶς καὶ συντόνως EA: συνεχῶς καὶ συντόμως St; συνεχῶς καὶ εὐτόνως Ma; σπουδαίως καὶ συντόνως C; συνεχῶς c
13–D3 συγκέχυται . . . φαιδρότερον hab. hic Ma: transp. ad cc. 17 et 19 ACcESt
D
7 ταχέως CESt: εὐχερῶς AMa; ῥαδίως c

1161

A
5 μέλισσαν μιμεῖται μοναχὸς πανοῦργος· ἔξωθεν [C ἢ ἔξωθεν; AC add. μὲν] φέρει τὰ ἄνθη, καὶ ἔσωθεν [C ἔσω] κηρίον ἐργάζεται post μοναχὸς συνετός add. ACcESt Syr Lat, cf. Muyldermans, 249
11 ὁδὸν νόμιζε τὸν παρόντα βίον, πειρατῶν [C παρατῶν; c ληστῶν; St πηρατῶν] πεπληρωμένην [A πληρωμένην; C πεπληρωμένον; c πεληρωμένων] καὶ πόλιν εὔνομον [om. C] τὸν μέλλοντα αἰῶνα. μὴ οὖν [om. ACc] κομπάσῃς ἐν τῇ ὁδῷ [St add. ταύτῃ σεαυτόν], ἀπειρόκαλον [Ec ἀπειροκάλων] γὰρ [om. A] τοῦτο καὶ τοὺς ἐπιβούλους ἐρεθίζει [E ἐρεθίζων; C ἐρεθίζον] ῥαδίως· ἐὰν δὲ [A οὖν] φθάσῃς εἰς τὴν πόλιν εἰσελθεῖν [St εἰσελθεῖν εἰς τὴν πόλιν], πάντων τῶν ἀγαθῶν [ECc om. τῶν ἀγαθῶν] ἀπολαύσεις [ACSt -ης] ἀκινδύνως λοιπόν [CSt om. λοιπόν], καὶ οὐδεὶς τοὺς σοὺς διαρπάσει [A διαρπάσῃ; C καρπώσηται] [τοὺς σοὺς διαρπάσει: St σου ἁρπάσει] πόνους post χρήσῃ σοῖς add. ACcESt, Syr (7. 14), Lat (7. 14–15), cf. Muyldermans, 249–50

1 συγχεῖται γραμμὴ ταραχθεῖσα [ACSt χαραχθεῖσα; c μὴ συμπαραχθεῖσα] καθ' ὕδατος, καὶ ἀρετῆς πόνος [c -οι] ἐν κενοδόξου [ACcSt -ῳ] ψυχῇ. ἐν [om. c] νυκτὶ ἤσθιε[AcSt ἔσθιε] κρέα τοῦ πάσχα [A κρέας τοῦ πάσχα; E τοῦ πάσχα κρέα], καὶ μὴ δημοσιεύσῃς [c add. σου] λανθάνουσαν ἐγκράτειαν, μηδὲ [C μὴ] ἐπιδείξῃς [Ec

ἐπιδείξῃ] ταύτην [ESt αὐτὴν] ὡς ἐν [A om.; St ἐπὶ] φωτὶ μάρτυσι πολλοῖς· ἵνα [ἵνα: C ἔστι γὰρ] ὁ βλέπων ἐν τῷ κρυπτῷ πατὴρ ἀποδώσῃ [ACcSt -ει] σοι τὸν μισθὸν φανερῶς [AcSt ἐν τῷ φανερῷ τὸν μισθόν]. λευκὴ γέγονε [St γίνεται] χεὶρ καλυπτομένη ἐν κόλπῳ [ἐν κόλπῳ om. C] καὶ κρυπτομένη πρᾶξις φωτὸς ἐκλάμπει φαιδρότερον [C λαμπρότερα] post θεοῦ add. ACcESt, Lat (7. 18)

9 δι' εὐτελῆ εὐφημίαν CcEMaSt: δι' εὐφημίαν εὐτελῆ A; δι' εὐφημίαν Pg
C
4–5 ὑπερηφανίας παρουσίαν εὐαγγελίζεται κενοδοξία [c -ος] CcESt
6 λίθος ἀπορραγεὶς [c ἀποραγὴς] ὄρους [E ἀπ' ὄρους; St ἀπὸ ὄρους] συντόμῳ ῥύμῃ καταφέρεται [C φέρεται; St κατέρχεται], καὶ [C add. ὁ] ἀποστὰς θεοῦ [ESt ἀπὸ θεοῦ] πίπτει ταχέως [Ec ταχέως πίπτει] post καταβάλλει add. ACcESt Syr, Lat, cf. Muyldermans, 251
13 χρησιμεύσει ACcEMaSt
D
6 μεθ' ἡμέραν ACcEMaSt

1164
A
5 τί φυσᾶσαι legendum: τῇ φύσει Pg: τί φυσιοῦσαι Ac²E; τί φυσάσαι cSt, τί φυσῇ C
11 ἔχεις καλόν ACcEMaSt
12 ἐναμβρύνῃ ACEMaSt: ἐναμβρύνει c; ἐναμβλύνῃ Pg
B
3 συνήργησεν ACcESt
5 ἄνθρωπος εἶ, μεῖνον ἐν τοῖς ὅροις τῆς φύσεως [E ἐντὸς τῆς φύσεως] post βέβαιος add. ACcESt, Lat, cf. Muyldermans, 251
6 αὐτῆς σοι CESt: αὐτῆς σου A; αὐτῆς Pg
6 δι' ἀλαζονείαν ACcEMaSt
9 κἂν ταπεινὸς ACcE, Lat
1164B9 ... ταπεινὸς ἐκεῖνος hic desinit E
9 σὺ μετέωρος ACSt, Lat: σὺ δὲ μετέωρος c; deest in E; σύμμετρος Pg
C
1 ... συντριβήσεται. hic desinit Lat, cf. Muyldermans, 261
1 σαθρὸν [C σαθρῶν] ὄχημα [A σαθρὰ κλίμαξ] [Ac add. ἢ] ὑπερηφανία καὶ ὁ ἐπιβαίνων αὐτῇ ταχέως ἔκδιφρος γίνεται [C πεσεῖται]· ὁ δὲ ταπεινὸς βέβαιος ἔστηκεν διὰ παντός, καὶ οὐ μὴ σαλεύσῃ αὐτὸν ποτὲ [om. C] πούς ὑπερηφανίας [C -είας; St ὑπερήφανος] post συντριβήσεται add. ACcSt, cf. Muyldermans, 251
6 post ὑπερηφάνου add. μετὰ θάνατον ACcSt
10 λίθος τίμιος ἐμπρέπει [C εὐπρεπῆ] σιαλώματι χρυσίου [σιαλώματι χρυσίου: c μετὰ χρυσίου; St στεφάνῳ χρύσῳ], καὶ πολλαῖς ἀρεταῖς ἐμφαιδρύνεται [C ἐνδέδεται] ταπείνωσις ἀνδρός post ὑπερηφάνου transp. ACcSt
10 στεφάνη δώματός ACcMaSt
15 Capita nonnulla a Muyldermans edita (251–2) hab. ACcSt post ταπείνωσις ἀνδρὸς [St post κινδυνεύει]

The line numbers below are those of Muyldermans' edition.

1 πολλάκις· ἄζυμον ACc: πολλάκις· ἄζυμα St
1 τις om. CcSt
3–4 τὸν μὲν ὑπερήφανον ACcSt
7 καθέξει cSt: καθέξῃ C; καθέξεται A; καθέζεται Muyld.
10 ἐκλύων τῇ συμπαθείᾳ Muyld.: ἐκλύων τῇ συνηθείᾳ C; ἐκλύων τῇ συμπνοίᾳ c; ἐκλύων τῆς συμπαθείας St
12 καὶ παιδείᾳ ἐμπρακτικῷ στηρίζει βίον ἀνδρὸς post χρησίμη· καὶ add. C
12 καὶ παιδεία ἐν πρακτικῷ βίον εὐθύνει [c εὐθύνει βίον] ἀνδρός· ῥάβδος ἀπορριφεῖσα [c ριφεῖσα] γέγονεν ὄφις post χρησίμη· καὶ add. cSt
13–14 μὴ φοβήσῃ σε ἐπὶ γῆς [C πηγῆς] ἰλυσπώμενος ὄφις CcSt
16 λυθήσεται A: αὖθις [om. c] ἔσται παιδεία CcSt
20 δάκνει CcSt
21 πλήσσει σφοδρῶς om. CcSt
21 δηχθέντος ἵππου ὑπὸ ὄφεως, ὁ ἱππεὺς πίπτει εἰς τὰ ὀπίσω, καὶ νοῦς φιληδόνου κλίνει εἰς κακίαν, δραξαμένου τοῦ πάθους. ὁ κλάσαντος ἵππου πεσὼν εἰς τὰ ὀπίσω ὁ ἐπιβάτης τὴν σωτηρίαν περιμένει ὑπὸ κυρίου, καὶ νοῦ ἀποπεσόντος, βοήθειαν ἐπικαλεῖται θεοῦ. χειρῶν ἔκτασις ἐτρόπωσεν τὸν ἀναλκῆ, καὶ πράξεις ἄνω προσεκτεινόμεναι ἐν ἀληθείᾳ νεκροῦσι τὰ πάθη. post ἅπτεται πάθους add. St
24 ὁμοίως καὶ ἀτιμία λυπεῖ C; καὶ ἀτιμία λυπεῖ cSt
24 καὶ ἀτιμία λυπεῖ μὲν τὸν κενόδοξον, παύει δὲ πάθη χαλεπά· κενοδοξίας ἐπιτυχία ὑπερηφανίαν γεννᾷ. κενοδοξίαν καὶ ὑπερηφανίαν ἐμίσησεν κύριος. λίθος τίμιος ἐμπρέπει σιαλώματι χρυσίου, καὶ πολλαῖς ἀρεταῖς φαιδρύνεται ταπείνωσις ἀνδρός. τοὺς δὲ ταπεινοὺς ἀνεγείρει ἐν δόξῃ. post τραύματος hab. St
St² add. hic in marg.   λίθος τίμιος ἐμπρέπει σιαλώματι χρυσίου, καὶ πολλαῖς ἀρεταῖς ἐμφαιδρύνεται ταπείνωσις ἀνδρός.

6. MONKS

Editions: H. Gressmann, 'Nonnenspiegel und Mönchsspiegel des Euagrios Pontikos', Texte und Untersuchungen, 39 (1913), 153–65.

MS Witnesses: AabCDE

A = Paris, Coislin 109, fols. 185r–189r, Title πρὸς τοὺς ἐν κοινοβίοις ἢ συνοδίαις μοναχοῖς   a = Vatican City, Vat. gr. 703 [Gressmann B], Title συμβουλείαι εἰς μοναχοὺς τοὺς θέλοντας σωθῆναι καταμόνας καὶ ἐν κοινοβίῳ   b = Vatican City, Barb. gr. 515, fols. 50v–57r [Gressmann A], Title Εὐαγρίου μοναχοῦ κεφάλαια διάφορα ψυχωφελῆ   C = Paris, Coislin 1188, fols. 125v–130v, Title τοῦ αὐτοῦ πρὸς τοὺς ἐν τοῖς κοινοβίοις ἢ ἐν συνοδίαις ἀδελφοῖς (sic); D = Athos, Protaton 26, fols. 13v–21r [Gressmann C], Title τοῦ αὐτοῦ πρὸς τοὺς ἐν κοινοβίοις ἢ ἐν συνοδίαις μοναχούς   E = Athos, Lavra Γ 93, fols. 235v–240v, Title τοῦ αὐτοῦ πρὸς τοὺς ἐν κοινοβίοις ἢ ἐν συνοδίαις μοναχούς.

Versions:

Latin: L = Jean Leclercq, 'L'ancienne version latine des Sentences d'Évagre pour les Moines', *Scriptorium*, 5 (1951), 195–213 *l* = Holstenius, PL 20. 1181–6/PG 40. 1277–82

Syriac: Syr = Vatican City, Vat. syr. 126, fols. 236v–238v

Note: For the variants of a b D and Syr, I have relied on the apparatus in the edition of Gressmann.

22 ἀφίπταται aDEF: ἀφίσταται Syr
25 μοναχὸς om. aDEF
39 ἐπὶ τῆς γῆς post παρὰ μοναχοῖς add. C, Ll, Syr
55 ἐν καιρῷ πάλιν ἐπωφελεῖ: L *in tempore luctum utilem, in tempore tristitiae l*; πάλιν: πλὴν C; ἐπωφελεῖ: ἐπωφελῆ AaF. I follow the reading ἐν καιρῷ πάλην ἐπωφελῆ according to the argument of Martin Mühmelt, 'Zu der neuen lateinischen Übersetzung des Mönchsspiegels des Euagrius', *Vigiliae Christianae*, 8 (1954), 101–3
112 θρόνου: χρόνου C, Ll
115 πνεύματος: μέλιτος ACDEF², Ll, Syr

VIRGIN

Editions: H. Gressmann, 'Nonnenspiegel und Mönchsspiegel des Euagrios Pontikos', *Texte und Untersuchungen*, 39 (1913), 146–51.

MS Witnesses: b

b = Vatican City, Barb. gr. 515, fols. 65v–68r [Gressmann A], *Title* παραίνεσις πρὸς παρθένον.

Versions

Latin: L = D. A. Wilmart, 'Les versions latines des Sentence d'Évagre pour les Vierges', *Revue Bénédictine*, 28 (1911), 143–53 (text 148–50) *l* = PL 20. 1185–8 = PG 40.1283–6.

Syriac: W. Frankenberg, *Euagrius Ponticus*, Abhandlungen der königlichen Gesellschaft der Wissenschaften zu Göttingen, Philolologisch-historische Klasse, new series, 13. 2 (Berlin: Weidmannsche Buchhandlung, 1912), 562–4

20a. Quae curat iunctum sibi opus cum diligentia inveniet mercedem magnam; quae autem neglegit neglegetur. L
54. Deus fundavit caelum et terram et providentiam habet omnium et condelectabitur in eis. Non est angelus incapax malitiae, et non est daemon natura malus; utrosque enim fecit sui arbitrii Deus. Sicut homo ex corpore corruptibili et anima constitit rationali, sic et Dominus noster natus est absque peccato, manducans vere manducabat et cum crucifigeretur vere crucifigebatur, et non erat

fantasma mendax in oculis hominum. Erit certa resurrectio mortuorum et mundus iste transibit et nos recipiemus spiritalia corpora. post μεταπείσῃ σε add. L
56. τῆς προσκυνητῆς καὶ ὁμοουσίου τριάδος bL*l*

8. PRAYER

Editions: Pg = PG 79. 1165–1200; Ph = *Philokalia* i. 176–89; M = J. Muyldermans, *Evagriana Syriaca*. *Textes inédits du British Museum et de la Vaticane*, Bibliothèque du Muséon, 31 (Louvain: Publications Universitaires, 1952), 39–46 (partial edition of the prologue according to Coislin 109 together with collations of other Paris manuscripts; cited below with the siglum M plus his letter-designation of the manuscript, e.g. M-B for Muyldermans' citation of a variant from Paris gr. 1140).

MS Witnesses: AcJMaStUZ
A = Paris, Coislin 109, fols. 126v–136r; c = Paris, Coislin 123, fols. 340r–349v; J = Athos, Vatopedi 57, fols. 133r–140v; Ma = Venice, Marc. gr. 131 (471), fols. 57v–68r; St = Jerusalem, Stavrou 55, fols. 56r–71v; U = Amorgos, Chozobiotissis 10, pp. 441–66; Z = Sinai, Sinai gr. 462, fols. 305r–310r.

Versions:
Syriac/Arabic: Syr/Ar = I. Hausherr, 'Le 'De oratione' d'Évagre le Pontique en syriaque et en arabe', *Orientalia Christiana Periodica*, 5 (1939), 7–71.

Prologue: Pg Ph A J St M(uyldermans)
Chapters: Pg Ph A c J Ma St U Z; Syr Ar

Variants are cited below in the following manner. The translation is based primarily on the Ph edition and so this is cited first, followed by variants separated by commas; sets of variants within a chapter are then separated by semicolons. In the translation, when the Ph text has proved to be deficient, I have followed for the most part the text of the manuscript family represented by A and St.

Prologue

References are to the line numbers of the *Philokalia*.

1–4 (Title) τοῦ ὁσίου πατρὸς ἡμῶν Νείλου ἀσκητοῦ πρόλογος τῶν περὶ προσευχῆς ἑκατὸν πεντήκοντα τριῶν κεφαλαίων Ph, τοῦ αὐτοῦ περὶ προσευχῆς λόγος εἰς ρνγ' κεφάλαια διειλημμένος, προοίμιον Pg, περὶ προσευχῆς προθεωρία A, τοῦ ἁγίου Νείλου, πρόλογος τῶν περὶ προσευχῆς ρνγ' κεφαλαίων πρὸς τὸν Εὐλόγιον J; Νείλου μοναχοῦ πρόλογος περὶ προσευχῆς ρνγ' κεφαλαίων St
15 ἐξαποστείλας Ph, ἀπέστειλα Pg, ἐξαπέστειλα AJSt
16–17 πεποιηκώς Ph, πεπληρωκώς PgAJSt
19 ὑπὸ χειρῶν PhPg, προχείρων AJSt
21 ὧν (ἴσως ἐν) Ph, ἐν PgAJSt

39–40 Legendum: ἀλλ' εἰ δὲ διὰ τῆς πληθύος τῶν ἀριθμῶν κομίζῃ τὸν ἑκατοστὸν πεντηκοστὸν τρίτον ... νόει
39 ἄλλως, εἰ δὲ PhPg M-AB, ἀλλ' εἰ δὲ A, ἀλλ' ἴδε J M-C, ἀλλ' εἰ δεῖ St
39 διὰ τῆς πληθύος, τὸν ἀριθμὸν PhJ, διὰ τῆς πληθύος τῶν ἀριθμῶν Pg M-ABC St, διὰ τῆς τῶν ἀριθῶν πληθύος A
39 κομίζειν PhSt, κομίζῃ PgA M-C, κομίζει J M-AB
39–40 τῶν ἑκατὸν πεντήκοντα τριῶν Ph, τῶν ἑκατὸν πεντήκοντα καὶ τριῶν M-AB, τὸν ἑκατοστὸν πεντηκοστὸν τρίτον A² M-C St; τὸν ἑκατοστὸν τρίτον PgA; τὸν ρνγ' J
40 νόει PhAJ M-C St, νοεῖν προσήκει Pg M-AB

Chapters

References for the variants given below follow the chapter numbers of the *Philokalia*. However, to avoid confusion, I have accepted the common practice of treating *Philokalia* c. 35 as c. 34a and *Philokalia* c. 77 as cc. 76–7, with the remaining chapters numbered sequentially. This was the numbering standarized by I. Hausherr, *Les leçons d'un contemplatif. Le Traité de l'Oraison d'Évagre le Pontique* (Paris: Beauchesne, 1960).

2 ἐντολῶν PhAcStZ, ἀρετῶν PgJMaUSyr
5 ἵνα...μαλάξῃς PgPhcJMaU, ἵνα δυνηθεὶς...μαλάξαι A, ἵνα δυνηθῆς...μαλάξαι StZSyr
6 πρὸς PgPhA²J²Ma, πρὸ AcJStUZ; προσευχομένου Ph, προσευχὴν δεχόμενος PgAcJMaStUZ
7 ἐὰν PhPg, κἂν AcJMaStUZ
8 ἐξετράπησαν PhAcJStZ, ἐξεπλάγησαν PgUSyr, ἐξέστησαν Ma
10 ἵνα κινηθεὶς Ph, ἵνα χαυνωθεὶς PgAJMaStUZ, ἵνα χαυνωθῆς c
12 ἢ post ἀντιλογία add. PgAcJMaStUZ; ἐξ ἐναντίας Ph, δι' ἐναντίας PgAcJMaStUZ; ἅμα Ph, ἄμυναν PgAStU, εἰς ἄμυναν A²J, ἄμυνα Ma, ἀμύνοντα cZ; τινα ἄσημον ῥῆξαι φωνήν PhJZ, τινὰ ἄσημον ῥῆξαι λόγον AcSt, ῥῆξαι φωνήν τινα Pg, τινὰ ῥῆξαι φωνήν MaU
34 μὴ ὀδυνῶ μὴ κομιζόμενος PhSt², μὴ ἐν δυνάμει κομιζόμενος AcMaStUZ, μὴ ἐνδύαζε μὴ κομιζόμενος A²J(Ar?)
34a ins. hic PhAcStZAr, om. PgJMa, ins. post c. 125 U
40 παρατάσει PhAcJSt, παραστάσει PgJ²MaUZAr
41 ἔθει PgPhZ, ἤθει A²cJMaStU, ἤθη A
42 αἴσθησις PhcJStZ, ἦθος PgAMaUAr
44 οἰκεῖα πάθη AStZ
47 τῇ τοῦ δικαίου προσευχῇ Ph, τῇ τοῦ σπουδαίου προσευχῇ AcJStZ, τὴν τοῦ σπουδαίου προσευχὴν PgMaU
50 post κινεῖσθαι hab. καὶ τὸν θεοῦ λόγον ἐπιζητεῖν PgAcMaSt, deest in Phc, καὶ τὸν θεὸν λόγον ἐπιζητεῖν JZ, καὶ τὸν θεὸν ἐπιζητεῖν U
51 οὐσιώσαντα λόγον Ph, οὐσιώσαντα κύριον Pg, οὐσιώδη λόγον AcStZ, οὐσιώσαντα θεόν JMaU

52 ante νοῦν add. καὶ πνευματικὸν PgAcJMaStUZ
63 κύριος Ph, θεὸς PgAJMaStUZ; ὢν βούλεται PhAcJStZ, ὡς βούλεται PgMaU
64 μέμψεως Ph, παραπληξίας PgAcJMaStUZ
68 τὴν μνήμην κινῆσαι PgPhcMaU, κινῆσαι τὸν νοῦν τῇ μνήμῃ A, τῇ μνήμῃ κινῆσαι τὸν νοῦν JStZ
69 τὴν αἴτησιν πληρῶσαι καὶ στῆναι Ph, καὶ στῆναι AcJZ, στῆναι PgU, καὶ στῆθι Ma⁽²?⁾St
71 καὶ οὐχ ἕξει στᾶσιν ἀκλόνητον Phc, καὶ οὐχ ἕξει στᾶσιν ἄκλονον AJStZ, καὶ οὐκ ἐξίσταται ἄκλονος MaU
72 ἔφρασε γνωστικὸς ἀνὴρ PhJ, ἔφρασεν ὁ γνωστικὸς ἀνὴρ MaU, ἔφρασε θαυμαστὸς καὶ γνωστικὸς ἀνήρ, ἔφρασε πρακτικὸς ἀνὴρ AcStZ; καὶ ἐν ταῖς φλεψὶ πάλλοντος AJMaStU, deest in Phc, καὶ ἐν ταῖς βλεψὶν βάλλοντος Z
84 ἤτοι (ἡ add. J) κρείττων καὶ εἰλικρινὴς χρῆσις αὐτοῦ PhJMaUZ, ἤτοι ἡ κρείττον (-ων J²) καὶ εἰλικρινὴς ἐνέργεια αὐτοῦ καὶ χρῆσις AJ²St, ἤτοι ἡ κρείττων καὶ εἰλικρινὴς ἐνέργεια καὶ χρῆσις αὐτοῦ c
85 ποικίλης² PgPhJMaUZ, ἀποικίλου Ac, [α]ποικίλου ut vid. St
94 σοῦ ἐμπείρως (ἐμπύρως cSt) τῇ βακτηρίᾳ τῆς πρὸς θεὸν ἐντεύξεως κεχρημένου AcSt(Ar?)
99 ἢ ὡς θῆρες ἀδικεῖν τὴν σάρκα σου PgAcJSt, deest in PhMaUZ
111 post ἴσχυσαν hab. κἂν πρὸς βραχὺ AcJSt
112 ἔννοιαν PhMa, πρόνοιαν PgAcJStUZ
113 ἀληθοῦς PgAcJMaStUZ, deest in Ph
114 σχῆμα ἢ χρῶμα AcJSt, deest in PgPhMaUZ
115 φρενήρης PhAcJMaStUZ, φρενιτικὸς Pg
117 νεωτέροις PgPhAc(-ος)JMaStUZ, ἐν ἑτέροις A²Ar
121 c. 121 post c. 122 transp. Ph
123 c. 123 ante c. 122 transp. PhMaZ
128 μηδὲν ἀνιμήσῃ PgPhMaUZ, μηδένα μίσει cJSt, μηδένα μήσει A (A² corr. μίσει), μηδένα μίσῃ U²; ἀπὸ σαρκὸς om. AcJStU
129 πιστεύων αὐτῷ PhPgMaZ, ἐμπιστεύων αὐτῷ AcJStU
137 τί εἰς τὸν πλησίον ἄτοπον AcSt
138 ἐπαχθείσας ἐκδέχου PhPg, ἐπαχθείας ἐκδέχου, ἐπαχθίσας ἐκδέχου Z, Ma ἐπαχθεὶς ἀεὶ προσδέχου AcSt, ἀεὶ (add. supra J²) ἐπαχθεὶς ἐκδέχου J
139 δυσπράττων PhMaZ, δυσπραγῶν PgAcJStU
149 οὐ καί τι ἄλλο ἔπεται Ph, εἰ καὶ τί ἄλλο παρέπεται (MaUZ ἔπεται) AMaUZ, εἰ καί τι ἄλλο μᾶλλον ἔπεται St, idem fort. sub ras. in J, εἰ κέ τι μᾶλλον ἄλλο ἔπεται c
150 θειοτέρα PgPhMaUZ, ἀνωτέρα AcJStAr

9. REFLECTIONS

Editions: J. Muyldermans, 'Note additionnelle à *Evagriana*', *Le Muséon*, 44 (1931), 369–83; repr. in *Evagriana, Extrait de la revue Le Muséon 44, augmenté de: Nouveaux fragments grecs inédits* (Paris: Paul Geuthner, 1931), 33–47.

MS Witnesses: M-A, M-B, eEMaU
M-A = ed. Muyldermans, Codex A: Paris gr. 913, *Title* τοῦ ὁσίου πατρὸς ἡμῶν Νείλου σκέμματα   M-B = ed. Muyldermans, Codex B: Paris gr. 3098, *Title* τοῦ αὐτοῦ κεφάλαια ξβ′   e = El Escorial, MS Y. III. 4: variants in J. Muyldermans, *Evagriana Syriaca. Textes inédits du British Museum et de la Vaticane*, Bibliothèque du Muséon 31, (Louvain: Publications Universitaires), 1952, pp. 34–8, *Title* Εὐαγρίου περὶ διαφόρων λογισμῶν   E = Athos, Lavra Γ 93, fols. 298v–301v, *Title* τοῦ αὐτοῦ Εὐαγρίου μοναχοῦ, σκέμματα   Ma = Venice, Marc. gr. 131 (471), fols. 26v–30r, *Title* – none; U = Amorgos, Chozobiotissis 10, fols. 383v–387v (nos. 24–49) [second half only; the order of the chapters is 40–4, 55, 45–6, S1, 51, 57, 55, 47–8, 50, 52–4, 58–62, S2–3.], *Title* τοῦ αὐτοῦ κεφάλαια διάφορα περὶ λογισμῶν.

Versions
Syriac: Syr = W. Frankenberg, *Euagrius Ponticus*, 422–71; S1–2 in J. Muyldermans, *Evagriana Syriaca*, 37–8.

Testimonia: Pal = Gregory Palamas, *To Xene on the Passions and the Virtues*, PG 150. 1081B4–14.

2. 4–5 θεοῦ γὰρ χρεία τοῦ ἐνεργοῦντος καὶ ἀναπνέοντος E: τοῦ συνεργοῦντος καὶ ἐμπνέοντος M-B; συνεργοῦντος καὶ ἀναπνέοντος Pal; συνεργοῦντος τοῦ ἀναπνέοντος M-AC, Ma
6. 1 καθαρὸς M-A²B, EMa
18. 3 E εἴπερ
22. 1 εἰς νόημα M-B, EMa, Syr
22. 2 εἰς θεώρημα [M-B θεωρίαν], καὶ πάλιν ἀπὸ νοήματος εἰς θεώρημα, καὶ ἀπὸ θεωρήματος ἐπὶ νόημα M-B, EMa, Syr
23. 6 ταύτην M-B, EMa
23. 7 αὐτῷ τοῦ φωτός M-A, Ma (cf. *Thoughts* 40.8): αὐτοῦ τοῦ φωτός M-B, E
25. 5 γῆς M-B, EMa, Syr
41. 2 ὑπερηφανίας M-A, EMa: ἐπιθυμίας Ue Syr
45. 1–5 τῶν λογισμῶν, οἱ μὲν ἐκ τοῦ χρόνου μόνον· οἱ δὲ ἐκ τοῦ χρόνου καὶ ἐκ τῆς κατ᾽ ἐνέργειαν ἁμαρτίας τὸν ἄνθρωπον βλάπτουσιν· καὶ ἐκ τοῦ χρόνου μὲν μόνου, οἱ φυσικοί· ἐκ τοῦ χρόνου δὲ καὶ ἐκ τῆς ἐνεργείας, οἱ παρὰ φύσιν· κοινὸν γὰρ πάντων τῶν λογισμῶν τὸ βλάπτειν ἐκ τοῦ χρόνου. Ue
45. 2 συγκαταθέσεως M-B, EMa
46. 2–3 τῷ δὲ πονηρῷ . . . ἀγγέλου M-A, EMa: τῷ δὲ πονηρῷ λογισμῷ τρεῖς

ἀντίκεινται λογισμοί· ὅ τε ἀγγελικὸς καὶ ὁ ἐκ τῆς ὀρθῆς προαιρέσεως καὶ ὁ ἐκ τῶν φυσικῶν σπερμάτων ἀναδιδόμενος Ue
47. 1 οἱ δὲ τῆς πορνείας M-B, EU
51. 1–2 πάντων τῶν λογισμῶν ἡδονὰς ἐχόντων οἰκείας, μόνοι τῆς λύπης οἱ λογισμοὶ οὐκ ἔχουσιν ἡδονάς. Ue, Syr
51. 1 χωρὶς τῶν τῆς λύπης λογισμῶν M-B, E
54. 2 εἰσίν U, M-B
56. 1 παρὰ φύσιν, εἰ δὲ κατὰ φύσιν E: παρὰ φύσιν, οἱ δὲ κατὰ φύσιν Ue, Syr; κατὰ φύσιν, οἱ δὲ παρὰ φύσιν M-A, Ma
58. 1 καὶ ἐκ τῆς συγκαταθέσεως post χρόνου add. Ue
62. 2 πράττοι U
62. 3 ἄγοι M-B, EMaU
62. 7 ἐκ δαιμόνων M-B, EMa

Supplementary Chapters in Ue, Syr (1–2)

1. Τῶν ἀκαθάρτων λογισμῶν, οἱ μὲν ἔξωθεν εἰσίασιν, οἱ δὲ ἐκ τῆς μνήμης γεννῶνται τῆς ψυχῆς· καὶ οἱ μὲν ἔξωθεν προϋπάρχουσιν (-ν om. U) τῆς ἑαυτῶν γνώσεως, οἱ δὲ ἔσωθεν μετὰ τὴν αὐτῶν γνῶσιν.
2. Λογισμὸς δαιμονιώδης ἐστὶ νόημα πράγματος αἰσθητοῦ, θυμὸν ἢ ἐπιθυμίαν παρὰ φύσιν κινῶν.
3. Χοῖρος βορβορώδης ἐστὶν ὁ τῆς πορνείας δαίμων, ὁ δὲ σύαγρος ὁ τῆς ὀργῆς ἐστίν· ὁ δὲ διασπῶν τοὺς ὀδόντας (e ὀδῶντας) αὐτῶν ἐν δυνάμει θεοῦ τὴν δύναμιν αὐτῶν καταθραύσει.

10. EXHORTATIONS 1–2

Editions: PG 79. 1236A–1240B; J. Muyldermans, 'Evagriana. Le Vat. Barb. Graec. 515', Le Muséon, 51 (1938), 198–204.

MSS Witnesses: bE
  b = Vatican, Barb. gr. 515, fols. 61r–65v [here I have relied on the collations and text of Muyldermans.], *Title* Παραίνεσις πρὸς μοναχούς; E = Lavra Γ 93, fols. 304r–304v / 304v–307r, *Title* 1. τοῦ αὐτοῦ παραίνεσις πρὸς μοναχούς, *Title* 2. τοῦ αὐτοῦ παραίνεσις δευτέρα εἰς μοναχούς.

Exhortation 1

2 ἐλεημοσύνη bE: ἀκτημοσύνη Pg
2 ἐλπὶς εἰς θεόν bE
4 om. bE sed add. E² in marg., adest in Syr
4 ἡ ἄμετρος bE
7 post κατάστασιν habet καθαρεῦσαι, εἰ μὴ μετὰ πάσης ἀκριβείας καὶ ὑπομονῆς ἡσυχάσῃ [-ει b] bE
12 προσθήσει b: E πορθήσει
16 πᾶς E: πῶς b

Exhortation 2

4 φρονήσῃ E: φρονήσει b
11 οὕτως θλίψις δικαιοσύνην αὔξει ἐν ψυχῇ b: οὕτω θλίψις διὰ δικαιοσύνην αὔξει ψυχὴν E
17 ἀγῶνος bE
18 ἴσος ὁ ζυγὸς PgE: ἰσόζυγος b
19 ἐπιμόνως bE: ἐπιμελῶς Pg
21 ὁ μὴ κεκοσμημένος E
21 κεκοσμημένος καὶ om. b
25 ὑπονοεῖ τὸ φάρμακον, οὕτω καὶ E
25 διαφυλαχθείη E: διαφυλαχθείν (?) b; διαφυλαχθῇ Pg
25 προέλθοι PgE: προέλθῃ b
26 ἑαυτῇ ἐμποιεῖται bE
27 αὐτὴν τὴν ἀπώλειαν bE
28 καρπὸν καλὸν bE
28 ἀπὸ Χριστοῦ bE
28 καρπὸν πνεύματος bE
29 τρωθῆναι PgE: τρωθέντα b
31 καταλάβοις PgE: καταλάβῃς b
31 οὐδ᾽εἰ Pg: οὐδὲ bE
31 ὁ θεὸς om. E
31 καθ᾽ὃ καὶ [ὁ add. b] κτίστης ἡμῶν bE
36 πρώτως E
37 βιῶν PgE: βιούς b
39 ῥύσεταί σε bE
39 ἀντιποιοῦ τῆς ζωῆς E
41 ἀνάπαυσιν ἀνεκλάλητον bE
42 πρὸς κατόρθωσιν ἐντολῶν θεοῦ καὶ ἀρετῶν bE

11. THIRTY-THREE CHAPTERS

Editions: PG 40.1264D–1268B; Paul Géhin (ed.), *Évagre le Pontique, Scholies aux Proverbes*, Sources Chrétiennes, 340 (Paris: Cerf, 1987), 486–9, for nos. 17–33.

MS Witnesses: DEMa
   D = Athos, Protaton 26, fols. 104v–106v (cited from Géhin's apparatus), *Title* τοῦ αὐτοῦ ὅροι παθῶν ψυχῆς λογικῆς   E = Lavra Γ 93, fols. 301v–302v, *Title* τοῦ αὐτοῦ ὅροι παθῶν ψυχῆς λογικῆς   Ma = Venice, Marc. gr. 131 (471), fols. 30r–31r, *Title* – none.

3. 1 σφακελισμός EMa
12. 1 ὠτότμητός ἐστι EMa
13. 1 ἐφήλωσίς ἐστι EMa

14.1 μογγιλαλία ἐστι EMa
14.2 σκανδαλιζόμενον EMa
18.2 μὴ ante δεξάμενα add. supra lin. E
19 ἀβασίλευτόν ἐστιν ἡ ἀκρίς, ψυχαὶ λογικαὶ μὴ βασιλευόμεναι ὑπὸ τοῦ θανάτου καὶ ὑπὸ τῶν τοῦ θεοῦ [τοῦ θεοῦ om. Ma] σπερμάτων διατρεφόμεναι. EMa
20.1 ἀσκαλαβώτης Ma
21.2 γεννωμένων DE
25.2 τῆς τοῦ θεοῦ θεωρίας DEMa
31.2 κακιῶν EMa: κακῶν D

12. MAXIMS 1

Editions: Pg = PG 79.1249C–1252B; El = A. Elter (ed.), Gnomica, i. *Sexti Pythagorici, Clitarchi, Evagrii Pontici sententiae* (Leipzig, 1892), p. lii.

MS Witnesses: bEMa
b = Vatican, Barb. gr. 515, fols. 82v–83r [variants cited from J. Muyldermans, 'Evagriana. Le Vat. Barb. Graec. 515,' Le Muséon 51 (1938): 219–20.] E = Lavra Γ 93, fols. 302v–303r, *Title* τοῦ αὐτοῦ Ma = Venice, Marc. gr. 131 (471), fols. 31r–v, *Title* none.

Testimonia: SP = John Damascene, Sacra parallela, PG 95.1040–1588; 96.9–442 (references can be found in the footnotes to the translation).

1 ἑαυτοῦ Pg, El, SP: σεαυτοῦ bEMa
2 εἰκῇ ἐμβάλλειν λίθον Pg: λίθον εἰκῇ βαλεῖν EMa, El, SP (βαλεῖν εἰκῇ)
3 σοὶ θέλεις πάντας Pg: σὺ θέλεις [E θέλῃς] τοὺς πάντας EMa, El
6 καὶ θαρρεῖν ἢ χρυσῆν Pg: κατακείμενον καὶ θαρρεῖν, ἢ ταράττεσθαι χρυσῆν EMa, El, SP
7 ἐκεῖνος ὁ φίλος Pg, SP: ἐκεῖνος φίλων EMa, El
7 μὴ τὴν ψυχὴν διαστρέφων b
8 θεὸν μὲν λόγοις ὕμνει, ἔργοις δὲ σέβου Pg: θεὸν ἔργοις μὲν σέβου, λόγῳ δὲ ὕμνει EMa, El; θεὸν ἔργοις σεμνοῖς, λόγοις δὲ ὕμνει, ἐννοίᾳ τίμα SP
10 πᾶσι Pg: πάθεσι EMa, El (Sextus 75a)
11 κήρυττε Pg: κήρυσσε EMa, El, SP
12 καλὸν νόμιζε Pg: καλὸν εἶναι νόμιζε EMa, El (Clitarchus 138)
12 καὶ ὑπὲρ ὧν δεῖ add. in fine b (Clitarchus 138)
14 ᾧ ξένα Pg: οὗ ξένα EMa, El
15 ἑαυτὸν ζημιοῖ Pg, El (Sextus 477): κόσμου post ζημιοῖ add. EMa, El-mss (cf. Muyldermans, p. 220); κόσμον add. b
15 κακῶς ante φθεγγόμενος add. bEMa, El
18 μὴ τοῖς ἡδέσιν b, SP
19 ὅμοιος ἔσο Pg: ἔσῃ ὅμοιος EMa, El
20 σου om. EMa, El

21 οὐ περισσεύει Pg, b: οὐ om. EMa, El (Clitarchus 83)
23 τὸν ἀνεπίληπτον EMa, El, SP (τὸν om. Pg)

MAXIMS 2

Editions: Pg = PG 79.1267C–1269B; El = A. Elter (ed.), *Gnomica*, i. *Sexti Pythagorici,
Clitarchi, Evagrii Pontici sententiae* (Leipzig, 1892), p. liii.

MSS Witnesses: EMa
E = Lavra Γ 93, fols. 303r–v, *Title* none, E² ἕτερον ἀλφάβητον   Ma = Venice,
Marc. gr. 131 (471), fols. 31v–32r, *Title* none.

Testimonia: SP = John Damascene, Sacra parallela, PG 95.1040–1588; 96.9–442
(references can be found in the footnotes to the translation).

1   τὸν PgMa: om. E; τὸ El, SP
2   σαυτόν E
9   ἐπίληπτος E
11 ἀκούσῃς E
13 νόσημα δὲ Ma
14 κολλύριον E²
15 αὐτοὺς Pg, SP: αὐτὸν EMa, El
16 μάλιστα Pg: μᾶλλον EMa, El
16 δυναμένους E, Pg, El: βουλομένους Ma
18 πραΰτης EMa, El
19 γήρου [l. γήρως] Pg: γήρως E, El, γήρους Ma
19 καὶ ante τὸ σπουδαῖον add. E
19 ἐν γήρει PgMa: ἐν γήρᾳ E, El
21 φιλήσεις Pg,El, Ma² (Sextus 141): φιλήσει EMa

MAXIMS 3

Editions: Pg = PG 79.1269B–D; El = A. Elter (ed.), *Gnomica*, i. *Sexti Pythagorici,
Clitarchi, Evagrii Pontici sententiae* (Leipzig, 1892), p. liii–liv.

MSS Witnesses: EMa
E = Lavra Γ 93, fols. 303v–304r, *Title* τοῦ αὐτοῦ   Ma = Venice, Marc. gr. 131
(471), fols. 33r–v, *Title* none.

Testimonia: SP = John Damascene, *Sacra parallela*, PG 95. 1040–1588; 96. 9–442
(references can be found in the footnotes to the translation).

2   ἐν πραύτητι EMa, El
3   λικμήτωρ EMa, El, SP

5 μεμολυμμένη Ma
7 θέλῃς E
8 καλὸς E
8 τοῦ ante θεοῦ om. EMa, El, SP
17 ὁ Χριστὸς E
17 ἀποθάνεις E
20 ἐπιλάθῃ PgMa: ἐπιλήσῃ E, El
20–21 capita iuncta sub num. 20 in El
22 μετὰ θεὸν ante ὁ κατὰ θεὸν transp. Ma (cf. Syr, Muyldermans, *Evagriana Syriaca*, p. 34)
22–23 capita iuncta sub num. 21 in El
23 ἤ om. EMa, El

APPENDIX 2: EULOGIOS—
TEXT OF LAVRA Γ 93

The text presented below is that of Athos, Lavra *Γ* 93(E), fols. 295v–298r. I have corrected orthographic errors, while noting the manuscript's readings in the footnotes. I have cited variants from other manuscripts (principally, C—Paris gr. 1188, fols. 103v–125v, which also represents the long recension of the text), where they are helpful in establishing the reading of the Lavra manuscript.

Εὐαγρίου μοναχοῦ Περὶ λογισμῶν ἐξηγορίας καὶ συμβουλίας. Πρὸς Εὐλόγιον

1. PROLOGUE

(1) Οἱ τὸν οὐράνιον χῶρον τοῖς πόνοις νεμόμενοι οὐ τῇ γαστρί, οὐδὲ τῇ μερίμνῃ τῶν φθαρτῶν ἐνατενίζουσι [1096A], καθάπερ οἱ κέρδους ἕνεκα τὰς εὐχὰς μισθούμενοι "νομίζοντες πορισμὸν εἶναι τὴν εὐσέβειαν", ἀλλὰ νοερᾷ ὁράσει τῆς τροφίμου τῶν ὑψηλῶν αὐγῆς μεταλαμβάνουσιν, ὥσπερ οἱ ἀσώματοι οἱ ἐκ τῆς θείας δόξης τὸ φῶς περιλαμπόμενοι. τοιγαροῦν καὶ αὐτός, ὦ μύστα τῶν ἀρετῶν Εὐλόγιε, τῇ τῶν ὑπερτάτων λαμπηδόνι τὴν νοερὰν οὐσίαν ἐκτρεφόμενος, ταῖς συναγωγαῖς τῶν λογισμῶν τὸν ὄγκον τῶν σαρκῶν ἀπόδυσαι, εἰδὼς ὅτι ὕλη σαρκῶν τροφὴ λογισμῶν καθίσταται, ὧνπερ τὰς μεθοδείας τῷ κέντρῳ τῶν πόνων κατειληφώς, ἐμὲ προχειρίζῃ στόμα σῶν ἔργων κατ᾽ αὐτῶν γενέσθαι, καὶ εἰ μὴ τολμηρὸν ἀγάπης ἐπίταγμα διαρρῆξαι, παρῃτησάμην ἂν ταύτην τοῦ πλοὸς τὴν ποντοπορίαν. ἐπειδὴ δὲ πείθεσθαι δεῖ μᾶλλον τοῖς ὁμοψύχοις καὶ οὐκ ἀντιτάσσεσθαι, ἔσο μοι σὺ τὰ πρὸς τὸν θεόν, ἵνα [1096B] μοι δοθῇ λόγος ἐν ἀνοίξει τοῦ στόματός μου, κἀγώ σοι ἔσομαι τὰ τῆς ὑπακοῆς, ἵνα δοθῇ σοι τοῦ σπόρου τοὺς καρποὺς ἀμήσασθαι.

2. VOLUNTARY EXILE

(2) Πρώτη τῶν λαμπρῶν ἀγωνισμάτων ἐστὶν ἡ ξενιτεία, μάλιστα ὅταν πρὸς ταύτην μόνος τις ἐκδημοίη, πατρίδα, γένος, ὕπαρξιν ἀθλητικῶς ἐκδυόμενος. οὕτως γὰρ ἂν ἐντὸς τῶν μεγίστων εὑρεθεὶς ἀγώνων, τῷ τέλει τῆς ὑπομονῆς σώαν

ταύτην ἀποσώζων, πτέρυξιν ἀρετῆς ἔσται περικεχρυσώμενος[1], τῶν οἰκείων τε
τόπων ἀφιπτάμενος, πρὸς αὐτὸν ἀναπτῆναι τὸν οὐρανὸν ἐπειχθήσεται. ἀλλὰ
τῇσδε τὰ πτερὰ τῆς πολιτείας ὁ [1096C] τῆς κακίας γενέτης μηχανᾶται περικόψαι
καὶ ποικίλαις αὐτὴν πειρᾶται καταβαλεῖν μηχαναῖς· καὶ παρὰ μὲν τὴν ἀρχὴν
ἀναχαιτίζει πρὸς ὀλίγον ἕως ἂν τὴν ψυχὴν περὶ τὰς θλίψεις καταμάθῃ ναυτιῶσαν·
καὶ τότε λοιπὸν τὴν τῶν λογισμῶν νύκτα ἐπιφερόμενος ὁ ζοφώδης νυκτικόραξ
ἐπισκοτίζει τὴν ψυχήν, τῆς τῶν κρειττόνων ἀκτῖνος ἀποστερῶν.

Εἰ δὲ καὶ παρατάττοιτό τις κατὰ μόνας ἐν τῇ τῆς ἐρήμου παλαίστρᾳ, τύχοι δέ
πως τὸ σῶμα ὑπὸ ἀρρωστίας τρωθῆναι, τότε μάλιστα χαλεπὴν ὑποδείκνυσι τῇ
ψυχῇ τὴν ξενιτείαν, οὐκ ἐν τόπῳ, ἀλλ' ἐν τρόπῳ κατορθοῦσθαι τὰ τῶν ἀρετῶν
ὑποβάλλων, καὶ ὅτι παράκλησιν ἔχων οἴκοι τὴν ἀπὸ τοῦ γένους, ἐκεῖσε μᾶλλον
ἀκόπως καὶ τὰ τῆς ἀκτημοσύνης ἆθλα διανύσειεν· ἔνθα τῆς ἀσθενείας [1096D]
προσηνὴς ὑπηρεσία καὶ οὐχ ὡς νῦν κακουχία καὶ ἐπώδυνος[2] λιποθυμία τῷ καὶ
μάλιστα σπανίσαι νῦν ἐκ τῆς ἀδελφότητος τὴν τῆς φιλοξενίας σπουδήν. θᾶττον
γοῦν, Ἄπιθι, φησί, χαρὰν τῷ σῷ γένει καὶ δόξαν σαυτὸν ἀποκομίζων, οἷς καὶ
τὸ πένθος ἀφόρητον καταλέλοιπας ἀσυμπαθῶς· πολλοὶ γὰρ καὶ πατρίδα μὴ
φυγόντες, ἐν μέσῳ τῷ γένει ἤλαντο ταῖς ἀρεταῖς.[3]

Ἀλλ' ὁ τὴν πορφυρίδα τῶν θλίψεων, τουτέστι τὴν ὑπομονήν, ἐν τῇ παρατάξει
τῆς ξενιτείας περιβεβλημένος, καὶ τῶν κόπων τὰς ἐλπίδας πίστει περιεστεμμένος,
ἀδιαλείπτῳ [1097A] εὐχαριστίᾳ τῶνδε τῶν λογισμῶν τὰς νιφάδας ἐκ τῶν ἐντὸς
ἐκτινάσσει· καὶ ὅσωπερ ἂν ὑποστρέφειν τὴν καρδίαν ἐκεῖνοι καταναγκάζωσι,
τοσούτῳ μᾶλλον ἡμεῖς ἔτι φεύγοντες, καταψαλοῦμεν αὐτῶν τὸ "Ἰδοὺ ἐμάκρυνα
φυγαδεύων, καὶ ηὐλίσθην ἐν τῇ ἐρήμῳ. προσεδεχόμην τὸν θεὸν τὸν σώζοντά με
ἀπὸ ὀλιγοψυχίας καὶ καταιγίδος·" καὶ γὰρ πειρασμοὺς ἐπιφέρουσι καὶ ἀνακάμψαι
κολακεύουσι καὶ ὀνειδίζοντες θλίβουσιν, ἵνα τῆς προθέσεως κενώσαντες καὶ τῆς
ἐν τῇ ὑπομονῇ εὐχαριστίας διακόψωσι· καὶ οὕτω λοιπὸν μετὰ πολλῆς τῆς ἀδείας
τὰς οἰκείας παγίδας ἐκ τῶν προσηκόντων εὐρύνωσιν. [1097B]

3. VIRTUE AND HUMAN HONOURS

(3) Διὰ τοῦτο ὁ ἀρχόμενος τῆς τοιαύτης ἀρετῆς ἐφάπτεσθαι λογιζέσθω καὶ τὸν
κατ' αὐτῆς ἐπιόντα πόλεμον, ἵνα μὴ ἀγύμναστος καταληφθείς, ὡς ἀνέτοιμος,
ῥαδίως κατασπασθῇ. ἐπαινετὴ μὲν οὖν ἡ τῶν πόνων ἐργασία καὶ εἰρήνης οὔσης·
ὑπερεπαινετὴ δὲ τούτων ἡ ἀνδραγαθία, πολέμου ἐπιστάντος· τοῦτο γὰρ κυρίως
ἀρετή, οὐ δι' ὧν πονεῖ τις μόνον, ἀλλὰ καὶ δι' ὧν πολεμεῖται κακῶν, τὴν ὑπομονὴν
ὡς ὅπλον προβάλλεσθαι· ἀπαθὴς γάρ ἐστιν ὁ διὰ πλείστων πολέμων τὸ πάσχειν
νικήσας, ἐμπαθὴς δὲ ὁ ἀρετὴν λέγων ἀπολέμητον κεκτῆσθαι. κατὰ παράταξιν γὰρ
τῆς ἐναρέτου τῶν πόνων στρατηγίας ἀντιπαρατάττεται καὶ ἡ τῶν ὑπεναντίων
κακία. ἀφῄρηται τὸ εἶναι ἐν ἀρετῇ καρδία πόλεμον οὐκ ἔχουσα· ἀρετὴ γὰρ ἐκ τῶν
ἀριστείων πρακτικὸν ὄνομα κέκτηται.

---

1 περικεχρυσομένος E   2 ἐπόδυνος E   3 ἤλαντο ταῖς ἀρεταῖς correxi: ἤλαντο
ταῖς ἀρεταῖς E, εἵλοντο τὰς ἀρετάς C; εἵλοντο τὴν ἀρετήν Pg

Ἀρετὴ τὰς παρὰ ἀνθρώπων εὐφημίας [1097C] οὐ ζητεῖ, οὐ γὰρ τέρπεται
τιμῇ, τῇ μητρὶ τῶν κακῶν. ἀρχὴ γοῦν τιμῆς ἀνθρωποδοξία, τὸ δὲ τέλος ταύτης
ὑπερηφανία· ὁ γὰρ τιμὰς ἀπαιτῶν ὑψοῖ ἑαυτὸν καὶ ἐξουδένωσιν φέρειν ὁ τοιοῦτος
οὐκ οἶδεν. τιμῆς ὄρεξις φαντασία πρὸς ἔπαρσιν καὶ ὁ ταύτης ἐρῶν καὶ κλῆρον
φαντάζεται. ἔστω σοι τιμὴ ὁ πόνος τῶν ἀρετῶν καὶ ἀτιμία ὁ κατὰ θέλησιν ἔπαινος·
δόξαν ἀπὸ σαρκὸς μὴ ζήτει ὁ τὰ σαρκὸς καταλύων πάθη· τὸ δὲ κρεῖττον ἐπιζήτει
καὶ ἔσται σου δόξα.

Ὁ τιμᾶσθαι θέλων τῷ παρευδοκιμοῦντι φθονεῖ καὶ τούτῳ τῷ ζήλῳ τὸ πρὸς τοὺς
πλησίον μῖσος σωρεύει⁴· ὁ ταῖς ἄγαν τιμαῖς ἡττηθεὶς ἑαυτοῦ προτιμᾶσθαι οὐδένα
θέλει, ἁρπάζει δὲ τὰ πρωτεῖα, μήπως ἥττων φανῇ δεδοικώς. οὐ βαστάζει, οὐδὲ
ἀπόντα τὸν εὐδοκιμοῦντα τιμώμενον, ἀλλ᾽ ἐν τοῖς αὐτοῦ πόνοις κωμῳδεῖν ζητεῖ
[1097D] τὴν χαμαίζηλον δόξαν. ἡ ὕβρις τῷ φιλοδόξῳ ὀξυτάτη σφαγὴ καὶ μῆνιν
ἐκ ταύτης οὐ πάντως ἐκφεύγει. (4) ὁ τοιοῦτος βαρβάρῳ δεσποίνῃ δουλεύει καὶ
πολλοῖς δεσπόταις μετεπράθη, ἐπάρσει, φθόνῳ, ζήλῳ καὶ ταῖς προρρηθείσαις τῶν
πνευμάτων λογάσιν, ὁ δὲ τῆς τιμῆς τὸ πνεῦμα τῇ ταπεινώσει ῥάσσων τὸν λεγεῶνα
τῶν δαιμόνων ὅλον καθαιρήσει· ὁ τῇ ταπεινώσει δοῦλον ἑαυτὸν πᾶσι παρέχων
ὁμοιούμενος ἔσται τῷ ταπεινώσαντι ἑαυτὸν καὶ μορφὴν [1100A] δούλου λαβόντι
Χριστῷ.

Ἐὰν μετρῇς τῷ ἐλαχίστῳ μέτρῳ σεαυτόν, οὐκ ἀντιμετρήσῃς⁵ ἑτέρῳ σαυτόν.
καὶ ὁ τῆς ψυχῆς τὴν ἀσθένειαν τοῖς θρήνοις ἐκκαλύπτων οὐ μέγα ἐπὶ τοῖς ὑπ᾽
ἑαυτοῦ πονουμένοις φρονήσει· οὐ μὴν οὐδὲ τοῖς τῶν ἄλλων ἐλαττώμασι προσέξει
τὸν νοῦν· χρὴ δὲ τῷ τοιούτῳ καὶ διαφερόντως ἀσφαλίζεσθαι. οἱ δαίμονες εὐτέλειαν
καὶ ὕβριν τοῖς ταπεινόφροσιν ἐπάγουσιν, ἵνα τὴν ἐξουδένωσιν μὴ φέροντες τὴν
ταπεινοφροσύνην ἐκφύγωσιν· ὁ δὲ τῇ ταπεινώσει τὰς ἀτιμίας γενναίως φέρων εἰς
φιλοσοφίας ὕψος δι᾽ ἐκείνων μᾶλλον ἀνωθεῖται.

4. ACCEPTANCE OF PERSONAL OFFENSES

Δαβὶδ ὑβριζόμενος οὐκ ἀντέλεγεν, ἀλλὰ καὶ τὴν Ἀβεσσὰ δυναστείαν κατέστελλεν.
καὶ σὺ ὑβριζόμενος μὴ ἀνθύβριζε, ἀλλὰ καὶ τὸν ἐκδικοῦντά σε αὐτὸς καταπράϋνε.
κἂν οὕτω ποιῇς, ἐμφράξῃς τοῦ θηρὸς τὸν θυμόν· ὕβριν φέρε, τὴν σὴν προκοπήν,
καὶ χείλεσι σύγκλειε τοῦ θυμοῦ τὸν θῆρα· ἀποκριθήσῃ τοῖς ἀπειλοῦσιν οὐδ᾽
ὅλως, ἵνα σιγῇ κοιμίσῃς τὰ καπνίζοντα χείλη. [1100B] τότε τοῖς ἀπειλοῦσι καὶ
ὑβρισταῖς δυνήσῃ, ὅταν χαλινὸν ταῖς σαῖς σιαγόσιν ἐπιθήσῃς. σὺ μὲν γὰρ σιγῶν
οὐ βρωθήσῃ τῇ ὕβρει, ὁ δὲ πολλῷ μᾶλλον δάκνεται ὑπὸ τῆς σιωπῆς, ἐπὰν ὕβρεις
τοῦ θρασέος μακροθύμως ὑπενέγκῃς. τὸν τῶν ἀνθρώπων ἔπαινον ἐκ τῶν ἐντὸς
ἀποσείου, ἵνα καὶ τὸν φιλενδείκτην λογισμὸν πρὸ αὐτοῦ ἐκτινάξῃς. ἐπιτήρει δὲ
καὶ τὸν αὐτάρεσκον μάλιστα καθ᾽ ἡσυχίαν, μὴ τότε σε μεγαλύνας ὑπὲρ τὸν θρασὺν
ἐξουδενώσει ἐκεῖνον.

Ὡς μὲν οὖν πολλαὶ καὶ διάφοροι ἀπὸ τῶν θείων γραφῶν παραινέσεις εἰσὶ περὶ
τοῦ μὴ ἀνταποδιδόναι, οὐδεὶς ἀντειπεῖν ἔχει· πρὸς δὲ ἀκριβεστέραν διδασκαλίαν,

4 σορεύει E   5 ἀντιμετρήσεις C

καὶ ὑπόδειγμα παραθήσομαι. τὶς τῶν ἀδελφῶν ὕβριν τε παρὰ εὐλαβοῦς καὶ ἀδικίαν
ὑπομείνας, ἀπίει χαρᾷ τε μεριζόμενος καὶ λύπῃ, τὸ μὲν ὅτι ἀδικούμενος ὑβρίσθη
καὶ οὐκ ἀντετάχθη, τὸ δὲ ὅτι ὁ εὐλαβὴς ἠπατήθη καὶ ἀπατήσας κατεχάρη. νόει
δέ μοι καὶ τὸν ἀπατεῶνα τὰ δύο πεπονθέναι ἐφ' ᾧ μὲν [1100C] ἐτάραξε πάντως
χαρέντα, ἐφ' ᾧ δὲ οὐκ ἐτάραξε καὶ μάλα λυπηθέντα.

5. RESENTMENT

(5) Ὅταν ἴδωσιν ἡμᾶς οἱ δαίμονες εἰς τὸ αὐτὸ ζέμα τῶν ὕβρεων μὴ ἐξαφθέντας,
τότε καθ' ἡσυχίαν ἐπιστάντες ἀναμοχλεύουσι τὸ ἡγεμονικόν, ἵνα οἷς παροῦσιν
εἰρηνεύσαμεν, τούτοις ἀποῦσι διαθρασυνώμεθα. ἐπὰν οὖν ἀντιλογίαν ἢ ὕβριν πρὸς
τὸν ἀδελφὸν ἐκτελέσῃς, σεαυτὸν λογίζου σφαλέντα διόλου, ἵνα μὴ καὶ ἡσυχάζων
μάχην λογισμῶν ἐν τῇ καρδίᾳ σου εὕρῃς· τοῦ μὲν ἐπονειδίζοντος τῶν ὕβρεων τὸν
τρόπον, τοῦ [1100D] δὲ ἀντονειδίζοντος ὡς τὰ δεινὰ καὶ σοῦ μὴ ἀνθυβρίζοντος.
Ὁπόταν παροξυσμὸς ἐκπικράνῃ τοὺς ἐν κοινοβίῳ ἀδελφούς, τότε οἱ λογισμοὶ
μακαρίζειν τὸν μόνον ἐμβάλλουσιν, ἵνα τῆς μακροθυμίας κενώσαντες καὶ τῆς
ἀγάπης ἀφορίσωσιν. ὁ δὲ μακροθυμίᾳ τὴν ὀργὴν καὶ ἀγάπῃ τὴν λύπην ἀνατρέπων
πονηροὺς δύο θῆρας διτταῖς ἀνδραγαθίαις ἀνατρέπει τοὺς θυμομαχοῦντας.
ὁ παρακαλῶν καὶ γονυπετῶν, ἵνα τὴν ὀργὴν ἀπελάσῃ, τὸν παροξύνοντα,
τοὺς ἀμφοτέρους ἐξ αὐτῶν ἀπελαύνει, ὅτι τὸ πνεῦμα τῆς ὀργῆς ἐκπολεμεῖ ὁ
τοὺς ὀργιζομένους εἰρηνεύων· μηνιάσει δὲ τούτῳ ὀργὴν ὁμογενῶν ἐπ' αὐτὸν
ἐκθρασύνων, ὅτι τὴν τῶν πλησίον εἰς ἑαυτὸν ἀνεδέξατο μάχην. ὁ [1101A] τὸν
θρασυκάρδιον βαστάζων ἕνεκεν εἰρήνης, οὗτος ἐκβιάζεται γενέσθαι τῆς εἰρήνης
υἱός.

6. PEACE AND JOY

Ἀλλ' οὐκ ἐπ' ἀνθρώπῳ[6] μόνον ζητητέος ὁ τῆς εἰρήνης σύνδεσμος, ἀλλὰ καὶ ἐν τῷ
σώματί σου καὶ ἐν τῷ πνεύματί σου καὶ ἐν τῇ ψυχῇ. (6) ὅταν γὰρ τῆς σῆς τριάδος
τὸν σύνδεσμον ἑνώσῃς τῇ εἰρήνῃ, τότε ὡς τῆς θείας τριάδος ἐντολὴ ἑνωθεὶς
ἀκούσεις· "Μακάριοι οἱ εἰρηνοποιοί, ὅτι αὐτοὶ υἱοὶ θεοῦ κληθήσονται." καὶ γὰρ
ἐὰν τὴν ἀντεπίθυμον τοῦ πνεύματος σάρκα εἰρηνεύσῃς τοῖς πόνοις, κλέος ἕξεις
τῶν μακαρισμῶν ἐπέκεινα αἰῶνος, νικήσας πόλεμον τὸν ἐν τῷ σώματί σου τὸν
ἀντιστρατευόμενον τῷ νόμῳ τοῦ νοός σου καὶ αἰχμαλωτίζοντά [1101B] σε τῷ
νόμῳ τῆς ἁμαρτίας τῷ ὄντι ἐν τοῖς μέλεσί σου. μέγας ὁ τῆς εἰρήνης σύνδεσμος ἐν
ᾧπερ ἥνωται καὶ ἡ χαρὰ φωτίζουσα[7] τὸ ὄμμα τῆς διανοίας εἰς τὴν τῶν κρειττόνων
θεωρίαν.
Εἴπερ οὖν ἐπικτησώμεθα τὴν εἰρηνικὴν ἐν τοῖς πόνοις χαράν, τὰ ἐπιόντα χαλεπὰ
εὐχαρίστως δι' αὐτῆς ἀποκρουσόμεθα καὶ τὸν τῆς ὀργῆς δαίμονα μυκώμενον οὐκ
εἰσδεξόμεθα, ὅστις ἀκρωτηρῶν ἐν ταῖς θλίψεσιν ἐφάλλεται μάλιστα τῇ ψυχῇ καὶ

6 ἀπ'ἀνθρώπων C   7 φωτίζουσα C: φωτίζων E

τῷ πνεύματι τῆς ἀκηδίας χώραν ἑτοιμάζεται, ὅπως τὴν ψυχὴν σκοτίσωσι καὶ ἅμα τοὺς πόνους ἀναλέξωσιν. ἔστω τοίνυν νόμος ἡμῶν τῆς καρδίας ἔγγραφος ἡ τῆς εἰρήνης χαρά, ἡ τὴν λύπην ἐξορίζουσα, ἡ τὸ μῖσος ἀπελαύνουσα καὶ τὴν μῆνιν ἀφανίζουσα, ἡ τὴν ἀκηδίαν καταλύουσα· ἐν γὰρ τῇ εἰρηνικῇ [1101C] μακροθυμίᾳ ἐμφωλεύουσα καὶ τῇ εὐχαριστίᾳ καὶ ὑπομονῇ ἐλλιμνάζουσα, πέλαγός ἐστιν ἀρετῶν τὴν ἀντιπαράταξιν τοῦ διαβόλου τῷ σταυρῷ καταποντίζουσα.

7. TWO TYPES OF JOY AND SADNESS

Νόει δέ μοι τὴν ἐναντίαν χαρὰν τεταραγμένην ἐφίστασθαι, μήπως ἄλλην ἀντ᾽ ἄλλης σκιασθεὶς ἀπατηθῇς κατέχειν. συσχηματίζονται γὰρ τοῖς πνευματικοῖς χαρίσμασι πολλάκις οἱ δαίμονες, ἵνα τῷ παρασκιάσματι τὸν νοῦν ἀποπλανήσαντες τῶν φρενῶν ἀποστήσωσιν· ἐφίσταται γὰρ χαρὰ δαιμονιώδης τῇ καρδίᾳ οὐδενὸς προκειμένου, ὅτι τὸν ἡγεμόνα τῆς κατὰ θεὸν λύπης μετέωρον εὑρίσκει, ἔπειτα δὲ καὶ τῷ πνεύματι τῆς λύπης τὴν ψυχὴν παραδίδωσιν, ὅτι τῆς πνευματικῆς αὐτὸν χαρᾶς αἰχμάλωτον ἐποίησεν. [1101D]

(7) Φημὶ δὲ καὶ τοῦτο, ὡς ὑπηγόρευσέ τινι τῶν ἀδελφῶν ἡ πεῖρα τῶν ζητουμένων, ὅτι ἀντὶ μὲν τοῦ χαίρειν ἐν κυρίῳ χαρὰν οἰκείαν ὁ ἀλάστωρ ἀντεισάγει· ἀντὶ δὲ τῆς κατὰ θεὸν λύπης, λύπην τὴν ἐναντίαν τῷ νῷ παραπετάζει, ἵνα ταῖς ἀντιστρόφοις μεταβολαῖς τῆς τῶν κρειττόνων μερίμνης τὴν ψυχὴν ἀμαυρώσῃ. διτταὶ τῆς κακίας αἱ λῦπαι τυγχάνουσιν ἐν ἑκάστῃ ἐργασίᾳ ἀπεζευγμέναι· καὶ ἡ μὲν ἐφίσταται τῇ καρδίᾳ λυπηρᾶς αἰτίας οὐ βλεπομένης, ἡ δὲ τίκτεται ἐξ ἀλλοκότων αἰτιῶν ὠθουμένη. ἡ δὲ κατὰ θεὸν [1104A] λύπη τοῖς δάκρυσι τὴν ψυχὴν ἀνακαλεῖται, τὴν ἀπεναντίας χαράν τε καὶ λύπην μὴ παραδεχομένη, τὸν δὲ ἐπιόντα θάνατον μεριμνᾷ καὶ κρίσιν· καὶ τοῦτο κατ᾽ ὀλίγον κέχηνε προσδεχομένη.

Ἐπιθυμίαι ἀποτυχοῦσαι φυτεύουσι λύπας· εὐχαὶ δὲ καὶ εὐχαριστίαι μαραίνουσι ταύτας. μεταξὺ ὀργιζομένων μέση λύπη δονεῖται. ὁ οὖν πρῶτος ἐκνήψας, ἐὰν τοῦ πάθους ἀναστῇ, καὶ τῷ ἑτέρῳ δώσῃ χεῖρα ἀπολογίᾳ, τὴν πικρὰν λύπην ἀπελαύνων. λύπη ψυχῆς καὶ σαρκὸς νόσος τυγχάνει· καὶ τὴν μὲν αἰχμαλώτιδα αἴρει, τὴν δὲ ἐπὶ τόπῳ μαραίνει. ἐξ ἐναντίων λύπη γεννᾶται· ἐκ δὲ λύπης μῆνις, τίκτεται δὲ ἐκ τούτων φρενῖτις, λοιδορία. λύπην καὶ μῆνιν εἰ θέλεις συμπατῆσαι, τὴν μακροθυμίαν τῆς ἀγάπης ἐναγκαλίζου καὶ τὴν χαρὰν τῆς ἀκακίας περιβαλοῦ. ἡ σὴ χαρὰ [1104B] ἑτέρῳ λύπη μὴ ἤτω· ἐπ᾽ ἀδικίᾳ ὁ χαίρων ἐπ᾽ εὐδοκίᾳ θρηνήσει, καὶ ὁ ὑποφέρων λύπας, πάσχων ἀδίκως, λαμπρῶς ἀγαλλιάσεται, τὰ γὰρ μέλλοντα τοῖς παροῦσιν ἐναντία.

8. ACEDIA

(8) Ἐν ταῖς θλίψεσιν εὐχάριστος ἔσο μάλιστα, ὅτι δι᾽ αὐτῶν τῆς ἀντιλήψεως τὴν χάριν σαφέστερον αἰσθάνῃ· οὕτω γὰρ τὰς ἐπιούσας θλίψεις εὐχαρίστως ἐκτινάσσων, οὐκ ἀμαυρώσεις τῆς καρτερίας τὸ λαμπρότατον κάλλος. ἐπάν σοι μάστιγα κατὰ σαρκὸς δαίμων καταρράξῃ, μεγίστου σοι μισθοῦ πρόξενος

[1104C] εὑρεθήσεται, ἐὰν εἰς ὑπόθεσιν εὐχαριστίας τὴν πληγὴν καταδέξῃ· οὕτω γὰρ καὶ ἑαυτὸν ἐκ σοῦ φυγαδεύσει. ἵνα μὴ πλεῖον ὁ μισθός σοι διὰ τῆς ὑπομονῆς ἐπομβρήσῃ, δι᾽ ὅλων τῶν ἐναντίων πόνων ἡ ὑπομονή σου στρατηγείτω, ὅτι διὰ πάσης κακίας καὶ ἡ ἀκηδία ἀντιστρατηγεῖ σοι, καὶ κατασκοποῦσά σου τοὺς πόνους ἅπαντας πειράζει· ὃν δὲ μὴ εὕρῃ τῇ ὑπομονῇ ἐνηλωμένον, τοῦτον καταβαρύνει ὑφ᾽ ἑαυτὴν καὶ κατακάμπτει. ἐὰν ὁ δαίμων τῆς ἀκηδίας πρὸς τὴν ὑπομονὴν τῶν πόνων ἀτονήσῃ, τῆς ἀπονοίας πάλιν ὁ θὴρ τὸ κατόρθωμα δάκνει. εἰ οὖν συνέσει τῆς ἀσφαλείας τοῦτον ἐλάσεις, καὶ τὸ κενόδοξον πνεῦμα σὺν αὐτῷ ἀπελάσῃς.

8. ACEDIA DURING PSALMODY

Ἐν καιρῷ συνάξεως, ἐπάν σοι τὸ τῆς ἀκηδίας ἐπιπέσοι πνεῦμα, ὡς φορτικὴν ἐπιψηφίζει τῇ ψυχῇ τὴν ψαλμῳδίαν, καὶ τὸν ὄκνον ὡς ἀντίπαλον τῇ ψυχῇ [1104D] παρεμβάλλει, ἵνα ἀψαύστῳ τάχει τὴν σάρκα ἀνακλίνῃ τῇ μνήμῃ, ὡς κοπωθεῖσαν δῆθεν ἔκ τινος αἰτίας. ἐπὰν οὖν ἐγρηγορότες ὦμεν νύκτωρ μὴ τὴν σύναξιν τῇ ἀκηδίᾳ ἀνακλίνωμεν, ἵνα μὴ οἱ δαίμονες ἐπιστάντες τὰ ζιζάνια τῶν λογισμῶν συνάξωσι καὶ ἅμα τῇ καρδίᾳ κατασπείρωσιν. ὅταν γὰρ τὴν σύνοδον τῶν ὕμνων ἀπολέσωμεν, τότε τὸν σύλλογον τῶν λογισμῶν ἐπισυνάξωμεν. πρὸ συνάξεως τοίνυν διυπνισθέντες, λογισμοὺς φωτὸς ἐν τῇ καρδίᾳ προγυμνάζωμεν, ἵνα εὐτρεπισθέντες ἔχωμεν, ἐν γρηγορούσῃ διανοίᾳ τῇ ψαλμῳδίᾳ παραστῶμεν.

[1105A]
(9) Πῇ μὲν ῥοίζῳ τὸν ψαλμὸν ἐν τῇ συνάξει λεκτέον, πῇ δὲ ἐνδελεχεῖν[8] τῇ ψαλμῳδίᾳ δοκιμαστέον· κατὰ γὰρ τὴν ἐνέδραν τοῦ ἐναντίου ἀνάγκη καὶ ἡμᾶς μεταμορφοῦσθαι, διότι ποτὲ μὲν ἐλαύνειν τὴν γλῶτταν ὑποτίθεται, τῆς ἀκηδίας τὴν ψυχὴν περιτρεχούσης, ποτὲ δὲ μελῳδεῖσθαι τὰς λέξεις ἐρεθίζει, τῆς αὐταρεσκίας τῇ ψυχῇ παρεμποδιζούσης. τῆς ἀκηδίας ὁ δαίμων ἐν μὲν τῷ ἀνίστασθαι εἰς προσευχὴν ὄκνον ποιεῖ, ἐν δὲ τῷ πάλιν προσεύχεσθαι ἢ ψαλμῳδεῖν κατεπείγων ταράττει. ἐντεῦθεν πρὸς τὴν θεωρίαν ὀφθαλμιῶσιν ἡμῶν αἱ ψυχαὶ καὶ ἄτονοι καθίστανται, μάλιστα ὅταν συνόντες τῇ τῶν λογισμῶν αἰχμαλωσίᾳ ἀνιστάμεθα καὶ μετ᾽ αὐτῶν πρὸς ἱκεσίαν ἱστάμεθα. ὁ δὲ λογισμοῖς βελτίστοις τὴν ψυχὴν προγυμνάζων ἐλλάμπεσθαι, τὴν στήλην τῆς εὐχῆς λαμπρὰν προαποσμήχει. ὁ λογισμοῖς ἀτόποις τὴν καρδίαν παίων τῆς εὐχῆς τὸν βότρυν αἰχμαλωσίᾳ λιθάζει· ὁ ἐκτενέστερον τῶν εὐχῶν τὴν ἔλλαμψιν ἐσοπτριζόμενος τῇ ἀνωτάτω θέᾳ τοὺς κάτω λογισμοὺς αἰχμαλωτίζει, τοῦ νοεροῦ ὄμματος καθάπερ τροφὴν τὴν ἰσχὺν ἐκ τοῦ φωτὸς λαμβάνοντος. ὁ γὰρ τῇ ὀπτασίᾳ τῶν ὑψηλῶν ἐπεκτεινόμενος ὀξυδερκέστερον ὄμμα λήψεται, καθὼς ἱστορεῖται Ἐλισσαῖος ὁ προφήτης. ὅταν λογισμὸς ἐπιστῇ σου τῇ καρδίᾳ πολέμιος, μὴ ἄλλα ἀντ᾽ ἄλλων δι᾽ εὐχῆς ἐπιζήτει, κατὰ δὲ τῶν πολεμίων τὸ ξίφος τῶν δακρύων ἀκόνα, ὅπως τῇ μάχῃ εὐτόνως προσράξας θᾶττον αὐτὸν ἀποστῆναί σου ποιήσῃς.

8 ἐνδελεχεῖν correxi: ἐνδελεχὴν C, ἀδολεσχεῖν Pg

10. MANUAL LABOUR AND PRAYER

Φιλοκάλει [1105B] σὺν τῷ ἔργῳ τῶν χειρῶν καὶ μάλα τῆς εὐχῆς τὴν μνήμην· τὸ μὲν γὰρ οὐ πάντοτε, τὸ δὲ ἀδιάλειπτον ἔχει τῆς ἐργασίας τὸν πόρον. μὴ συναναβάλλου δοῦναι τῆς εὐχῆς τὸ χρέος, λογισμοῦ ἀκούων διὰ πρόσβασιν ἔργου καὶ μὴ θορυβοῦ ἐν τῷ ἔργῳ πράττων⁹ τὸ σῶμα, ἵνα μὴ συνταράξῃς καὶ τῆς ψυχῆς τὸ ὄμμα. ὥσπερ ὁ ἐκτὸς ἡμῶν ἄνθρωπος χερσὶν ἐργάζεται πρὸς τὸ μὴ ἐπιβαρῆσαί τινα, οὕτω καὶ ὁ ἐντὸς φρεσὶν ἐργαζέσθω, πρὸς τὸ μὴ ἐπιβαρηθῆναι τὸν νοῦν. τότε γὰρ οἱ λογισμοὶ τὴν ἐναντίαν ἐργασίαν τῇ ψυχῇ προσφέρουσιν, ὅταν αὐτὴν ταῖς κατὰ θεὸν ἐννοίαις ἀργὴν καταλάβωσιν. ἀροτρία γοῦν τὰ μὲν ἔργα τῶν χειρῶν εἰς τὸ φιλάνθρωπον, τὴν δὲ φρένα τοῦ λογιστικοῦ εἰς τὸ φιλόσοφον, ἵνα τὸ μὲν ᾖ ξένων ξενισμὸς [1105C] καὶ ὀκνηρίας ἐμπρησμός, τὸ δὲ θεωρίας στρατηγὸς καὶ λογισμῶν ἀποβρασμός.

11. IRASCIBILITY AND GENTLENESS

Τὰς ἡδονὰς τῶν κολάκων λογισμῶν μετὰ θράσους ἐπιπλήξωμεν, ἅπασαν τὴν ὀργὴν εἰς αὐτοὺς περιτρέποντες, ἵνα μὴ ἡδονῇ τὰ παρ᾽ αὐτῶν δεχόμενοι πρᾶοι πρὸς αὐτοὺς ἀντιστρόφως γενώμεθα. (10) ἑτοίμαζε σαυτὸν πρᾶον εἶναι καὶ μαχητήν, τὸ μὲν τῷ ὁμοφύλῳ, τὸ δὲ τῷ πολεμίῳ· ἐν τούτῳ γὰρ ἡ χρῆσις τοῦ θυμοῦ, ἐν μὲν τῷ κατὰ τὴν ἔχθραν ἀντιμάχεσθαι τῷ ὄφει, ἐν δὲ τῷ κατὰ τὸ πρᾶον καὶ ἐπιεικὲς κατὰ τὴν ἀγάπην μακροθυμεῖν τῷ ἀδελφῷ καὶ πολεμεῖν τῷ λογισμῷ. ὁ πραὺς οὖν ἔστω μαχητής, διαιρουμένης τῆς πραΰτητος ἐκ τῶν δολοφόνων [1105D] λογισμῶν, καθάπερ καὶ τῆς μάχης ἐκ τῶν τῆς φύσεως ὁμογενῶν. μὴ ἀντιστρέψῃς τοῦ θυμοῦ τὴν χρῆσιν εἰς τὴν παρὰ φύσιν, θυμοῦσθαι μὲν τῷ ἀδελφῷ κατὰ τὴν ὁμοίωσιν τοῦ ὄφεως, φιλιοῦσθαι δὲ τῷ ὄφει κατὰ τὴν συγκατάθεσιν τῶν λογισμῶν. ὁ πρᾶος, κἂν πάσχῃ τὰ δεινά, τῆς ἀγάπης οὐκ ἐξίσταται, ἕνεκεν γὰρ ταύτης μακροθυμεῖ καὶ στέγει, χρηστεύεταί τε καὶ ὑπομένει. εἰ γὰρ τῆς ἀγάπης τὸ μακροθυμεῖν, οὐ τῆς ἀγάπης τὸ θυμομαχεῖν· θυμὸς γὰρ μῖσος καὶ φθόνον καὶ μῆνιν ἐγείρει, ἀγάπη δὲ τὰ τρία μισεῖ. εἰ παγίαν ἔχεις ἐν τῇ ἀγάπῃ τὴν βάσιν, μᾶλλον πρόσεχε ταύτῃ, ἤπερ τῷ πταίοντί σε. φόβῳ καὶ ἀγάπῃ δούλευε τῷ θεῷ, τὸ μὲν ὡς δεσπότῃ καὶ κριτῇ [1108A], τὸ δὲ ὡς φιλανθρώπῳ, καὶ τροφεῖ. ὁ τῆς ἀγάπης τὰς ἀρετὰς κτησάμενος τὰ φαῦλα τῶν παθῶν αἰχμαλωτίζει· καὶ ὁ παρὰ τῆς ἁγίας τριάδος ἔχων τὰ τρία ταῦτα, πίστιν, ἐλπίδα, ἀγάπην, τρίτειχος ἔσται πόλις ταῖς ἀρεταῖς πυργωθεῖσα.

12. POVERTY

Οὐκ ἐν τῷ μὴ λαμβάνειν μόνον παρ᾽ ἑτέρου ἀγαπητικὸς ἀναδειχθήσῃ, ἀλλ᾽ ἐν τῷ διδόναι ἀφειδῶς ἀποτακτικὸς¹⁰ ἐπιγνωσθήσῃ. ἐν τῷ μεταδιδόναι σε τὰς ὕλας ἀγωνίζου τὰ σπέρματα καθαρὰ¹¹καταβάλλειν, ἵνα μὴ ἀντὶ πυροῦ ἐξέλθῃ σοι κνίδη. θεοῦ ἐφ᾽ οἷς παρέχεις μνημόνευε καὶ δότην καὶ λήπτορα, ὅπως σοι μετ᾽ ἐγκωμίων λογίσηται τοὺς τῆς ἀποταξίας μισθούς. [1108B]

9 ταράσσων C   10 ἀποτακτηκὸς E   11 καθαρὰ C: καθ᾽ ὥραν E

(11) Ὁ ἀκτήμων ἀμέριμνον ἔχει τοῦ βίου τὴν ἡδονήν, ὁ δὲ φιλοκτήμων μέριμναν ἔχει διὰ παντὸς τὴν ὀδύνην τοῦ πλούτου. τότε δῆμον λογισμῶν αἰχμάλωτον ἐλάσεις¹², ὅταν ταῖς φροντίσι τῶν ὑλῶν τὴν καρδίαν μὴ δῷς. τότε καὶ τὸν σταυρὸν ἀπερισπάστως βαστάσεις, ὅταν τοῦ κτᾶσθαι τὴν ἐπιθυμίαν ἀρνήσῃ. ἀλλ' ὁ τῆς ὕλης λογισμὸς γῆράς σοι μαντεύεται, λιμούς τε καὶ νόσους, ἵνα σου τὴν εἰς θεὸν ἐλπίδα τοῖς χρήμασι μερίσῃ. ὁ τὴν ἀποταγὴν ἀσκεῖν προῃρημένος πίστει τειχιζέσθω καὶ ἐλπίδι κραταιούσθω καὶ ἀγάπῃ βεβαιούσθω. ἔστι γὰρ πίστις, οὐκ ἐγκατάλειψις, ἀλλὰ τῶν κρειττόνων ὑπόστασις ἐν τῇ ἐλπίδι τῆς ὑπομονῆς καὶ τῇ ἀγάπῃ τῆς ζωῆς.

Ὅταν ἀποταξάμενος ἀπαθῶς ταῖς [1108C] ἔξωθεν ὕλαις, ἐν ὁδῷ τῶν κρεττόνων βαδίζεις, τότε οἱ ξιφαῖοι λογισμοὶ καιρὸν κατασκοπήσαντες τὴν πενίαν σοι καὶ τὴν ἔνδειαν ἐπονειδίζουσιν, εὐτέλειαν καὶ ἀδοξίαν σοι προσφέροντες, ἵνα τῆς τοιαύτης λαμπρᾶς ἀρετῆς μετάγνωσιν οἱ φόνιοι δολοφόνως ἐργάσωνται. ἐὰν οὖν συνέσει τῇ νίκῃ τῆς ἀθλήσεως πρόσχῃς, μᾶλλον ἢ ἐκείνοις τότε εὑρήσεις, ὅτι δι' ὧν σε ὀνειδίζουσι, δι' αὐτῶν σοι στέφανος πλέκεται· καὶ γὰρ ἀποτασσόμενος δι' ἐκείνων ἀποτάσσῃ, δι' ὧν ἄθλων ὀνειδίζῃ. μὴ οὖν τῇ πάλῃ τῶν ἔνδον λογισμῶν ὑπενδώσῃς, ὅτι οὐκ ἐν ἀρχῇ τῆς ἀποταγῆς τὸ τέλος εὐφημεῖται, ἀλλ' ἐν τῷ τέλει τῆς ὑπομονῆς αἱ ἀρχαὶ στεφανοῦνται· οὐδὲ ἐν τῇ σωματικῇ γυμνασίᾳ μόνον οἱ ἀγῶνες συγκροτοῦνται, ἀλλὰ καὶ ἐν τῇ τῶν λογισμῶν πάλῃ τὸ πέρας τοῦ στεφάνου ζητεῖται. [1108D]

13. THOUGHTS

(12) Δίκαζε τοὺς λογισμοὺς ἐν τῷ βήματι τῆς καρδίας σου, ἵνα τῶν λῃστῶν ἀναιρουμένων ὁ ἀρχιλῃστὴς φοβῆται· ὁ γὰρ ἀκριβὴς ὢν τῶν λογισμῶν ἐξεταστὴς καὶ τῶν ἐντολῶν ἔσται ἀληθῶς ἐραστής. ἐπὰν λογισμὸς ἐπιστῇ σου τῇ καρδίᾳ δυσεύρετος¹³, τότε ἐπὶ πλεῖον συντόνους πόνους κατ' αὐτοῦ ἐκπύρωσον· ἢ γὰρ τὴν θέρμην ὡς ἐναντίαν ἀποδρᾷ οὐ φέρων ταύτην, ἢ ὑπομένει ὡς οἰκεῖος ὢν τῆς εὐθείας ὁδοῦ. ἔστι δ' ὅταν οἱ δαίμονες λογισμὸν δῆθεν καλὸν ὑποβάλλουσί σου τῇ καρδίᾳ, καὶ παρευθὺ μεταμορφούμενοι ἐναντιοῦσθαι τούτῳ προσποιοῦνται, ἵνα ἐκ τῆς ἐναντιώσεως νομίσῃς αὐτοὺς καὶ τὰς ἐνθυμήσεις τῆς καρδίας σου εἰδέναι· οὐ μόνον δέ, ἀλλ' ἵνα καὶ δικάζωνται [1109A] τῇ συνειδήσει σου κρίνειν σε, ὡς τῇ ἐναντιότητι τοῦ κακοῦ ἡττηθέντα τῷ καλῷ· ἔστι δ' ὅταν πάλιν τὴν οἰκείαν σκαιωρίαν ὑπεμφαίνουσί σοι ἵνα παρὰ σεαυτῷ δόξῃς φρόνιμος εἶναι.

Ὁ τῆς ἀσελγείας δαίμων, πῇ μὲν τῇ παρθένῳ κατὰ διάνοιαν τὰς ἀκολάστους συμπλοκὰς ὑπεισφέρει, πῇ δὲ τούτων νεάνισιν δι' ὀνειράτων συμπλέκεσθαι φαντάζει, ὅπως εἰ μὲν τῇ μνήμῃ τοῦ φαντασθέντος κλίνοιτο πρὸς ἡδονήν, τοῖς λογισμοῖς χρήσοιτο πρὸς πόλεμον· εἰ δὲ οὐ κλίνοιτο ἀλλ' ἀνταγωνίζοιτο, κἂν αἴσθηται τὸ πάθος τῇ φύσει μεμενηκός, οὐ πρότερον συγκροτοῦσι πόλεμον οἱ τῆς αἰσχύνης λογισμοί, πρὶν ἢ χώραν ἕξουσι τοῦ τῇ ψυχῇ συνομιλεῖν· οὐδ' αὖ πάλιν κινηθείη πρὸς τὸ πολεμεῖν ἡ ψυχή, πρὶν ἢ μάθῃ ἀντιπαρατάττεσθαι τοῖς

---

12 ἐλάσεις correxi: ἐάσεις E, ἐλάσῃς C   13 δυσεύρετος C: δυσέρευτος E

ἀντιπάλοις λογισμοῖς. ὅταν οἱ δαίμονες τὴν ἔννοιαν ταῖς αἰσχίστοις ἡδοναῖς πειρῶνται σαλεύειν, τότε καὶ τὸν τῆς λαιμαργίας πόλεμον προσάγουσιν, ὅπως ταῖς ὕλαις τὴν γαστέρα προπυρώσαντες, ἀκοπωτέρως τὴν ψυχὴν τῇ ἀσελγείᾳ βαραθρόσωσιν. ἐν τῇ ῥᾳθυμίᾳ τῆς ψυχῆς περιδράσσονται ἡμῶν οἱ δαίμονες τοῦ λογιστικοῦ καὶ ἐν τοῖς λογισμοῖς ἀπερεύγονται τὰς τῆς κακίας ἡδονάς. πῇ μὲν οἱ λογισμοὶ ἐφέλκονται τὰ πάθη, πῇ δὲ τὰ πάθη τοὺς λογισμούς. τὸ τηνικαῦτα καὶ οἱ λογισμοὶ διὰ τοῦ πάθους, πολεμοῦσι τὴν ψυχήν.

Ὅταν οἱ λογισμοὶ μεταστήσωσιν ἡμᾶς εἰς οὓς ὑπέβαλον ἐρᾶν τόπους, τότε μεταμελεῖσθαι πάλιν ποιοῦσιν, ἵνα ἀστάτους ἡμᾶς πανταχόθεν καταστήσωσι καὶ ἀκάρπους. διὸ μὴ πετάζωμεν ἑαυτοὺς ἀπὸ τόπων εἰς τόπους, ἀλλὰ καμπτώμεθα μᾶλλον εἰς ἡσυχίαν καὶ κόπους, ὅτι ἐκ τῆς ἡμετέρας ῥᾳθυμίας λαμβάνουσι καθ᾽ ἡμῶν οἱ λογισμοὶ τὴν δύναμιν. ὁ δὲ εἰδὼς πολέμου πεῖραν ἐν ᾧ τόπῳ ἐκλήθη, ἐν τούτῳ μένει παρὰ θεῷ, ὁ δὲ μὴ εἰδὼς, ὡς ἄπειρος ἔτι βαδίζει. οἱ ἀπὸ τόπων εἰς τόπους μετερχόμενοι μετιέτωσαν εἰς τὰ πνευματικώτερα καὶ μὴ εἰς τὰ ἀναπαυστικώτερα· ὑπομονὴ γὰρ καὶ μακροθυμία [1109B] καὶ ἀγάπη ἐν ταῖς θλίψεσι πάντοτε εὐχαριστεῖ· ἀκηδία δὲ καὶ ἐλαφρία καὶ φιλαυτία ἐν ταῖς ἀναπαύσεσι χαίρει. ὁ ἀνήσυχος ἐκ τῶν περὶ τὰς ὄψεις αἰσθήσεων τὴν ψυχὴν πολεμεῖται, ὁ δὲ φιλήσυχος, τὰς αἰσθήσεις φυλάσσων, τοὺς λογισμοὺς πολεμεῖ.

(13) Τῷ οὖν διατάγματι τοῦ νόμου τῶν αἰσθήσεων τὴν τάξιν ὁ ἡγεμών σου συναγέτω, ἵνα μὴ βλέμματι καὶ ἀκοῇ μάστιγας κακῶν τῇ ψυχῇ σου καταταράξῃς· ἐν [1109C] δυσὶν οὐσίαις ὑπάρχων, ἑκάστῃ διανέμειν τὴν τάξιν φυλάττου, ἵνα ἡ μὲν ἀριστεύῃ, ἡ δὲ μὴ ἀνταίρῃ· καὶ τῷ τυράννῳ ἐπιτάγματα μὴ δίδου, ὅτι τῷ πυρὶ τούτου δοθέντος, καὶ τὸν ἔσχατον κοδράντην ἀποδώσεις.

14. ASCETIC ACHIEVEMENT AND PRIDE

Ὁπηνίκα τὰς τῶν παθῶν αἰτίας ἀντιπολεμῶν τροπώσῃ, τὸ τηνικαῦτα μή σε λογισμὸς μεγαλύνῃ δολουργῶς, μήπως πνεύματι πλάνης πιστεύσας τῶν φρενῶν ἐκπλαγῇς. ἐπιζήτει δὲ λογιστεύων τὰς ἐφ᾽ οἷς πονεῖς ὑποβολάς, ὅπως τὰ τέλη τῶν κατορθωμάτων διὰ τῶν ἔνδον μὴ παραφθαρῇ. τινὲς ἐπὶ κατορθώμασιν εὐφημηθέντες, τῷ χρόνῳ τοὺς πόνους ἠκηδίασαν καὶ ἡ μὲν εὐφημία διώδευσεν, οἱ δὲ πόνοι ἐλύθησαν. τινὲς δι᾽ ὄγκον κακῶν σκληρουχούμενοι, μεγάλοι ἐνομίσθησαν καὶ τῆς μὲν ψυχῆς τὸ συνειδὸς εἱλκοῦτο, τῆς δὲ εὐφημίας ἡ νόσος ηὐρύνετο, οἱ δὲ λογισμοὶ τῶν [1109D] τραυμάτων τὴν ψυχὴν ἀποπλανήσαντες ἐν ταῖς εὐφημίαις τοὺς πόνους ἀπέφερον. ὁπηνίκα ταῖς παρ᾽ ἀνθρώπων τιμαῖς οἱ πονικώτατοι πλουτήσωσι, τὸ τηνικαῦτα καὶ τὰς ἀτιμίας οἱ δαίμονες σκευάσαντες ἐπάγουσι τούτοις, ἵνα, ἀπὸ τῶν τιμῶν ὄντες, τὰς ἀτιμίας μὴ φέρωσι καὶ τὰς ὕβρεις μὴ βαστάσωσιν.

Ὅταν ἐφ᾽ ἁμαρτίαις μεγάλην μετάνοιαν διδῷς, τότε οἱ λογισμοὶ τοὺς ἀγῶνας τῶν πόνων μεγαλύνοντες τὰς ἁμαρτίας σμικρύνουσι καὶ πολλάκις τῇ λήθῃ καλύπτουσιν, ἢ καὶ συγχωρεῖσθαι ταύτας σημαίνουσιν, ἵνα ὑπενδοὺς τοῖς πόνοις, μὴ ἀναλογίζῃ τῶν πταισμάτων τοὺς θρήνους τοῦ κατ᾽ αὐτῶν ὠρύεσθαι πλείονας.

(14) ὁ δὲ τὰ προσπεσόντα πάθη πυκτεύων ἐκκόψαι [1112A] πλείονας παθῶν

ὁπλίτας ἐπιστρατηγήσει τῇ μάχῃ. μὴ ἀμνημόνει πταίσας, κἂν μετανοήσῃς, ἀλλὰ
μνήμην ἔχε τῆς σῆς ἁμαρτίας τὸ πένθος πρὸς ταπείνωσίν σου, ὅπως ταπεινωθεὶς
ἀνάγκῃ τὴν ὑπερηφανίαν ἐμέσῃς.

Εἴ τις τῶν ἄθεσμα δρασάντων βούλοιτο μεταβιῶσαι ἀρίστως, κατ᾽ ἄντικρυ
τῶν ἐναντίων πράξεων στήτω τῇ τῶν κρειττόνων ἐναλλαγῇ· καὶ γὰρ ὁ ἐν ἑκάστῃ
πονηρίᾳ τὴν ἀντικειμένην πρᾶξιν ἀνθιστῶν τῇ συνετῇ τῶν ἀρετῶν βελοθήκῃ
τοξεύει τὸν δράκοντα· τοῦ δὲ θηρὸς ὀξύτατον ὅπλον ἐστὶν ἡ κενοδοξία, τοὺς πόνους
κατατοξεύουσα, ἥνπερ ὁ ταῖς κρυπταῖς τῶν ἔργων στρατηγίαις προκαταλαβών,
ἤγγικεν ἅπασαν τὴν τοῦ διαβόλου κατενέγκαι κεφαλήν.

Τὰ ἀρώματά σου τῶν πόνων σφράγισον τῇ σιγῇ, ἵνα μὴ γλώττῃ λυθέντα ὑπὸ
δόξης κλαπῶσι. κρύπτε σου τὴν γλῶτταν ἐν τῷ [1112B] πρακτικῷ τῆς ἀσκήσεως
τρόπῳ· σοῦ γὰρ σιγῶντος, μάρτυρας σχοίης τοῦ βίου τοὺς ἀξιοπίστους συμβιώτας
σου πόνους. ὁ μαρτυρεῖσθαι ἀπὸ τῶν παρόντων πόνων οὐκ ἔχων τίς ἦν ποτέ,
ἑαυτῷ μὴ γλώττῃ μαρτυρείτω. τινὲς γὰρ τῶν πόνων τῆς σκληρουχίας ἑαυτοὺς
ἐκδύσαντες, ὡς προκάλυμμα τῆς ῥᾳθυμίας τῶν ἀπελθόντων χρόνων τὰς πράξεις
προβάλλουσι, μάρτυρας ἐκδήμους ἔργοις οὐ παροῦσιν ἀβεβαίως παρέχοντες.

Ὥσπερ ἐκ τῶν ἀνθρώπων κρύπτεις σου τὰς ἁμαρτίας, οὕτω καὶ τοὺς
πόνους ἐξ αὐτῶν ἀπόκρυπτε· καὶ γὰρ τὸ ἀντίτεχνον τῶν κρυφίων τῆς καρδίας,
σκελλισμάτων τὰ κρυφῇ καὶ τὰ ἀναπαλαίσματα, κατ᾽ αὐτῶν ἀντιστηρίζειν σε· εἰ
δὲ τὰ μὲν πλημμελήματα ἀσφαλῶς ἀποκρύπτομεν, τὰ δὲ κατ᾽ αὐτῶν ποιήματα
ἀνασφαλῶς[14] ἀνακαλύπτομεν, καὶ ἐν τοῖς [1112C] ἀμφοτέροις τὰ ἐναντία
διαπραττόμεθα. ἀλλ᾽ ἐπαισχύνῃ τῶν αἰσχρῶν τὴν δημοσίευσιν, μήπως ὄνειδος καὶ
ἐξουδένωσιν ποιήσῃς τὰς τῆς ψυχῆς σου συμφοράς. οὐ φοβῇ δὲ καὶ τῶν πόνων τὴν
ἐπίδειξιν, μήπως ἐγκλήματι ἀνθρωπαρέσκῳ κομίσῃ τὸν τῆς ψυχῆς σου ὄλεθρον; εἰ
δὲ μόνῳ θεῷ ἐκφαίνεις τὰ τῆς αἰσχύνης παραπτώματα, μὴ ἀνθρώποις ἔκφαινε τὰ
κατ᾽ αὐτῶν ἀνταγωνίσματα ἵνα μὴ νομισθῶσιν ἤδη νίκης εἶναι στεφανώματα.

(15) Οἱ τὴν δύναμιν τῶν πόνων ἀπὸ τῆς χάριτος λαβόντες [1112D] μὴ ὡς ἐξ
οἰκείας ἰσχύος ἔχειν ταύτην νομιζέτωσαν· αἴτιος γὰρ πάντων τῶν καλῶν ἡμῖν
ἐστιν ὁ τῶν ἐντολῶν λόγος, ὥσπερ οὖν καὶ τῶν κακῶν ὁ τῶν ὑποβολῶν ἀπατηλός.
ἅπερ οὖν διαπράττῃ καλά, τῷ αἰτίῳ τὴν εὐχαριστίαν πρόσφερε· ἃ δὲ διοχλεῖ σοι
κακά, τῷ ἀρχηγέτῃ τούτων πρόσριπτε. πάσης πραγματείας τὸ τέλος πρόσφερε
εὐχαριστίαν τῷ κρείττονι, ἵνα τῆς προσφορᾶς σου νομίμως προσενεχθείσης ἡ
κακία καταισχύνηται. ὁ γὰρ τῇ πράξει τὴν εὐχαριστίαν συνάψας, ἀπόρθητον ἕξει
τὸν θησαυρὸν τῆς καρδίας, διπλοῦν κατὰ τῆς κακίας πυργώσας τὸ τεῖχος.

15. SPIRITUAL DIRECTION

Ἐπαινετὸς οὗτος ἀνὴρ ὁ τῇ πρακτικῇ τὴν γνωστικὴν συζεύξας, ἵνα ἐξ ἀμφοτέρων
πηγῶν τὸ τῆς ψυχῆς χωρίον ἀρδεύοιτο πρὸς ἀρετήν· ἡ μὲν γὰρ γνωστικὴ πτεροῖ
τὴν νοερὰν οὐσίαν [1113A] τῇ τῶν κρειττόνων θεωρίᾳ, ἡ δὲ πρακτικὴ "νεκροῖ τὰ
μέλη τὰ ἐπὶ τῆς γῆς, πορνείαν, ἀκαθαρσίαν, πάθος, κακίαν, ἐπιθυμίαν κακήν".

---

14 ἀνασφαλῶς fort. recte C: ἀνασφάλτως E, σφαλερῶς Pg

οἱ οὖν διὰ τῶν ἀμφοτέρων τούτων τῇ πανοπλίᾳ περιπεφραγμένοι, εὐκόλως κατεπιβήσονται λοιπὸν τῆς τῶν δαιμόνων πονηρίας.

Οἱ δαίμονες διὰ τῶν λογισμῶν τὴν ψυχὴν πολεμοῦσι, κἀκεῖνοι δὲ χαλεπωτέρως διὰ τῆς ὑπομονῆς ἀντιπολεμοῦνται, καὶ δειλιῶντες προσίασι λοιπὸν τῇ μάχῃ, κραταιὸν τὸν στρατηγὸν τῆς πυγμῆς ὑφορῶντες. εἰ βούλει στρατηγῆσαι κατὰ τῆς φάλαγγος τῶν δαιμόνων, ἡσυχίᾳ φράσσε τὰς τῆς ψυχῆς σου πύλας, θῆγε δὲ καὶ τὸ οὖς σου τοῖς τῆς πατροσύνης λόγοις, ἵνα τότε μᾶλλον λογισμῶν ἀκάνθας παθῶν[15] ἐμπρήσῃς.

Ἐπὰν πατρικῆς νουθεσίας ἀκροάσῃ, μὴ τῶν ἔργων ἔσο τούτου δικαστής, ἀλλὰ τῶν ῥήσεων ἐξεταστής. [1113B] (16) ἔθος γὰρ τοῖς τοιούτοις λογισμοῖς εἰς τὸ πρακτικὸν τοῦ νουθετοῦντός σε ἀπάγειν, ἵνα δεινόν σε τούτου καταστήσαντες κριτὴν τῆς ἐπωφελοῦς νουθεσίας ἀποστήσωσι. [new hand 284r] μὴ ἀπαναίνου νουθετούμενος, κἂν γνωστικὸς ὑπάρχῃς· ἐὰν γὰρ τὸ πρακτικὸν τῆς γνωστικῆς ἀποζευχθῇ, χρεία τοῦ ζευγνύντος τὴν ὁποτέρων τῶν ἀρετῶν ἁρμονίαν τῇ φρικτῇ τῆς κρίσεως δίκῃ. ὁ τὴν πατρῴαν ἐντολὴν ἐκ τοῦ ὠτὸς ἐκτινάσσων καὶ νομικῆς ἐντολῆς παρήκοος ἔσται.

Μὴ μόνον κατορθώματα πατέρων τερπόμενος λάλει, ἀλλὰ καὶ σεαυτὸν ἐργάτην τούτων πονικώτατον ἀπαίτει. ὁ πονικώτερον ἐπιζητῶν, οἷος οἴῳ πόνῳ λογισμὸς [1113C] ἀντίκειται, τεχνίτης ἐν πάλῃ κατὰ τῆς πλάνης εὑρίσκεται. ἐν ὅλοις δὲ τοῖς νοεροῖς σου πόνοις, εἰς ἐὰν ἐλλείψῃ, ὁ τούτων συλήσας ἀντ' αὐτοῦ παρεισδύνει. μνημόνευε τῇ συνέσει τῶν πόνων συντηρεῖν τὴν καρδίαν, μήπως ἡ λήθη τῆς τῶν κρειττόνων μερίμνης ταύτην συλήσασα τῇ τῶν λογισμῶν αἰχμαλωσίᾳ παραδῷ· ἡ γὰρ λήθη τῆς αἰχμαλωσίας προπηδᾷ τῇ κακίᾳ, ἵνα ὑπ' ἐκείνης τοῦ νοῦ κλαπέντος ἑτοίμως αὕτη παρεισέλθοι. νοῦς κλεπτόμενος ἀπὸ θεοῦ καὶ μνήμῃ μακρυνόμενος, καὶ διὰ τῶν ἐκτὸς αἰσθήσεων ἀδιαφόρως ἁμαρτάνει· ἀκοὴν γὰρ καὶ γλῶτταν ὁ τοιοῦτος ἀδυνατεῖ παιδαγωγῆσαι, ὅτι τὸ φίλτρον τῶν πόνων ἐκ τῶν ἐκτὸς ἐξαφῆκεν.

16. MALICIOUS GOSSIP

Ὁ φιλῶν εἰσακούειν τοῦ ψέγοντος τὸν δεῖνα, δυσὶ συνεργοῖς πνεύμασι συνεργοῦσιν [1113D] οἱ δύο· ἡ γὰρ κακηκοΐα τῆς κακηγορίας συνεργὸς τυγχάνει, καὶ ἐρῶσιν ἀλλήλων εἰς λύμην καρδίας. (17) ἐκ τῶν καταλαλιῶν τὰ ὦτά σου φράξον, ἵνα μὴ διττῶς σὺν αὐτοῖς ἀνομήσῃς, σαυτὸν μὲν δεινῷ πάθει ἐθίζων, γλωσσαλγεῖν δὲ ἐκείνους οὐκ ἀνακόπτων. ψυχὴν τῶν κρειττόνων ὁ φιλοσκώπτης[16] ληστεύει, σαθρὰν ἀκοὴν διαβολαῖς διορύττων· ὁ δὲ διαδρῶν τὴν τοῦ πέλας λοίδορον γλῶτταν καὶ τὴν οἰκείαν λοιδορίαν φυγαδεύει. ἡδεῖς ἀκοὰς τῷ λοιδόρῳ παρέχων, ἰὸν θηρὸς τοῖς ὠσὶν ἀμέλγει. μὴ γευέσθω τὸ οὖς σου τῆς τοιαύτης [1116A] πικρᾶς ἀντιδότου, μήπως τοιαύτην καὶ σὺ συγκεράσεις ἑτέρῳ. μὴ γοήτευεν καταλαλιαῖς τὸ οὖς σου, ἵνα μὴ πάθει πραθεὶς πολυπαθείᾳ δουλεύσῃς· ἐν γὰρ τῶν πολλῶν πάθος τόπον ἐν σοὶ εὑρόν, εἰς τὸν αὐτὸν σηκὸν καὶ ἄλλα συνεισφέρει· τότε πλήθει κακῶν ὁ ἡγεμὼν δουλοῦται, ὅταν πάθει ζευχθεὶς τοὺς πόνους ἀποζεύξῃ.

15 μᾶλλον παθῶν λογισμῶν ἀκάνθας C   16 φιλοσκόπτης CE

Ὁ τὰς ἑτέρων σκώψεις¹⁷ πειρώμενος ἐρευνᾶν τὰς ἑαυτοῦ πράξεις ἔργῳ οὐκ
ἐρευνᾷ. μὴ ὡς ἀμελῶς ζήσαντα τὸν ἀποβιώσαντα σκῶπτε¹⁸, ἵνα μὴ ὡς ἐκ
συνηθείας τῶν ζώντων καὶ τοῦ νεκροῦ πικρὸς γένῃ δικαστής. μὴ τοῖς πταίουσιν
ἔπεχε λογισμῷ ἀλαζόνι ἐπαίροντί σε ὡς δικαστήν, ἀλλὰ σαυτῷ πρόσεχε λογισμῷ
νήφοντι καὶ τῶν σῶν πράξεων δοκιμαστῇ. στένε πταίων καὶ μὴ φυσῶ κατορθῶν
ἀκαταφρόνητος εἶναι. μὴ μεγαλαύχει, ὅπως μὴ ὡς κόσμον [1116B] τὸ κακὸν
ἐνδύσῃ.

Τινὲς γὰρ ἀπὸ εὐλαβείας μὴ δυνάμενοι γνωσθῆναι ἔσπευσαν, κἂν ἀπὸ κακίας
οὕτω γνωσθῆναι· ἕτεροι δὲ αὐξηθέντες τῷ φθόνῳ, προφάσεις ἀκροβολοῦσι καὶ τοὺς
εὐσταθοῦντας ταῖς ἀρεταῖς ἐξουδενοῦσι τοῖς πέριξ. τινὲς εἰς φαῦλα θρυλούμενοι
βίον σεμνὸν ἀμφιέννυνται, οὐχ ἵνα τὰ πταίσματα τοῖς πόνοις θρηνήσωσιν, ἀλλ᾽ ἵνα
τῶν ψόγων τὰς φήμας σκιάσωσιν. ἀλλὰ μὴ τῷ ἀπατῶντί σε καλλωπίζου, μηδὲ τῷ
ἀπατᾶσθαι ἐναγάλλου· ἐὰν γὰρ δι᾽ ὄνομα ψιλὸν τῶν σπουδαίων ἐφάπτῃ, οὐ θεῷ,
ἀλλ᾽ ἀνθρώποις ἐργάζῃ.

17. JEALOUSY

Μὴ παρρησίαν ἄγε τῷ ἀπόνως βιοῦντι, κἂν ὄνομα τούτῳ μέγα πομπεύῃ· ἔστι
φίλος προσώπου χάριν, καὶ χρόνος κατήγορος τούτου γίνεται. [1116C] (18)
Δεδοικότα φίλον σκώπτην¹⁹ κτῆσαι, ἵνα σκέπην εὕρῃς τῶν σῶν πταισμάτων, τὸ
δὲ φθονούμενον ἐν σοὶ κρύπτε μάλιστα τοῦ φθονοῦντος. ὅταν ὁ σὸς φίλος ἐπὶ ταῖς
σαῖς τῶν πόνων εὐφημίαις ἐλαττούμενος εἰς φθόνον ἐκτραπῇ, ὡς καὶ τοῖς πέριξ
ῥήματα κενοδοξίας ἀκοντίζειν σου τοῖς πόνοις, ὅπως τὴν διατρέχουσαν περὶ σοῦ
δόξαν συσκιάσῃ τοῖς σοῖς σκώμμασι²⁰, τότε μὴ τῇ ἐκείνου βασκανίᾳ προσέχων
δηχθῇς, ἵνα μὴ ἰὸν πικρὸν τῇ ψυχῇ σου σιφωνίσῃς²¹. τοῦτο γὰρ ἔργον τοῦ Σατανᾶ,
ἵνα ἐκεῖνον²² μὲν τῷ φθόνῳ ἐκπυρώσῃ, σὲ δὲ πικρίᾳ ἀναλώσῃ. ταπεινούμεθα δὲ
μᾶλλον καὶ τῇ τιμῇ τοὺς τοιούτους προηγούμεθα, ἐξημεροῦντες αὐτῶν καὶ διὰ
τραπέζης τὸ ἀγριωθὲν [1116D] τῷ ζήλῳ φρόνημα.

Μὴ ὡς ἐξ ἑτέρου προσώπου ψέγε ζήλῳ τὸν φίλον, ἵνα ὡς ἐξ ἄλλου δῆθεν
στόματος ψέγων ἐκεῖνον, σεαυτὸν ὡς ἀθῷον ποιήσῃς καὶ ὡς ἄψογον ὑψώσῃς·
τοῦτο γὰρ μετασχηματισμὸς τοῦ Σατανᾶ, τοῦ ἐκ ὄφεως τὸν ὕψιστον
ψέγοντος, ἵνα, ὡς ἐξ ἑτέρου δῆθεν στόματος, τὸν ἑαυτοῦ φθόνον τῷ θεῷ προσάψας,
αὐτὸς ὡς ἄφθονος νομίζηται.

Μὴ ὡς ὑπόδουλον θέλων ἔχειν τὸν ἀδελφὸν πειρῶ τούτου πταίσματα
καταλαβεῖν, ἵνα μὴ συνεργὸς εὑρεθῇς τοῦ Σατανᾶ. ὁ πταίσας ἑτέρους ψέγειν ἢ
πταίειν μὴ ἐπιχειρείτω, ὡς ἵνα μὴ μόνος ᾖ συμπεσὼν [1117A] τῷ κακῷ, ὅπερ τῆς
ἐκπτώσεως τοῦ διαβόλου πρῶτον καὶ τοῦτο ἔργον ἐστίν. ἔστω δὲ μεταμελούμενος
ἐφ᾽ οἷς ἀτόποις ἔπραξεν ἔργοις, τὸν τῆς λύπης θρῆνον κατ᾽ αὐτῶν ἐπιγινώσκων,
ἐπισπάσεται δὲ καὶ τὴν πρωτοστάτην τῶν πόνων ἡσυχίαν, φαίνουσαν αὐτῷ τὴν
πολυόμματον τῶν ἀρετῶν θεωρίαν. ὁ ἡσυχάζων τῇ γλώττῃ κατὰ τῶν λογισμῶν

---

17 σκόψεις CE   18 σκόπτε E, σκόπται C   19 σκόπτην E, σκόπτειν C
20 σκόμμασι E, σκόμμασιν C   21 σιφωνήσῃς E   22 ἐκεῖνον C: ἐκείνῳ E

ἀνδριζέσθω· ἡ γὰρ τῆς ψυχῆς ἀνδρεία οὐκ ἐν τῇ ἡσυχίᾳ μόνον δείκνυται τοῦ σώματος, ἀλλὰ καὶ ἐν τῇ τῶν λογισμῶν ἀνδραγαθίᾳ καὶ τῇ τῶν ὕβρεων καὶ ἀδικιῶν εὐσταθείᾳ. ἐντεῦθεν γὰρ αἱ δειναὶ μάστιγες τοῦ διαβόλου περιτινάσσονται ἐν ταῖς συντυχίαις. [1117Β]

18. FORNICATION

(19) Μὴ στόμα μόνον, ἀλλὰ καὶ καρδία τηρείσθω. τότε γὰρ ἀμαυροῦται τῆς ψυχῆς τὸ ὄμμα τῷ τῆς ἀρεσκείας πνεύματι, τοῦ νοῦ πασσομένου²³. ἔστω σου πηρὸς ὁ νοῦς περὶ τὰ αἴσχιστα, "κύριος γὰρ σοφοῖ τοὺς τοιούτους τυφλούς", διορατικὸς δὲ περὶ τὰ κάλλιστα, ἵνα ἐκτυφλώττῃ τὰ κάκιστα.

Νόει δέ μοι πορνείας εἶναι δύο ἐν διαιρέσει ἐζυγωμένας, τὴν τοῦ σώματος καὶ τὴν τοῦ πνεύματος²⁴, καθ᾽ ὧν καὶ ἡ παρθένος "ἵνα ᾖ ἁγία τῷ σώματι καὶ τῷ πνεύματι". ὅταν λογισμὸς πορνείας τῇ ψυχῇ σου μίγνυται, τότε ἐκτυπώματι πλάνης ἡ ψυχή σου συγγίνεται. προσώπῳ θηλείας σχηματίζεται δαίμων, ἵνα φαρμάξῃ σὴν ψυχὴν μετ᾽ αὐτοῦ συμμιγῆναι· μορφῆς γλύμμα φορεῖ ἄσαρκος φάσμα ἵνα λογισμῷ ἀκολάστῳ τὴν ψυχὴν ἐκπορνεύσῃ. μὴ [1117C] οὖν συγκατακάμπτου εἰδωλείῳ ἀνυπάρκτῳ, ἵνα μὴ καὶ τῇ σαρκὶ τὸ ὅμοιον δράσῃς. πνεύματι πορνείας ἐπλανήθησαν οἱ τοιοῦτοι, οἱ τὰς ἔνδον μοιχείας τῶν πνευμάτων τῷ σταυρῷ μὴ σοβοῦντες.

Αἴκιζε τοὺς λογισμοὺς ἀσιτίᾳ βρωμάτων, ἵνα μὴ πορνείᾳ, ἀλλὰ πείνῃ λαλῶσιν εὐχῆς· ἀγρυπνίαν στῆσον δακρύων, ἵνα βοήθειαν λάβῃς τοῦ παρόντος πολέμου. ἐν καιρῷ τοῦ τῆς πορνείας πολέμου²⁵ τὰς κλήσεις τῶν ἑστιατόρων παραίτησαι· καὶ τὸν μὲν ξένον ἐπιστάντα ὑπηρετῶν ἀναπαύσεις, σεαυτὸν δὲ περικεκαλυμμένως ἀσιτίᾳ περιφράξεις. διπλοῦς ἔστω σοι τῶν ἀμφοτέρων ἔργων ὁ μισθὸς ἑνὶ ἑκάστῳ τὸ πρακτικὸν δι᾽ ἀρετὴν ἀπονέμοντι. μὴ εἵνεκεν γαστρὸς συνεστία τῷ ἀδελφῷ, ἀλλ᾽ εἵνεκεν Χριστοῦ συναυλίζου²⁶ ἀγάπῃ. ὁ κόρος σιτίων λογισμοὺς σιτίζει καὶ μέθυσος ὕπνον φαντασίας ποτίζει. [1117D] τέθνηκε μετὰ τὸν φάραγγα τῆς τρυφῆς ἡδονὴ καὶ ὑπνεῖ ἐν τῷ τάφῳ τὰ τῆς γαστρὸς λαγνεύματα. οἱ πόνοι τῆς σκληρουχίας τελευτῶσιν εἰς ἀνάπαυσιν, οἱ δὲ τρόποι τῆς τρυφηλίας τελευτῶσιν εἰς κατάκαυσιν. ὁ τῆς σαρκὸς τὸ ἄνθος τῇ ἀσκήσει μαραίνων καθ᾽ ἡμέραν ἐν τῇ σαρκὶ μελετᾷ τὴν ἑαυτοῦ τελευτήν. ἡ τῆς καρδίας λογιστεία τὸ σῶμα συμμετρείτω, ἵνα μὴ τούτου πληγέντος καὶ αὐτὴ κοπιάσῃ. ἀρκείσθω σὰρξ τὰ φυσικὰ περικόπτουσα· ἡ σωματική σου γυμνασία ἐν τοῖς ἤθεσιν οἰκονομείσθω, ἵνα μάθῃς καρδίαν πονεῖν καὶ ψυχὴν συμπονεῖν.

19. SELF-SATISFACTION

(20) Οἱ τοῦ προσώπου τὴν ὠχρίαν ἐν τῇ ἀσκήσει λάμποντες τὸν παρὰ τῶν ἀνθρώπων ἔπαινον καὶ πρὶν [1120A] ἐλθεῖν ῥιπτέτωσαν τούτων, τοῦ λογισμοῦ καὶ πρὸ τῆς συντυχίας ἔνδον ἐκβάλλοντες. ὅταν χρονίσῃς ἀπεχόμενος οἴνου καὶ

---

23 πασσομένου ACEMa: παυσομένου Pg   24 τὴν τοῦ σώματος καὶ τὴν τοῦ πνεύματος
PgSyr   25 πολέμου C: στολισμοῦ E   26 συναυλίζου C: συναυλίζων E

ἐλαίου καὶ τῶν περιττῶν, τότε οἱ λογισμοὶ τοὺς χρόνους σοι μετ᾽ ἐγκωμίων
ψηφίζοντες ὑπενδοῦναί σε τοῖς πόνοις διὰ τὸ σῶμα γυμνάζουσιν. εἰκότως οὖν
τοῖς κακογνώμοσιν ἀντιφθέγξῃ διαψηφισταῖς, ὅσα πρὸς ἀνατροπὴν τῆς ἐκείνων
σκαιωρίας ἀντίκειται.

Τὶς τῶν ἀδελφῶν διὰ τῶν λογισμῶν τοὺς πόνους ὑπὸ δαιμόνων τῶν ἔνδον
ἐπαινούμενος ἔψαλλεν. "Ἀποστραφήτωσαν παραυτίκα οἱ λέγοντές μοι· εὖγε,
εὖγε." μὴ τῶν λογισμῶν ἀνάσχῃ πολυετῆ σοι κύκλον ἐν τῷ μονήρει βίῳ φερόντων,
ἵνα μή σου τοὺς πόνους τοῖς χρόνοις κρεμάσωσι, μηδὲ ἐν τῇ ὑπομονῇ τῇ τῆς
ἐρημίας καυχήσῃ ζωγρηθείς· ἀλλ᾽ ἐν τῇ ὑπομονῇ τῆς εὐτελείας τὸ δοῦλος [1120B]
ἀχρεῖος εἶναι μνήσθητι.

Διὰ γῆρας βαθύ τινα τῶν καρτερικῶν μονηρεμίτην πρεσβύτην ἐκ τῆς ἐρημίας
αἴρειν ἐβιάζετο. ὁ δὲ πρὸς αὐτόν· παῦσαι, φησί, τῆς βίας, οὔπω γὰρ τῆς ἐξορίας
ὁ κακοῦργος ἀνακέκλημαι. ζητοῦντος δέ μου τοῦτον τὸν τῆς διδασκαλίας λόγον
μαθεῖν, ἔφη· ζητεῖτε πρῶτον ἐμπόνως τὸν ἔμφυτον φόβον, καὶ τότε ἔνδον εὑρήσεις
τὸν ἔμπυρον λόγον τὸν διδάσκοντα ἄνθρωπον γνῶσιν. ὁ δ᾽ αὐτὸς ἐπερωτηθεὶς καὶ
περὶ φόβου, οὕτως ἀπεκρίνατο· ὁ μέριμναν ἔχων ἀεὶ τοῦ θανάτου τὴν μνήμην
ὁδηγεῖται καὶ εἰς τὸν τῆς κρίσεως φόβον.

Φόβῳ τῶν θείων γραφῶν καθ᾽ ἑκάστην συνόμιλος γίνου· τῇ γὰρ τούτων
συνουσίᾳ λογισμῶν ἐξοίσεις ὁμιλίας.²⁷ ὁ μελέτῃ τὰς θείας γραφὰς ἐκθησαυρίζων
τῇ καρδίᾳ τοὺς λογισμοὺς ἐκ ταύτης ῥᾳδίως ἐκβάλλει. ἀναγνώσει νυκτερινῇ ἐν
[1120C] ταῖς ἀγρυπνίαις τῶν θείων γραφῶν ἀκροώμενοι, μὴ τὰς ἀκοὰς τῷ ὕπνῳ
νεκρώσωμεν, μηδὲ τῇ τῶν λογισμῶν αἰχμαλωσίᾳ τὴν ψυχὴν προδώσωμεν, ἀλλὰ
τῷ κέντρῳ τῶν γραφῶν τὴν καρδίαν κατανύξωμεν, ὅπως τῇ τῆς ἐπιμελείας
κατανύξει τὴν ἀντίζυγον ἀμέλειαν διχοτομήσωμεν.

20. MISCELLANEOUS COUNSELS

(21) Τινὲς διὰ φήμην καὶ οὐκ ἐπιμέλειαν ψυχῆς τοῖς εὐλαβέσι φιλιοῦνται, ἵν᾽
ἑαυτοῖς κόσμον περιποιήσωσιν ἀπόνως.

Ὁ δὲ διὰ μνήμην τῶν ἐπουρανίων τῇ ἀγάπῃ πυρούμενος τὴν ἀρέσκειαν τῶν
ἐπιγείων ἐκ τῆς ἐννοίας ἐκκαθαίρεται.

Τὸ διαμαρτυροῦν σοι [1120D] συνειδὸς μὴ παραπέμπου λογισμῷ καταφρονοῦντι
καὶ γλυκολογοῦντι τὸ πταῖσμα.

Τῷ φιλονεικοῦντι μὴ συνδιατείνου, ἵνα μὴ πάθει πάθος στρατεύσας τῆς ἀρετῆς
ἡττηθῇς.

Τῷ ὑπερηφάνῳ μὴ συνεπαίρου λογισμῷ ἀντιφυσῶντι εἰς ἀντάνεμον πνεῦμα.

Οὐκ ἔπαινος γλώσσῃ τροχαλῶς φθεγγομένῃ, ἀλλὰ χείλεσι δόξα εὐσταθῶς
κινουμένοις.

27 λογισμῶν ἐξοίσεις ὁμιλίας correxi: λογισμὸν ἔξοις [ἔξεις E²] εἰς ὁμιλίας E, λογισμὸν
ἐξοίσις ὁμιλία C

324 Appendix 2

Ἀκροώμενος λόγον, ἐρώτα τὸν νοῦν σου καὶ τότε διακρίνας τὸ ψήφισμα δώσεις·
Μὴ παραλογίζου τὸν νοῦν σου ἀβουλίᾳ ῥημάτων, ἵνα μὴ κρημνισθείη ἡ χανανιτὶς
σου γλῶσσα.

Μή σε πνεῦμα πολυρῆμον πλανήσῃ, ἐν αὐτῷ γὰρ φωλεύει τὸ δόλιον ψεῦδος·
[ὅπλισαι δὲ σοφίας λόγον ἀληθῆ, ἵν᾽ ἐκπολεμήσῃς τὸ πολυμήχανον ψεῦδος.²⁸]

Ὁ ταῖς παρ᾽ ἑτέρων λοιδορίαις [1121A] δακνόμενος καὶ μὴ ταύτας τῷ διαβόλῳ
προσρίπτων τὸν τῶν λογισμῶν αὐτοῦ δῆμον ἑαυτῷ ἐπεγείρει, καὶ ἑαυτὸν δὲ βέλη
σκευάζειν ἔτι μᾶλλον ἐρεθίζει, ἐν τῷ τὴν ψυχὴν διὰ τῶν τοιούτων τιτρωσκομένην
συμπίπτειν.

Ἕνεκεν διακονίας ἐπ᾽ ἀλλοδαπῆς ἐὰν βαδίσῃς, μὴ φιλοξενεῖσθαι παρὰ πάντων
εὐτρεπίζου, ἀνάξιον ἑαυτὸν τῆς δοχῆς καταλέγων ἵνα οὕτως τὸν τῆς λοιδορίας
λογισμὸν φυγαδεύσῃς, κἂν λέγειν τἀληθῆ νομίζῃ.

Ὡς οὐκ οὔσης ἀγάπης λοιδορούμενος τὰ μέγιστα ἢ ἀδικούμενος, οὐ μνησικακήσεις,
ἀλλ᾽ εὐλογήσεις. ὁ γὰρ δαίμοσι μνησικακῶν ἀνθρώποις ἀμνησικακεῖ· εἰρηνεύει δὲ
μετὰ δαιμόνων, ὁ τῷ ἀδελφῷ μνησικακῶν.

Ἐμπρησμὸς καρδίας μῆνις ἀντιλογίας, ψυχαὶ δὲ ἀμνησικάκων δροσίζονται
πνευματικῶς.

Ἄνθρακες πυρὸς σπινθῆρας ἐρεύγονται, [1121B] καὶ μνησίκακοι ψυχαὶ λογισμοὺς
πονηρούς.

Ὥσπερ πληγὴ σκορπίου δριμύτατον ἔχει τὸν πόνον, οὕτω καὶ μνησίκακος ψυχὴ
πικρότατον ἔχει τὸν ἰόν.

21. FORNICATION AND VAINGLORY

(22) Πνεύματι πορνείας μνησικάκει καὶ κενοδοξίας, δυσὶ πικροῖς δαίμοσιν
ἐναντίοις ἀλλήλων· ὁ μὲν γὰρ πρόσωπα φεύγει, ὁ δὲ προσώποις χαίρει. [καὶ
ὁ μὲν τῆς ἀσελγείας δαίμων τῷ τῆς ἀσκήσεως ἀγωνιστῇ τὰς ῥυπαρίας ἄφνω
ἀκοντίσας, ἀφάλλεται ὀξέως τῆς διαπύρου τῶν πόνων δαδουχίας, τὴν θέρμην
μὴ φέρων. [1121C] τῷ δὲ τῆς ἐγκρατείας χαυνωθέντι κολακείᾳ ἡδονῶν τὸ κατ᾽
ὀλίγον ἐπιβουλεύει συνομιλεῖν τῇ καρδίᾳ, ἵν᾽ ἐξαφθεῖσα ταῖς κακίας διαλογαῖς
αἰχμαλωτισθῇ καὶ τὸ τῆς ἁμαρτίας μῖσος²⁹ εἰς πέρας ἀγάγῃ. ὁ δὲ τῆς κενοδοξίας
πλάνος, δημοχαρὴς]³⁰ τυγχάνων, παρεσκιασμένως ἐφίπταται τῇ ψυχῇ τῶν
ἐθελοπόνων, τὴν δι᾽ ὧν πόνων ἐργάζονται δόξαν ἑαυτῷ θηρώμενος. εἴ τις
οὖν βούλοιτο τούτων σὺν θεῷ περιγενέσθαι, λεπτυνέτω τὴν σάρκα κατὰ τῆς
πορνείας, ταπεινούτω δὲ τὴν ψυχὴν κατὰ τῆς κενοδοξίας· οὕτω γὰρ ῥᾳδίως τοῦ

28 ὅπλησαι δὲ σοφίας λόγον ἀληθῆ, ἵν᾽ ἐκπολεμήσῃς τὸ πολυμήχανον ψεῦδος C, deest in
E per homoioteleuto   29 μῦσος E   30 καὶ ὁ μὲν πρῶτος ὀξὺς τοξότης
ἀκοντιστὴς ὑπάρχει, μετέπειτα δὲ καὶ κόλαξ ταῖς κατὰ μέρος κακίαις περιπτυσσόμενος
τὴν καρδίαν· ὁ δὲ δεύτερος δημόχαρις..... C

μὲν τὴν ματαίαν δόξαν ἐξώσομεν καὶ θεῷ εὐαρεστήσομεν, τοῦ δὲ τὰς ἀκαθάρτους φαντασίας φυσήσομεν καὶ καθαρὰν ἡδονῶν τὴν καρδίαν ποιήσομεν. Χαλεπώτατόν ἐστι συνηθείᾳ ἡδονῶν συνάπτεσθαι τὴν καρδίαν καὶ πολλῶν χρεία κόπων [1121D] τὴν νομὴν κακῶν εἰς ἄκρον ἐκκόψαι. μὴ οὖν ταῖς ἡδοναῖς τῶν λογισμῶν συνομιλεῖν ἐθίσῃς· ἐν γὰρ συλλόγῳ κακῶν ἐκκαίεται πῦρ. οὕτω γὰρ ἐκθερμαίνοντές σε, λογίζεσθαι ποιοῦσι κόπον εἶναι τὴν πυρὰν τῆς φύσεως κρατῆσαι, καὶ ὅτι πολὺς ὁ τῆς καρτερίας χρόνος καὶ βαρὺς ὁ τῆς ἐγκρατείας βίος· ἀναφέρουσι δέ σοι καὶ μνήμας ὧν σε νύκτωρ φαντάζουσιν αἰσχρῶν, μορφάζοντές σοι πυρωτικὰ τῆς πλάνης εἴδωλα. εἶτα καὶ σφοδρότερον[31] ἐν τῇ σαρκὶ ἐξάψαντες τὸν πυρετόν, τῷ νόμῳ τῆς ἁμαρτίας γνωμοδοτοῦσί σοι ἔνδον, ὅτι ὅσον οὐκ ἰσχύεις κατασχεῖν τὴν τῆς φύσεως βίαν, κἂν σήμερον ἁμαρτήσῃς δι᾽ ἀνάγκην, ἀλλ᾽ αὔριον μετανοήσεις διὰ τὴν ἐντολήν· φιλάνθρωπος γὰρ ὁ νόμος καὶ συγχωρῶν ἀνομίας τοῖς μετανοοῦσι. καὶ φέρουσί σοί τινας τῶν μετ᾽ [1124A] ἐγκρατείας πταισάντων καὶ πάλιν μετανοησάντων, ἵνα ἐκ τούτων πιθανοποιήσωσι τῆς ἑαυτῶν ἀπάτης τὴν συμβουλίαν· ὅπως τῇ ἀντιστρόφῳ μετανοίᾳ ψυχὴν ἀνακλάσαντες τὸν ναὸν τῆς σωφροσύνης πορνεῖον ποιήσωσιν· οὕτως ὑποσυρίζοντες οἱ δίγλωσσοι τῶν λογισμῶν ὄφεις ἐν τῷ κινουμένῳ τῆς καρδίας ἐργαστηρίῳ.

(23) Σὺ δέ, ὦ τῆς ἐγκρατείας ἄνθρωπε, μὴ προφάσει [1124B] πάλιν μετανοίας δελεάζου ἐλπίσιν ἀδήλοις, πολλοὶ γὰρ πεσόντες εὐθὺς ἀνηρπάσθησαν, ἕτεροι δὲ ἀναστῆναι οὐκ ἴσχυσαν τῇ τῶν ἡδονῶν συνηθείᾳ ὡς ὑπὸ νόμον δεθέντες. τί γὰρ οἶδας, ἄνθρωπε, εἰ ζήσεις, ἵνα καὶ μετανοήσῃς, ὅτι χρόνους ζωῆς ἑαυτῷ ὑπογράφεις; κἀνταῦθα πταίων, τῇ σαρκί σου χαρίζῃ, τὸ μᾶλλον χάρισαι σεαυτῷ θανάτου τὴν μνήμην καὶ ἀναζωγράφει σου τῇ καρδίᾳ τὴν φοβερὰν τῆς κρίσεως δίκην, εἴ πως δυνηθείης τὸ πυρέττον τῆς σαρκὸς φρόνημα κατασβέσαι· Οὐ γὰρ ἄλλως κατασβέσῃς τὰ πάθη, πρὶν ἢ τῇ σαρκί σου συγκεράσεις τῆς ἀνασκευῆς αὐτῆς πόνους. οὔτε μὴν ψυχικά, πρὶν ἢ τῇ καρδίᾳ ἐξομβρήσεις τοὺς καρποὺς τῆς ἀγάπης. τὰ μὲν σωματικὰ πάθη ἐκ τῶν φυσικῶν τῆς σαρκὸς τὴν ἀρχὴν λαμβάνει, καθ᾽ ὧν [1124C] καὶ ἡ ἐγκράτεια, τὰ δὲ ψυχικὰ ἐκ τῶν ψυχικῶν τὴν κύησιν ἔχει, καθ᾽ ὧν καὶ ἡ ἀγάπη. ἡ ἀγάπη ἀπαθείας ἐστὶ συνάφεια, παθῶν δὲ ἀπαλειφή, τὴν μακροθυμίαν προφέρουσα καὶ τὸν ζέοντα θυμὸν καταψύχουσα, τὴν ταπείνωσιν προβάλλουσα καὶ τὴν ὑπερηφανίαν καταφέρουσα. ἡ ἀγάπη ἔχει μὲν ἴδιον οὐδὲν πλὴν τοῦ θεοῦ· αὐτὴ γάρ ἐστι καὶ ὁ θεός.

22. THE MONASTIC NOVICE

Ὁ εἰς τὴν φαιδρὰν τῶν μοναχῶν σύγκλητον νεοπαγὴς τυγχάνων, τοὺς λογισμοὺς ἀπωθείσθω τοὺς προσσείοντας εὐφημίας αὐτῷ ἀπὸ τῆς συγγενείας, ἵν᾽ ὅπως μὴ τὸν ἐξ ἀνθρώπων ἔπαινον, ἀλλὰ τὸν ἐκ τῶν ἐντολῶν μακαρισμὸν ἐπιζητοίη. τῶν δὲ τὰς δειλίας εἰσβαλλόντων δαιμόνων καταθαρσείτω· "οὐ γὰρ ἐλάβετε πνεῦμα δειλίας πάλιν εἰς φόβον." διὰ τοῦτο πνεύματι δειλίας ἑαυτοῦ μὴ καταπτησσέτω, μήτε τοὺς νυκτερινοὺς κτύπους [1124D] τῶν δαιμόνων τρεμέτω, ὁπότε οὔτε κατὰ

31 σφοδρότερον C: φαιδρότερον E

χοίρων ἔχουσιν ἐξουσίαν. ἐν ταῖς ὀψιναῖς οὖν ἐξιὼν τῆς κέλλης, μὴ θροείσθω καὶ
φεύγων ἀνώπιν εἰσπηδάτω, ὡς τῶν δαιμόνων δῆθεν κατατρεχόντων, ἀλλὰ κλίνας
τὰ γόνατα ἐν ᾧ τόπῳ δειλιᾷ εὐξάσθω, οὐ γάρ σοι ἐπιπεσοῦνται κἂν οὕτω σε
θροοῦσιν. ἐπειδὰν δὲ ἀναστῆς θάρρυνε τὴν καρδίαν καὶ παρακάλει τῇ ψαλμῳδίᾳ,
"Οὐ φοβηθήσῃ, λέγων, ἀπὸ φόβου νυκτερινοῦ, ἀπὸ βέλους πετομένου³² ἡμέρας,
ἀπὸ πράγματος ἐν σκότει διαπορευομένου, ἀπὸ συμπτώματος καὶ δαιμονίου
μεσημβρινοῦ." οὕτω γὰρ ἅπαξ καὶ πολλοστὸν ποιήσας, τὸν δαίμονα τῆς δειλίας
θᾶττον ἀφ' ἑαυτοῦ ἀπελάσεις. ἀδυνατοῦντες γὰρ ἔργῳ βλάπτειν, ταῖς φαντασίαις
τὴν ψυχὴν δειλοκοποῦσιν, ἵνα [1125A] τοὺς ἀσθενεῖς καὶ τοὺς ἀδυνάτους, ἰσχυροὺς
καὶ δυνατοὺς εἶναι νομίσωμεν.

23. THE PRACTICAL LIFE

(24) Καλλίστοις ἱματίοις μὴ σεαυτὸν περιστολίσῃς, ἵνα μὴ τὸν τῆς κενοδοξίας
δαίμονα προφανέστερον ἐνδύσῃ· οὐ γὰρ ἐν κάλλει ἱματίων αἱ ἀρεταὶ φοροῦνται,
ἀλλ' ἐν κάλλει ψυχῆς οἱ πόνοι χρυσοφοροῦνται. τὸν δὲ τοῦ θεοῦ φόβον ἐπενδύου
τῶν τῆς κρίσεως κολαστηρίων, ὅπως φόβῳ πυρὸς ἀκατασβέστου τὴν ἀδιαίρετον
τῶν πόνων στολὴν ἐπενδύσῃ καὶ θᾶττον κατὰ τῆς κακοτεχνίας τῶν λογισμῶν
σοφισθήσῃ, "ἀρχὴ γάρ ἐστιν ὁ φόβος τῆς σοφίας."
Ὁ τῶν λογισμῶν τὴν πλάνην διὰ πείρας ἐξαγγέλλων, οὐ πᾶσιν εὔγνωστος
ἔσται πλὴν τῶν ἐν [1125B] πείρᾳ· ὁδὸς γὰρ τῆς ἐν τούτῳ τῷ μέρει γνωστικῆς ἡ
πεῖρα καθέστηκεν. αἰτία γὰρ ἀμφοτέρων ἐστὶν ἡ πρακτική, ἥνπερ πονικώτερον
κατέχοντες, ἑαυτοὺς ἐπιγνωσόμεθα καὶ λογισμῶν καταγνωσόμεθα, καὶ θεὸν
ἐπιγνωσόμεθα. ὁ ἐκ πρακτικῆς ἐκδημίας καὶ γνωστικῆς ἐνδημίας τῶν λογισμῶν
τὴν τέχνην τοὺς ἀφελεῖς ἀλείφων, βλεπέτω, μὴ εἰς ἔνδειξιν δόξης τὴν γνωστικὴν
κομπαζέτω. εἰ δὲ λογισμὸς τοῦτον μεγαλύνων ληστεύει, εἰς βοήθειαν λαμβανέτω
τὸν νέηλυν Ἰοθόρ, Μωϋσῇ τῷ³³ μεγάλῳ προφήτῃ τὴν ἀπὸ τῆς χάριτος σοφὴν
συμβουλίαν καὶ διάκρισιν ἐκδόντα.
Ἤτω σου λόγων³⁴ ἡ δύναμις τὰ ἔργα· τὰ γὰρ πρακτέα τῶν λεκτέων ἐστὶ
φιλοσοφώτερα, καθάπερ καὶ ἐπιπονώτερα. πράξεως παρούσης ὥσπερ οἱ λόγοι
ἐξαστράπτουσιν· [1125C] ἔργων δὲ μὴ παρόντων, οἱ λόγοι τὴν τῶν ἔργων δύναμιν
οὐκ ἀπαστράπτουσι. πολιῶν ἔγκλημα, λόγος νεώτερος καὶ χείλη πέρπερα
τινασσόμενα γέλωτι, ὁ δὲ ταράττων καὶ ταραττόμενος εἰκῇ γαλήνης ἐκτὸς ἔσται
καὶ κλύδωνος οὐκ ὄντος χειμάζεται.

24. FRATERNAL RELATIONS

(25) Μὴ τὴν ἄκαιρον γλῶσσαν λεξιθήρει, ἵνα μὴ τὸ αὐτὸ ὑφ' ὧν οὐ θέλεις
ὑπομείνῃς. φεῦγε πτερνίσαι τοῦ πλησίον τὴν γλῶτταν, ἵνα καὶ σὺ τοῦ διαβόλου
τὸν πτερνισμὸν διαφύγῃς. φεῦγε ὀνειδίσαι ἀδελφοῦ σου πταίσματα, ἵνα μὴ τῆς
συμπαθείας ὡς ἀλλόφυλος ἐκπέσῃς.

32 πετομένου C: πετωμένου E   33 τῷ C: τὸ E   34 λόγων C: λογισμῶν E

Ὁ τὴν χρηστότητα καὶ τὴν ἀγάπην εἰς τὸν ἀδελφὸν μὴ ἔχων, πῶς τῆς χριστοφόρου
[1125D] ἀγάπης μέλος ἂν εἴη; ἐπὰν τῇ συντόνῳ σου νηστείᾳ καὶ ἡσυχίᾳ ἀδελφός
σοι παραβάλῃ, μὴ τῶν λογισμῶν τὴν ἀηδίαν παραδέξῃ ὑποτιθεμένων σοι ὄχλησιν
τῇ ἡσυχίᾳ, ἐκκοπὴν δὲ τῇ νηστείᾳ· ποιοῦσι δὲ τοῦτο ἵνα ἰδὼν τὸν ἀδελφόν σου
μὴ ὡς θεὸν αὐτὸν ἴδῃς. τὰς συνεχεῖς τῶν ἀδελφῶν ἐπιστασίας ὀχλήσεις εἶναι μὴ
φάσκωμεν, συμμαχίαν δὲ μᾶλλον κατὰ τῆς φάλαγγος τοῦ ἀντιπάλου τὴν αὐτῶν
χοροστασίαν ἐμπιστεύσωμεν· οὕτω γὰρ τῷ φίλτρῳ τῆς ἀγάπης ἑνωθέντες, τὴν
κακίαν ἐξωθήσομεν καὶ τὰ ἔργα τῶν χειρῶν εἰς τὸν τῆς φιλοξενίας θησαυρὸν
μετακομίσωμεν. [1128A]
    Μὴ ὡς χάριν παρέχοντες τοῖς ἀδελφοῖς τούτοις δεξιωσώμεθα, ἀλλ᾽ ὡς ὑπόχρεοι
ὄντες τῷ δανείσματι μεθ᾽ ἱκεσίας ξενίζωμεν, καθὼς ὑπέδειξε Λώτ. τινὲς ἐπὶ ξένῳ
ἀξιώματι καὶ ξένως ἐπαίρονται, καὶ ὅταν μὲν ξένον γνώριμον καλῶσιν, οὐδ᾽ ὅλως
παρακαλοῦσιν, ἀλλὰ καὶ τὸν τῆς κλήσεως λόγον τῷ τύφῳ πλατύνουσιν· τὸν δὲ
παραιτούμενον ὡς ἐφ᾽ ὑβρικότα μέμφονται. διὰ τοῦτο μέγα φύσημα ἐντεῦθεν
ἀνακαίεται· οἱ γὰρ λογισμοὶ τὸ ὄμμα τῆς ψυχῆς παρακεντοῦντες τυφλώττουσιν,
ἵνα ταῖς καλλίσταις τῶν ἐντολῶν κακίστως χρησώμεθα.
    (26) Ὅταν λογισμὸς ἐκκόψῃ σε, μὴ ἄγαν βιάσασθαι [1128B] τῇ τραπέζῃ τὸν
ἀδελφόν, τότε δι᾽ αὐτοῦ κωμῳδεῖ σε, μὴ βεβιασμένην ἔχειν τὴν βίαν τῆς ἀγάπης.
σοὶ μὲν γὰρ ἴσως ὑποβάλλει τὸν ἀδελφὸν ἕνα τῶν κυκλευτῶν ὑπάρχειν, καὶ ὅτι
ἄρτοις ἀρκεσθεὶς ἀφικέσθω, ἐκείνῳ δὲ ἐμβάλλει φιλοξενίαν παρὰ σοὶ τὸ παράπαν
μὴ εὑρηκέναι. τῆς γὰρ πρακτικῆς αὐτοῦ μεταβολῆς τὸ ὄμμα βαστάζων, ἕνα τῷ ἑνὶ
ἐν ταῖς καρδίαις ἐμβάλλει, ἵνα τοῦ μὲν τὴν φιλοξενίαν ὑπεκκόψῃ, τοῦ δὲ λοιδορίαν
ἐκβλαστήσῃ.
    Ἀβραὰμ καθήμενος πρὸ τῆς σκηνῆς, εἴ πού τινα τῶν παριόντων ἑώρα, ἔργῳ
προσεδέχετο· καὶ τοῖς ζώοις ἐν ἀσεβείᾳ ἐξήπλου τὴν τράπεζαν, καὶ ὁ βαρβάρους
δεχόμενος, ἀγγέλων οὐκ ἀπέτυχεν. ἴσασι τὴν τῆς φιλοξενίας γλυκύτητα ὅσοι
ξενιτεύσαντες ὑπ᾽ αὐτῆς ἐξενίσθησαν, ὅτε καὶ λόγος [1128C] προσηνὴς γλυκεῖαν
ἀρτύσῃ τὴν τράπεζαν τῇ καρδίᾳ. μετὰ πολλῆς οὖν σπουδῆς τὴν φιλοξενίαν
χρηστοποιώμεθα, ἵνα μὴ μόνον ἀγγέλους, ἀλλὰ καὶ θεὸν ὑποδεξώμεθα. "Ἐφ᾽ ὅσον,
γάρ φησιν ὁ κύριος, ἐποιήσατε ἑνὶ τούτων τῶν ἐλαχίστων, ἐμοὶ ἐποιήσατε."
    Τὶς τῶν γνωστικωτέρων τὴν πρακτικὴν μετιόντων οὕτως ἀπεκρίνατο· τὰς
ἐνηχούσας τῶν δαιμόνων ἐν τῇ καρδίᾳ φαντασίας εἴωθεν ἐξαφανίζειν ἢ τῆς
φιλοξενίας σπουδὴ καὶ δαψιλὴς ὑπηρεσία προθύμως γινομένη, εἴπερ τις τῶν ὑλῶν
ὁπωσδηποτοῦν ἀπήλλακται· ταῦτα δὲ γινόμενα μετὰ ταπεινώσεως καὶ συντριβῆς
καρδίας θᾶττον ἀπαλλάττειν τῶν φαντασιῶν τὸν κάμνοντα.

25. HUMILITY

Σφόδρα γὰρ δεδοίκασιν τὴν ταπείνωσιν οἱ δαίμονες, εἰδότες ταύτην δεσποτικὴν
γεγενῆσθαι στολήν. τίς τῶν δοκιμωτάτων[35] περὶ ταπεινώσεως [1128D]
λόγον κινῶν καὶ τοῦτο κατεμήνυσεν, ὅτι πατήρ, φησί, τῶν πάνυ δοκίμων ὑπὸ
δαιμονῶντος καὶ δεινῶς ἀφραίνοντος[36] τὴν σιαγόνα[37] κρουσθεὶς εὐθὺς ἐναλλάξας

35 δοκιμοτάτων E   36 ἀφρένοντος E   37 σιαγῶνα E

καὶ τὴν ἄλλην ἑτοίμην παρέθηκεν· ὁ δὲ ὡς ὑπὸ ἀστραπῆς τῆς ταπεινώσεως ἀντικρουσθεὶς καὶ κραυγάσας ἀθρόως τοῦ πλάσματος ἀφήλλατο.

(27) Ἐπιφανίου τοῦ ἁγίου ἐπισκόπου καὶ οὗτος ὁ λόγος ἐφέρετο, ὅτι, φησί, χήρας πιστῆς υἱὸς ἔχων [1129A] δαίμονα πύθωνα, ἐν τῇ πληγῇ χρονίσας θεραπείαν οὐχ ὑφίστατο. τῆς δὲ τούτου μητρὸς ἐπιταπεινωθείσης τῷ πένθει, εὐχαριστία τὸ πάθος κατέψυξεν, ἥπερ ἐκ τοῦ σταυροῦ τὴν ψυχὴν κρεμάσασα, τὸν δαίμονα τοῦ παιδὸς ταῖς εὐχαῖς ἀπέρρηξε· τοῦ γὰρ νέου ἐν τοῖς μέρεσι τοῖς πέριξ πλανωμένου καὶ τῆς μητρὸς οἴκοι εὐχομένης, τὸ ταύτης ὄνομα βοῶν ὁ δαίμων βασάνοις ἠλαύνετο· ἡ δὲ αὐτὸ τοῦτο ἀκούσασα, οὐκ ἐπέδραμε τῷ πράγματι τὴν μάχην τῆς φύσεως τῇ ταπεινώσει[38] δεσμεύουσα, ἑλκομένη δὲ παρ᾽ ἄλλων ἀβουλήτως ἀπήγετο, ἐπέκεινα δὲ καὶ ὁ δαίμων χρῆσθαι[39] τῇ φυγῇ ἐμαίνετο. ἡ μὲν οὖν ἐπιστᾶσα καὶ τοῖς δάκρυσι τὸν παῖδα περιπτυξαμένη, τὴν εὐχαριστίαν καὶ ταπείνωσιν κατὰ τοῦ δαίμονος προὐβάλλετο· πικρῶς δὲ κλαύσασα καὶ Χριστὸν ἱκετεύσασα, [1129B] καὶ τὸν σταυρὸν τυπώσασα, πρὶν μαστίγων πολλῶν θᾶττον τοῦ παιδὸς ὁ δαίμων ἀπέδρασε.

26. SPIRITUAL SUBMISSION

Σφόδρα ζηλοῦσιν οἱ δαίμονες τοὺς ἐν ὑποταγῇ πατρὸς ἀστράπτοντας καὶ τρίζουσι κατ᾽ αὐτῶν τοὺς ὀδόντας, ὅτι ἐν τῇ ὑποταγῇ τὴν ἀποταγὴν[40] ἀμερίμνως ἐζύγωσαν· καθ᾽ ὧν καὶ προφάσεις ἀκριβολογοῦντες παροξυσμοὺς ἀρτύουσι καὶ τῇ συμβαινούσῃ ὀργῇ, τὴν μνήμην ἐγγλύφουσιν· ἔπειτα δὲ καὶ μῖσος πρὸς τὸν πατέρα κατ᾽ ὀλίγον ἐψοῦσιν, ὡς ἄτε δῆθεν ἀδίκως ἐπιπλήττοντος καὶ κατὰ πρόσωπον προσέχοντος· ἵνα ἐκ διαφόρων τρόπων τὴν ψυχὴν περιτινάξαντες, τῶν πατρικῶν[41] ἀγκαλῶν σκορπίσωσιν. ὁ οὖν ἐν ὑποταγῇ πατρὸς ὑπάρχων ὕβρεσι μὴ ἡττάσθω καὶ ταπεινώσει νικάτω, καὶ μακροθυμίᾳ ῥυθμιζέσθω, καὶ [1129C] μὴ τῶν λογισμῶν ὑπογογγυζόντων ἀνεχέσθω πρὸς πατρὸς[42] αὐστηρότητα καὶ ἔργων βαρύτητα καὶ ἀδελφῶν θρασύτητα.

(28) Καὶ ὅτι μοχθηρᾶς δουλείας ἡ ἐλευθερία ἰσόζυγος τυγχάνει, εἰσβάλλουσι γὰρ μάλιστα καὶ περαιτέρω τούτων, ἵνα αὐθάδη τὸν ὑπεξούσιον ποιήσαντες εὐχερῶς εἰς ὕλας περιπείρωσι· τοὺς μὲν γὰρ καὶ διὰ τούτων τῆς πατροσύνης χωρίσαι σπουδάζουσι, τοὺς δὲ καὶ δι᾽ ἑτέρων. ἔργασαι καὶ κτῆσαι καὶ ξένισαι[43], ἔνδον ἐπάδοντες, ὅπως ὄνομα καλὸν σαυτῷ περιποιήσῃ· ἀπὸ γὰρ τῶν δῆθεν καλῶν τὰ ζιζάνια τῆς πονηρίας τὸ κατὰ μέρος ἐνσπείρουσι[44]

Καὶ παρὰ μὲν τὰς ἀρχὰς ἀφιᾶσιν αὐτὸν ἐν τῇ κενοδοξίᾳ [1129D] ἐγγλυκαίνεσθαι καὶ νήφειν ἐν τῇ συνεχεῖ νηστείᾳ καὶ προθύμως ἀνίστασθαι ἐν ταῖς προσευχαῖς καὶ ἐν ταῖς συνάξεσιν, ὡς ἵνα λογίζηται, ὅτι ὑπεξούσιος ὢν τοιοῦτος οὐκ ἐτύγχανεν· ἐκεῖ γὰρ καὶ ὕβρεις καὶ λύπαι καὶ ταραχαί, ἐνταῦθα δὲ εἰρήνη καὶ γαλήνη καὶ χαρά· ἐκεῖ πατρὸς αὐστηρία καὶ φόβος καὶ ἐπιπληξία[45] ἐνταῦθα δὲ καὶ ἀμεριμνία

38 ταπεινώσει C: ταπεινῶσαι E   39 χρῆσθε E   40 τὴν ἀποταγὴν C: om. E
41 πρακτικῶν E, πατρικῶν E² in marg.   42 πατρὸς ACMa: om. E   43 ξένισε E
44 ἐμπείρουσι E, σπείρῃ C   45 ἐνταῦθα δὲ εἰρήνη καὶ γαλήνη καὶ χαρά· ἐκεῖ
πατρὸς αὐστηρία καὶ φόβος καὶ ἐπιπληξία om. E

καὶ ἀφοβία καὶ ἀπληξία. καὶ τότε ἐν τοῖς τοιούτοις κλέψαντες αὐτοῦ τὸν νοῦν ὑφαρπάζουσιν· ἄφνω ἐπιστάντες ὕπνῳ τε ὑπερορίῳ⁴⁶ τὴν ψυχὴν φόβῳ ῥαντίζουσι καὶ τὰς συνάξεις ἀμελείᾳ καὶ ἀκηδίᾳ⁴⁷ ἐκκόπτουσι· καὶ τὴν ξενοδοχίαν ὄχλησιν εἶναι ὑπομνηματίζουσι, καὶ πάντα μάγγανα τῆς κακίας ἐπάγουσιν, ἵνα τὴν ἀκηδίαν αὐτῷ προσρίψαντες καὶ πρὸς αὐτὸν τὸν βίον μῖσος ἐργάσωνται, καὶ οὕτω γυμνὸν αὐτὸν τῶν [1132A] ἀρετῶν στήσαντες τοῖς ἀγγέλοις δειγματίσωσιν.

27. DEMONIC DECEPTIONS

Ποτὲ μὲν οἱ δαίμονες διὰ τῶν λογισμῶν τοὺς πόνους μεγαλύνουσι, ποτὲ δὲ τούτους εὐτελίζουσιν ὡς μηδὲν ἀνύοντας, ἵν᾽ ὅπου μὲν ἀπόνοιαν ἐνθήσωσιν, ὅπου δὲ ἀπόγνωσιν ἐνσπείρωσι. τοὺς μὲν μὴ καμπτομένους χαυνῶσαι τοὺς πόνους μεγαλύνουσιν, ἵνα ἀπόνοιαν ἐνθήσωσι, τοὺς δὲ ἀπονοίᾳ κάμπτεσθαι μὴ πειθομένους οὐδὲν πλέον ἀλλ᾽ ἢ τοὺς πόνους ἐπάδουσιν ἀνύειν, ἵνα χαυνώσαντες ἀπόγνωσιν ἐνσπείρωσιν. (29) ὅταν οὖν οἱ λογισμοὶ τοὺς πόνους μεγαλύνωσι, τούτους ἀποπτύοντες, τὴν ψυχὴν εὐτελίζωμεν· ὅταν [1132B] δὲ πάλιν τοὺς πόνους σμικρύνωσιν ὡς μηδὲν ἀνύοντας, ἡμεῖς ὅσῃ δύναμις τὰ ἐλέη Χριστοῦ μεγαλύνωμεν.

Ὅσῳ γὰρ ἐπὶ πλείω σκληραγωγεῖς σου τὸ σῶμα, τοσοῦτον διέλαυνόν⁴⁸ σου τὸ συνειδός. ἐπίγνωθι σαυτόν, ἐπαισθανόμενος τὰς ἐν κρυφῇ τῶν λογισμῶν διαρπαγάς, μήπως ἀναισθήτως φερόμενοι περὶ τὰς κρυπτὰς αὐτῶν λῃστείας σκιασθῶμεν μόνῃ τῇ σκληρουχίᾳ τρυγᾶν τὰς ἀρετάς. οὕτω γάρ τινες φαντασθέντες τῶν φρενῶν ἐξετινάχθησαν ὡσεὶ ἀκρίδες, τῶν δαιμόνων φαντασιοκοπούντων καὶ τὰς ὁράσεις παραφερόντων, ἐσθ᾽ ὅτε δὲ καὶ δειλίᾳ τὴν ψυχὴν διαρπαζόντων.

Τινὶ τῶν ἀδελφῶν ἐγρηγορότι νύκτωρ φοβερὰς φαντασίας ἐξετύπουν οἱ δαίμονες, οὐ μόνον τῷ ἔξωθεν ὄμματι, ἀλλὰ καὶ τῷ ἔνδοθεν [1132C] βλέμματι, ὥστε μερίμνῃ τῆς ἐπιούσης νυκτὸς ἀγωνιῶντα κινδυνεύειν τὴν τῶν φρενῶν διαρπαγήν, καὶ γὰρ ἐπὶ πλείους νύκτας ὁ πόλεμος τῇ ψυχῇ ἐφίστατο. ὁ δὲ κινδυνεύων ἔνδον κατέχειν τὸν ἡγεμόνα τῶν φρενῶν ἐβιάζετο, τῷ τῆς εὐχῆς δοτῆρι τὴν ψυχὴν ἀποκρεμαννῶν· καὶ τὰς πράξεις τῶν πταισμάτων καθ᾽ ἑαυτοῦ προφέρων, εἰσιδεῖν ἑαυτὸν ἠγωνίζετο· ἔπειτα καὶ τῇ πυρᾷ τῆς κρίσεως τὴν ψυχὴν περισπῶν ἐξεφόβει, ἵνα φόβῳ φόβον συγκρούσας τὴν δειλίαν ἀποκρούσηται. ὥσπερ καὶ γέγονεν, ὡς ἔφησεν ὁ πεπονθὼς τὸν πόλεμον. τῶν γὰρ δαιμόνων πολυτρόπως τὴν ψυχὴν ἐκφοβούντων, ὁ κάμνων τὸν θεὸν τῇ εὐχῇ ἐπεζήτει· ἐκείνων δὲ ταῖς φαντασίαις τὴν ψυχὴν περισπώντων, οὗτος τῶν πταισμάτων τὸν ὄγκον ἀναλέγων τῷ παντεπόπτῃ θεῷ ἐπεδείκνυ· [1132D] τῶν δὲ πάλιν τῆς εὐχῆς τὸ ὄμμα κατασπώντων, ἐκεῖνος τὸν φόβον τῆς κρίσεως ἀνταμείψας τὸν φόβον τῶν φαντασμάτων ἐξηφάνισε⁴⁹· τὸ γὰρ ἕτερον μέρος τοῦ φόβου πλεονάσαν τοῦ ἄλλου τῆς πλάνης σὺν θεῷ περιεγένετο. τῇ γὰρ μνήμῃ τῶν ἁμαρτημάτων ἡ ψυχὴ ταπεινωθεῖσα καὶ τῷ φόβῳ τῆς κρίσεως διυπνισθεῖσα, τὰ φόβητρα τῶν δαιμόνων ἐκ τῶν ἐντὸς ἀπεφύσησε. τὸ δὲ πᾶν τῆς ἄνωθεν χάριτος γέγονε, τῶν

46 ὑπερωρίῳ E   47 φόβῳ add. E   48 διελαύνων E, διερευνῶν C   49 ἐξηφάντωσεν C

μὲν δαιμόνων ἀπελάσαι τὰ φόβητρα, τὴν δὲ ψυχὴν καταπίπτουσαν ὑποστηρίξαι. "Ὑποστηρίζει γὰρ κύριος πάντας τοὺς καταπίπτοντας καὶ ἀνορθοῖ πάντας τοὺς κατερραγμένους." [1133A]

28. PURE PRAYER

(30) Ἔστιν ὅτε βιαζόμεθα καθαρὰν τὴν εὐχὴν ποιῆσαι, καὶ ἴσως οὐ δυνάμεθα. ἔστι δὲ καὶ πάλιν ὅτε, οὐ βιαζομένων ἡμῶν, καθαρὰ προσευχὴ τῇ ψυχῇ ἐγγίνεται, ὅτι τὸ μὲν τῆς ἡμῶν ἀσθενείας, τὸ δὲ τῆς ἄνωθεν χάριτος ἐκκαλουμένης ἡμᾶς ἐπανελθεῖν εἰς τὴν τῆς ψυχῆς καθαρότητα, ἅμα δὲ καὶ δι' ἀμφοτέρων παιδευούσης ἡμᾶς μὴ ἑαυτοῖς ἀποδιδόναι ἐν τῷ καθαρῶς εὔχεσθαι, ἀλλ' ἐπιγινώσκειν τὸν δωρούμενον· "τὸ γὰρ τί προσευξόμεθα καθ' ὃ δεῖ οὐκ οἴδαμεν." ὅταν οὖν καθαρθῆναι τὴν εὐχὴν βιαζώμεθα καὶ οὐ δυνάμεθα, ἀλλ' ἐσκοτίσμεθα, τότε δάκρυσι τὰς παρειὰς καταβρέξαντες, τὸν θεὸν ἱκετεύσωμεν ἐπὶ τὸ διαλυθῆναι τοῦ πολέμου τὴν νύκτα καὶ ἐλλαμφθῆναι τῆς ψυχῆς τὸ φέγγος.

Ἕνεκεν διακονίας [1133B] ἐπὰν ὁ συμβιώτης ἀδελφὸς ἐκδημοίη, κατὰ τὸ ἔθος τῶν εὐχῶν, ἀνακαίνιζε τούτου τὴν μνήμην· πέρα δὲ τοῦ μέτρου τοῦτον μὴ φαντάζου, μήπως τὴν ἀρχὴν τῆς μερίμνης ἀπὸ σοῦ λαβόντες οἱ δαίμονες, ταύτην ἀκονῶντες⁵⁰ ἐπὶ πλεῖον ἐποξύνουσι, σκιάζοντές σοι τοῦτον ἐν τῇ τῶν ψαλμῶν ὑμνῳδίᾳ καὶ ἐκτυποῦντες ἐν καιρῷ τῆς κατὰ θεὸν μερίμνης, ἵνα μερίμνῃ μέριμναν ἀντικρούσαντες αἰχμαλώτους ἡμᾶς τῶν κρειττόνων ἀπαγάγωσιν εἰς τὸ μὴ λογίζεσθαι τό· "Ἐπίρριψον ἐπὶ κύριον τὴν μέριμνάν σου."

Ἴσασι γὰρ ὡς ἐκ τῆς περιττῆς περὶ τὸν ἀδελφὸν φροντίδος, ὅτι καὶ λύπας ἐντορνεύουσιν, ὑποταράττοντες τὸ ἡγεμονικόν. ἔτι δὲ καὶ μέμψεις βραδύτητος ὑφάπτουσιν, ὡς ἀμελήσαντος τοῦ ἀδελφοῦ περὶ τὴν τῆς διακονίας [1133C] σπουδήν, ὅπως ὁ πολυμέριμνος πόθος ἴσως καὶ εἰς μῖσος ἐκτραπῇ. ἔθος δὲ ἐν ταῖς περὶ τὸν ἀπόδημον μερίμναις καὶ τοῦτο ποιεῖν τοῖς δαίμοσιν, ἐν ᾗ ἴδωσιν αὐτὸν παραγινόμενον ἡμέρᾳ κατ' ὄναρ τοῦτον ἐσοπτρίζειν, ἵνα ὡς ἐκ τοῦ ἀποβάντος ἐνυπνίου ποιήσωσιν ἡμᾶς ἐν καιρῷ τῶν ἀποδήμων τοὺς προφήτας τῶν ἐνυπνίων καὶ πάλιν προσδέχεσθαι, οὓς ἀποστρέφεσθαι δεῖ μᾶλλον καὶ σφόδρα ἐκτρέπεσθαι, μήπως ἐκ τούτων καὶ εἰς ἕτερα τὴν ψυχὴν ἀποπλανήσωσι. (31) προΐσασι γὰρ οὗτοι μὲν οὐδέν, ἃ δὲ βλέπουσι γινόμενα, [1133D] ταῦτα μηνίουσι καὶ φαντάζουσι. πολλάκις γοῦν καθ' ἡσυχίαν ὄντων ἡμῶν, θεασάμενοι ἀδελφὸν πρὸς ἡμᾶς ἐρχόμενον, διὰ τῶν λογισμῶν προεσήμαναν, οἷς οὐ χρὴ πιστεύειν, κἂν λέγειν τ' ἀληθῆ νομίζωσι· διὰ γὰρ τῆς δῆθεν ἀληθείας τὸ ψεῦδος παρεισφέρουσιν, ἵνα ἐκ τούτων κατὰ μέρος ταῖς ἔμπροσθεν ὁδοῖς τοὺς βρόχους ὑπορράψωσιν.

29. COMMUNITY AND ANACHORESIS

Ὥσπερ ἀνέργαστος χρυσὸς ἐν χωνευτηρίῳ βαλλόμενος καθαρώτερος γίνεται, οὕτω καὶ νέηλυς μοναχὸς ἐν κοινοβίῳ τὰ ἤθη ἀναχωνευόμενος φαιδρὸς ταῖς

50 ἀκωνῶντες Ε

ἀποκαρτερίαις ἀποκαθίσταται. διὰ γὰρ τῆς ἐπιταγῆς τῶν ἀδελφῶν τὴν ὑπακοὴν
μανθάνειν κατεργάζεται· διὰ δὲ τοῦ ἐπιπλήττοντος ἑτοιμάζεται τὴν φύσιν
[1136A] μακροθυμίαν ἔχειν. ἐπὰν οὖν χαρᾷ τὰς ὕβρεις καταδέχεται καὶ εὐτελείᾳ
τὴν ταπείνωσιν ἀσπάζεται, ἀνώτερος τῶν ἄντικρυς παθῶν γενόμενος, ἐπέκεινα
στίλβειν ταῖς ἀρεταῖς ἐπαγωνίζεται, τῆς χάριτος αὐτῷ ἐπὶ πλεῖον τὴν δύναμιν
δωρουμένης. ὥσπερ οἱ εἰς τὰς ῥίζας τῆς γῆς κατιόντες τὸν χρυσὸν ἀνορύττουσιν,
οὕτως οἱ εἰς τὴν χρυσῖτιν ταπείνωσιν καταβαίνοντες ἀρετὰς ἀναφέρουσι. τότε ὁ
νοῦς ἀναπαύσεως αἰσθεται, ὁπότε τὰς τῶν παθῶν αἰτίας ἀποτεμὼν περὶ θεωρίαν
ἠσχόληται· πρὶν δὲ τῆς τούτων κοπῆς, κόπου καὶ ταλαιπωρίας ἐπαισθάνεται, τῇ
τῶν ἐναντίων μάχῃ ἀσθενῶς προσερχόμενος. [1136B]
(32) Βαθμῷ τὴν ἀναχώρησιν γινομένην οἱ γέροντες ἄγαν ἀποδέχονται, εἴπερ
τις τὰς ἐν κοινοβίῳ τελέσας ἀρετὰς εἰς τοῦτο παρελήλυθε. καὶ εἰ μὲν δύναιτο ἐν
τῇ ἀναχωρήσει προκόπτειν, ἑαυτὸν δοκιμαζέτω· εἰ δὲ ἀδυνάτως ἔχων τῆς ἀρετῆς
ἐλαττοῦται, εἰς τὸ κοινόβιον ἀνακαμπτέτω, μήπως ταῖς μηχαναῖς τῶν λογισμῶν
οὐ δυνηθεὶς ἀπαντῆσαι τῶν φρενῶν ἀποπέσοι.

30. TRUE UNDERSTANDING

Ὥσπερ χήρας πενθούσης παραμύθιον οἱ υἱοί, οὕτω καὶ ψυχῆς πταισάσης
παρηγορία πόνοι, οἵτινες τὴν ἀπόγνωσιν τῶν λογισμῶν σκορπίζουσι καὶ τὴν
πίστιν τῆς μετανοίας κατασπείρουσι καὶ τὰ ἐλέη Χριστοῦ ἀνακηρύττουσι καὶ
τὰ πραχθέντα ἁμαρτήματα ἀποκηρύττουσιν. οὐκ ὀφείλομεν οὖν ὡς συνήθεας
μόνον τοὺς πόνους ἐργάζεσθαι, ἀλλὰ καὶ [1136C] ἐν συνέσει εὐχαριστίας, ἵνα μὴ
γυμνὴ τῆς τοιαύτης φιλοσοφίας ἡ ψυχὴ εὑρίσκοιτο. ἐὰν γὰρ ἐφ᾽ ἑκάστῃ πράξει
συνήσωμεν τὸν διδόντα τὰ τέλη τῶν πόνων, εὐχαριστίᾳ σφραγίζομεν. ὥσπερ
ἄρτον ἀπὸ βρέφους ἐνεδρεύει σκύλαξ ἐξαρπάσαι, οὕτω σύνεσιν ἀπὸ καρδίας
λογισμὸς πονηρός. μὴ οὖν ἐνεάζωμεν51 τῶν ἐναντίων ἔργων τῇ κακίᾳ χρωμένων,
ἵνα μὴ εἰς διαρπαγὴν τούτοις τὴν ψυχὴν προεκδώσωμεν. ὥσπερ ἡ τῶν ἄστρων
χορεία δᾳδουχοῦσα φαιδρύνει τὸν οὐρανόν, οὕτως ἡ τῶν ῥημάτων ἀλήθεια
λαμπαδουχοῦσα φαιδρύνει τὸν ἄνθρωπον, ἵνα οὖν τὸν τῆς ἀληθείας τρόπον ἐπὶ
γλώττης βαστάζωμεν, ὅτι "κύριος κατοικίζει μονοτρόπους ἐν οἴκῳ." ὥσπερ
ἀστραπαὶ σφοδροὶ προπηδῶσαι προμηνύουσι βροντήν, οὕτω καὶ ῥήσεις ἀκριβεῖς
προσιοῦσαι προσημαίνουσι πίστιν. [1136D]
Πιστοὶ οὖν εἶναι τῇ ἀληθείᾳ σπουδάσωμεν, ἵνα καὶ εἰς τὴν μητρόπολιν τῶν
ἀρετῶν ἀγάπην προκόπτωμεν. ὡς ἥλιος ταῖς χρυσαυγέσιν ἀκτίσιν ἁπάσῃ
προσμειδιᾷ τῇ γῇ, οὕτως ἀγάπη ταῖς φωταυγέσι πράξεσιν ἁπάσῃ προσχαίρει
ψυχῇ· ἥνπερ ἐὰν κατάσχωμεν, τὰ πάθη ἐσβέσαμεν καὶ εἰς οὐρανοὺς ἐλάμψαμεν·
ἅπαντα πόνον ποιήσεις ἕως τῆς ὁσίας ἀγάπης ἐπιτεύξῃ, ὅτι, ταύτης ἀπούσης,
ὄφελος τῶν παρόντων οὐδέν· καὶ γὰρ ὀργὴ ἀγριαίνεται καὶ ἤθη χαλεπαίνεται καὶ
πόνοι ἀπονοούμενοι τῇ δόξῃ συμμίγνυνται. διὰ ψυχῆς ταπείνωσιν Δαβὶδ μετὰ
πένθους [1137A] ἐνήστευσε, καὶ ἡμεῖς διὰ νηστείας τὴν ψυχὴν ταπεινώσωμεν.

51 ἐννεάζωμεν Pg

31. DEMONIC CONCEIT

(33) Ὁ τοῖς σωματικοῖς πόνοις τραχυτέρως ἀσκούμενος, μήτε ἐπαίνῳ ἐργαζέσθω, μήτε δόξῃ ἐπαιρέσθω. εἰ γὰρ ἐν τούτοις οἱ δαίμονες ὀφρυώσουσι τὴν ψυχήν, καὶ τὴν τραχύτητα καὶ τὴν ἄσκησιν τοῦ σώματος ἐνισχύσουσι τῇ δόξῃ καὶ μειζόνων ἐφάπτεσθαι πόνων ἐφελκύσωσιν, ἵνα καὶ μειζόνως ἐπαίρηται. συλλαλοῦσι γὰρ ἔνδοθεν διὰ τῶν λογισμῶν ἐμβάλλοντες ταῦτα, ὅτι καθὼς ὁ δεῖνα ἀποσκλήρως ἀσκήσας, καὶ ὁ δεῖνα μεγάλως ὠνομάσθη καὶ θανὼν ἔτι λαλεῖται, οὕτω καὶ αὐτὸς εἰς ἀκρότατον ἐπασκήσεως [1137B] ἀνάβηθι ὕψος, ἵνα δόξαν σαυτῷ περιποιήσῃ καὶ μέγα σου τὸ ὄνομα ἐξέλθῃ, ἐπὶ τῷ καὶ μετὰ θάνατον ὑπερβαλλόντως λαλεῖσθαι. διὰ δὴ τῶν οὕτως ἀπατηθέντων, οὐ μόνον τοὺς σωματικούς σου πολεμοῦσι πόνους, ἀλλὰ καὶ μᾶλλον εἰς συμμαχίαν καλοῦσιν, ὅτι δι᾽ αὐτῶν ἐν τοῖς χαλεπωτέροις ψαύουσι τὴν ψυχήν.

Καὶ γὰρ ἐνθρονίζουσιν αὐτὸν καὶ εἰς τὸν διδασκαλικὸν ἐξυψοῦσθαι λόγον, ἵν᾽ ὡς ἐκ τούτων τὰ πρῶτα τῶν μεγαλοπόνων τε καὶ γνωστικῶν ἔχειν εὐφημισθῇ. ζηλοῦν δὲ καὶ φθονεῖν εἰσβάλλουσι τοῖς ἐπὶ κατορθώμασιν εὐφημουμένοις, καὶ ὧν μάλιστα θαυμαστὴ πρᾶξις καὶ γνῶσις γειτνιᾷ. ἔσθ᾽ ὅτε δὲ καὶ τῆς σαρκὸς αὐτοῦ τὴν πύρωσιν ἀποκοιμίζουσι δολουργῶς, τοὺς ἀκαθάρτους λογισμοὺς ἐκ τῶν ἐντὸς [1137C] ὑποτοπίζοντες, ὡς ἵνα νομισθῇ τὸ πνεῦμα τῆς πορνείας τῇ σκληρουχίᾳ νενικηκέναι καὶ κατὰ τὴν λαμπρότητα τῶν ἁγίων τὴν καρδίαν ἡγνικέναι καὶ εἰς τὴν τῆς ἁγιωσύνης ἁψῖδα ἀναβεβηκέναι.

Περὶ δὲ ὧν τε καὶ ὧν ἀπέσχετο βρωμάτων καὶ συναπτῶν ἀσιτιῶν, ἐπιψηφίζουσιν αὐτῷ τοὺς χρόνους ἐν οἷς ὀφείλει ὡς ἀριστεὺς ἐγκαυχᾶσθαι καὶ τῆς ἀδελφότητος ὡς εὐτελοῦς κατεπαίρεσθαι· οὕτω δὲ ἐκδιηγεῖσθαι ποιοῦσιν αὐτὸν τοὺς ἀγῶνας ὡς ἐκ μόνης τῆς ἰσχύος αὐτοῦ κατορθωθέντας, ὅτι ἐποίησα τάδε καὶ ἤσκησα τοιῶσδε καὶ ἐκακουχήθην, ἀποστομῶντες ἔτι τοῦ λέγειν, οὐκ ἐγὼ δὲ ἀλλ᾽ ἡ ἐν ἐμοὶ βοήθεια. θεὸν γὰρ βοηθὸν ἐφ᾽ οἷς μεγαλαυχεῖν αὐτὸν ποιοῦσιν ὁμολογεῖν οὐκ ἐῶσιν, ἵν᾽ ὡς ἐξ οἰκείας δῆθεν ἰσχύος τὸ πᾶν τὸ τῶν ἀγώνων τελέσας, τοὺς ἐπαίνους τῶν [1137D] ἄθλων ὁλοκλήρως ἀπαιτοίη, ὅπως καὶ εἰς τὸν τῆς βλασφημίας βυθὸν ποντοθείη, αὐτοβόηθον ἑαυτὸν ἀναισθήτως παρεμφαίνων.

(34) Οὕτω τοιγαροῦν τῆς καρδίας διὰ τῆς τῶν λογισμῶν δόξης ἐνηχουμένης καὶ μὴ ἀντιταττομένης, οὐκ ἐκτὸς ἔσται τῆς ἐν ἀποκρύφῳ τῶν φρενῶν παραπληξίας, τοῦ ἡγεμόνος τῶν φρενῶν ἐκτιναχθῆναι κινδυνεύοντος ἢ δι᾽ ὀνειράτων πιστουμένης ἢ ἐν ἀγρυπνίαις μεταμορφουμένης ἢ ἐν μετασχηματισμῷ [1140A] φωτὸς ὀπτανομένης. "αὐτὸς γὰρ ὁ Σατανᾶς μετασχηματίζεται εἰς ἄγγελον φωτὸς" πρὸς ἀπάτην ἡμετέραν, ἴσως χαρίσματα δώσειν ἐνδεικνύμενος, ὡς ἵνα πεσὼν προσκυνήσῃς, ἢ ἀναλαμβάνειν ὡς ἅγιον εὐαγγελιζόμενος, ἢ ἁγιάζειν ὑπισχνούμενος, ὧν τινες τὴν πίστιν δεξάμενοι περὶ τὴν ἀλήθειαν ἠστόχησαν καὶ φρενοβλαβεῖς ἐγενήθησαν.

32. CONCLUSION

Σὺ οὖν, ὦ τῆς ἁγίας τριάδος ἱκέτα, εἰδὼς ταῦτα ἐν οἷς φιλοπονοῖς, πάσῃ φυλακῇ τήρει σὴν καρδίαν, μήπως τοῖς ἔξωθεν πόνοις προσέχων, τοῖς ἔσωθεν δελέασι βροχισθῇς. οἱ ἐμοὶ λόγοι εἴρηνται πρὸς σέ, τὰ δὲ ῥήματά μου τηρείτω σὴ καρδία· μέμνησο Χριστοῦ τοῦ φυλάξαντός σε καὶ μὴ ἐπιλάθῃ τῆς προσκυνητῆς καὶ ἁγίας τριάδος.

BIBLIOGRAPHY

Arras, Victor, *Collectio monastica*, CSCO, 238–9 (Louvain: Secrétariat du CSCO, 1963).

Augst, Rüdiger, *Lebensverwirklichung und christlicher Glaube. Acedia—Religiöse Gleichgültigkeit als Problem der Spiritualität bei Evagrius Ponticus*. Saarbrücker theologische Forschungen, 3 (Berne/Frankfurt am Main: Peter Lang, 1990).

Augustin, Pierre, 'Note critique sur deux traités d'Évagre', *Revue des Études Augustiniennes*, 39 (1993), 203–13.

Bacht, Heinrich, 'Pachomius und Evagrius', in Klaus Wessel (ed.), *Christentum am Nil: Internationale Arbeitstagung zur Ausstellung 'Koptische Kunst' Essen, Villa Hügel, 23.–25. Juli 1963* (Recklinghausen: Bongers, 1964), 142–57.

——'Agrypnia. Die Motive des Schlafentzuges im frühen Mönchtum', in Gunther Pflug, B. Eckhart, and H. Friesenhahn (eds.), *Bibliothek-Buch-Geschichte. Kurt Köster zum 65. Geburtstag*, Sonderveröffentlichungen der Deutschen Bibliothek, 5 (Frankfurt am Main: Klostermann, 1977), 353–69.

——'Evagrius Ponticus und Pachomius von Tabennesi: Das Vermächtnis des Ursprungs', in Joseph Sudbrack (ed.), *Zeugen christlicher Gotteserfahrung* (Mainz: Matthias-Grünewald, 1981), 34–63.

——'Euagrios Pontikos', in Gerhard Ruhbach and Josef Sudbrack (eds.), *Grosse Mystiker. Leben und Werken* (Munich: Beck, 1984), 36–50.

Balthasar, Hans Urs von, 'Die Hiera des Evagrius', *Zeitschrift für katholische Theologie*, 63 (1939), 86–106, 181–206.

——'Metaphysik und Mystik des Evagrius Pontikus', *Zeitschrift für Askese und Mystik*, (1939), 31–47.

——'The Metaphysics and Mystical Theology of Evagrius', *Monastic Studies*, 3 (1965), 183–95.

Bamberger, John Eudes, 'Evagrius Ponticus: the *Practicos* and *Chapters on Prayer*', *Cistercian Studies*, 3 (1968), 137–46.

——(trans.), *Evagrius Ponticus: The Praktikos, Chapters on Prayer*, Cistercian Studies Series, 4 (Kalamazoo, Mich.: Cistercian Publications, 1970).

——'Desert Calm. Evagrius Ponticus: the Theologian as Spiritual Guide', *Cistercian Studies*, 27 (1992), 185–98.

Berthold, George C., 'History and Exegesis in Evagrius and Maximus', in Lothar Lies (ed.), *Origeniana Quarta*, Innsbrucker theologische Studien, 19 (Innsbruck: Tyrolia Verlag, 1987), 390–404.

Bettiolo, Paolo (trans.), *Per conoscere lui* (Mangano:Qiqajon, 1996).

——(ed.), *L'Epistula fidei di Evagrio Pontico : temi, contesti, sviluppi : atti del III Convegno del Gruppo*, Atti del III Convegno del Gruppo Italiano di Ricerca su 'Origene e la Tradizione Alessandrina', (Rome: Institutum Patristicum Augustinianum, 2000).

Beyer, Hans-Veit, 'Die Lichtlehre der Mönche des vierzehnten und des vierten Jahrhunderts', *Jahrbuch der Österreichischen Byzantinistik*, 31 (1981), 473–512.

Bigotius, Emericus, (ed.), *Palladii episcopi Helenopolitani de vita S. Johannis Chrysostomi dialogus. Accedunt homilia Sancti Johannis chrysostomi in laudem Diodori, Tarsensis episcopi, Acta Tarachi, Probi et Andronici, Passio Bonifatii Romani, Evagrius de octo cogitationibus, Nilus de octo vitiis* (Paris: Apud viduam Edmundi Martini, 1680).

Bundy, David, 'The Philosophical Structures of Origenism: the Case of the Expurgated Version (S1) of the Kephalaia Gnostica of Evagrius', in Robert J. Daly, *Origeniana Quinta* (Leuven: Leuven University Press, 1992), 577–84.

Bunge, Gabriel, 'Évagre le Pontique et les deux Macaire', *Irénikon*, 56 (1983), 215–27; 323–60.

——(trans.), *Evagrios Pontikos: Briefe aus der Wüste*, Sophia, 24 (Trier: Paulinus, 1986).

——'The "Spiritual Prayer": On the Trinitarian Mysticism of Evagrius of Pontus', *Monastic Studies*, 17 (1986), 191–208.

——'Origenismus-Gnostizismus. Zum geistesgeschichtlichen Standort des Evagrios Pontikos', *Vigiliae Christianae*, 40 (1986), 24–54.

——*Das Geistgebet: Studien zum Traktat De oratione des Evagrios Pontikos*, Schriftenreihe des Zentrums Patristischer Spiritualität Koinonia im Erzbistum Cologne, 25 (Cologne: Luthe, 1987).

——*Geistliche Vaterschaft. Christliche Gnosis bei Evagrios Pontikos*, Studia patristica et liturgica, 23 (Regensburg: Pustet, 1988).

——' "Priez sans cesse." Aux origines de la prière hésychaste', *Studia Monastica*, 30 (1988), 7–16.

——(trans.), *Evagrios Pontikos: Praktikos oder der Mönch. Hundert Kapitel über das geistliche Leben*, Schriftenreihe des Zentrums Patristischer Spiritualität Koinonia im Erzbistum Köln, 32 (Cologne: Luthe, 1989).

——'Hénade ou monade? Au sujet de deux notions centrales de la terminologie évagrienne', *Le Muséon*, 102 (1989), 69–91.

——'*Mysterium unitatis*. Der Gedanke der Einheit von Schöpfer und Geschöpf in der evagrianischen Mystik', *Freiburger Zeitschrift für Philosophie und Theologie*, 36 (1989), 449–69.

——' "Nach dem Intellekt leben": Zum sogennanten "Intellektualismus" der evagrianischen Spiritualität', in Wilhelm Nyssen (ed.), *Simandron, der Wachklopfer. Gedenkschrift für Klaus Gamber (1919–1989)*, Schriftenreihe des Zentrums Patristischer Spiritualität Koinonia im Erzbistum Köln, 30 (Cologne: Luthe, 1989).

——*Akèdia. La doctrine spirituelle d'Évagre le Pontique sur l'acédie*, Spiritualité orientale, 52 (Bégrolles-en-Mauges: Abbaye de Bellefontaine, 1991).

——(trans.), *Evagrios Pontikos: Über die acht Gedanken* (Würzburg: Echter, 1992).

——*Paternité spirituelle. La gnose chrétienne chez Évagre le Pontique*, Spiritualité Orientale, 61 (Bégrolles-en-Mauges: Abbaye de Bellefontaine, 1994).

Bunge, Gabriel, 'Der mystische Sinn der Schrift. Anlasslich Der Veröffentlichung der *Scholien zum Ecclesiasten* des Evagrios Pontikos', *Studia Monastica*, 36 (1994), 135–46.

——*Akedia: Die geistliche Lehre des Evagrios Pontikos vom Überrdruß*, 4th rev. edn. (Würzburg: Der Christliche Osten, 1995).

——(trans.), *Évagre le Pontique, Traité Pratique ou Le Moine*, Spiritualité Orientale, 67 (Bégrolles-en-Mauges: Abbaye de Bellefontaine, 1996).

——'Evagrios Pontikos: Der Prolog des "Antirrhetikos"', *Studia Monastica*, 39 (1997), 77–105.

——*Drachenwein und Engelsbrot: Die Lehre des Evagrios Pontikos von Zorn und Sanftmut* (Würzburg: Der Christliche Osten, 1999).

——'Aktive und kontemplative Weise des Betens im Traktat *De oratione* des Evagrios Pontikos', *Studia Monastica*, 41 (1999), 211–27.

——'La montagne intelligible. De la contemplation indirecte à la connaisance immédiate de Dieu dans le traité *De oratione* d'Évagre le Pontique', *Studia Monastica*, 42 (2000), 7–26.

—— and Adalbert de Vogüé, *Quatre ermites égyptiens d'après les fragments coptes de l'Histoire Lausiaque*. Spiritualité Orientale, 60 (Bégrolles-en-Mauges: Abbaye de Bellefontaine, 1994).

Clarke, Elizabeth, 'New Perspectives on the Origenist Controversy: Human Embodiment and Ascetic Strategies', *Church History*, 59 (1990), 145–62.

Contreras, E., 'Evagrio Póntico: su vida, su obra, su doctrina', *Cuadernos Monásticos*, 11 (1976), 83–95.

Cotelerius, Johannes Baptista (ed.), *Ecclesiae graecae monumenta*, 4 tom. (Paris: François Muguet, 1677–86).

Crouzel, Henri, 'Recherches sur Origène et son influence', *Bulletin de littérature ecclésiastique*, 6th ser., 62 (1961), 3–15; 105–13.

Dechow, Jon F., *Dogma and Mysticism in Early Christianity: Epiphanius of Cyprus and the Legacy of Origen*, North American Patristic Society Patristic Monograph Series, 13 (Macon, Ga.: Mercer University Press, 1988).

Dempf, Alois, 'Evagrios Pontikos als Metaphysiker und Mystiker', *Philosophisches-Jahrbuch*, 77 (1970), 297–319.

Draguet, René, 'L'Histoire Lausiaque, une oeuvre écrite dans l'esprit d'Évagre', *Revue d'Histoire Ecclésiastique*, 41 (1946), 321–64; 42 (1946–47), 5–49.

——'Un morceau grec inédit des vies de Pachôme apparié à un texte d'Évagre en partie inconnu', *Le Muséon*, 70 (1957), 267–307.

Dräseke, Johannes, 'Zu Evagrios Pontikos', *Zeitschrift für wissenschaftliche Theologie*, 37 (1894), 125–37.

Driscoll, Jeremy, 'Listlessness in *The Mirror for Monks* of Evagrius Ponticus', *Cistercian Studies*, 24 (1989), 206–14.

——'A Key for Reading the *Ad Monachos* of Evagrius Ponticus', *Augustinianum*, 30 (1990), 361–92.

——'Gentleness in the *Ad Monachos* of Evagrius Ponticus', *Studia Monastica*, 32 (1990), 297–321.

——*The* Ad Monachos *of Evagrius Ponticus. Its Structure and a Select Commentary*, Studia Anselmiana, 104 (Rome: Pontificio Ateneo S. Anselmo, 1991).

——*The Mind's Long Journey to the Holy Trinity. The 'Ad Monachos' of Evagrius Ponticus* (Collegeville, Minn.: Liturgical Press, 1993).

——'Penthos and Tears in Evagrius Ponticus', *Studia Monastica*, 36 (1994), 147–63.

——'Spiritual Progress in the Works of Evagrius Ponticus', in Jeremy Driscoll and Mark Sheridan (eds.), *Spiritual Progress. Studies in the Spirituality of Late Antiquity and Early Monasticism*, Studia Anselmiana, 115 (Rome: Pontificio Ateneo S. Anselmo, 1994), 47–83.

——'Spousal Images in Evagrius Ponticus', *Studia Monastica*, 38 (1996), 243–56.

——'Evagrius and Paphnutius on the Causes for Abandonment by God', *Studia Monastica*, 39 (1997), 259–86.

——'Apatheia and Purity of Heart in Evagrius Ponticus', in Harriet A. Luckman and Linda Kulzer (eds.), *Purity of Heart in Early Ascetic and Monastic Literature* (Collegeville, Minn.: The Liturgical Press, 1999), 141–59.

——'The Fathers of Poemen and the Evagrian Connection', *Studia Monastica*, 42 (2000), 27–51.

——'Love of Money in Evagrius Ponticus', *Studia Monastica*, 43 (2001), 21–30.

Durand, Georges-Matthieu de , 'Évagre le Pontique et le *Dialogue sur la vie de saint Jean Chrysostome*', *Bulletin de Littérature Ecclésiastique*, 77 (1976), 191–206.

Dysinger, Luke, 'The Significance of Psalmody in the Mystical Theology of Evagrius of Pontus', *Studia Patristica*, 30 (1997), 176–82.

Elm, Susannah K., 'The *Sententiae ad virginem* by Evagrius Ponticus and the Problem of the Early Monastic Rules', *Augustinianum*, 30 (1990), 393–404.

——'Evagrius Ponticus' *Sententiae ad Virginem*', *Dumbarton Oaks Papers*, 45 (1991), 265–95.

——'The Polemical Use of Genealogies: Jerome's Classification of Pelagius and Evagrius Ponticus', *Studia Patristica*, 30 (1997), 311–18.

Frankenberg, Wilhelm, *Euagrius Ponticus*, Abhandlungen der königlichen Gesellschaft der Wissenschaften zu Göttingen, Philolologisch-historische Klasse, new series, 13. 2 (Berlin: Weidmannsche Buchhandlung, 1912).

Gallandius, Andreas (ed.), *Bibliotheca veterum patrum antiquorumque scriptorum ecclesiasticorum, postrema lugdunensi longe locupletior atque accuratior*, 14 tom. (Venice: Ex typis J. B. Albritii Hieronymi fil., 1765–81).

Garzya, Antonio, 'Osservazioni su un epistola di Evagrio Pontico', in *Mémorial Dom Jean Gribomont (1920–1986)*, Studia Ephemeridis 'Augustinianum', 27 (Rome: Institutum Patristicum Augustinianum, 1988), 299–305.

Géhin, Paul, 'Un nouvel inédit d'Évagre le Pontique: son commentaire de l'Ecclésiaste', *Byzantion*, 49 (1979), 188–98.

——(ed.), *Évagre le Pontique, Scholies aux Proverbes*, Sources Chrétiennes, 340 (Paris: Cerf, 1987).

——'À propos d'Évagre le Pontique', *Revue des Études Grecques*, 103 (1990), 263–7.

——'Un recueil d'extraits patristiques: Les *Miscellanea Coisliniana* (Parisinus

Coislinianus 193 et Sinaiticus Gr. 461)', *Revue d'Histoire des Textes*, 22 (1992), 89–130.

——(ed.), *Évagre le Pontique, Scholies à l'Ecclésiaste*, Sources Chrétiennes, 397 (Paris: Cerf, 1993).

——'Nouveaux fragments grecs des Lettres d'Évagre', *Revue d'Histoire des Textes*, 24 (1994), 117–47.

——'Evagriana d'un manuscrit basilien (*Vaticanus gr. 2028; olim Basilianus 67*)', *Le Muséon*, 109 (1996), 59–85.

——'Évagre le Pontique. Une anachorèse spirituelle vers le "Lieu de Dieu"', *Connaissance des Pères de l'Église*, 72 (1998).

Gendle, Nicholas, 'Cappadocian Elements in the Mystical Theology of Evagrius Ponticus', *Studia Patristica*, 16.2 (1985), 373–84.

Gould, Graham, 'An Ancient Monastic Writing Giving Advice to Spiritual Directors (Evagrius of Pontus, *On Teachers and Disciples*)', *Hallel*, 22 (1997), 96–103.

Grébaut, Sylvain, 'Sentences d'Évagre', *Revue de l'Orient Chrétien*, 20/22 (1915–20), 211–14 and 435–9.

Gressmann, H., 'Nonnenspiegel und Mönchsspiegel des Euagrios Pontikos', *Texte und Untersuchungen*, 39 (1913), 143–65.

Gribomont, Jean, 'L'édition romaine (1673) des Tractatus de S. Nil et l'Ottobonianus gr. 25', *Texte und Untersuchungen*, 133 (1987), 187–202.

Guillaumont, Antoine (ed.), *Les Six Centuries des 'Kephalaia Gnostica' d'Évagre le Pontique*, Patrologia Orientalis, 28. 1 (Paris, 1958).

——*Les 'Kephalaia Gnostica' d'Évagre le Pontique et l'histoire de l'origénisme chez les grecs et chez les syriens*, Patristica Sorbonensia, 5 (Paris: Seuil, 1962).

——'Le texte syriaque édité des Six Centuries d'Évagre le Pontique', *Semitica*, 4 (1951–2), 59–66.

——'Évagre et les anathématismes antiorigénistes de 553, *Studia Patristica* 3 [*Texte und Untersuchungen*, 78] (1961), 219–26.

——'De l'eschatologie à la mystique: histoire d'une sentence d'Évagre', in *Mémorial du cinquantenaire de l'École des Langues orientales anciennes de l'Institut Catholique de Paris*, Institut Catholique, Travaux, 10 (Paris: Bloud & Gay, 1964), 187–92.

——'Le dépaysement comme forme d'ascèse dans le monachisme ancien', in *École Pratique des Hautes Études, Ve section: Sciences religieuses, Annuaire 1968–1969*, 76 (1968), 31–58 [Origines 5:89–116].

——'Un philosophe au désert: Évagre le Pontique', *Revue de l'Histoire des Religions*, 181 (1972), 29–56 [Origines 12:185–212].

——'Le problème des deux Macaire dans les *Apophthegmata patrum*', *Irénikon*, 48 (1975), 41–59.

——'Fragments syriaques des "Disciples d'Évagre"', *Parole de l'Orient*, 6–7 (1975–6), 115–24.

——'Histoire des moines aux Kellia', *Orientalia Lovaniensia Periodica*, 8 (1977), 187–203 [Origines 10:151–67].

——'Les fondements de la vie monastique selon Évagre le Pontique', *Annuaire du Collège de France*, 78 (1977–8), 467–77.

——'L'ascèse évagrienne', *Annuaire du Collège de France*, 79 (1978–9), 395–9.

——'La vie gnostique selon Évagre le Pontique', *Annuaire du Collège de France*, 80 (1979–80), 467–70.

——*Aux origines du monachisme chrétien. Pour une phénoménologie du monachisme*, Spiritualité Orientale, 30 (Bégrolles-en-Mauges: Abbaye de Bellefontaine, 1979).

——'La métaphysique évagrienne', *Annuaire du Collège de France*, 81 (1980–1), 407–11.

——'Evagrius Ponticus. Leben, Werk, Nachwirkung, Quellen/Literatur', *Theologische Realenzyklopädie*, 10 (1982), 565–70.

——'Les versions syriaques de l'oeuvre d'Évagre le Pontique et leur rôle dans la formation du vocabulaire ascétique syriaque', *Orientalia Christiana Analecta*, 221 (1983), 35–41.

——'Preghiera pura di Evagrio e l'influsso del neoplatonismo', *Dizionario degli Istituti de Perfezione*, 7 (1983), 591–5.

——'La vision de l'intellect par lui-même dans la mystique évagrienne', in *Mélanges de l'Université Saint-Joseph* 50 (*Mélanges in memoriam Michel Allard et Paul Mwyia*) (Beirut: Université Saint-Joseph, 1984), 255–62 (*Études* IX. 143–50).

——'Le rôle des versions orientales dans la récupération de l'oeuvre d'Évagre le Pontique', *Comptes rendus des séances de l'Académie des inscriptions et belles-lettres*, (1985), 64–74.

——'Le gnostique chez Clément d'Alexandrie et chez Évagre le Pontique', in *Alexandrina: Hellénisme, judaïsme et christianisme à Alexandrie. Mélanges offerts au P. Claude Mondésert*, (Paris: Cerf, 1987), 195–201.

——'Une nouvelle version syriaque du Gnostique d'Évagre le Pontique', *Le Muséon*, 100 (1987), 161–9.

——*Études sur la spiritualité de l'Orient chrétien*, Spiritualité Orientale, 66 (Bégrolles-en-Mauges: Abbaye de Bellefontaine, 1996).

Guillaumont, Antoine and Claire, 'Le texte véritable des "Gnostica" d'Évagre le Pontique', *Revue de l'Histoire des Religions*, 142 (1952), 156–205.

——'Évagre le Pontique', *Dictionnaire de spiritualité*, 4 (1961), 1731–44.

——'Evagrius Ponticus. Persönlichkeit, Leben, Wirkung', *Reallexikon für Antike und Christentum*, 6 (1966), 1088–1107.

——(eds.), *Évagre le Pontique, Traité Pratique ou Le Moine*, Sources Chrétiennes, 170–1 (Paris: Cerf, 1971).

——(eds.), *Évagre le Pontique. Le Gnostique*, Sources Chrétiennes, 356 (Paris: Cerf, 1989).

Guillaumont, Antoine and Claire, and Paul Géhin, *Évagre le Pontique. Sur les Pensées*, Sources Chrétiennes, 438 (Paris: Cerf, 1998).

Guillaumont, Claire, 'Fragments grecs inédits d'Evagre le Pontique', *Texte und Untersuchungen*, 133 (1987), 209–21.

Hagedorn, Ursula and Dieter, *Die älteren griechischen Katenen zum Buch Hiob, i.: Einleitung, Prologe und Epiloge, Fragmente zu Hiob 1,1–8,22*, Patristische Texte und Studien, 40 (Berlin: W. de Gruyter, 1994).

Haidacher, S., 'Nilus-Exzerpte im Pandektes des Antiochus', *Revue Bénédictine* 22 (1905), 244–9.

Hausherr, Irénée, 'Les versions syriaque et arménienne d'Évagre le Pontique, leur valeur, leur relation, leur utilisation', *Orientalia Christiana*, 22. 2 (1931), 69–118.

—— 'Par delà l'oraison pure grâce à une coquille. À propos d'un texte d'Évagre', *Revue d'Ascétique et de Mystique*, 13 (1932), 184–8.

—— 'L'origine de la théorie orientale des huit péchés capitaux', *Orientalia Christiana*, 30.3 (1933), 164–75.

—— 'Evagrii Pontici tria capita de Oratione', *Orientalia Christiana*, 30. 3 (1933), 149–52.

—— 'Le *De oratione* de Nil et Évagre', *Revue d'Ascétique et de Mystique*, 14 (1933), 196–8.

—— 'Une énigme d'Évagre le Pontique: *Centurie* II. 50', *Recherches de Sciences Religieuses*, 23 (1933), 321–5.

—— 'Le *Traité de l'Oraison* d'Évagre le Pontique (Pseudo-Nil)', *Revue d'Ascétique et de Mystique*, 15 (1934), 34–93, 113–70.

—— 'Ignorance infinie', *Orientalia Christiana Periodica*, 2 (1936), 351–62.

—— 'Nouveaux fragments grecs d'Évagre le Pontique', *Orientalia Christiana Periodica*, 5 (1939), 229–33.

—— 'Le "De oratione" d'Évagre le Pontique en syriaque et en arabe', *Orientalia Christiana Periodica*, 5 (1939), 7–71.

—— 'Eulogios-Loukios', *Orientalia Christiana Periodica*, 6 (1940), 216–20.

—— 'Ignorance infinie ou science infinie?" *Orientalia Christiana Periodica*, 25 (1959), 44–52.

—— 'Le *Traité de l'Oraison* d'Évagre le Pontique: Introduction, authenticité, traduction française et commentaire', *Revue d'Ascétique et de Mystique*, 35 (1959), 3–26, 121–46, 241–65; 361–85; 36 (1960), 3–35, 137–87.

—— *Les leçons d'un contemplatif. Le Traité de l'Oraison d'Évagre le Pontique* (Paris: Beauchesne, 1960).

Heussi, Karl, *Untersuchungen zu Nilus dem Asketen*, Texte und Untersuchungen, 42. 2 (Leipzig: J. C. Hinrichs, 1917).

Joest, Christoph, 'Die Bedeutung von Akedia und Apatheia bei Evagrios Pontikos', *Studia Monastica*, 35 (1993), 7–53.

Jourdan-Gueyer, Marie-Ange, and Marie-Odile Goudet (trans.), *Évagre le Pontique. De la prière à la perfection* (Paris: Migne, 1992).

Kline, Francis, 'The Christology of Evagrius and the Parent System of Origen', *Cistercian Studies*, 20 (1985), 155–83.

Kohlbacher, Michael, 'Unpublizierte Fragmente des Markianos von Bethlehem', in Michael Kohlbacher and M. Lesinski (eds.), *Horizonte der Christenheit. Festschrift für Friedrich Heyer zu seinem 85. Geburtstag*. Oikonomia, 34 (Erlangen: Lehrstuhl für Geschichte und Theologie des Christlichen Osten, 1994), 155.

Labate, Antonio, 'L'esegesi di Evagrio al Libro dell'Ecclesiaste', in Enrico Livrea and G. Aurelio Privitera (eds.), *Studi in onore di Anthos Ardizzoni*, Filologia e critica, 25 (Rome: Edizioni dell'Ateneo e Bizzarri, 1978), 485–90.

———'Nuove catene esegetiche sull'Ecclesiaste', in Jacques Noret (ed.), *Antidoron: Hommage à Maurits Geerard* (Wetteren: Cultura, 1984), 241–63.

Lackner, W., 'Zur profanen Bildung des Euagrios Pontikos', in *Hans Gerstinger. Festgabe zum 80. Geburtstag* (Graz: Akademische Druck- und Verlagsanstalt, 1966), 17–29.

Lanne, Emmanuel, 'La *xeniteia* d'Abraham dans l'oeuvre d'Irénée. Aux origines du thème monastique de la "peregrinatio"', *Irénikon*, 47 (1974), 163–87.

Lantschoot, Arnold van, 'Un opuscule inédit de F. C. Conybeare', *Le Muséon*, 77 (1964), 121–35.

Larchet, Jean-Claude, *Thérapeutique des maladies mentales. L'expérience de l'Orient chrétien* (Paris: Cerf, 1992).

———*Thérapeutique des maladies spirituelles* (Paris: Cerf, 2000).

Leanza, Sandro, 'Le catene esegetiche sull'Ecclesiaste', *Augustinianum*, 17 (1977), 545–52.

———'A proposito di una recente edizione del presunto 'Commentario all'Ecclesiaste' di Evagrio Pontico', *Rivista di Storia e Letteratura Religiosa*, 33 (1997), 365–98.

Leclercq, Jean, 'L'ancienne version latine des Sentences d'Évagre pour les Moines', *Scriptorium*, 5 (1951), 195–213.

Lefort, L. Théophile, 'À propos d'un aphorisme d'Evagrius Ponticus', *Bulletin de l'Académie Royale de Belgique, Classe des Lettres, 5e série*, 36 (1950), 70–9.

Linge, David E., 'Leading the Life of Angels: Ascetic Practice and Reflection in the Writings of Evagrius of Pontus', *Journal of the American Academy of Religion*, 68 (2000), 537–68.

Leloup, Jean-Yves (ed.), *Praxis et gnosis d'Évagre le Pontique, ou la guerison de l'esprit: textes choisis*, Spiritualités Vivantes, 103 (Paris: Albin Michel, 1992).

Levasti, Arrigo, 'Il più grande mistico del deserto: Evagrio il Pontico (m. 399)', *Rivista di Ascetica e Mistica*, 13 (1968), 242–64.

Louf, André, 'L'acédie chez Évagre Le Pontique', *Concilium (France)*, 99 (1974), 113–17.

Louth, Andrew, and Jill Raitt, *Wisdom of the Byzantine Church: Evagrios of Pontos and Maximos the Confessor. Four Lectures*, Paine Lectures in Religion, 1997 (Columbia, Mo.: Department of Religious Studies, University of Missouri, 1998).

Maier, Barbara, 'Apatheia bei den Stoikern und Akedia bei Evagrios Pontikos: Ein Ideal und die Kehrseite seiner Realität', *Oriens Christianus*, 78 (1994), 230–49.

Melcher, Robert, *Der achte Brief des hl. Basilius: Ein Werk des Evagrius Pontikus*, Münsterische Beiträge zur Theologie, 1 (Münster i.W: Aschendorff, 1923).

Mercati, Giovanni, 'Intorno ad uno scolio creduto di Evagrio', *Revue Biblique*, 23 (1914), 534–42.

Messana, Vincenzo, 'La chiesa orante nella catechesi spirituale di Evagrio Pontico', in *Biblioteca de Scienze Religiose*, 46 (Rome: Libreria Ateneo Salesiano, 1982), 173–86.

———'Le definizioni di προσευχή nel *De oratione* di Evagrio Pontico', in *Oeconomus Gratiae: Studi per il 20 anniversario di episcopato di Alfredo M. Garsia*, Quaderni di Presenza Culturale, 32 (Caltanissetta: Edizioni del Seminario, 1995), 69–87.

Messana, Vincenzo, (trans.), *Evagrio Pontico. La Preghiera*, Collana di Testi Patristici, 117 (Rome: Città Nuova, 1994).

Molinier, Nicolas, *Ascèse, contemplation et ministère d'après l'Histoire Lausiaque de Pallade d'Hélénopolis*, Spiritualité Orientale, 64 (Bégrolles-en-Mauges: Abbaye de Bellefontaine, 1995).

Moscatelli, Francesca (trans.), *Evagrio Pontico. Gli otto spiriti della malvagità; Sui diversi pensieri della malvagità* (Milan: San Paolo, 1996).

Moÿescu, I., Εὐάγριος ὁ Ποντικός, Βίος, Συγράμματα, Διδασκαλία (Athens, 1937).

Mühmelt, Martin, 'Zu der neuen lateinischen Übersetzung des Mönchsspiegels des Euagrius', *Vigiliae Christianae*, 8 (1954), 101–3.

Murphy, Francis Xavier, 'Evagrius Ponticus and Origenism', in R. P. C. Hanson and F. Crouzel (eds.), *Origeniana Tertia* (Rome: Ateneo, 1985), 253–69.

Muyldermans, Joseph, 'La teneur du *Practicus* d'Evagrius le Pontique', *Le Muséon*, 42 (1929), 74–89.

——'Le discours de Xystus dans la version arménienne d'Évagre le Pontique', *Revue des Études Arméniennes*, 9 (1929), 183–201.

——*Evagriana, Extrait de la revue Le Muséon 44, augmenté de: Nouveaux fragments grecs inédits* (Paris: Paul Geuthner, 1931).

——'Note additionnelle à *Evagriana*', *Le Muséon*, 44 (1931), 369–83.

——*À travers la tradition manuscrite d'Évagre le Pontique. Essai sur les manuscrits grecs conservés à la Bibliothèque Nationale de Paris*, Bibliothèque du Muséon, 3 (Louvain: Bureaux du Muséon, 1932).

——'Miscellanea armeniaca', *Le Muséon*, 47 (1934), 293–6.

——'Évagre le Pontique. Les *Capita cognoscitiva* dans les versions syriaque et arménienne', *Le Muséon*, 47 (1934), 73–106.

——'Evagriana. Le Vat. Barb. Graec. 515', *Le Muséon*, 51 (1938), 191–226.

——'Une nouvelle recension du *De octo spiritibus malitiae* de S. Nil', Le Muséon, 52 (1939), 235–74.

——'Fragment arménien du 'Ad Virgines' d'Évagre', *Le Muséon*, 53 (1940), 77–87.

——'Evagriana de la Vaticane', *Le Muséon*, 54 (1941), 1–15.

——'S. Nil en version arménienne', *Le Muséon*, 56 (1943), 77–113.

——'*Sur les Séraphins* et *Sur les Chérubins* d'Évagre le Pontique dans les versions syriaque et arménienne', *Le Muséon*, 59 (1946), 367–79.

——*Evagriana Syriaca. Textes inédits du British Museum et de la Vaticane*, Bibliothèque du Muséon, 31 (Louvain: Publications Universitaires, 1952).

——'À propos d'un feuillet d'un manuscrit arménien (Brit. Mus., Cod. Arm. 118)', *Le Muséon*, 55 (1952), 11–16.

——'Les manuscrits arméniens d'Évagre le Pontique à Jérusalem', *Bazmavēp*, 113 (1955), 72–8, 108–14.

——'Les citations bibliques dans la version arménienne de l'*Antirrheticus* d'Évagre le Pontique', *Handès Amsoreay*, 75 (1961), 441–8.

——'Evagriana coptica', *Le Muséon*, 76 (1963), 271–6.

O'Laughlin, Michael Wallace, *Origenism in the Desert: Anthropology and Integration in Evagrius Ponticus* (Harvard, Mass.: Dissertation, Harvard University, 1987; UMI ProQuest (http://www.umi.com/)).

——'The Bible, the Demons and the Desert: Evaluating the *Antirrheticus* of Evagrius Ponticus', *Studia Monastica*, 34 (1992), 201–15.

——'Elements of Fourth-Century Origenism: The Anthropology of Evagrius Ponticus and Its Sources', in Charles Kannengiesser and W. L. Petersen (eds.), *Origen of Alexandria: His World and his Legacy* (Notre Dame, Ind.: University of Notre Dame Press, 1988), 357–73.

——'Evagrius Ponticus in Spiritual Perspective', *Studia Monastica*, 39 (1997), 224–30.

——'New Questions Concerning the Origenism of Evagrius', in Robert J. Daly (ed.), *Origeniana Quinta* (Leuven: Leuven University Press, 1992), 528–34.

Otto, Stephan, 'Esoterik und individualistische Gnosis: der mönchische Platonismus des Euagrios Pontikos', in Stephan Otto (ed.), *Die Antike im Umbruch. Politisches Denken zwischen hellenistischer Tradition und christlicher Offenbarung bis zur Reichstheologie Justinians*, (Munich: List, 1974), 65–81.

Ousley, David Alan, *Evagrius' Theology of Prayer and the Spiritual Life* (Chicago, Ill.: Dissertation, University of Chicago, 1979; UMI ProQuest (http://www.umi.com/)).

Paramelle, Joseph, '*Chapitres des disciples d'Évagre* dans un manuscrit grec du Musée Bénaki d'Athènes', *Parole de l'Orient*, 6–7 (1975–6), 101–14.

Parmentier, M., 'Evagrius of Pontus, "Letter to Melania"', *Bijdragen, tijdschrift voor filosofie en theologie*, 46 (1985), 2–38.

Patrucco, Marcella Forlin (ed.), *Basilio di Cesarea, Le lettere*, i. (Turin: Società editrice internazionale, 1983).

Peterson, E., 'Zu griechischen Asketikern, I. Zu Euagrius Ponticus', *Byzantinisch-neugriechische Jahrbücher*, 4 (1923), 5–8.

——'Zu griechischen Asketikern, II. Noch einmal zu Euagrius Ponticus', *Byzantinisch-neugriechische Jahrbücher*, 5 (1926), 412–14.

——'Zu griechischen Asketikern, III. Zu Euagrius', *Byzantinisch-neugriechische Jahrbücher*, 9 (1930–32), 51–4.

Quecke, Hans, 'Auszüge aus Evagrius' "Mönchsspiegel" in koptischer Übersetzung', *Orientalia Christiana Periodica*, 58 (1989), 453–63.

Rahner, Karl, 'Die geistliche Lehre des Evagrius Ponticus', *Zeitschrift für Aszese und Mystik*, 8 (1933), 31–47.

Refoulé, François, 'Rêves et vie spirituelle d'après Évagre le Pontique', *Supplément de la Vie Spirituelle*, 59 (1961), 470–516.

——'La christologie d'Évagre et l'origénisme', *Orientalia Christiana Periodica*, 27 (1961), 221–66.

——'Évagre fut-il origéniste', *Revue des Sciences Philosophiques et Théologiques*, 47 (1963), 398–402.

——'La mystique d'Évagre et l'origénisme', *Supplément de la Vie Spirituelle*, 66 (1963), 453–63.

Rondeau, Marie-Josèphe, 'Le commentaire sur les Psaumes d'Évagre le Pontique', *Orientalia Christiana Periodica*, 26 (1960), 307–48.

——*Les commentaires patristiques du Psautier (IIIe–Ve siècles)*, i, Orientalia Christiana Analecta, 219 (Rome: Pontificium Institutum Studiorum Orientalium, 1982).

Rubenson, Samuel, 'Evagrios Pontikos und die Theologie der Wüste', in Hanns Christof Brennecke, Ernst Grasmück, and Christoph Markschies (eds.), *Logos. Festschrift für Luise Abramowski*, Beihefte zur Zeitschrift für die neutestamentliche Wissenschaft und die Kunde der älteren Kirche, 67 (Berlin: W. de Gruyter, 1993), 384–401.

Samir, Khalil, 'Évagre le Pontique dans la tradition arabo-copte', in Marguerite Rassart-Derbergh and Julien Ries (eds.), *Actes du IVe Congrès Copte. Louvain-la-Neuve, 5–10 septembre 1988*, Publications de l'Institut Orientaliste de Louvain, 41 (Louvain-la-Neuve: Institut Orientaliste, 1992), ii:123–53.

Sargisean, H. Barsegh V., *Srboy hōrn Ewagri Pontac'woy Vark' ew Matenagrut'iwnk* (Venice, 1907).

——*Le opere di Evagrio Pontico nell'antica versione armena*, annotated by E. Teza, (Venice, 1909).

Schenke, Hans-Martin, 'Ein koptischer Evagrius', in P. Nagel (ed.), *Graeco-Coptica: Griechen und Kopten im byzantinischen Ägypten*, Wissenschaftliche Beiträge der Martin-Luther-Universität (Halle–Wittenberg, 1984), 219–30.

——'Das Berliner Evagrius-Ostrakon (P. Berol. 14 700)', *Zeitschrift für ägyptische Sprache und Altertumskunde*, 116 (1989), 90–107.

Sims-Williams, N., *The Christian Sogdian Manuscript C 2*, Schriften zur Geschichte und Kultur des Alten Orients, Berliner Turfantexte, 12. (Berlin: Akademie Verlag, 1985).

Spies, Otto, 'Die äthiopische Überlieferung der Abhandlung des Evagrius περὶ ὀκτὼ λογισμῶν', *Oriens Christianus*, 3rd ser., 7 (1932), 203–28.

Stewart, Columba, 'Imageless Prayer and the Theological Vision of Evagrius Ponticus', *Journal of Early Christian Studies*, 9 (2001), 173–204.

Suaresius, Josephus Maria (ed.), *Sancti Patris nostri Nili Abbatis Tractatus seu Opuscula ex codicibus manuscriptis Vaticanis, Cassinensibus, Barberinis et Altaempsianis eruta* (Rome: Ex typis Barberinis, 1673).

Toda, Satoshi, 'Les *Apophthegmata patrum* et Évagre le Pontique', in The Mediterranean Studies Group (eds.), *Mediterranean World*, 16 (Tokyo: Hitotsubashi University, 2001), 77–87.

Turner, Henry J. M., 'Evagrius Ponticus, Teacher of Prayer', *Eastern Churches Review*, 7 (1975), 145–8.

Vitestam, Gösta (ed.), *La seconde partie du traité qui passe sous le nom de 'La Grande Lettre d'Évagre le Pontique à Mélanie l'Ancienne*, Scripta Minora Regiae Societatis Humaniorum Litterarum Lundensis, 1963–4, no. 3 (Lund: Glerrup, 1964).

Vivian, Tim, 'Coptic Palladiana II: The Life of Evagrius (*Lausiac History* 38)', *Coptic Church Review*, 21 (2000), 8–23.

Vögtle, Anton, 'Woher stammt das Schema der Hauptsünden?', *Theologische Quartalschrift*, 122 (1941), 217–37.

de Vogüé, Adalbert, 'La lecture du Matin dans les Sentences d'Évagre et la *De Virginitate* attribué à saint Athanase', *Studia Monastica*, 26 (1984), 7–11.

—— and Gabriel Bunge, 'Palladiana III. La version copte de l'Histoire Lausiaque. II. La vie d'Évagre', *Studia Monastica*, 33 (1991), 7–21.

——*Quatre ermites égyptiens d'après les fragments coptes de l'Histoire Lausiaque*. Spiritualité Orientale, 60 (Bégrolles-en-Mauges: Abbaye de Bellefontaine, 1994).

Ware, Kallistos, and Alois Dempf, 'Nous and Noesis in Plato, Aristotle and Evagrius of Pontus: Evagrios Pontikos als Metaphysiker und Mystiker', *Diotima*, 13 (1985), 158–63.

Watt, John W., 'Philoxenus and the Old Syriac Version of Evagrius' "Centuries"', *Oriens Christianus*, 64 (1980), 65–81.

——'The Syriac Adapter of Evagrius' Centuries', *Studia Patristica*, 17.3 (1982), 1388–95.

Wilmart, André, 'Les versions latines des Sentences d'Évagre pour les Vièrges', *Revue Bénédictine*, 28 (1911), 143–53.

Young, Robin Darling, 'The Armenian Adaptation of Evagrius' Kephalaia Gnostica', in Robert J. Daly (ed.), *Origeniana Quinta* (Leuven: Leuven University Press, 1992), 535–41.

——'Evagrius the Iconographer: Monastic Pedagogy in the *Gnostikos*', *Journal of Early Christian Studies*, 9 (2001), 53–71.

Zigmund-Cerbu, A., 'La préface du *De Oratione* d'Évagre', *Acta Philologica (Societas Academica Daco-Romana)*, 2 (Rome, 1959), 251–7.

Zöckler, Otto, *Evagrius Pontikus, seine Stellung in der altchristlichen Literatur- und Dogmengeschichte*, Biblische und kirchenhistorischen Studien, 4 (Munich: Beck, 1893).

INDEX LOCORUM

The following abbreviations are used for the works of Evagrius:

8Th.	*Eight Thoughts*	*Pry.*	*Prayer*
Eul.	*Eulogios*	*Rfl.*	*Reflections*
Exh.	*Exhortations*	*33Ch.*	*Thirty-Three Chapters*
Fnd.	*Foundations*	*Th.*	*Thoughts*
Max.	*Maxims*	*Vic.*	*Vices*
Mn.	*Monks*	*Vg.*	*Virgin*
Pr.	*Praktikos*		

Old Testament (Septuagint)

Genesis:

1: 31	*Exh.* 2.36
2: 15	*Pry.* 48
3: 1–5	*Eul.* 17.18
3: 6, 23	*8Th.* 1.10
3: 15	*Eul.* 11.10
3: 24	*Exh.* 2.39
9: 3	*Fnd.* 10
12: 1	*Th.* 12
18: 1–5	*Eul.* 24.26
18: 27	*8Th.* 8.12; *Exh.* 1.6
19: 2–3	*Eul.* 24.25
29: 20–30	*Pry. Prol.*
31: 20–7	*8Th.* 8.22
31: 39–40	*Th.* 17
31: 39	*Th.* 17
32: 7	*Pr.* 26
32: 10	*8Th.* 8.23
49: 17–18	*8Th.* 8.29

Exodus:

2: 11–12	*8Th.* 1.32
3: 1–6	*Th.* 17
3: 5	*Pry.* 1
3: 8	*Max.* 3.22
4: 3	*8Th.* 8.25
4: 4	*8Th.* 8.26
4: 6	*8Th.* 7.19

5: 7–12	*Th.* 36
7: 9	*Th.*17
11: 9–10	*Th.* 17
12: 8	*8Th.* 7.18
12: 18–20	*8Th.* 8.21
17: 11	*8Th.* 1.29
18: 13–27	*Eul.* 23.24
24: 9–11	*Th.* 39; *Rfl.* 2
25: 18–22	*Max.* 2.18
25: 29, 31	*Th.* 8
27: 1–3	*Th.* 8
30: 34–5	*Pry.* 1

Leviticus:

11: 22	*Pr.* 38
15: 19–24	*Th.* 37
21: 18	*33Ch.* 4, 11, 12, 15
21: 20	*33Ch.* 13
22: 4	*33Ch.* 6, 8
22: 22	*8Th.* 4.19, 7.16
26: 16	*33Ch.* 1, 3

Numbers:

6: 3	*Th.* 5
12: 3	*Th.* 13
13: 27	*Max.* 3.22
21: 6	*8Th.* 8.27
21: 9	*8Th.* 8.28

New Testament

Apocrypha

INDEX RERUM